# Biology
## for Cambridge IGCSE

### Gareth Williams

Richard Fosbery • Janet Adams

Series Editor:

Lawrie Ryan

Nelson Thornes

Published in 2009 by:
Nelson Thornes Ltd
Delta Place
27 Bath Road
CHELTENHAM
GL53 7TH
United Kingdom

13 / 10 9 8 7 6

A catalogue record for this book is available from the British Library.

ISBN 978 1 4085 0017 0

Cover photograph by Photolibrary/Michael Fogden

Illustrations include artwork drawn by Barking Dog Art and
GreenGate Publishing

Page make-up by GreenGate Publishing, Kent

Printed in China

# Contents

# Contents

This book is designed specifically for Biology IGCSE (Syllabus 0610) and is fully endorsed by University of Cambridge International Examinations (CIE). CIE IGCSE Principal Examiners have been involved in all aspects of the book, including detailed planning to ensure that the content gives the best match possible to their syllabus.

Using this book will ensure that you are well prepared for the Biology IGCSE examination and for studies beyond IGCSE level in pure sciences, in applied sciences or in science-dependent vocational courses. The features of the book outlined below are designed to make learning as interesting and effective as possible:

## LEARNING OUTCOMES

- These are at the start of each spread and will tell you what you should be able to do at the end of the spread

**Extension**
- Some outcomes will only be needed if you are taking Paper 3 and these are clearly labelled, as is any Supplementary content in the spread

## EXAMINER SAYS...

This provides a chance for the IGCSE Principal Examiners to share their experience of many years marking and setting examinations with you. They give you hints on how to avoid common errors or give useful advice on how to tackle questions.

## DID YOU KNOW?

These are not needed in the examination but are found throughout the book to stimulate your interest in biology.

## PRACTICAL

These show the opportunities for practical work. The results are included to help you if you do not actually tackle the experiment or are studying at home.

## KEY POINTS

These summarise the most important things to learn from the spread.

## SUMMARY QUESTIONS

These questions are at the end of each spread and allow you to test your understanding of the work covered in the spread.

At the end of each unit there is a double page of examination-style questions written by the very CIE Examiners that set the papers for the Biology 0610 exams. In most cases the questions are only set on the contents of the unit. In the examination you will find questions that deal with the contents of two or more units. In Papers 2 and 3 you may have to complete graphs by adding labels and units for axes, plotting points, adding bars to bar charts or joining points or giving lines of best fit. You will not have to draw the axes yourself. You can also expect to have photographs which are not included in these questions.

At the end of the book you will also find: 'Alternative to practical' section – this provides guidance if you are taking Paper 6 instead of coursework or the practical test.

A useful Revision checklist is also provided to help you prepare for the examination in Paper 1, 2 and 3.

# 1 Characteristics and classification of living organisms

## 1.1 Characteristics of living organisms

Biology is the study of living things or living organisms, which are classified into five major groups called **kingdoms**:

animals, plants, fungi, protoctists and prokaryotes (bacteria)

There are seven characteristics of living organisms. These characteristics are often described as life processes:

nutrition, respiration, movement, growth, excretion, sensitivity, reproduction.

### Nutrition

Nutrition is the obtaining of food to provide energy and substances needed for growth and repair. Nutrients are compounds that may be large and complex (like carbohydrates, proteins and vitamins) or simple (like mineral ions).

Nutrition in green plants involves **photosynthesis**, in which the energy from sunlight is absorbed and used to turn carbon dioxide and water into simple sugars. Plants then convert these simple sugars into complex compounds, such as cellulose and proteins. They need mineral ions from the soil to make proteins.

Animals cannot make their own food like plants, so they have to eat plants or other animals to gain energy and nutrients. The process of taking in food is called **ingestion**. The food is digested, absorbed into the blood and then assimilated by cells for growth and repair. Food which is not digested and absorbed is egested in faeces.

Salmon provide nutrition for bears.

### Respiration

All living organisms respire because they all need energy. Respiration involves chemical reactions that occur in cells to break down nutrients, such as glucose, to release energy. Oxygen is usually needed for respiration to happen. This is the word equation for respiration involving oxygen:

$$\text{glucose} + \text{oxygen} \longrightarrow \text{carbon dioxide} + \text{water} + \text{energy released}$$

Living things use this energy for movement, growth, repair and reproduction.

### Movement

Organisms move themselves or move parts of themselves into new areas or to change position.

Plants move slowly when they grow. Their roots move down into the soil and their leaves and stems move up towards the light. Leaves can move to face the Sun so they can absorb as much light as possible.

Most animals are able move their whole bodies. They move to obtain their food or to avoid being caught by predators. Some animals remain fixed to one place throughout their lives, but they are able to move parts, such as the tentacles on a sea anemone.

Sea anemone.

## Growth

Growth is a permanent increase in size and the dry mass of an organism. It can involve an increase in cell number, cell size or both. It always involves making more complex chemicals, such as proteins, which is why the dry mass increases. Plants carry on growing throughout their lives. Animals stop growing when they reach a certain size.

## Excretion

All living organisms produce toxic (poisonous) waste substances as a result of metabolism. **Metabolism** is all the chemical reactions that occur in an organism. Respiration is a major part of metabolism.

Excretion is the removal of these waste substances from the body. Plants store waste substances in their leaves, so the waste chemicals are removed when the leaves fall off. Animals breathe out carbon dioxide; other waste substances leave the body in the urine.

## Sensitivity

Living organisms are able to detect or sense changes in their environment. A change like this is a **stimulus** (plural: stimuli). Sensitivity is the ability to detect these stimuli and **respond** to them.

Plants respond to movement of the Sun by moving their leaves to face the light. The flowers of some plants open in the morning and close at night. Animals have sensory cells and sense organs for detecting light, sound, touch, pressure and chemicals in the air and in food.

### Reproduction

Organisms reproduce to make new individuals. **Asexual reproduction** involves one parent giving rise to offspring that are often identical to each other and to the parent. **Sexual reproduction** involves two parent organisms producing **gametes** (sex cells) which fuse to give rise to the next generation. The offspring show **variation**. They are not identical to each other or to their parents.

**SUMMARY QUESTIONS**

1 A visitor from outer space lands on Earth. The first thing that it sees is a motor car passing by.
   a  Give two reasons why the visitor thinks that the car is alive.
   b  Give two reasons why you think that the visitor is wrong.

2 Plants and animals are two groups of living organisms. Find out and then describe how plants differ from animals in the ways in which they:
   a  feed,  b  move,  c  grow,  d  use their senses.

**KEY POINTS**

The mnemonic, 'Mrs Gren' can help you remember the seven characteristics of living organisms:

**M**ovement causes an organism to change its position or place.

**R**espiration involves chemical reactions that release energy in cells.

**S**ensitivity is being able to detect and respond to stimuli.

**G**rowth is a permanent increase in size and mass.

**R**eproduction results in the formation of new individuals.

**E**xcretion is the removal of waste chemicals made in the cells during metabolism.

**N**utrition involves the use of food for energy and growth.

# Classification

A meerkat.

**EXAMINER SAYS...**

Remember that the name of a species is <u>both</u> names. If a name has been used once then it can be shortened like this: <u>H. sapiens</u>.

We classify organisms into groups. The largest grouping is the **kingdom** (see previous spread) and the smallest is the **species**. The organisms in a kingdom share some similar features. For example, within the plant kingdom, all plants are green and carry out photosynthesis. Each kingdom is subdivided into groups known as **phyla** (singular: **phylum**). In this spread we deal with three such phyla (nematodes, annelids and molluscs) within the animal kingdom. But first we must explain how organisms are named.

## The binomial system

Meerkat, suricate and Sun angel are names for a type of mongoose that lives in the Kalahari Desert in southern Africa. To avoid confusion organisms are given scientific names using the **binomial system** (binomial means 'two names').

A **species** is a group of individuals that look alike. They live in the same habitat and breed together to give offspring which are fertile and can also breed together.

Each species is given two names: the first name is for the **genus** and the second name is the **trivial** name that applies to one species within the genus. The trivial name should never be used on its own.

A genus is a group of species that are closely related, but do not interbreed with each other. Some genera (plural of genus) only consist of one species, as is the case with meerkats. This may be because other species in that genus are extinct.

The binomial system is used by biologists all over the world as it is an international language for naming organisms. The table has some examples.

| common name | scientific name |
|---|---|
| meerkat | *Suricata suricatta* |
| human | *Homo sapiens* |
| baobab tree | *Adansonia digitata* |
| cholera bacterium | *Vibrio cholerae* |
| malarial parasite | *Plasmodium falciparum* |
| oyster mushroom | *Pleurotus ostreatus* |

## Invertebrates

**Invertebrates** are animals that *do not* have a **vertebral column** or backbone. On the next page is information about three phyla of invertebrates: nematodes, annelids and molluscs.

## Nematodes

Nematodes or roundworms are a group of worms that have thread-like bodies that taper at mouth and anus. They have no obvious head and no legs. Their bodies are not made up of segments. Most are very tiny and live in soils and water. There are many types of nematodes: some species are **parasites** living inside another animal, the **host**.

## Annelids

Annelids are worms with soft bodies made up of segments. Some have paddle-like extensions for moving and they have chaetae or bristles for making contact with mud or soil. Most species of annelids live in the sea, but some live in the soil and in fresh water (streams, lakes and rivers).

Earthworms burrow through soil. To help them move through the soil, earthworms have a pointed front end to their body and they make mucus as a lubricant.

## Molluscs

Molluscs have soft bodies that are not segmented. They have a muscular 'foot' that they use for burrowing or movement. Many species of molluscs have one or two shells for protection. The animal is able to retreat inside the shell if a predator is close by, or if they need to avoid excessive water loss. Some, like the octopus, do not have a shell. Other animals in this phylum are snails, slugs, clams and squids.

*Ascaris lumbricoides*, a parasitic nematode.

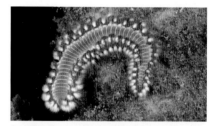

Bearded fireworm – an annelid.

Banded snail – a mollusc.

### SUMMARY QUESTIONS

1 Copy and complete the sentences using the words below:

**fertile   genus   shared   trivial
classification   binomial   breed**

The system of putting organisms into groups is called _____. The _____ system is used for naming organisms. Each organism has two names. The first is called the _____ name and the second the _____ name. A species is a very similar group of individuals that can _____ together and produce _____ offspring. We classify living things on the basis of their _____ features.

2 a  State three ways in which nematodes differ from annelids.

   b  State two features that are shown by both annelids and molluscs.

3 a  Explain the term *binomial system*.

   b  Find the scientific names of two plant species and two animal species not mentioned in this spread and write them alongside their common names.

4 In the 18th century, Carl Linnaeus worked out the binomial system of naming living things. Find out about his life and work and then write a brief biography in your own words.

### KEY POINTS

1 The binomial system uses two names for each species: the genus name and the trivial name.

2 A species is a group of individuals, living in the same habitat that breed together to produce fertile offspring.

3 Invertebrates are animals without a vertebral column (backbone).

4 Three invertebrate phyla are nematodes, annelids and molluscs.

# Arthropods

Woodlouse or slater. Notice its antennae for detecting stimuli.

Sally lightfoot crab, *Grapsus grapsus*. Notice its large claws for feeding and defence.

Arthropods is the largest of the phyla in the animal kingdom as it contains the largest number of species. Each species in this phylum has a segmented body, an external skeleton (**exoskeleton**) and jointed legs.

The hard exoskeleton allows arthropods to live on dry land. When they grow too big for their exoskeleton, they moult and grow a new one. Some moult all through their lives, others only moult during the early stages of their life.

Each phylum is divided into classes. We will now consider four of the classes in the arthropod phylum:

crustaceans, myriapods, insects and arachnids

## Crustaceans

Crustaceans have a body divided into a **cephalothorax** (head-thorax) and abdomen. Many have a chalky exoskeleton that provides a very hard and effective protection against predators. Crustaceans have two pairs of **antennae** and **compound eyes**. They have between five and 20 pairs of legs. They breathe using **gills**.

Nearly all crustaceans live in water. Some crabs live on land but return to water to breed. Woodlice (also known as slaters) and some land crabs are exceptions as they do not use water for breeding. Examples of crustaceans include crabs, shrimps, crayfish and lobsters.

## Myriapods

These are the **centipedes** and the **millipedes**. They have long bodies made up of many segments.

Their bodies are not divided into separate regions such as the thorax and abdomen. Centipedes have one pair of legs on each segment so that the total number of legs depends upon how many segments there are. Centipedes are fast-moving carnivores. They have powerful jaws and can paralyse their prey.

Millipedes have two pairs of legs on each body segment. They are slow-moving herbivores. You can often find them feeding in leaf litter.

Millipede – with its many legs for moving efficiently.

Centipede – a fast-moving carnivore.

## Insects

Insects have bodies that are divided into three parts: head, thorax and abdomen.

On the thorax there are three pairs of legs and many species have two pairs of wings. They have one pair of antennae on the head and compound eyes that are made of many tiny individual components. They breathe through holes in the sides of the thorax and abdomen called **spiracles**.

Insects have colonised most habitats in the world, although there are very few species that live in the sea. Two reasons why they are so successful on land is that they are covered by a waterproof **cuticle** that stops them losing too much water, and they can fly!

This is the largest group within the arthropods. Examples include beetles, flies, locusts, cockroaches, dragonflies, butterflies, moths, bees and wasps.

## Arachnids

These arthropods have bodies divided into two parts, the cephalothorax and abdomen.

Arachnids have four pairs of legs and no wings. They have no antennae but do have several pairs of simple, not compound, eyes. They paralyse their prey with poison fangs. Spiders are able to weave silken webs with their **spinnerets**. This class of arthropod also includes scorpions, ticks and mites.

Monarch butterfly, *Danaus plexippus*. Notice its wings for its migration over long distances.

Tarantula – a large spider with venom to paralyse its prey.

### SUMMARY QUESTIONS

1 a   Name four classes of arthropod.

   b   List the key features of insects.

   c   State three ways in which arachnids look different from insects.

2 Distinguish between the following on the basis of visible features:

   a   centipedes and millipedes

   b   crustaceans and arachnids.

3 Describe the features of insects that adapt them for living successfully on land.

4 Copy and complete the table:

| feature | myriapods | crustaceans | insects | arachnids |
|---|---|---|---|---|
| number of pairs of legs | | | | |
| body regions | | | | |
| number of pairs of antennae | | | | |
| type of eyes | | | | |
| wings | | | | |

### DID YOU KNOW?

There are over a million known species of insects and it is estimated that there may be 30 million species altogether, but no one knows.

### KEY POINTS

1 Arthropods are segmented animals with jointed legs and an exoskeleton.

2 Arthropods are classified into four different classes:

   crustaceans, myriapods, insects and arachnids

# Vertebrates

This dace has fins, tail and a streamlined shape – adaptations for swimming.

The bright red eyes of this tree frog are thought to startle predators, giving time for the frog to escape.

American crocodile, *Crocodylus acutus*.

Animals that have a vertebral column or backbone are called **vertebrates**. All vertebrates have an internal skeleton made of either bone or cartilage. They all belong to the phylum chordata which includes some invertebrates that share common features with the vertebrates.

There are five main classes of vertebrates: fish, amphibians, reptiles, birds and mammals.

## Fish

Most fish live in water permanently, but there are some species, such as the mud skipper, that can survive out of water for varying lengths of time.

Typically, fish are streamlined and have fins for swimming and for balance. They have eyes and a lateral line for detecting pressure changes in water. They breathe dissolved oxygen from the water using their gills. Their skin is covered with scales. Examples include tuna, herring, shark, catfish and cod.

Unlike fish, the other classes of vertebrates have ears for detecting sound and four limbs, although some have evolved into legless forms like snakes and some lizards.

## Amphibians

These vertebrates have smooth, moist skin. Although most amphibians live on land, they return to water to breed. Fertilisation is external because sperm and eggs are released into the water (not inside a female body). Development is external: the fertilised eggs hatch into swimming tadpoles which have gills for breathing.

On land, the adult amphibians breathe using lungs, but when they are in water, they can breathe through their skin. Examples of amphibians include frogs, toads and salamanders.

## Reptiles

Reptiles have dry, scaly skin to cut down water loss. They can live in dry regions as they do not have to return to water to breed.

Fertilisation takes place inside the female's body. However, development is external as they lay eggs with leathery, waterproof shells which stop them from drying out. Reptiles have lungs to breathe air. Crocodiles, lizards, snakes, turtles and tortoises are all reptiles.

## Birds

Birds have feathers and their front limbs are modified as wings. Most of them are able to fly but some, like penguins and ostriches, cannot. Birds have no teeth but different species have beaks adapted to deal with different types of food.

Fertilisation is internal and development is external as the females lay eggs which are protected by hard shells.

Birds are **homeothermic** (warm-blooded). This means that they are able to regulate their body temperature. They can keep it constant even though the outside temperature changes. Examples of birds include hawks, eagles, sparrows, parrots and starlings.

## Mammals

Mammals are the vertebrates that have hair or fur. Fertilisation is internal and so is development. The young develop in a womb and they are born already well developed. Female mammals suckle their young on milk from mammary glands. All mammals, even aquatic ones like whales and dolphins, use lungs for breathing.

Like birds, mammals are also homeothermic, maintaining a constant internal temperature. Leopards, bats, dolphins, bears, lemurs and wolves are all mammals.

Grey Heron, *Ardea cinerea* – a bird with a long beak for catching fish.

A chimpanzee has hands and feet adapted to living in trees.

**EXAMINER SAYS...**

Make a table to help you learn the features of these five classes. Do this in the same way as shown in question 4 on page 7. Making the table will help you learn this topic.

**DID YOU KNOW?**

Many amphibian species are threatened with extinction. Some rare Panamanian golden frogs were filmed for Sir David Attenborough's BBC TV series *Life in Cold Blood*. After the filming the frogs were removed to a zoo to protect them from disease, habitat loss and pollution.

## SUMMARY QUESTIONS

1 Copy and complete these sentences using the words below:

**development five wings scaly moist land water classes breed fly fish fur feathers**

There are _____ different groups or _____ of vertebrate. Sharks belong to the class called _____ and spend all their time in _____. Amphibians have _____ skin and return to water to _____. Reptiles have _____ skin and lay their eggs on _____. Birds have front limbs that are modified to form _____. They also have _____ and most are able to _____. Mammals have _____ or hair and give birth to their young in an advanced state of _____.

2 a State the features that are shown by all vertebrates.

b Name the five classes of vertebrates.

c Give an example of each of class.

3 To which class of vertebrates does each of the following belong:

a turtle, b bat, c whale, d salamander, e snake, f hawk, g shark?

**KEY POINTS**

1 Vertebrates are animals that have a vertebral column or backbone.

2 The vertebrates are divided into five classes:

fish, amphibians, reptiles, birds and mammals.

# 1.5 Microorganisms

Bacteria, viruses and fungi are all **microorganisms** or microbes. Bacteria and fungi are in separate kingdoms (see page 2). Viruses are not living organisms like the others we have considered so they are classified in a different way.

Many species of bacteria and fungi break down dead and decaying material and these are called **decomposers** (see page 230). Some species of bacteria and fungi are used in making our food, for example yoghurt, bread, cheese and wine. We have made use of viruses in genetic engineering (see page 221). Microbes that cause disease are called **pathogens**.

## Bacteria

Bacteria have a simple cell structure that you can see in the diagram. Some bacteria are spherical and some are rod-shaped. Many exist in short chains of cells. Most bacteria are a few micrometres in length and can only be seen with light and electron microscopes. (One micrometre is one-thousandth of a millimetre.)

Bacterial cells are surrounded by cell walls. The cells of some bacterial species are surrounded by slime capsules.

There is no nucleus, just a loop of DNA within the cytoplasm. Bacteria often have additional loops of DNA inside their cytoplasm called **plasmids** (see page 221). The structure of bacteria differs from animal and plant cells as they do not have chloroplasts or mitochondria. Some bacteria have extensions called flagella (singular flagellum) for moving through water or other fluids.

Bacteria are found everywhere – in the air, in water and in the soil. Under good conditions, bacteria may divide every 20 minutes, so it does not take long to have a very large number of bacteria that you can see on agar as a colony. Each colony starts from just one cell.

Bacteria feed by secreting enzymes onto their food source. The food is broken down and simple molecules such as sugars are absorbed.

Bacteria which can survive harsh conditions, such as heat, cold and drought, produce spores within their cells. These have a protective covering so they can survive for a long time. When suitable conditions return, the spores germinate and divide again.

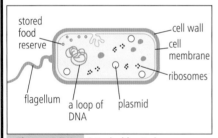

stored food reserve — cell wall — cell membrane — ribosomes — flagellum — a loop of DNA — plasmid

**Figure 1.5.1** A typical bacterium.

*Staphylococcus*, a type of bacterium.

## Fungi

Fungi are visible under a light microscope. Many are also visible to the naked eye. Most fungi are multicellular although yeasts are single-celled. Each cell has a nucleus and cell wall which is made out of chitin, not cellulose as in plants. They do not have chlorophyll and cannot carry out photosynthesis.

The main fungus body is called the **mycelium**. It consists of a branching network of threads or **hyphae** which grow over the surface of its food source, releasing **enzymes** which digest the food outside the fungus. The digested food is then absorbed by the hyphae.

Fungi reproduce by making spores that can be carried by the **wind**. Most fungi are **saprotrophs**, which means they feed on dead or decaying matter, but some are **parasites**.

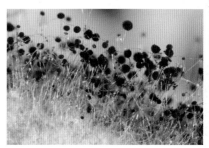

Bread mould, *Rhizopus nigricans*. The black structures contain spores.

## Viruses

Viruses are extremely small; far smaller than bacteria and fungi. For example, the virus that causes influenza is about 120 nanometres in size. (One nanometre is one-thousandth of a micrometre.) Viruses are only visible under an electron microscope.

Viruses are not cells. They are particles made up of genetic material (DNA or RNA) surrounded by a protein coat. The genetic material is composed of a few genes that code for the proteins that form the coat and maybe other proteins that help it reproduce. Viruses are **parasites** that enter the cells of another organism (the **host**) in order to multiply. Viruses take over the host cell and direct it to make new viruses.

If you breathe in the viruses that cause colds or influenza, they enter the cells of your nose and throat. Here they reproduce and make lots of new viruses. These are able to invade more cells to make even more viruses.

Viruses can be very harmful because they can reproduce so quickly and do not respond to antibiotics. They are constantly changing into new strains.

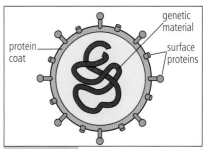

**Figure 1.5.2**  Structure of a human virus.

### SUMMARY QUESTIONS

1 Copy and complete the sentences using the words below:

  **nucleus  decay  inside  parasites  hyphae  protein  antibiotics  reproduce  colony  genes**

  Viruses are not cells but are made up of a few _____ surrounded by a _____ coat. Viruses are _____ that can only reproduce _____ healthy cells. Bacteria are cells with no _____ . They can _____ very quickly to form a bacterial _____ .

  Bacteria inside the human body can be killed by chemicals called _____ . Fungi are made up of a network of threads called _____ . Fungi act as saprotrophs when they cause dead materials to _____ .

2 Each of the following diseases is caused by a bacterium or fungus. In each case, state whether the pathogen (disease-causing organism) is a bacterium or a fungus and then find out how the disease is spread:

  a  cholera, b  typhoid, c  tuberculosis (TB), d  syphilis, e  athlete's foot, f  candidiasis.

### KEY POINTS

1 Bacteria are cells but have no nucleus. They can be seen under a light microscope.

2 In favourable conditions, bacterial cells can divide quickly to form a colony.

3 Viruses can only be seen under an electron microscope. They are not cells but a few genes inside a protein coat.

4 Viruses are parasites that invade healthy cells, reproducing to produce many new virus particles.

5 Fungi are made up of threads called hyphae. These grow over the food supply, digest it externally and then absorb it.

# Flowering plants

## Features of flowering plants

Like all plants, flowering plants are multicellular. They are green in colour because many of their cells contain **chloroplasts**. These chloroplasts contain the green pigment **chlorophyll**, which absorbs light for photosynthesis. Each cell is surrounded by a cell wall made of cellulose.

Flowering plants have stems, roots and leaves. They have transport systems consisting of tiny tubes. These are called **xylem vessels**, which carry water and mineral salts, and **phloem tubes**, which transport dissolved food.

Flowering plants reproduce by means of flowers which make seeds. The seeds are produced inside the ovary within the flower.

## Shoots and roots

The **shoot** is the part of the plant above ground. The shoot is made up of a **stem** bearing leaves, buds and flowers. The **apical bud** is the part where the stem grows new leaves. The stem supports the structures of the shoot, and spaces out the leaves so that they can receive adequate light and air (see page 66.) It holds the flowers in a position which enables **pollination** to take place.

The stem allows transport of water from the soil up to the leaves and food from the leaves to other parts of the plant, such as the roots.

The **roots** are the parts of flowering plants found below ground. Roots are usually white since they do not contain chlorophyll. Roots anchor the plant firmly in the ground and prevent it from being blown over by the wind. Roots also absorb water and mineral ions from the soil (see page 90).

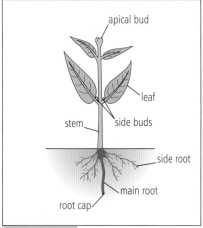

**Figure 1.6.1**  Structure of a typical dicotyledonous plant.

apical bud
leaf
stem
side buds
side root
main root
root cap

## Dicotyledonous and monocotyledonous plants

Flowering plants can be divided into two main groups:

**dicotyledons** and **monocotyledons**

*Magnolia* is a dicotyledon.

Maize, *Zea mays*, is a monocotyledon.

Dicotyledons look like the plant at the top of the opposite page.

Their leaves are often broad with a network of branching veins. The parts of the flower, for example the male parts known as stamens, are in multiples of four or five in each flower. Dicotyledons have *two* **cotyledons** (seed leaves) in a seed.

Grasses and cereals, like the maize plant opposite, are monocotyledons.

The leaves of most monocotyledons have parallel veins. Grasses and cereals have long, narrow leaves. Other monocotyledons have leaves with a variety of shapes, such as those of palm trees. The parts of the flower are in multiples of three. Monocotyledons have *one* cotyledon inside each seed.

## PRACTICAL

### Comparing dicotyledons and monocotyledons

Obtain two plants, one a dicotyledon and the other a monocotyledon.

   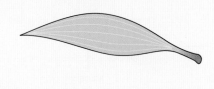

leaf of dicotyledon            leaf of monocotyledon

Compare the shape of their leaves and look carefully at the pattern of their veins.

How do they differ?

In what other ways do the two plants differ?

Make labelled drawings to illustrate your answers.

clusters of flowers

leaf

**Figure 1.6.2**  Structure of a typical monocotyledon plant.

## SUMMARY QUESTIONS

1  Copy and complete the sentences using the words below:

**parallel   two   narrow   flowering
broad   network   one**

Monocotyledons are _____ plants that often have _____ leaves with _____ veins. They have _____ cotyledon inside the seed. Dicotyledons often have _____ leaves with a _____ of veins. They have _____ cotyledons inside each seed.

2  Find the names of five dicotyledonous plants and five monocotyledonous plants that grow where you live.

3  Find out and list the functions (jobs) of each of the following:
   a  leaves,  b  stems,  c  roots,  d  flowers.

## KEY POINTS

1  Flowering plants are multicellular – each cell is surrounded by a cellulose cell wall and those in leaves and some stems contain chloroplasts.

2  Monocotyledons have one cotyledon in their seeds and leaves with parallel veins.

3  Dicotyledons have two cotyledons and broad leaves with a network of branching veins.

- Use simple dichotomous keys to identify plants and animals
- Identify external features of animals and plants that are useful for making a key

In this section, we have used external features to identify and classify organisms. Cladistics is the method used by scientists to classify organisms using other features to show how they evolved. They use many techniques including comparing the DNA of different species to see how closely related they are.

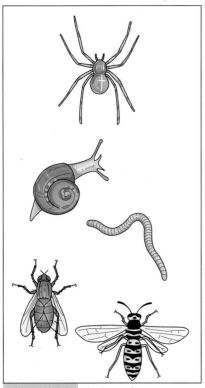

**Figure 1.7.2** Five invertebrates.

## Sorting things out

To identify the name of a plant or animal you could look through the pictures in a book until you found the right one. However, that would take a lot of time and effort.

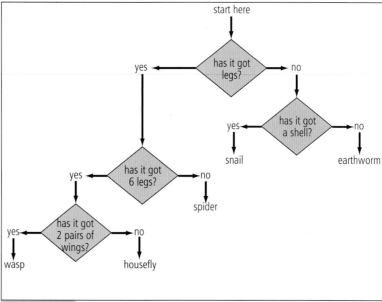

**Figure 1.7.1** A branching dichotomous key.

Scientists use **dichotomous keys** to identify living things. Dichotomous means dividing into two.

A key has a number of steps – you can see them in the branched key and the numbered key on this page. At each step in the branching key you find a question or statement. Start at the beginning and answer 'yes' or 'no' to the first question or statement. This takes you to another question or to an identification. Use the branching key above to identify the animals to the left.

Use the numbered key below to identify the same animals. It is set out differently from the first key, but it works in the same way. Start at the beginning and answer the questions at each stage.

**1** Has legs      Go to 2
    Has no legs      Go to 4
**2** Has 6 legs      Go to 3
    Has 8 legs      Spider
**3** Has 1 pair of wings      Housefly
    Has 2 pairs of wings      Wasp
**4** Has a shell      Snail
    Has no shell      Earthworm

**Making a leaf key**

Now try making a key of your own.

Take six different leaves and label them A to F.

Put the six leaves out in front of you.

Think of a question that will divide them into two groups.

Write down the question.

Now think up questions to divide each group into two.

Write these down.

Carry on until you come to the last pair of leaves.

Write out your key as a branching key or a numbered key.

## Pond animals key

Now try making a key of these pond animals below.

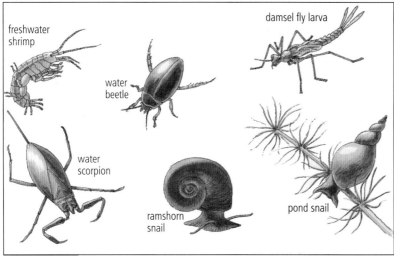

**Figure 1.7.3**  Pond animals.

**KEY POINTS**

1  Dichotomous keys are used to identify organisms, such as plants and animals.

2  A dichotomous key includes a series of paired statements or questions which lead to an identification. Dichotomous means dividing into two.

**SUMMARY QUESTIONS**

1  When a scientist visited an island she discovered some insects.

   She made some drawings and brought them back to the laboratory. Her drawings are shown on the right.

   a  Give each insect a suitable name.

   b  Make a dichotomous key to identify them. Present your key either as a branching key or as a numbered key.

2  Write down the features that would enable you to classify a fish, an amphibian, a reptile, a bird and a mammal. (You can use the photos on pages 8 and 9 to help you.) Now make a key that you could use to identify each of these vertebrate groups.

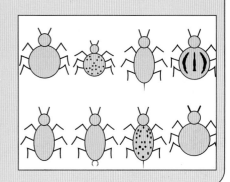

1 Write definitions of the following terms:

   excretion, growth, movement, nutrition, reproduction, respiration, sensitivity.

2 The binomial system is used to give scientific names to organisms. State what the two words in a binomial, such as *Homo sapiens*, stand for.

3 Write out the full scientific names of the following:

   meerkat
   malarial parasite
   American crocodile
   maize
   Monarch butterfly.

4 List the external features used to identify the following phyla of animals:

   annelids, arthropods, molluscs, nematodes.

5 List the external features used to identify the following classes of the arthropod phylum:

   arachnids, crustaceans, insects, myriapods.

6 Vertebrates are divided into five classes. Name these classes and state three external features shown by the animals in each class.

7 State the differences between monocotyledons and dicotyledons that are used to classify these two groups of flowering plants.

8 State what is meant by dichotomous when used in the term dichotomous key.

9 List the main features used to classify the following groups of microorganisms:

   viruses, bacteria, fungi.

10 Explain how viruses, bacteria and fungi are adapted to survive in their environments.

Extension

1 Which process is carried out by all the organisms that live in a forest?

   A moulting
   B photosynthesis
   C pollination
   D respiration

   *(Paper 1)* [1]

2 What are characteristics of all organisms?

   A excretion and respiration
   B ingestion and growth
   C photosynthesis and egestion
   D respiration and photosynthesis

   *(Paper 1)* [1]

3 Which group of animals includes those with a segmented body, an exoskeleton and jointed limbs?

   A annelids
   B arthropods
   C molluscs
   D vertebrates

   *(Paper 1)* [1]

4 Which class of vertebrate includes those with dry scaly skin and four legs?

   A amphibians
   B fish
   C mammals
   D reptiles

   *(Paper 1)* [1]

5 The drawings show five animals, **A** to **E**. They are not drawn to scale.

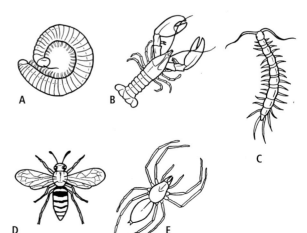

(a) Name (i) the phylum, and (ii) the class into which each of these animals, **A** to **E**, is classified. [6]

(b) Give three reasons for the choice of phylum, and one reason for each choice of class that you made in part (a). [8]

(Paper 2)

6 Draw and complete the table using ticks and crosses to indicate whether the four phyla show the features or not.

| feature | annelids | nematodes | arthropods | molluscs |
|---|---|---|---|---|
| segmented body | | | | |
| jointed limbs | | | | |
| exoskeleton | | | | |
| internal or external shell | | | | |

(Paper 2) [4]

7 (a) Define the term *vertebrate*. [1]

There are five classes within the vertebrate group.

(b) List three external features shared by the following classes of vertebrates: amphibians, reptiles, birds and mammals. [3]

(c) State two external features of mammals that are *not* seen in reptiles. [2]

(d) State two external features shared by amphibians and fish. [2]

(Paper 2)

8 The drawings show leaves from three species of flowering plant, **A** to **C**. They are not drawn to scale.

A          B          C

(a) (i) Identify the group of flowering plants to which each species belongs.

(ii) State the features that you used to make your identifications. [5]

(b) List five features shown by the leaves that would be useful in devising a dichotomous key to identify species of flowering plants. [5]

(Paper 2)

9 The drawing shows a giant pangolin, *Smutsia gigantea*. Pangolins are mammals with bodies covered in plates made of the protein keratin, which is also found in skin, hair, claws and nails. The body covering makes pangolins look similar to reptiles.

(a) Explain what the giant pangolin's scientific name tells us about how this animal is classified. [2]

(b) State two external features that pangolins share with reptiles *other than* the body covering. [3]

(c) Explain why pangolins are classified as mammals and *not* as reptiles. [3]

(d) The table shows the features shown by some microorganisms. Copy and complete the table using ticks and crosses.

| feature | viruses | bacteria | fungi |
|---|---|---|---|
| have nuclei | | | |
| can make capsules | | | |
| produce spores | | | |
| have hyphae | | | |

[4]

(e) Explain how:

(i) a fungus, such as *Rhizopus nigricans* shown on page 11, is adapted to feed and disperse from one source of food to another; [5]

(ii) bacteria survive adverse conditions; [2]

(iii) viruses increase in number. [3]

(Paper 3)

## 2.1

# Structure of cells

## Cells

Cells are the small building blocks that make up all living organisms. Very small living things such as bacteria are made of only one cell.

An insect such as a fly may contain millions of cells. No one knows for certain how many cells there are in a human being – estimates vary between $10 \times 10^{12}$ and $50 \times 10^{12}$.

### Animal cells

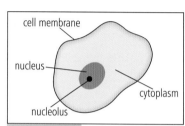

**Figure 2.1.1**  A cheek cell (stained with a blue dye).

### Plant cells

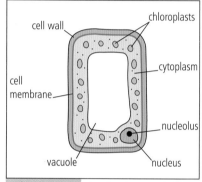

**Figure 2.1.2**  A palisade mesophyll cell from a leaf.

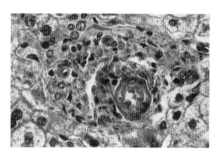

Liver cells magnified by ×300.

## Differences between plant and animal cells

The differences between plant and animal cells are summarised in this table.

| feature | plant cell | animal cell |
|---|---|---|
| cellulose cell wall | present | absent |
| shape | permanent shape determined by the cell wall; shapes can be nearly spherical, box-like or cylindrical | shapes vary as there is no cell wall |
| chloroplasts | present in some cells | absent |
| vacuole | large permanent vacuole containing cell sap | small vacuoles, do not contain cell sap |
| nucleus | present (often at the side of the cell close to the cell wall) | present (found anywhere within the cell) |

# Functions of cell structures

| cell structure | functions |
|---|---|
| cell membrane | • forms a barrier between the cell and its surroundings<br>• keeps contents of cell inside<br>• allows simple substances to enter and leave the cell, e.g. oxygen, carbon dioxide and water<br>• controls movement of other substances into and out of cell, e.g. glucose<br>• often described as partially permeable (see page 28) |
| nucleus | • controls all activities in the cell<br>• controls how cells develop |
| cytoplasm | • place where many chemical reactions take place, e.g. respiration and making proteins for the cell |
| chloroplast | • photosynthesis<br>• stores starch |
| cell wall | • stops cells from bursting when they fill with water<br>• gives shape to cells<br>• allows water and dissolved substances to pass through freely (often described as freely or fully permeable) |
| sap vacuole | • full of water to maintain shape and 'firmness' of cell<br>• stores salts and sugars |

**EXAMINER SAYS...**

Make drawings of liver cells and palisade mesophyll cells, label the structures and underneath each label write the functions. You can use your diagram to help your revision.

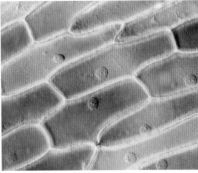

Cells of onion epidermis magnified by ×250.

## SUMMARY QUESTIONS

1 Copy and complete this table by using ticks and crosses to indicate if the structures are present or not.

| cell structures | cheek cell (animal) | onion cell (plant) | leaf cell (plant) |
|---|---|---|---|
| nucleus | | | |
| cell wall | | | |
| chloroplasts | | | |
| large vacuole | | | |
| cytoplasm | | | |

2 State the functions of the following parts:
  a chloroplast, b cell membrane, c cell wall, d nucleus.

**KEY POINTS**

1 A cell membrane, cytoplasm and a nucleus are found in both plant and animal cells.

2 All plant cells have a cellulose cell wall; some have chloroplasts and a vacuole containing cell sap. Animal cells do not have these parts.

# Different types of cell

To function efficiently, many-celled organisms have cells that are specialised to carry out certain functions. This means that the functions of the body are divided between different groups of cells. As an organism develops from a fertilised egg, new cells are produced. These cells grow and change to become specialised for certain functions. In this spread we look at some examples of specialised cells.

## Specialised cells

**Ciliated cells** are found in the air passages in the lungs (trachea and bronchi) and in the oviducts in the female reproductive system. These cells have **cilia** on their surfaces. Cilia beat back and forth to create a current in the fluid next to the cell surfaces.

In the airways, cilia move the mucus that traps dust and pathogens up to the nose and throat. In the oviducts, cilia move the egg from the ovary to the uterus.

**Root hair cells** have long extensions that give them a large surface area to absorb water and ions from the soil.

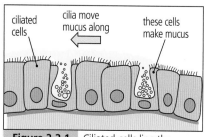

**Figure 2.2.1** Ciliated cells line the airways.

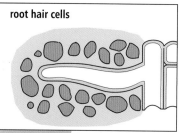

**Figure 2.2.2** Root hair cells are long and thin to absorb water from the soil.

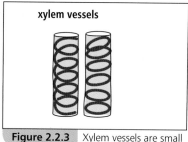

**Figure 2.2.3** Xylem vessels are small tubes that carry water up the stem.

**Xylem vessels** are cylindrical and empty. They are arranged into columns like pipes. The cell walls are thickened with bands or spirals of cellulose and a waterproof material called lignin. These cells allow water and ions to move from the roots to the rest of the plant. They also help to support the stem and leaves.

**Muscle cells** make up fibres that are able to shorten or contract. Some muscles are attached to the skeleton; when they contract they move bones at joints. Muscle cells are also in the gut and in the heart.

**Red blood cells** contain the protein **haemoglobin** that carries oxygen. They are shaped like flattened discs. This shape provides a large surface area compared with their volume which makes for efficient absorption of oxygen.

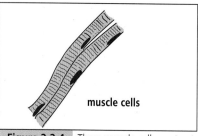

**Figure 2.2.4** These muscle cells contract to move bones.

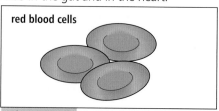

**Figure 2.2.4** Red blood cells have a substance called haemoglobin that carries oxygen.

## Size of cells and specimens

Look at the photograph of some human cheek cells.

The cells are 1000 times larger than in real life.

This means that they have been *magnified* 1000 times.

To work out the *actual size* of a cell measure the length of one magnified cell in millimetres. Let's say that it measures 13 mm.

Now we can use this formula to work out actual size:

$$\text{actual size} = \frac{\text{image size}}{\text{magnification}}$$

So the actual size of our cell $= \dfrac{13}{1000} = 0.013 \, \text{mm}$

There are 1000 micrometres (µm) in a millimetre. We can convert the answer to micrometres by multiplying by 1000 to give 13 µm.

We can use a similar technique when the image size has been reduced, as in this photograph of a goldfish. This time there has been a *reduction* of actual size in the photograph. If you calculate the fish's actual size using the same formula you will find it is 90 mm long.

To calculate the magnification of an image we reorganise the formula:

$$\text{magnification} = \frac{\text{image size}}{\text{actual size}}$$

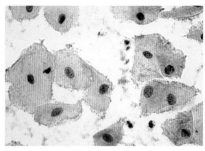

Human cheek cells.

The image of this goldfish is one third (×0.33) actual size.

### SUMMARY QUESTIONS

1 Draw a table matching the type of cell in the first column with its correct shape and function:

| Type of cell | Shape | Function |
|---|---|---|
| red blood cells | hollow tube | keep the air passages free from dust |
| ciliated cells | long banded threads | transport water and ions |
| root hair cells | flat discs | contract (shorten) to move muscles |
| muscle cells | long and thin | transport oxygen |
| xylem vessels | have cilia that move | absorb water from the soil |

2 Here are some other specialised cells. Use this book to find out the functions of these cells and how they are adapted to carry out their functions.

  a sperm cell, b nerve cell, c white blood cell,

  d human egg cell, e palisade mesophyll cell.

3 Calculate the actual sizes of the liver cells and the onion cells on pages 18 and 19.

### KEY POINTS

1 During development, cells change their structure and often their shape.

2 Specialised cells have a structure that enables them to carry out a particular function, e.g. ciliated cells have cilia to move mucus along the windpipe.

3 We can calculate both the magnification and actual sizes of images of biological specimens.

# Levels of organisation

## Tissues and organs

A group of similar cells is called a **tissue**. All the cells in a tissue look the same and they work together to carry out a shared function. Muscle tissue is made up of identical **muscle** cells. These cells work together and so the muscle tissue contracts.

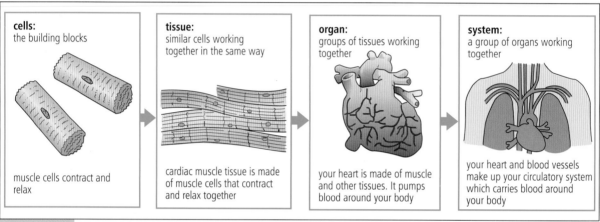

**cells:**
the building blocks

muscle cells contract and relax

**tissue:**
similar cells working together in the same way

cardiac muscle tissue is made of muscle cells that contract and relax together

**organ:**
groups of tissues working together

your heart is made of muscle and other tissues. It pumps blood around your body

**system:**
a group of organs working together

your heart and blood vessels make up your circulatory system which carries blood around your body

**Figure 2.3.1**  Levels of organisation in the human circulatory system.

An **organ** is made up of a group of different tissues that work together to perform specific functions.

The heart is an example of an organ. It is made up of different tissues such as cardiac muscle, nervous tissue, fibrous tissue and blood that work together to pump blood around the body.

The stomach, lungs, brain and kidneys are all organs.

Different organs work together as part of an **organ system**. Organ systems consist of a group of organs with related functions, working together to perform body functions. For example, the heart and blood vessels work together as part of the circulatory system. Here are some other organ systems:

- The digestive system is made up of the gullet, stomach, pancreas, liver and intestines.
- The excretory system is made up of the kidneys, ureters and bladder.
- The nervous system is made up of the brain, spinal cord and nerves.
- The reproductive system in females is the ovaries, oviducts, uterus and vagina; in males it is the testes, sperm ducts, prostate gland and penis.

All the different organ systems make up a living **organism**.

## Plant tissues and organs

The diagrams show the tissues in a leaf. The tissue that carries out photosynthesis in leaves is called **mesophyll**. The cells making up the upper layer of the mesophyll are called palisade cells. These cells are closely packed and full of chloroplasts so that they are well adapted to absorb lots of light. The palisade cells make up the **palisade mesophyll tissue**. All the cells making up this tissue look alike and do the same function – they absorb light for photosynthesis.

A leaf is an organ. Other plant organs are roots and stems. Other structures, such as flowers and fruits, are modified leaves.

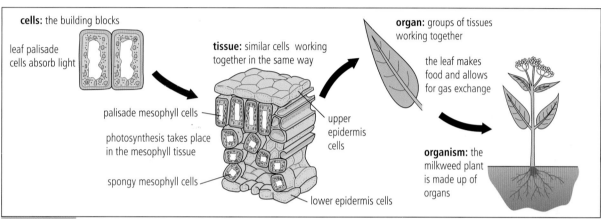

**Figure 2.3.2**  Levels of organisation in a flowering plant.

**SUMMARY QUESTIONS**

1 Copy and complete the sentences using the words below:

**organ system      cells      tissues      function**

A tissue is made up of _____ that carry out the same _____.
An organ is formed from a group of _____ working together.
An _____ is a group of organs working together to perform several body functions.

2 Copy out the organs listed on the left. Match each with the correct system from those listed on the right.

| Organs | System |
|---|---|
| lungs and trachea | digestive |
| heart and blood vessels | nervous |
| brain and spinal cord | gas exchange |
| ovaries, oviducts and uterus | excretory |
| gullet, stomach and intestines | reproductive |
| kidneys and bladder | circulatory |

3 Arrange the following words into the correct sequence, starting with the smallest and ending with the largest:

**organ      organ system      tissue      organism      cell**

**EXAMINER SAYS...**

Make sure you can explain how a palisade mesophyll cell is adapted to carry out photosynthesis by listing the features and explaining how each one helps.

**KEY POINTS**

1 Cells that have the same function are grouped together to form tissues.

2 Different tissues make up organs which work together to do a particular function.

3 Different organs work together as organ systems.

1 State three structures that are present in both plant and animal cells.

2 State three structures present in plant cells that are never found in animal cells.

3 Match the cell types with their functions:

| cell type | function |
|---|---|
| red blood cells | movement of mucus |
| root hair cells | contraction and movement |
| muscle cells | absorption of water and ions |
| xylem vessels | transport of oxygen |
| ciliated cells | conduction of water and ions |

4 Write definitions of the following:
   (a) tissue
   (b) organ
   (c) organ system.

5 (a) Name three animal tissues.
   (b) Name three plant tissues.

**Extension**

6 The following structures are present in both plant and animal cells:

   cell membrane, cytoplasm and nucleus.

   State the functions of each of these structures.

7 All plant cells have cell walls; some plant cells have chloroplasts and large vacuoles. State the function of each of these structures.

1 Which structure is found *only* in plant cells?
   A cell membrane
   B chloroplast
   C cytoplasm
   D nucleus

*(Paper 1)* [1]

2 Which of the following structures is *not* found in animal cells?
   A cell membrane
   B cell wall
   C cytoplasm
   D nucleus

*(Paper 1)* [1]

3 Which is the correct sequence, starting with the smallest and ending with the largest?
   A tissue, organ system, organ, cell
   B cell, tissue, organ system, organ
   C tissue, cell, organ, organ system
   D cell, tissue, organ, organ system

*(Paper 1)* [1]

4 A student made a drawing of a biological specimen. The length of the specimen in the drawing is 140 mm. The magnification is ×40. What is the actual size of the specimen?
   A 5600 mm    B 56 mm
   C 35 mm      D 3.5 mm

*(Paper 1)* [1]

5 The palisade mesophyll cell is a type of plant cell. A liver cell is a type of animal cell. Copy and complete the table to compare these two cells. Copy the table and put a tick (✔) if you think the structure is present and a cross (✗) if you think it is absent.

| cell structure | palisade mesophyll cell | liver cell |
|---|---|---|
| cell wall | | |
| cell membrane | | |
| cytoplasm | | |
| nucleus | | |
| chloroplast | | |
| large vacuole | | |

[6]

*(Paper 2)*

**6** The diagram shows three animal cells.

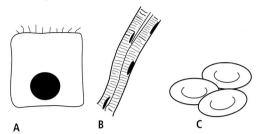

**A**          **B**          **C**

(a) Identify the cells **A**, **B** and **C**. [3]

(b) State the functions of the three cells. [3]

(c) State where in the body these cells are found. [3]

(d) The magnification of cell **A** is ×1000. Calculate its actual size. [2]

*(Paper 2)*

**7** The diagram shows three plant cells.

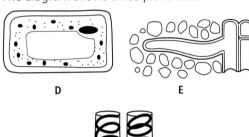

**D**          **E**

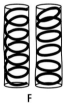

**F**

(a) Identify the cells **D**, **E** and **F**. [3]

(b) State the functions of the three cells. [3]

(c) For each cell, **D**, **E** and **F**, state a plant organ where it is found. In each case give a different organ. [3]

(d) The actual length of cell **D** is 0.05 mm. Calculate the magnification of the drawing. [2]

*(Paper 2)*

**8 (a)** Name:

(i) an animal cell which does not have a nucleus; [1]

(ii) a plant cell that does not have a nucleus; [1]

(iii) the organ system for transport in mammals; [1]

(iv) the plant tissue that transports sugars. [1]

(b) Distinguish between the following pairs of terms.

(i) Organs and tissues. [2]

(ii) Cytoplasm and nucleus. [2]

(iii) Cell membrane and cell wall. [2]

(iv) Organ system and organism. [2]

*(Paper 2)*

**9 (a)** Match each cell structure on the left with its function on the right.

| | |
|---|---|
| nucleus | controls the entry and exit of materials from the cell |
| cell membrane | full of cell sap as a store of water and ions |
| cell wall | contains chlorophyll and carries out photosynthesis |
| large vacuole | place where most chemical reactions in the cell take place |
| chloroplast | contains the instructions for the cell |
| cytoplasm | made of cellulose to withstand pressure of water inside the cell |

[6]

(b) A student looked at a cell under a light microscope. She made a drawing of the cell and showed the diameter of the nucleus in her drawing as 70 mm. She calculated the magnification of her drawing as ×10 000. What is the actual size of the nucleus? [2]

*(Paper 3)*

# 3 Movement in and out of cells

## 3.1        Diffusion

Molecules in gases move about in a random way. They bump into one another and spread out to fill up all the space available. Molecules in a liquid do this as well, although it takes longer for them to fill the space. Movement in a gas is faster as the molecules are more spread out. The difference in speed between movement in gases and liquids is important for organisms.

This movement of molecules is called **diffusion**.

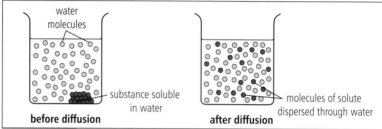

Figure 3.1.2    Diffusion in a liquid.

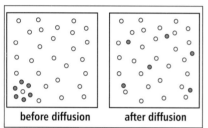

**Figure 3.1.1** Diffusion in a gas. Molecules of a coloured gas spread out through the container.

When molecules diffuse they spread out from where there are lots of them in a given volume (a high concentration) to where there are not as many of them (a low concentration). The difference between the concentration of molecules in two places is a **concentration gradient**. Molecules carry on diffusing until they are spread out evenly. When this happens the molecules keep moving, but there is no longer a difference in concentrations so diffusion has stopped.

**Diffusion is the net movement of molecules from a region of high concentration to a region of lower concentration down a concentration gradient.**

Cells gain some of the substances they need by diffusion from their surroundings. They also lose some of their waste substances to their surroundings by diffusion. These substances have to cross cell membranes that are **partially permeable** as they allow the movement of small molecules such as oxygen, carbon dioxide and water to pass through easily, but not larger molecules. The movement of molecules by diffusion across cell membranes is **passive movement** as cells do not need to use energy to move the molecules.

## Factors that affect diffusion

These factors influence the efficiency of diffusion.

- The distance molecules have to travel – note that cell membranes are very thin.
- The concentration gradient – cells use the substances that diffuse in as quickly as possible, so they keep a low concentration inside the cytoplasm. This means that molecules keep diffusing into the cell because the cell is maintaining a steep concentration gradient.

- The surface area – some cells have cell membranes that are folded to give a large surface to allow many molecules to cross by diffusion.
- The temperature – molecules move faster and collide more often as the temperature increases. Diffusion is faster at warmer temperatures.
- The size of molecule – small molecules diffuse faster than large ones.

## Gas versus liquid

Animals and plants exchange the gases oxygen and carbon dioxide with their surroundings at gas exchange surfaces. In mammals, the gas exchange surface is formed of the alveoli in the lungs (see page 121). Blood transports these two gases between the lungs and all the cells in the body. In the alveoli, oxygen diffuses across a very thin layer of cells into the blood. Carbon dioxide diffuses in the opposite direction. Breathing constantly refreshes the air in the alveoli and blood constantly removes oxygen and brings carbon dioxide, so the concentration gradients are always steep. There are many alveoli to give a very large surface area for gas exchange.

In plants, gas exchange occurs inside the leaves. The spongy mesophyll cells provide a large surface area for exchange of gases. There are air spaces between the cells in a plant and each cell exchanges gases with this air (see page 66). This is efficient because diffusion through the air is 300 000 times faster than through water.

## Water as a solvent

A **solution** is made up of two parts, the **solute** and the **solvent**. The solute dissolves in the solvent. If you dissolve sugar in water you make a sugar solution. The sugar is the solute and the water is the solvent. The solute is not always a solid like sugar. Liquids and gases can be solutes as they can dissolve in solvents too. Something which dissolves in a solvent is described as being **soluble**.

Water is sometimes called the universal solvent. About 75% of cytoplasm is water and it is the main component of transport fluids like blood, and xylem sap and phloem sap in plants. Everything transported in plants and animals has to dissolve in water and most of the chemical reactions that occur in cells happen in water.

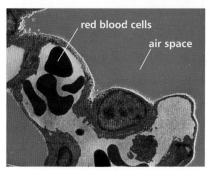
There is a short distance between the red blood cells and the air in the alveoli. Magnification ×1500.

## SUMMARY QUESTIONS

1 Copy and complete the sentences using the words below :

**liquid   random   diffusion   low   gas   high**

_____ is the net movement of molecules of a _____ or a _____ from an area of _____ to an area of _____ concentration as a result of the _____ movement of molecules.

2 State how the following factors affect diffusion into cells:
  a  distance,   b  size of molecule,   c  surface area,
  d  concentration gradient,   e  temperature.

3 What do the terms *solution* and *concentration gradient* mean?

4 Explain why water is an important solvent for animals and plants.

## KEY POINTS

1 Diffusion is the net movement of molecules from a region of high concentration to a region of low concentration down a concentration gradient.

2 Factors that affect diffusion are: size of molecule, distance, surface area, temperature and the steepness of the concentration gradient.

**Extension**

### LEARNING OUTCOMES

- Define the term *osmosis*
- Describe the effect of osmosis on plant and animal tissues
- Explain the movement of water into and out of cells using the term water potential

### EXAMINER SAYS...

If asked to define osmosis or write about it, make sure you say that it is the diffusion of water molecules.

Each cell is surrounded by a cell membrane. It separates the contents of the cell from the outside. The cell membrane has tiny holes in it which allows small molecules to pass through but not large ones. The cell membrane is described as being **partially permeable**.

**Osmosis** is a special kind of diffusion involving water molecules. It occurs when two solutions are separated by a **partially permeable membrane**.

Osmosis is the diffusion of water from a dilute solution into a more concentrated solution through a partially permeable membrane.

The tiny holes in the membrane allow small water molecules to pass through, but the large solute molecules are too big to pass through the partially permeable membrane. Water is diffusing from a place where there is a dilute solution with a **high concentration of water** to a place where there is a concentrated solution with a **low concentration of water**.

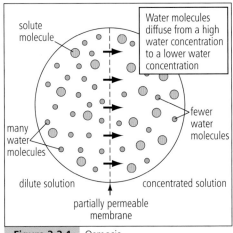

Labels in figure: solute molecule; Water molecules diffuse from a high water concentration to a lower water concentration; many water molecules; fewer water molecules; dilute solution; concentrated solution; partially permeable membrane

**Figure 3.2.1**  Osmosis.

**Extension**

Water potential is a way of thinking about the ability of water to move by osmosis. This is influenced by how much water is available, but also by other factors such as the pressure exerted on water in plant cells by the cell wall. It is more accurate to say that a dilute solution (containing a lot of water molecules) has a **high water potential**. A concentrated solution (containing fewer water molecules) has a **low water potential**.

In the diagram above, there is a **water potential gradient** between the two sides of the membrane. The water molecules diffuse *down* this water potential gradient, from a region of high water potential to a region of lower water potential.

### A model cell

**Dialysis tubing** (Visking tubing) is partially permeable. We can use dialysis tubing to represent the cell membrane and the sugar solution to represent the cytoplasm.

Cut two pieces of dialysis tubing, each 12 cm long. Tie one end of each with cotton.

Fill one model cell with a dilute sugar solution (cell A). Fill the other model cell with water (cell B).

Tie the other end of both model cells and weigh them on a balance. Put 'cell A' into a beaker of water and put 'cell B' into a beaker containing a concentrated solution of sugar. After 30 minutes take out the model cells and weigh them again.

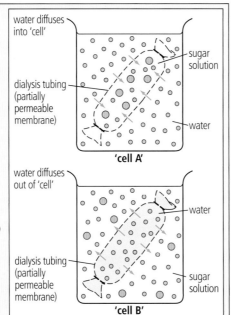

'Cell A' increases in mass because water has diffused *into* the 'cell' by osmosis. 'Cell B' decreases in mass because water has diffused *out of* the cell by osmosis.

**An osmometer**

You can see the effects of osmosis if you set up this apparatus.

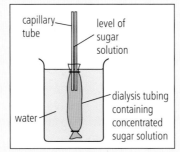

Fill the partially permeable membrane with a very concentrated solution of sugar.

Tie it to a capillary tube and stand it in water.

Very quickly you will see the liquid moving up the tube. You can measure how fast it is moving using a ruler and a stopwatch. Use your ideas about osmosis to explain why the liquid rises in the tube.

**SUMMARY QUESTIONS**

1 Define the following terms:

   **diffusion   osmosis   partially permeable membrane**

2 Describe how you can find out how fast water diffuses by osmosis into a sugar solution. Remember to include all practical details.

3 Explain in terms of water potential, how water passes into plant cells placed in distilled water.

Extension

**KEY POINTS**

1 Osmosis is the diffusion of water molecules from a region of their higher concentration (dilute solution) to a region of their lower concentration (concentrated solution) through a partially permeable membrane.

2 A partially permeable membrane allows small molecules such as water to pass through but not large solute molecules.

# Osmosis in plant and animal cells

- Describe how water can enter and leave plant cells by osmosis
- Describe how osmosis can affect animal cells

**EXAMINER SAYS...**

When describing the cell membrane always say that it is <u>partially</u> permeable, not semi-permeable.

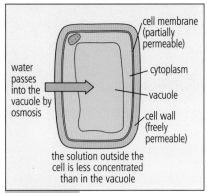

the solution outside the cell is less concentrated than in the vacuole

cell membrane (partially permeable)

cytoplasm

vacuole

cell wall (freely permeable)

water passes into the vacuole by osmosis

**Figure 3.3.1** Osmosis in a plant cell.

**EXAMINER SAYS...**

In Paper 3 you may be expected to use the term 'water potential' in writing about osmosis and plant or animal cells and tissues. You can also refer to 'water potential gradients' to explain water movement into and out of cells and tissues.

Extension

## PRACTICAL

**Osmosis in potato cells**

Cut nine cores from a potato so that they are exactly the same length. Record this length.

Feel the cores to see how firm and 'bendy' they are.

Set up the following test-tubes:

test-tube **A** – distilled water

test-tube **B** – dilute sugar solution

test-tube **C** – concentrated sugar solution.

Place three cores of potato into each test-tube and leave them for 60 minutes.

Remove the cores and measure their lengths. Calculate the average length of the cores in each test-tube.

A – distilled water
tissue swells up

B – dilute sugar solution
no change

C – concentrated sugar solution
tissue shrunken and flaccid

**A** – Cores will be longer and feel firmer than at the start.

**B** – Cores will be about the same length and firmness as at the start.

**C** – Cores will be shorter and feel much softer and 'bendier' than at the start.

These results are explained in the text.

## Turgidity

The cell membrane of the plant cell is partially permeable and the cell sap inside the vacuole is a solution of salts and sugars. When plant cells are placed in water, the water enters the cells. This is because there is a water concentration gradient so that water molecules diffuse into the cells by osmosis.

As water enters it makes the cell swell up. The water pushes against the cell wall. Eventually the cell contains as much water as it can hold. It's like a blown-up balloon. The strong cell wall stops the cell bursting. We say that the cell is **turgid**. This is what has happened to the cells in the potato cores in tube A. The cells have absorbed water, swollen and caused the core to get slightly longer.

Turgid cells give the plant support. They keep the stems of many plants upright. However, when these cells lose water, they are no longer firm and turgid. Plant stems and leaves that have lost water **wilt**.

## Plasmolysis

When plant cells are placed into a concentrated sugar or salt solution water passes *out* of the cells by osmosis. As water passes out, the sap vacuole starts to shrink. These cells are no longer firm, and become limp. We say that they are **flaccid**. As more water leaves the cells the cytoplasm starts to move away from the cell wall. These cells are now **plasmolysed**. This is what has happened to the cells in the potato cores in **C**. The cells have decreased in volume so the whole core is shorter than at the start.

The cores in **B** did not change in length very much because the water concentration of the sugar solution was about the same as the water concentration of the cell sap in the potato cells. There has been no overall diffusion of water into or out of the cells so they have stayed about the same length.

## Osmosis in animal cells

This diagram shows what happens to red blood cells when they are placed in different concentrations of a salt solution. Remember that the cell membrane is partially permeable.

The red blood cells in the picture have been placed into different liquids. Their cytoplasm is a concentrated solution of proteins, salts and sugars.

The cells in **D** were in distilled water. Water passes *into* the cells by osmosis. However, animal cells have no cell wall to stop them swelling so they burst. When red blood cells are put into a concentrated salt solution (**F**), they shrink as water passes *out* of the cells by osmosis. The cells in **E** have not changed in size as they are in a solution which has the same water concentration as the cells. This is how they are in the blood when surrounded by blood plasma.

**Figure 3.3.3**  This shows what happens when red blood cells are put into distilled water (D) and a concentrated solution of salt (F). E shows red blood cells as they appear when suspended in blood plasma.

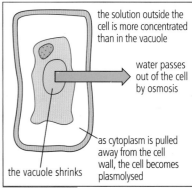

**Figure 3.3.2**  Water passes out of a plant cell by osmosis.

the solution outside the cell is more concentrated than in the vacuole

water passes out of the cell by osmosis

the vacuole shrinks

as cytoplasm is pulled away from the cell wall, the cell becomes plasmolysed

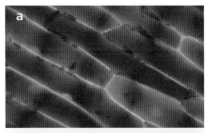

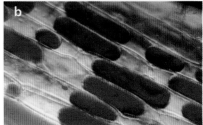

These epidermal cells from a red onion are (a) turgid and (b) plasmolysed.

### SUMMARY QUESTIONS

1 Explain what is meant by each of the follow terms.

**turgid   flaccid   plasmolysis**

2 Some potato cores were weighed and then placed into a dilute sugar solution. After 2 hours, they were taken out of the solution, dried on a paper towel and weighed again.

The mass of the potato cores had stayed unchanged.

   a  What does this tell you about the concentration of the sugar solution?

   b  Explain your answer to part **a** in terms of osmosis.

3 Explain, using the term *water potential*, what happens to cores of potato when they are placed into distilled water for 60 minutes.

**Extension**

### KEY POINTS

1 Water passes into plant cells by osmosis. A plant cell that is full of water is turgid. Turgid cells provide support for leaves and young stems.

2 If plant cells are placed into a concentrated sugar solution, water passes out by osmosis. These cell are no longer firm, they are flaccid. As the vacuole shrinks, the cell membrane moves away from the cell wall – the cell is now plasmolysed.

3 Animal cells burst if they are placed into water as they have no cell wall to resist the increase in size.

# Active transport

## LEARNING OUTCOMES

- Define the term *active transport*
- Explain the importance of active transport as an energy-consuming process
- Describe the active transport of ions in plant roots
- Describe the active uptake of glucose by epithelial cells in villi

### Active transport

Cells take up molecules and ions and keep them in high concentrations.

Look at the concentration of magnesium ions in the root hair cell and the concentration of magnesium ions in the soil solution:

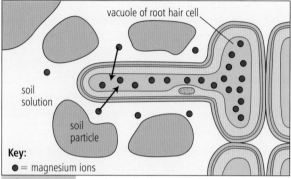

**Figure 3.4.1**   Root hair cells absorb ions by active transport.

The concentration of magnesium ions is far greater inside the vacuole of the root hair cell than it is in the water in the soil. We might expect magnesium ions to diffuse out of the root hair cell into the soil water down a diffusion gradient. The magnesium ions are maintained at a high concentration inside the root hair cell by a process called **active transport**.

Active transport is the movement of ions or molecules in or out of a cell through the cell membrane against a concentration gradient, using energy released during respiration.

### EXAMINER SAYS...

Notice the use of the term 'concentration gradient' in the definition of active transport. 'Against a concentration gradient' means from a low concentration to a high concentration.

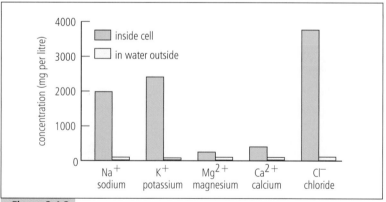

**Figure 3.4.2**

The bar chart shows the concentrations of some ions inside the cells of a freshwater plant and in the water in which it lives. These ions cannot have been taken into the plant by diffusion. They are taken in against a concentration gradient by active transport.

# Active transport needs energy

The cell membrane contains **carrier proteins**. These carrier proteins span the cell membrane and provide means by which ions and molecules can enter or leave a cell by active transport. First the molecule or ion combines with a carrier protein. Energy from respiration enables the carrier protein to change its shape to carry the ion or molecule to the inside of the membrane. The molecule or ion is released to the inside of the membrane and the carrier protein reverts to its original shape.

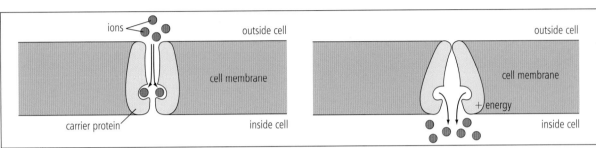

**Figure 3.4.3**  Carrier proteins in membranes carry out active transport.

Epithelial cells lining the **villi** in the small intestine absorb glucose by active transport (see page 84). These cells have high rates of respiration to provide energy for this active transport.

Active transport relies upon respiration to take up ions or molecules against a concentration gradient. Any factor that affects the rate of respiration will also affect the rate of active transport. So a lack of oxygen would reduce respiration rate and active transport.

An increase in temperature would increase the rate of respiration, up to a point, so would also have the same effect on active transport. The presence of poisons such as cyanide can stop respiration, so active transport would stop altogether.

> ## EXAMINER SAYS...
>
> Root hair cells and epithelial cells of villi are adapted for active transport by having many carrier proteins in their cell membranes and a high rate of respiration to provide energy.

## SUMMARY QUESTIONS

1 a  Explain what is meant by active transport.
  b  Describe the role of carrier proteins and respiration in active transport.
  c  Give two examples of active transport taking place.

2 Make a table to compare diffusion with active transport.

  Make sure that you have three columns headed 'features', 'diffusion' and 'active transport'. For features you can include 'needs energy from the cell', 'concentration gradient'. You may be able to think of some other features to use in your table.

3 State what effect each of the following would have on active transport, in each case give reasons for your answer:
  a  a lack of oxygen
  b  an increase in temperature
  c  the presence of a poison, such as cyanide.

## KEY POINTS

1 Active transport is the movement of ions or molecules across the cell membrane, against a concentration gradient, using energy from respiration.

2 Active transport enables root hair cells to take up ions, and epithelial cells of the villi to take up glucose.

## SUMMARY QUESTIONS

1 Define the terms *solvent*, *solute* and *soluble*.

2 Explain why diffusion occurs faster in a gas than in a liquid.

3 Name the process by which each of the following occur:
 (a) molecules of oxygen move from the air spaces in the alveoli in the lungs into the blood
 (b) molecules of carbon dioxide move from respiring cells into the blood
 (c) water molecules move into root hair cells.

4 Define the following terms:
 (a) concentration gradient
 (b) diffusion
 (c) partially permeable membrane
 (d) osmosis.

5 Water forms about 75% of the cytoplasm of cells and a higher proportion of body fluids such as blood. Explain the importance of water as a solvent in the body.

6 Describe what happens to animal and plant cells when they are placed in (a) water, and (b) concentrated solutions of salt.

7 Explain your answers to question 6 (a) and (b) using the terms *partially permeable membrane* and *osmosis*.

8 Use the term *water potential* to explain why plant cells increase in size when placed in water and decrease in size when placed in very concentrated solutions of salt or sugar.

9 Some resources required by cells, such as molecules and ions, are often in very low concentrations in their surroundings. Describe how root hair cells and epithelial cells from the gut obtain resources from their surroundings under these circumstances.

10 Explain why root hair cells have to provide energy for the absorption of ions from the soil.

11 Explain what is meant by the term *concentration gradient* and explain how the term is used when describing the movement of molecules across cell membranes.

## EXAM-STYLE QUESTIONS

1 Which of the following is *not* partially permeable?
 A cell membrane of palisade mesophyll cell
 B cell membrane of red blood cell
 C cell wall
 D dialysis tubing
 *(Paper 1)* [1]

2 Which of the following is the *best* definition of diffusion?
 A movement of molecules down a concentration gradient
 B movement of molecules up a concentration gradient
 C movement of solvent molecules through a partially permeable membrane down a concentration gradient
 D random movement of molecules in a gas or a liquid
 *(Paper 1)* [1]

3 Which of the following is the *best* definition of osmosis?
 A diffusion of molecules through a partially permeable membrane from a dilute solution to a concentrated solution
 B diffusion of molecules through a partially permeable membrane from a high concentration to a low concentration
 C diffusion of water molecules from a region with a dilute solution to a region with a concentrated solution through a partially permeable membrane
 D diffusion of water molecules through a partially permeable membrane
 *(Paper 1)* [1]

4 Some fresh plant tissue was put into a concentrated salt solution for 60 minutes. Which *best* explains why the tissue became softer?
 A The cells became turgid.
 B The cells lost water to their surroundings.
 C Water diffused from a dilute solution in the cells to a more concentrated solution outside the cells.
 D Water diffused by osmosis from the cell sap in the vacuoles into the more concentrated solution outside the cells.
 *(Paper 1)* [1]

**5 (a)** State *three* factors that increase the rate of diffusion. [3]

In the lungs, oxygen and carbon dioxide are exchanged between the blood and the air in the alveoli by diffusion.

**(b)** State three ways in which the alveoli in the lungs are adapted for efficient gas exchange. [3]

*(Paper 2)*

**6** A student set up some apparatus as shown in the diagram below.

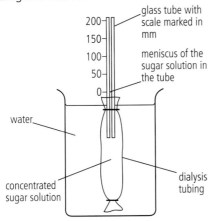

The student measured the level of the meniscus in the glass tube every minute and the results are shown in the table.

| time (minutes) | position of the meniscus in the tube (mm) |
|:--------------:|:-----------------------------------------:|
| 0 | 0 |
| 1 | 24 |
| 2 | 52 |
| 3 | 73 |
| 4 | 102 |
| 5 | 127 |
| 6 | 138 |
| 7 | 180 |
| 8 | 190 |

**(a)** Draw a graph of the results. [6]
**(b)** Describe the results shown by your graph. [2]

**(c)** Calculate the rate of movement in millimetres per minute of the meniscus over the 8 minutes. [2]
**(d)** Explain what caused the sugar solution to move up the tube. [4]

*(Paper 2)*

**7** An experiment was set up to investigate the factors influencing the uptake of ions by plant roots. Some roots were cut from a plant, washed and placed in three solutions, **A**, **B** and **C**, containing potassium ions. A mixture of gases was bubbled through each of the solutions. A gas mixture rich in oxygen was bubbled through solution **A**; solution **B** received a gas mixture with a very low concentration of oxygen; solution **C** received no oxygen in the gas mixture. The roots were left for 24 hours and then the rate of uptake of potassium ions was determined.

The rate of uptake of potassium ions was highest in solution **A** and lowest in solution **C**.

**(a)** Explain how the supply of oxygen to roots influences their uptake of potassium ions. [3]

The experiment was repeated with solutions containing roots kept at different temperatures. They were all provided with the gas mixture that had been given to solution **A**. The results are shown in the table.

| temperature (°C) | rate of uptake of potassium ions (arbitrary units) |
|:----------------:|:--------------------------------------------------:|
| 5 | 3 |
| 10 | 5 |
| 20 | 10 |
| 30 | 20 |
| 40 | 15 |

**(b)** Draw a graph of the results. [6]
**(c)** Describe the results shown in your graph. [4]

**(d)** Explain the effect of temperature on the uptake of potassium ions by the roots. [3]

*(Paper 3)*

# 4 Enzymes

## 4.1 Structure and action of enzymes

This computer-generated image of an enzyme (on the right) shows its 3D shape.

A **catalyst** speeds up a chemical reaction and remains unchanged at the end of the reaction. Enzymes are proteins, produced by organisms, that speed up chemical reactions. They are known as **biological catalysts**.

### How enzymes work

Many chemical reactions take place in organisms. These reactions happen too slowly to keep organisms alive unless they are speeded up by enzymes. There are many different types of enzyme as each one catalyses a different reaction. Most enzymes work inside cells, but many of those that we will discuss here work outside cells, for example in the gut (see pages 78 and 82).

The reactions that enzymes catalyse can be divided into three types.

### 1 Breaking large molecules into small ones

This is important in nutrition when large food molecules are broken down into small ones so that they can be absorbed and then used. Bacteria and fungi release enzymes to break down their food and we release enzymes into the gut for the same reason.

### 2 Building up large molecules from small ones

Small molecules, such as glucose, are joined together to make large molecules. These enzymes work inside cells to speed up the formation of storage molecules, such as starch, and structural molecules such as cellulose for cell walls of plants.

### 3 Converting one small molecule into another

Many of the chemical reactions that occur inside cells involve small changes to molecules, such as adding or removing atoms or groups of atoms. For example, there are enzymes that remove hydrogen from compounds during respiration.

Figure 4.1.1 shows the way in which an enzyme catalyses the breakdown of a molecule.

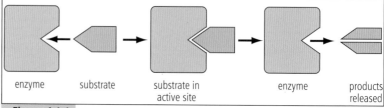

| enzyme | substrate | substrate in active site | enzyme | products released |

**Figure 4.1.1**

Figure 4.1.2 shows how an enzyme is involved in building a molecule from two smaller molecules.

## Enzymes are made of protein

All enzymes have five important properties.

1  They are all proteins.
2  Each enzyme catalyses one reaction.
3  They can be used again and again.
4  They are influenced by temperature.
5  They are influenced by pH.

Extension

Enzymes are made of protein molecules. These can be folded into many different shapes. Each enzyme molecule has a shape that makes it suitable for catalysing one reaction. This explains why there are many different enzymes – one enzyme for each reaction. Proteins are influenced by the conditions of their surroundings. If the conditions become too hot, too acid or too alkaline they tend to change shape. Enzymes stop acting as catalysts when they change shape.

## 'Lock and key' model

Enzymes work on substances called **substrates**. The reaction takes place on a part of the surface of the enzyme called the **active site**.

Look at Figure 4.1.2. Notice the shape of the active site. Only a substrate molecule with a shape that fits into the active site will take part in the reaction catalysed by this enzyme. Other substrates have the wrong shape to fit in and will not be involved in the reaction. This way of describing how enzymes work is known as the 'lock and key' model. The substrate (the 'key') must have a shape that fits exactly into the active site (the 'key hole') of the enzyme (the 'lock').

Only a small number of enzyme molecules are needed to catalyse a reaction because they can be used over and over again. Once the products leave the active site, more substrate molecules can enter and the enzyme will keep on working until all the substrate is used up. A small quantity of the enzyme can catalyse a large quantity of substrate.

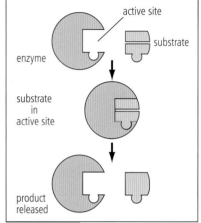

**Figure 4.1.2**  This shows how an enzyme can join two molecules together.

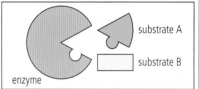

**Figure 4.1.3**  Only substrate A will fit the enzyme's active site.

---

### SUMMARY QUESTIONS

1  Copy and complete the following sentences using the words below:

**substrate   speed   catalysts   proteins   reactions**

Enzymes are biological _____ that _____ up the rate of chemical _____. Enzymes are all _____ and each enzyme acts on one type of _____.

Extension

2  Explain what is meant by the 'lock and key' model of enzyme action.

3  Use the 'lock and key' model to explain:
   a  why each enzyme will only act on one substrate
   b  why an enzyme can be used to catalyse a large quantity of substrate
   c  why destroying the active site by heating the enzyme to a high temperature stops the enzyme from working.

### KEY POINTS

1  Enzymes are biological catalysts that increase the rate of chemical reactions.

2  All enzymes are protein molecules. The active site is the part of the enzyme molecule where the substrate binds with the enzyme and the reaction takes place.

# Factors affecting enzyme action

## LEARNING OUTCOMES

- Describe the effects of temperature and pH on enzyme activity
- Explain the effects of temperature and pH on enzyme activity

The activity of an enzyme is determined by measuring the rate of the reaction that the enzyme catalyses. This may be done either by measuring how much product is formed or by measuring how much substrate is used over a period of time. The rate is like the speed of the reaction measured in quantity of product or substrate per unit of time, e.g. per minute.

## Effect of temperature on enzymes

The activity of enzymes is influenced by temperature. This graph shows the effect of increasing temperature on the rate of an enzyme-catalysed reaction.

Look at the graph and observe that the rate of reaction:

- is slow at low temperatures, e.g. at 10°C
- increases as the temperature increases to 40°C
- reaches a maximum at 40°C
- decreases at temperatures greater than 40°C
- is zero at 60°C.

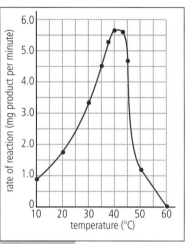

**Figure 4.2.1**

The temperature at which the maximum rate of reaction occurs is called the **optimum temperature**. This is the best temperature for the enzyme. Here are some examples of optimum temperatures:

- fungal and plant enzymes: approximately 20°C (see pages 41 and 230)
- human enzymes: 37°C (body temperature – see pages 78 and 82)
- some of the enzymes produced by bacteria for use in industry: 90°C.

As we saw in the previous spread, an enzyme molecule is folded into a shape that accepts the substrate molecules. The shape of an enzyme's active site is maintained by bonds between different parts of the molecule. Remember that the shape of the active site determines whether the substrate will fit into the enzyme for the reaction to occur.

At first, increasing the temperature of an enzyme-controlled reaction will increase the rate. This is because enzyme and substrate molecules have greater **kinetic energy**. They move around more quickly and there are more chances of them colliding, the substrate fitting into the active site and a reaction taking place.

At higher temperatures the bonds holding the enzyme molecule together start to break down. This changes the shape of the active site, so the substrate no longer fits.

We say that the enzyme has been **denatured** and it can no longer catalyse the reaction.

## Enzymes and pH

Enzymes are influenced by the pH of their surroundings.

Many enzymes work best in neutral conditions, but some prefer acidic and some alkaline conditions.

Look at the graph below showing the action of enzymes X and Y.

- Enzyme X works best at pH 2.0 – that is its optimum pH.
- The optimum pH for enzyme Y is pH 8.0.
- Up to pH 2.0 the rate of reaction increases for enzyme X and then between pH 2.0 and pH 5.5 it decreases. There is no reaction above pH 5.5.
- Between pH 4.5 and pH 8.0 the rate of reaction increases for enzyme Y and then between pH 8.0 and pH 10.0 it decreases. There is no reaction below pH 4.5 and above pH 10.0.

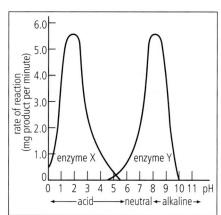

Figure 4.2.3

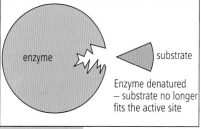

Figure 4.2.2

**Extension**

The shape of the active site can be altered by changes in pH. The bonds that hold the enzyme molecule in shape are broken by changes in pH. When the rate of reaction is zero the shape of the active site has changed and the substrate molecules no longer fit. At these values of pH enzymes are denatured.

### KEY POINTS

1 Increasing the temperature of an enzyme-controlled reaction increases the rate of reaction up to a maximum, which occurs at the optimum temperature.

**Extension**

This is because greater kinetic energy is causing a greater number of collisions between enzyme and substrate molecules.

2 At higher temperatures the rate of reaction decreases quickly until it stops acting as a catalyst.

**Extension**

This is due to a change in the shape of the active site which means the substrate can no longer fit. The enzyme is now denatured.

3 Most enzymes work best at one value of pH.

**Extension**

At some values of pH the shape of the active site changes so that substrate molecules no longer fit.

### SUMMARY QUESTIONS

1 a Sketch a graph to show the effect of increasing temperature on the rate of a reaction catalysed by a human enzyme, such as salivary amylase.

b Describe, in words, what is shown by your graph.

2 Sketch a graph to show the effect of increasing pH on the rate of an enzyme-catalysed reaction where the optimum pH is 7.0 and there is no activity below pH 4.0 and none above pH 10.0.

**Extension**

3 Suggest what each of the following would do to the rate of an enzyme-catalysed reaction and give an explanation:

a a temperature below 10 °C

b a decrease in pH to below the optimum pH for the enzyme.

4 Use the 'lock and key' model to explain what happens when enzymes are denatured at high temperatures and at extremes of pH.

# Enzymes in industry

## LEARNING OUTCOMES

- Explain the role of enzymes in the breakdown of stored materials in seeds during germination
- Describe the role of enzymes in malting
- Describe the role of enzymes in biological washing powders and the role of pectinase in the production of fruit juices
- Describe the role of microorganisms and fermenters in production of the antibiotic penicillin

Industrial fermenters.

## EXAMINER SAYS...

Fermenters provide suitable conditions for growth and metabolism of microorganisms, such as bacteria and fungi. If the temperature is too high, enzymes in the microbes denature and the organisms die.

Enzymes have become very important in industry. Some processes can use enzymes instead of other catalysts. Enzymes work at lower temperatures than other catalysts so reducing the cost of fuels. As enzymes are not destroyed they can be used over and over again and only small quantities are needed.

The first stage in making beer is to get barley seeds to germinate by placing them in warm, moist conditions. Enzymes in the seeds become active and convert the stored starch into the sugar, maltose. This is the sugar used by yeast in the fermentation process to produce alcohol in the beer. Starch is stored in the seeds as a source of energy for respiration.

Seeds of plants such as sunflower and olive contain oils as their energy store. The enzyme lipase is produced inside these seeds to break down the oils when they germinate. If these seeds are harvested for their oils, we do not allow them to start germinating as the oil would be broken down.

## Extracting fruit juice

**Pectinases** are enzymes that break down pectins, which are molecules that act like a 'glue' in plant cell walls. Pectinases are used for extracting fruit juices and for softening vegetables.

## Industrial fermentation

You may recognise the word 'fermentation' as meaning 'respiration without oxygen' (see page 116). However, in this industrial context it refers to any process that uses microorganisms to produce a useful product or to carry out a useful process for us. The organisms involved may respire with or without oxygen. Industrial fermenters are large tanks (see left) that can hold as much as $500\,000\,dm^3$ of fermenting mixture. Conditions inside these huge tanks are carefully controlled. We will use the production of the antibiotic **penicillin** to show how these fermenters work.

- The **fermentation vessel** is made of stainless steel and is filled with a medium containing the required nutrients. These include sugars and ammonium salts. To this some of the fungus *Penicillium* is added.
- The fungus grows well in the conditions inside the fermenter. Sugars provide energy for respiration and ammonium salts are used by the fungus to make proteins and nucleic acids (DNA and RNA). After a few days the fungus starts to produce penicillin, which accumulates in the fermenter.
- A **stirrer** keeps the microorganisms suspended so they always have access to nutrients and oxygen. Stirring also helps to maintain an even temperature throughout the fermenter.
- An **air supply** provides oxygen for the aerobic respiration of the fungus. (In brewing, no oxygen is supplied as the yeasts respire without oxygen to make alcohol.)
- A **water-cooled jacket** removes the heat produced by fermentation to give a constant temperature of 24°C.

- **Probes** monitor the temperature and make sure the pH is constant at 6.5 by adding alkalis if necessary.

Once the fermentation has started it takes about 30 hours for penicillin production to start. After 6 days, fermentation is complete and the mixture is drained and filtered. The penicillin is then extracted as a salt-like material.

## Biological washing powders

Microorganisms produce enzymes to digest complex carbohydrates, proteins and fats. These enzymes are released outside the cells to break down their substrates. Bacteria, e.g. *Bacillus*, and fungi, e.g. *Aspergillus*, are grown in fermenters to produce enzymes for biological washing powders. The fermentation process is similar to that described for penicillin production. The enzymes released by the microorganisms are extracted from the material in the fermenter by filtration.

Biological washing powders may contain one or more of the following types of enzymes:

- **proteases** – break down protein stains, e.g. blood, grass and egg
- **lipases** – break down fats in grease stains, e.g. butter, lipstick and mayonnaise
- **amylases** – break down starch, e.g. food stains containing starch
- **cellulases** – break down cellulose fibres on the outside of cotton fabrics to remove the dirt attached to them.

The enzymes listed above have been modified so that they withstand the high temperatures and alkaline conditions required for some washing powders. During a washing cycle, the enzymes break down stains; the products of the reactions dissolve or are suspended in water and are removed when the washing machine empties. For example, proteins are broken down into amino acids; starch and cellulose are broken down into glucose.

The newest biological washing powders work at quite low temperatures, e.g. 15°C, thus saving energy as the temperature is lower than for non-biological washing powders. The enzymes are broken down into harmless products after they have been used. Unlike chemicals used in some washing powders, they do not harm the environment.

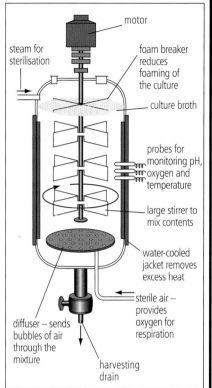

**Figure 4.3.1**   Large industrial fermenter.

### SUMMARY QUESTIONS

1 Describe what each of the following enzymes do:
   a  amylase,  b  protease,       c  lipase,  d  pectinase.

2 Explain the function of each of the following in an industrial fermenter:
   a  a stirrer,  b  an air supply,   c  a water-cooled jacket,
   d  temperature and pH probes.

3 Explain the advantages of using enzymes in washing powders.

4 Explain the role of *Penicillium* in the production of penicillin.

5 State the conditions necessary for the production of penicillin in a fermenter.

### KEY POINTS

1 Stored starch in seeds is broken down by amylase to maltose during germination. Stored fat is broken down by the enzyme lipase.

2 Biological washing powders contain enzymes that work at low wash temperatures and in alkaline conditions.

3 Pectinase is used to extract fruit juice by breaking down the pectin in the cell walls in fruits such as apple.

4 Microorganisms reproduce quickly in the ideal conditions found inside large, industrial fermenters producing useful products such as penicillin.

1 Write definitions of the following terms:
  (a) catalyst
  (b) enzyme
  (c) substrate
  (d) product
  (e) optimum temperature.

2 Explain the following statements.
  (a) Only small quantities of enzymes are required inside cells.
  (b) Amylase digests starch, but trypsin does not.
  (c) When investigating the effect of pH on enzymes, the reaction mixtures must always be kept at the same temperature.

3 Describe the three types of reaction that are catalysed by enzymes.

4 The table shows the effect of temperature on the relative activity of an enzyme kept at pH 7.

| temperature (°C) | relative activity |
| --- | --- |
| 5 | 4 |
| 15 | 8 |
| 25 | 16 |
| 35 | 32 |
| 45 | 30 |
| 55 | 7 |

  (a) Draw a graph of the results in the table.
  (b) Describe the results as shown in the graph.

5 The table shows the relative activity of an enzyme in solutions of different pH kept at 35 °C.

| pH | relative activity |
| --- | --- |
| 3 | 5 |
| 5 | 14 |
| 7 | 32 |
| 9 | 10 |
| 11 | 4 |

  (a) Draw a graph of the results in the table.
  (b) Describe the results as shown in the graph.

1 Which of the following gives the features of enzymes?
  A  Enzymes are made of carbohydrates and are catalysts.
  B  Enzymes are made of carbohydrates and are chemical messengers.
  C  Enzymes are made of proteins and are biological catalysts.
  D  Enzymes are made of proteins and are chemical messengers.

  *(Paper 1)*                                    *[1]*

2 Starch and human salivary amylase were mixed together at different temperatures. Which temperature will give the fastest rate of starch digestion?
  A  20 °C
  B  60 °C
  C  37 °C
  D  10 °C

  *(Paper 1)*                                    *[1]*

3 The pH of enzyme-controlled reactions may be changed from pH 7 to pH 8. How does this affect the rate of the reactions?
  A  always increases the rate
  B  always decreases the rate
  C  has no effect on the rate
  D  may change the rate or have no effect on the rate.

  *(Paper 1)*                                    *[1]*

**Extension**

6 Describe the 'lock and key' model of enzyme action.

7 Explain the results shown in the graphs you drew for questions 4 and 5.

8 Describe the roles of enzymes in:
  (a) the germination of seeds
  (b) washing clothes with biological washing powders
  (c) the production of apple juice.

9 Describe how the fungus *Penicillium* is grown in fermenters.

**4** A student investigated the effect of temperature on amylase.

An amylase solution was divided equally between six test-tubes, **A** to **F**.

Starch solution was put into six test-tubes, **1** to **6**.

The test-tubes were put into water baths at the temperatures given in the table.

After 10 minutes the solutions were mixed: **A** added to **1**, **B** to **2**, etc.

The contents of the test-tubes were stirred and then they were put back into the water baths.

After 5 minutes the contents of the test-tubes were tested for the presence of starch.

The results are in the table.

| test-tubes | temperature (°C) | presence (✓) or absence (✗) of starch |
|---|---|---|
| A + 1 | 5 | ✓ |
| B + 2 | 15 | ✓ |
| C + 3 | 25 | ✗ |
| D + 4 | 35 | ✗ |
| E + 5 | 45 | ✗ |
| F + 6 | 55 | ✓ |

**(a)** Describe how to test for starch. [2]

**(b)** Explain why the test-tubes were left for:

    **(i)** 10 minutes before mixing amylase with starch

    **(ii)** 5 minutes before testing for starch. [4]

**(c)** State in which test-tubes amylase was active. [1]

*(Paper 2)*

**5** The diagram shows an enzyme-catalysed reaction.

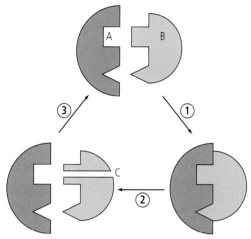

**(a)** State the names of **A**, **B** and **C**. [3]

**(b)** Use the diagram to describe what happens when an enzyme catalyses a reaction. [4]

**(c)** Explain why the model is known as 'lock and key'. [2]

**(d)** Use the model to explain what happens when the enzyme molecule changes shape in high temperatures or extremes of pH. [4]

*(Paper 3)*

**6** Look at the diagram of the fermenter on page 41.

*Penicillium* is grown in fermenters to produce an antibiotic.

**(a)** Name the antibiotic produced by *Penicillium*. [1]

**(b)** State five conditions that are maintained inside the fermenter. [5]

**(c)** For each condition, describe how it is maintained and explain why it must be maintained. [5, 5]

**(d)** Describe how the antibiotic is obtained from the fermenter. [2]

*(Paper 3)*

## 5.1    Nutrients

- Define the term *nutrition*
- List the elements present in carbohydrates, fats and proteins
- Describe the synthesis of large molecules from smaller molecules

**EXAMINER SAYS...**

Be careful how you use the word 'nutrient'. In most cases you should use a more precise term. For example, rather than write about plant nutrients, you should write about mineral ions and perhaps give some examples (such as magnesium).

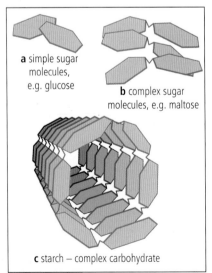

**a** simple sugar molecules, e.g. glucose

**b** complex sugar molecules, e.g. maltose

**c** starch – complex carbohydrate

**Figure 5.1.1**    Different types of carbohydrate.

## Nutrition

You will remember from Unit 1 that nutrition is the obtaining of food to provide energy and substances needed for growth and repair. All living organisms need useful substances, called **nutrients**, which they take into their bodies. Nutrients are compounds that may be large and complex (like carbohydrates, proteins and vitamins) or simple (like mineral ions).

Green plants make the complex chemical compounds that they need from simple raw materials. Carbon dioxide and water are the raw materials for **photosynthesis**. The simple sugars produced in photosynthesis are used to make a wide range of other compounds. Plants need minerals to make some of these complex compounds. Minerals, such as magnesium, are sometimes called plant nutrients.

Animals eat plants and/or other animals that feed on plants. Nutrients that animals require are present in their **diet**.

The seven different nutrients needed for a balanced diet for humans are:

carbohydrates, proteins, fats, vitamins, minerals, fibre, water

These provide energy and the molecules that we need for making and repairing cells and tissues as well as a variety of other functions, such as maintaining a healthy gut. In this spread we look at the different nutrient groups.

## Carbohydrates

These contain the elements carbon (C), hydrogen (H) and oxygen (O). Carbohydrates include sugars and starches.

**Glucose** is a simple sugar which is made in photosynthesis, used in respiration and transported in the blood. It consists of six carbon atoms arranged into a ring.

Two molecules of simple sugars like glucose are joined by chemical bonds to form a complex (or 'double') sugar. Complex sugars include **sucrose** (the sugar you add to food and drinks), **maltose** (malt sugar – see page 40) and **lactose** (milk sugar). All these sugars are sweet and soluble and provide energy in a ready-to-use form.

Complex carbohydrates are made by joining many simple sugar molecules together by chemical bonds. Plants store **starch** as an energy store. They have enzymes that catalyse the reactions that join glucose together into long chains. **Glycogen** (sometimes called animal starch) is another complex carbohydrate made from glucose by animals as a store of energy. It is stored in the liver and muscles. Starch and glycogen, unlike sugars, are insoluble and do not taste sweet.

## Proteins

Proteins are complex molecules made up of carbon, hydrogen and oxygen, but they also contain nitrogen (N) and many have sulfur (S). Proteins are long-chain molecules made up of smaller molecules called **amino acids**. After formation they are either folded into different shapes (see page 37) or become arranged into long fibres.

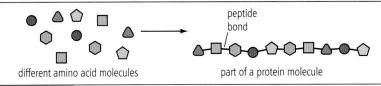

**Figure 5.1.2**   How a protein is made from amino acids.

There are about 20 different types of amino acid. Molecules of amino acids are made into chains as you can see in the diagram. It is the sequence of the different amino acids in the chain which determines the type of protein that is formed. Each individual amino acid joins the chain by means of a chemical bond called a peptide bond.

Haemoglobin, enzymes, antibodies and some hormones (e.g. insulin) are soluble proteins. They dissolve in water in cytoplasm or in the blood. There are also insoluble proteins that are used to make fibres in the body. **Keratin** is a fibrous protein found in skin and hair. Proteins are vital for growth and repair of cells and tissues as they form important components of cell membranes.

## Fats

Fats and oils are made up of the elements carbon, hydrogen and oxygen. Each fat molecule is made up of one molecule of **glycerol** and attached to this are three **fatty acids**. There are different types of fatty acid and these can form different fats with different properties. Fats are used for energy storage and thermal insulation in the body.

EXAMINER SAYS...

You may be asked to compare these three groups of nutrients. Make a table to compare them using headings such as 'Name of nutrient group' and 'Elements'. You will be able to add to this table as you go through the rest of this unit. When naming the elements always use their full names, not their symbols.

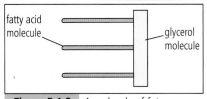

**Figure 5.1.3**   A molecule of fat.

### KEY POINTS

1 Carbohydrates and fats are made up of the elements carbon, hydrogen and oxygen. Proteins are made up of the same elements plus nitrogen and sulfur.

2 Carbohydrates are simple sugars (e.g. glucose), complex sugars (e.g. sucrose) and complex carbohydrates such as starch and glycogen.

3 Small molecules are joined together to make long chain molecules. Sugars are made into starch and glycogen. Amino acids are made into proteins.

4 A molecule of a fat is made by combining three fatty acid molecules with a molecule of glycerol.

### SUMMARY QUESTIONS

1 a   List the components of a balanced diet for a human.

  b   Give one example of each of the following:
       i a simple sugar, ii a complex ('double') sugar,
       iii a complex carbohydrate.

2 a   Which elements are present in proteins, but are not found in carbohydrates and fats?

  b   Name the small molecules that are joined together to make protein molecules.

  c   Give three examples of proteins that are made in the body.

  d   State the function of each protein that you named in part c.

3 a   Name the molecules that are reacted together to make a molecule of fat.

  b   Give two uses of fats in the body.

# Chemical tests for nutrients

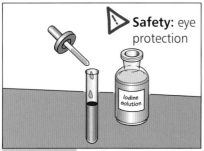

⚠️ **Safety:** eye protection

**Figure 5.2.1**   Test for starch.

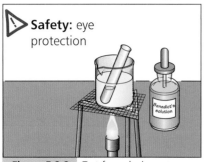

⚠️ **Safety:** eye protection

**Figure 5.2.2**   Test for reducing sugars.

Simple chemical tests can be used to identify starch, sugars, proteins and fat.

First it is important to carry out these tests on pure forms of these compounds. For example, if you are testing a food for reducing sugars, you should first carry out the chemical test on a glucose solution. Then keep the results to compare with your results from testing other materials, such as foods or animal and plant tissues. You should also do a test with water so that you can see the negative result as well.

You will need to make an **extract** from the material you are testing. This involves grinding up a small amount of the material with some water with a pestle and mortar or putting it into a blender. The chemicals will be in solution in the extract.

**Safety:** Some of the chemicals used in these tests are corrosive, so always wear eye protection.

## Testing for starch

- Half fill a test-tube with the food extract you wish to test for starch.
- Add two or three drops of **iodine solution**.

  Iodine solution usually looks yellow or light brown.

- A positive result for starch is if the iodine solution turns **blue–black**. If the extract remains a yellow or light brown colour it does *not* contain starch.

## Testing for reducing sugars

- Put a known volume of the extract you wish to test for reducing sugars in a test-tube.
- Place a beaker on a heat-proof mat.
- Carefully half fill the beaker with boiling water from a kettle (or place the beaker on a tripod and gauze and boil the water with a Bunsen burner).
- Add the same volume of **Benedict's solution** to the test-tube containing the food extract and a put it into the hot water.
- Benedict's solution is bright blue.
- A positive test for simple sugars is when Benedict's solution turns red or orange (if you look carefully you can see it turn green and then yellow before turning orange). If you leave the test-tube to cool you will also see a precipitate.
- You can use Benedict's test to tell you how much simple sugar is present. If the colour changes to green, the extract only contains a little of the reducing sugars. If it goes a deep orange colour then it contains a lot of reducing sugars.
- If the colour remains blue then the extract does *not* contain any reducing sugars.

The sugars that give a positive result change the copper ions in the Benedict's solution when the mixture is heated. The type of reaction that occurs is a reduction reaction that you will learn about in chemistry. Reducing sugars are simple sugars, such as glucose, and some complex sugars, such as maltose and lactose. Sucrose is *not* a reducing sugar and gives a negative result.

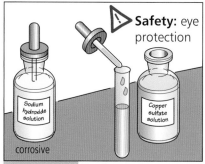

**Safety:** eye protection

**Figure 5.2.3** Test for protein.

## Testing for protein

- Half fill a test-tube with the extract you wish to test for protein.
- Add five to six drops of **biuret solution** (this solution contains copper sulfate solution and sodium hydroxide solution).

**Safety:** Take care as sodium hydroxide solution is corrosive.

- Biuret solution usually looks blue in colour.
- A positive test for protein is if the biuret solution turns **purple**, **violet** or **lilac**.
- If the colour remains blue, then the extract does *not* contain protein.

## Testing for fats

Fats will not dissolve in water but they will dissolve in **ethanol**. If a solution of fat in ethanol is added to water a cloudy white emulsion is formed.

- Chop up or grind a small amount of material you wish to test for fats. (Do not add water to make the extract this time.)
- Put the extract into a clean test-tube and add enough ethanol to cover it.
- Put a stopper over the open end of the test-tube and shake up the contents.
- Add some distilled water to make the test-tube half full.
- Shake the contents of the test-tube once more.
- A white emulsion that looks cloudy white or a milky colour is a positive test for fats.
- If this does not happen, the extract does *not* contain fat.

# 5.3

# Sources of nutrients

## Eating healthily

Diets in different parts of the world vary. However, we should all eat from each of the food groups shown in the food guide pyramid.

## Carbohydrates

Carbohydrates include sugars and starches, which provide us with a ready source of energy that is easily respired. Simple sugars are absorbed almost immediately by the stomach into the blood to give an immediate source of energy. This energy is released as a result of respiration. Good sources of carbohydrates are rice, potatoes, bread, yams, sugar and honey.

## Proteins

In order for your body to grow and develop, it needs protein to make new cells. You digest protein into amino acids and then use these to make your own proteins. There are 20 different types of amino acid and your body must have all of these to make its own protein.

Cell membranes and cytoplasm contain a great deal of protein. Your body may need to replace old or damaged cells so you need enough protein in your food for this as well. If protein is not used for growth and repair it may be respired to provide energy. Good sources are meat, fish, milk and nuts.

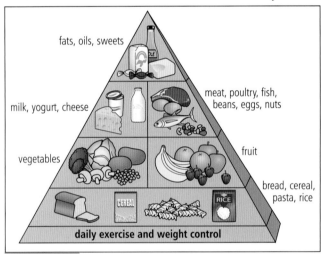

**Figure 5.3.1** The food guide pyramid.

## Fats

Fats are important as a long-term energy store. The fat is stored under the skin and around the heart and kidneys. One gram of fat releases more than twice as much energy than can be released from one gram of carbohydrate or protein. When we are short of energy our body uses the fat.

Fats are also good thermal insulators, since they cut down heat loss. Fats also give buoyancy to marine animals, for example whales have a thick layer of blubber. Good sources are butter, cheese, fat in meats and fish, nuts.

## Water

Water makes up two-thirds of your body mass. You take in water when you drink or eat.

You could go without food for a number of weeks, but you would die in a few days without water. Water is needed for chemical reactions to take place in solution. The blood transports substances dissolved in water. Waste chemicals are passed out of our bodies in solution in the urine, and water in our sweat cools us down. It is important that your intake of water each day equals your loss of water in urine, faeces, sweat and breath.

**EXAMINER SAYS...**

You can now add more information to the table you started in the first spread in this unit. For each feature you include (e.g. energy content in kJ) make sure you write something for each nutrient even if the answer is 0 (e.g. fibre, vitamins, minerals and water do not provide any energy).

## Vitamins and minerals

We need small, regular amounts of vitamins and minerals if we are to be healthy. If these are lacking in the diet we can develop symptoms of deficiency diseases:

| name | rich food source | use in body | deficiency symptoms (deficiency disease) |
|------|------------------|-------------|------------------------------------------|
| vitamin C | oranges, lemons, other citrus fruits | tissue repair, resistance to disease | bleeding gums (scurvy) |
| vitamin D | fish oil, milk, butter (also made by skin in the Sun) | strengthens bones and teeth | soft bones, legs bow outwards (rickets) |
| iron | liver, meat, cocoa, eggs | used in formation of haemoglobin in red blood cells for transport of oxygen | tiredness, lack of energy (anaemia) |
| calcium | milk, fish, green vegetables | strengthens bones and teeth | weak, brittle bones and teeth (rickets), muscle weakness and cramps |

## Fibre

Dietary fibre or roughage comes from plants. It is made up mainly of cellulose from plant cell walls. Although it cannot be digested, it is an important part of the diet. High-fibre foods include bran cereals, cabbage, sweetcorn and celery.

Fibre adds bulk to our food. Since it is not digested, it passes down the entire gut from mouth to anus and does not provide any energy.

The muscles of the gut wall need something to push against. Fibre helps the movement of food in the alimentary canal by peristalsis so preventing constipation (see page 75). Fibre absorbs poisonous wastes from bacteria in our gut. Many doctors believe that a high-fibre diet lowers the concentration of **cholesterol** in the blood. Fibre reduces the risk of heart disease and bowel cancer.

Tangerines are a good source of vitamin C.

### KEY POINTS

1 Carbohydrates are a quick source of energy, while fats are an energy store.

2 Protein is needed for growth and repair of tissues.

3 Lack of calcium and vitamin D can cause rickets (soft bones); lack of iron causes anaemia and lack of vitamin C causes scurvy.

4 Roughage helps the passage of food through the gut.

### SUMMARY QUESTIONS

1 List the nutrients in the human diet and give a good source of each one.

2 Explain why the diet must contain each nutrient.

3 Explain the term *deficiency disease*.

# Uses of microorganisms in industry

Extension

Food production is an important part of biotechnology, the branch of industry in which microorganisms or their products are used. Bacteria are used to produce yoghurt and a fungus is used to make mycoprotein (a form of single-cell protein) which is manufactured into a meat substitute.

Microorganisms grow and reproduce very quickly in suitable conditions. They do not make complex bodies, so much of the energy they use is converted into material we can eat as is the case with mycoprotein. Yoghurt production relies on the respiration of bacteria and the end product (lactic acid) causes a change to the milk so that it becomes semi-solid and good to eat. In many of these processes microorganisms are fed on waste materials of other industries and this helps to reduce the costs.

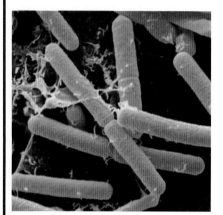

Yoghurt bacteria.

## Yoghurt

Milk is first pasteurised to kill the disease-causing bacteria. The milk is thickened with skimmed milk powder.

Yoghurt production needs a temperature of about 40 °C, which is the ideal temperature for growth of the bacteria. Once the milk is at the ideal temperature, bacteria are added. These bacteria respire anaerobically (without oxygen) and use the complex sugar **lactose** (milk sugar) as their source of energy. They cannot respire lactose completely to water and carbon dioxide as there is no oxygen available. The end product of their anaerobic respiration is **lactic acid**, which lowers the pH of the milk and causes the milk to coagulate (try adding vinegar to milk to see how this happens).

When the yoghurt is ready, it is cooled before it undergoes the final stage of production. This often involves mixing the yoghurt with fruit to create the many different types of yoghurt now available. Some yoghurts are treated to kill all bacteria, whilst others contain 'live' cultures. These bacteria supplement the bacteria naturally found in the gut helping our digestion.

Yoghurt manufacture is an example of a **batch culture**. The fermentation takes place in large, stainless steel fermentation tanks and when the yoghurt is removed all the equipment is cleaned and sterilised before starting again with a new batch.

## Mycoprotein

Microorganisms are very good at producing protein. In the UK in the 1960s, the food producers Rank Hovis McDougall (RHM) began a research programme that led to the production of **mycoprotein**.

Mycoprotein is a high protein material produced by a fungus called *Fusarium*. (Mycos is ancient Greek for fungus.)

Mycoprotein is made by **continuous culture**. This means that the nutrients are *continually* added and the product *continually* removed. The fermenter works continually without having to be emptied regularly and sterilised. The fungus is supplied with oxygen, glucose (as an energy

Adding bacteria to pasteurised milk.

source), mineral salts and ammonia as a source of nitrogen for the fungus to make amino acids. The fermenter is kept at 30°C. The hyphae are processed to give a meat-like texture. Flavourings are added so that it can be made into a variety of products, such as burgers, sausages and pies.

Mycoprotein makes an ideal meat substitute for those who wish to reduce or cut out meat from their diet. Like meat it is high in protein, but a great advantage is that it is low in fat. High-fat diets are linked with a variety of diseases, such as obesity, diabetes and heart disease. Foods made of mycoprotein are good to include in the diet to reduce the risk of developing these conditions.

In the 1970s, there were several research programmes trying to develop single-cell protein from bacteria using by-products of the oil industry. None of these were successful as the price of oil increased and protein from plants, especially soya, became available and was cheap.

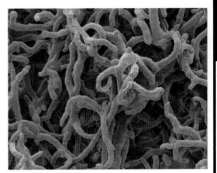
Fungal hyphae used to make mycoprotein.

Meat substitutes derived from mycoprotein.

## SUMMARY QUESTIONS

1 Microbes are commonly used in biotechnology.

Explain the advantage of each of the following features.

a Microbes can reproduce quickly.

b Microbes can grow easily on waste material.

c Microbes are very efficient protein producers.

2 a What is the name of the fungus from which mycoprotein is produced?

b Give two advantages of this fungus for food production.

c Explain how the production of mycoprotein differs from the production of penicillin.

This table shows a comparison between mycoprotein and beef:

| nutrient | mycoprotein (% dry mass) | beef (% dry mass) |
|---|---|---|
| protein | 40 | 60 |
| fat | 10 | 30 |
| minerals | 3 | 1 |
| fibre | 30 | 0 |

d Use this information to explain why mycoprotein is a healthy alternative to meat.

## KEY POINTS

1 Bacteria act on lactose in pasteurised milk to form lactic acid during yoghurt production.

2 Mycoprotein is a meat substitute made by a type of fungus. It has some advantages over meat, e.g. low in fat so reducing the risk of heart disease if included in the diet.

# 5.5 Food additives

**LEARNING OUTCOMES**

- Describe the uses and benefits of food additives
- Describe the hazards associated with food additives

**SHERBERT FRUITS**

An assortment of fruit flavour sweets with a sherbert cracknel centre

INGREDIENTS
Glucose Syrup, Sugar, Hydrogenated Vegetable Oil, Flavourings, Colours: E124, E141, E100, E110; Contains 23% Sherbert

**250g**

**Figure 5.5.1** A food label including details of food additives.

**DID YOU KNOW?**

Florida oranges, which are green when they are ripe, are made orange by colouring them to make them more appealing to customers.

**EXAMINER SAYS...**

You can read more about food additives in different countries by reading information on relevant websites, e.g. the New Zealand Food Safety Authority.

## Uses and benefits of food additives

Substances have been used to preserve food for centuries. Pickled foods contain vinegar which is ethanoic (acetic) acid and acts as a preservative. The low pH prevents microorganisms growing on the food, causing its decay and so ruining its taste and flavour. Sugar and salt are two other traditional preservatives. The food industry makes large quantities of processed foods and a large number of substances are deliberately added to our food. These substances are **food additives**.

Additives can colour, preserve and add flavour to our foods. Many additives are natural substances that are added during processing. Some, like tartrazine – a food colouring, are artificial substances.

All food additives are given an identification number that is recognised all over the world. In Europe the numbers are prefaced by an 'E' for Europe and food additives are often known as 'E numbers'. They are used on food labelling.

## Colourings

When foods are processed, much of the natural colour is lost. This tends to make the food look less appetising, so food scientists discovered substances that put the colour back into processed food. Other compounds are used to make sweets and soft drinks brightly coloured so that they look more attractive to children.

## Preservatives and anti-oxidants

Fresh foods can soon 'go off' as they are decomposed by bacteria and fungi or oxidised by oxygen in the air. For example, fats in food are oxidised to acids making the food rancid.

Preservatives and anti-oxidants protect the food and give it a longer shelf life so benefiting shops and consumers.

## Flavourings

Food scientists use compounds to reproduce the exact natural flavours of many foods. For example the smell of strawberry is a complex mixture of 280 different compounds. But the main compounds have been identified and used as artificial flavourings. Flavour enhancers act like salt, to increase the taste sensation of a food. Monosodium glutamate (MSG) is used in many products where it enhances the original flavour of the food.

## Emulsifiers and stabilisers

These enable fats and oils to mix with water. For example, a chocolate cake bar contains emulsifiers 471 and 475. Look at the label on the next bar of chocolate that you eat to find out the emulsifiers used.

## International numbering system for food additives

| additive number range | use of additive |
|---|---|
| 100–181 | colouring (tartrazine is 102) |
| 200–290 | preservatives (ethanoic acid is 260) |
| 296–385 | anti-oxidants and acids (ascorbic acid – vitamin C – is 300) |
| 400–495 | emulsifiers and stabilisers |
| 500–585 | anti-caking agents and mineral salts |
| 620–640 | flavour enhancers (monosodium glutamate is 621) |
| 900–1520 | others, such as sweeteners and wax glazes on fruit |

## Disadvantages of food additives

People are becoming more and more aware of health issues and they are looking more closely at the things that they eat and want more information about the additives in food.

We have looked at the benefits of food additives, but there are worries about some of the compounds used.

Tartrazine (102) is a yellow colouring used in sweets, jams, drinks and snack foods. However, it can provoke asthma attacks and cause hyperactivity in children. There are also claims of other side effects. It is now banned in Norway, and the UK Food Standards Agency wants food manufacturers to stop using it.

Butylated hydroxyanisole (320) is another controversial compound. It was banned in Japan as early as 1958 as it was linked to a variety of health hazards including cancer. Experts recommended its ban in the UK. However, due to pressure from industry it was not banned. McDonald's stopped using this additive in the USA in 1986.

954 is saccharin, the artificial sweetener. It was banned in the USA in 1977 following a study on rats who were given very high doses of saccharin. It was later allowed to be used in foods if a health warning was put on product labels. In 2000, legislation was passed making this no longer necessary as further research had not shown any hazards to human health.

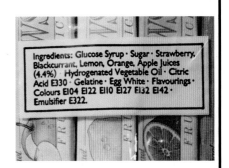

Ingredients: Glucose Syrup · Sugar · Strawberry, Blackcurrant, Lemon, Orange, Apple Juices (4.4%) · Hydrogenated Vegetable Oil · Citric Acid E330 · Gelatine · Egg White · Flavourings · Colours E104 E122 E110 E127 E132 E142 · Emulsifier E322.

### SUMMARY QUESTIONS

1 Explain why the following types of food additive are used:
   a colourings,   b preservatives and anti-oxidants,
   c emulsifiers and stabilisers,   d flavourings.

2 Look at some food labels in your home. Make a list of the additives and their numbers (if given).
   Use the table above to find out why they have been put into the food and add to your list.

3 Find out about health issues associated with food additives other than those given in this spread. Write a report on your findings.

### KEY POINTS

1 Colourings replace the original colour lost when processing food.

2 Preservatives prevent food from decomposing and anti-oxidants prevent the oxidation of some chemicals, e.g. fats present in food.

3 Flavourings reproduce natural flavours and can enhance flavours.

4 Some food additives are thought to cause health problems such as hyperactivity and asthma in children.

1 Give definitions of the following terms:

nutrition, nutrients, deficiency symptoms.

2 Explain the importance in the diet of the following:

carbohydrates, fats, proteins, vitamins C and D, calcium, iron, fibre and water.

3 Name the chemical elements found in
(a) both carbohydrates and proteins
(b) proteins but not in fats or carbohydrates.

4 Describe how cells make the following large molecules:
(a) starch and glycogen
(b) proteins
(c) fats and oils.

5 State one difference between each of the following pairs:
(a) starch and glycogen
(b) fats and proteins
(c) starch and proteins.

6 Write out the details of the food tests in a table with the following headings:
• name of test
• substance tested for
• practical procedure
• positive result
• negative result.

7 Describe the symptoms that are shown by people who have a deficiency in their diet of:
(a) vitamin C
(b) vitamin D
(c) calcium
(d) iron.

Extension

8 Describe how: (a) bacteria are used in the production of yoghurt, and (b) how a fungus is involved in the production of single-cell protein (mycoprotein).

1 What are the chemical elements in proteins?
  A carbon, hydrogen and oxygen
  B carbon, hydrogen, nitrogen, and oxygen
  C carbon, hydrogen, nitrogen, oxygen and sulfur
  D carbon, nitrogen, oxygen, and sulfur

*(Paper 1)* [1]

2 The small molecules that are built up into proteins are:
  A amino acids
  B fatty acids
  C glucose
  D glycerol

*(Paper 1)* [1]

3 Which gives the positive results for the four chemical tests?

|   | Benedict's test | biuret test | iodine test | emulsion test |
|---|---|---|---|---|
| A | green | violet | yellow | no suspension |
| B | blue | blue | yellow | no suspension |
| C | yellow | red | blue | cloudy suspension |
| D | orange | violet | blue-black | cloudy suspension |

*(Paper 1)* [1]

4 Which gives the deficiency symptoms for vitamin C, vitamin D, calcium and iron?

|   | vitamin C | vitamin D | calcium | iron |
|---|---|---|---|---|
| A | gums bleed | bowing of leg bones | muscle weakness and cramps | tiredness |
| B | bowing of leg bones | gums bleed | tiredness | muscle weakness and cramps |
| C | scurvy | rickets | rickets | anaemia |
| D | tiredness | muscle weakness | soft bones | gums bleed |

*(Paper 1)* [1]

**5** The diagram shows how a starch molecule increases in length.

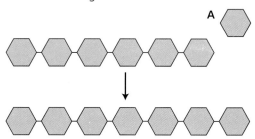

(a) Name molecule **A**. *[1]*

(b) Name two places where starch is stored in plants. *[2]*

(c) Describe how you would find out whether a plant tissue contained starch. Include the practical details of the test in your answer. *[4]*

(d) What is the importance of starch in the human diet? *[2]*

*(Paper 2)*

**6** The diagram shows a protein molecule:

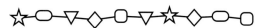

(a) Name the sub-unit molecules that are assembled into the protein. *[1]*

(b) Name two proteins found in the human body. *[2]*

(c) State two places in the human body where many proteins are made. *[2]*

(d) State two functions of protein in the human diet. *[2]*

(e) Some seeds are rich in proteins. Describe the chemical test that you would use to determine whether different types of seed are rich in proteins. Include the practical details of the test in your answer. *[4]*

*(Paper 2)*

**7** The table shows the composition of 100 g of a low fat fruit yoghurt and 100 g of sausages made from mycoprotein.

| | low fat fruit yoghurt | sausages made from mycoprotein |
|---|---|---|
| energy (kJ) | 348 | 474 |
| protein (g) | 4.1 | 14.9 |
| fat (g) | 0.9 | 3.7 |
| carbohydrates (g) | 16.5 | 4.9 |
| calcium (mg) | 143 | 0 |
| fibre (g) | 0.5 | 3.3 |
| additives | colouring | flavouring colouring |

(a) Fat provides 39 kJ of energy per gram. What percentage of the energy content of yoghurt is provided by the fat content? *[4]*

(b) The recommended daily intake of calcium for a 14 year old male is 1000 mg. Calculate the percentage of the RDI for calcium that 100 g of yoghurt provides for a 14-year-old male. Show your working. *[2]*

(c) Describe the benefits of adding food additives to foods. *[3]*

(d) State the type of microorganism used in making: **(i)** yoghurt, and **(ii)** mycoprotein. *[2]*

(e) Outline the roles of the microorganisms you have named in part **(d)** in the production of the two foods. *[4]*

*(Paper 3)*

### The process of photosynthesis

When you look at some leaf cells under the microscope you see many round, green structures called **chloroplasts**. Green plants use light energy to convert raw materials from their surroundings into simple sugars. This process is called **photosynthesis**.

This is the word equation for the whole process:

$$\text{carbon dioxide} + \text{water} \xrightarrow{\text{light and chlorophyll}} \text{glucose} + \text{oxygen}$$

**Extension**

This is the chemical equation for photsynthesis:

$$6CO_2 + 6H_2O \xrightarrow{\text{light and chlorophyll}} C_6H_{12}O_6 + 6O_2$$

During photosynthesis the energy from light becomes converted into chemical bond energy in the simple sugars. This provides energy for the plant and also for other organisms that feed on plants directly or indirectly (see page 224). The equation shows that oxygen is produced as a by-product. The plant may use oxygen in its own respiration or it may diffuse out into the atmosphere where it is used by other organisms.

Photosynthesis is not a simple reaction as suggested by the equation. There are many chemical reactions that take place in chloroplasts to form simple sugars and oxygen. Each reaction is catalysed by an enzyme. The equations above just summarise what happens during photosynthesis.

### Investigating photosynthesis

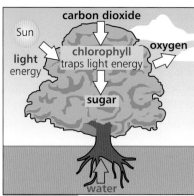

**Figure 6.1.1**   A simple overview of photosynthesis.

Green plants make simple sugars from carbon dioxide and water. However, if too much simple sugar is dissolved in the cell sap of plant cells it would make a very concentrated solution. This would make water move in from other cells by osmosis and cause the cells to swell so much that they would need to make very thick cell walls. To prevent this, the glucose molecules are linked up to form larger starch molecules which are insoluble.

These plant cells are full of chloroplasts.

## PRACTICAL

### Testing a leaf for starch

Submerge a leaf in boiling water for one minute. This kills the leaf as it destroys membranes, making it easier to extract the chlorophyll.

At this point, **turn off** any Bunsen burners used to boil the water.

Put the leaf into a test-tube of ethanol. The chlorophyll is extracted by dissolving into the ethanol.

Stand the test-tube in a beaker of hot water for about 10 minutes.

Wash the leaf in cold water. This removes the ethanol and rehydrates the leaf which softens it and makes it easy to spread out.

Spread the leaf out flat on a white surface and put some drops of iodine solution on it.

If the leaf goes blue-black, starch is present. If it stays red/brown there is no starch.

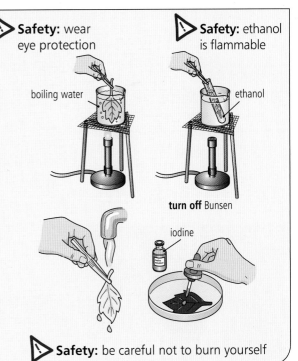

**Safety:** wear eye protection

**Safety:** ethanol is flammable

boiling water

ethanol

**turn off** Bunsen

iodine

**Safety:** be careful not to burn yourself

## SUMMARY QUESTIONS

1 Copy and complete the following sentences using the words below:

**oxygen starch chlorophyll dioxide energy water photosynthesis**

Green plants make their own food by _____. Green _____ in the chloroplasts of the leaves traps the Sun's _____. Raw materials for this process are carbon _____ and _____. Simple sugars are made in the leaves and some are changed to _____. The waste product of this process is the gas _____.

2 To find out if photosynthesis has taken place in a leaf we can carry out a test.

Copy out the stages listed on the left. Match each one with the correct reason on the right.

| Stage in test | Reason |
| --- | --- |
| wash the leaf in cold water | to test for starch |
| boil the leaf in ethanol | to soften it |
| add drops of iodine solution to the leaf | to remove the ethanol and rehydrate the leaf |
| dip the leaf in boiling water | to extract the chlorophyll |

3 Write out the word equation for photosynthesis and identify the raw materials and products.

4 Using only information in this spread, explain why plants are vital to our survival.

### KEY POINTS

1 Chlorophyll absorbs light energy that is used in photosynthesis.

2 Photosynthesis is the process by which plants make glucose from raw materials using energy from light.

3 Carbon dioxide and water are the raw materials for photosynthesis.

4 A leaf that has been exposed to light will give a positive test for starch.

# What is needed for photosynthesis?

It is important to understand the factors that affect photosynthesis in order to increase crop yields.

## The requirements for photosynthesis

Green plants need the following in order to carry out photosynthesis:

- **light**, which provides energy for the process
- **chlorophyll**, a green pigment that absorbs the energy from light. Chlorophyll is in the chloroplasts of the leaf
- **carbon dioxide**, which diffuses into the leaves from the air
- **water**, which is absorbed by the plant's roots from the soil.

Water and carbon dioxide are the **raw materials** for photosynthesis.

Investigations demonstrate that chlorophyll, carbon dioxide and light are needed for photosynthesis.

If the plant carries out photosynthesis it will make simple sugars and store them as starch. If it cannot photosynthesise then it will not make starch.

To be certain that the investigation is valid, we must make sure that the leaves have no starch at the start. To do this a plant is left in the dark for at least 48 hours. This is called **de-starching**. The plant is then given all the things that it needs *except* for the substance that we are testing. (It is difficult to show that water is needed for photosynthesis, as water is required by a plant for so many other things; most of the plant is water so you can hardly 'take it away'.)

### PRACTICAL

#### Showing that chlorophyll is needed for photosynthesis

Take a de-starched, variegated plant such as a geranium.

('Variegated' means some parts of the leaves are white because there is no chlorophyll there.)

Place the plant in sunlight for about 6 hours.

Draw one leaf to show the white and green parts.

Now test this variegated leaf for starch using the starch test described on page 57.

Variegated geranium leaves.

You should find that only the green parts of the leaf go blue-black.

The green parts contain chlorophyll which is needed for photosynthesis to make starch.

The white parts contain no chlorophyll, so no photosynthesis occurs here.

Therefore the white parts of the leaf give a negative result with the starch test.

▷ **Safety:** wear eye protection

## Showing carbon dioxide and light are needed for photosynthesis

You could prove that a plant needs **carbon dioxide** to make its own food by providing it with everything it needs for photosynthesis *except* carbon dioxide. Then test to see if it has made starch.

EXAMINER SAYS...

You must be able to explain why we need controls in these experiments.

### PRACTICAL

**Showing that carbon dioxide is needed for photosynthesis**

Take a de-starched plant. Enclose it in a plastic bag with a chemical that absorbs carbon dioxide. (**Soda lime** absorbs carbon dioxide.)

Leave the plant in the light for a few hours. Test a leaf for starch as described on page 57. The leaf should show a negative result for the starch test. Deprived of carbon dioxide the leaf is unable to photosynthesise and make starch.

A **control** experiment should be set up in exactly the same way but without the soda lime. This means the plant in the control experiment does not have carbon dioxide removed. Then we can be sure it was the absence of carbon dioxide that caused the lack of starch and not keeping the plant inside the plastic bag.

plastic bag

soda lime

elastic band

You can also show that a plant needs **light** to carry out photosynthesis.

### PRACTICAL

**Showing that light is needed for photosynthesis**

Take a de-starched plant. Cover part of the leaf with some aluminium foil to prevent light getting through.

Leave the plant in the light for a few hours.

Test the leaf for starch as described on page 57. Only the parts of the test leaf that were left uncovered go blue-black. The parts of the leaf that were covered did not receive light and could not carry out photosynthesis and so could not make starch.

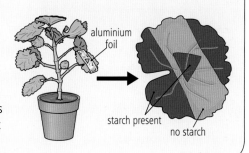

aluminium foil

starch present

no starch

### SUMMARY QUESTIONS

1 a Describe how you would de-starch a plant.

  b Explain why it is necessary to use a de-starched plant to show that plants need light to carry out photosynthesis.

  c What is a variegated leaf?

  d Describe how you could carry out an investigation to show that carbon dioxide is needed for photosynthesis.

2 State whether the following statements are true or false.

  a Plants get all their food from the soil.

  b Plants need chlorophyll to carry out photosynthesis.

  c Water for photosynthesis is absorbed through the leaves.

  d Leaves that are de-starched give a blue-black colour when tested with iodine.

3 Explain what is meant by a *control experiment*.

### KEY POINTS

1 Plants need light, chlorophyll, carbon dioxide and water in order to carry out photosynthesis.

2 We can test to see that light, chlorophyll and carbon dioxide are needed for photosynthesis by not giving plants each of these and testing leaves for starch.

# Products of photosynthesis

Photosynthesis makes food in these wheat plants.

## EXAMINER SAYS...

Make a diagram or a concept map to show how plants use the simple sugars made in photosynthesis. This will help you learn them all.

How much of this food depends upon plants?

The products of photosynthesis are simple sugars, such as glucose, and oxygen.

Most of the sugars which the plant needs for food are made in the leaves.

- Some of the **glucose** is used for respiration in the leaf.
- Some of the glucose is changed into **starch** and stored in the leaves for use in the future, e.g. at night.
- Some of the glucose is used to make **cellulose**, which is needed to make cell walls.
- Glucose is converted to **sucrose** and transported to other parts of the plant in the phloem (see page 96).

Glucose can also be converted to other substances:

- Plants get nitrogen by absorbing nitrate ions from the soil.
- Glucose and nitrate are used to form **amino acids**, which are built up into **proteins**.
- Plants need proteins for growth and cell repair and for making enzymes and hormones.
- **Sugars** are converted to **oils**, which are an efficient way to store energy in seeds.

## The importance of photosynthesis

Think about the food you have eaten in the last 24 hours. A lot of what you eat comes from plants like rice, maize, wheat, potatoes, soya beans and nuts.

If you eat meat or fish then that comes from animals that have eaten plants.

Products like cooking oil and margarine are made from plants.

## Oxygen is a by-product of photosynthesis

Oxygen is a product of photosynthesis. It is not the main product. Some is used by the plant's respiration, but usually there is more than needed so most diffuses out of the leaves into the atmosphere. That is why it is called a **by-product**.

## Plant products

Plants provide us with our food and also food for our livestock. There is more about this on page 228.

Plants also provide a range of raw materials for industry, such as timber and cotton. Many medicines have been discovered in plants including digitalis, which is a heart drug, and two anti-cancer drugs extracted from the rosy periwinkle from Madagascar.

Plants are the dominant organisms in almost all environments. As such they provide habitats for animals and microorganisms. The rainforests make up only 6% of the Earth's land surface, but they support more than half the world's species of animals and plants.

The concentrations of gases in the atmosphere are kept constant by photosynthesis. Without green plants, the concentration of carbon dioxide in the air would increase and the concentration of oxygen would decrease.

## PRACTICAL

### Oxygen produced in photosynthesis

Set up the apparatus to collect bubbles of gas given off by the Canadian pondweed (*Elodea canadensis*).

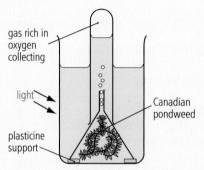

gas rich in oxygen collecting

light

Canadian pondweed

plasticine support

A lamp provides the light energy that the plant needs. Carbon dioxide is dissolved in the water. Add some sodium hydrogencarbonate powder to the water and stir to dissolve.

This is to make sure that there is always enough carbon dioxide in the water.

If there is not enough carbon dioxide then photosynthesis slows down.

Place the apparatus in the light and allow a few hours for the gas to collect.

Test the gas for oxygen with a glowing splint.

Standing the funnel on Plasticine gives a gap to allow carbon dioxide dissolved in the water to reach the pondweed so photosynthesis does not slow down.

A water plant is used because it is easy to collect the gas by downward displacement of water.

**EXAMINER SAYS...**

Remember that some of the oxygen produced in photosynthesis is used by the plant for its respiration. This means that some oxygen produced is not released into the atmosphere or water.

## SUMMARY QUESTIONS

1 What are the following products made in plants used for:
   a glucose, b starch, c cellulose, d protein, e oils?

2 a Describe how you would show that plants produce oxygen as a by-product of photosynthesis. Remember to include all practical details.

   b How would you show that light is necessary for oxygen production?

3 Plants are important because they provide us with:

   a food, b fuels, c building materials, d medicines.

   Give three examples of plants that provide us with each of these.

## KEY POINTS

1 Products of photosynthesis include glucose, which is used to make starch, cellulose, amino acids (and then proteins).

2 Photosynthesis is important as it provides us with food and medicines; it helps to keep constant concentrations of carbon dioxide and oxygen in the atmosphere.

## 6.4    Rate of photosynthesis

- Describe the effect of varying light intensity and temperature on the rate of photosynthesis
- Explain the term *limiting factor*

the rate increases as the light intensity increases – light intensity is the limiting factor

rate remains constant because something else is limiting the rate

rate of photosynthesis

light intensity

when there is no light there is no photosynthesis

**Figure 6.2.1**

When plants carry out photosynthesis they produce oxygen. We can determine how fast or slow photosynthesis occurs by measuring the oxygen produced in a certain time. This can be done by counting bubbles or by measuring the volume of oxygen produced. The rate of photosynthesis can also be measured by how much starch is made. This may be done by measuring the change in dry mass in a given time.

Farmers and agricultural scientists are keen to increase crop growth. The faster photosynthesis takes place the bigger the plant will grow and the more food is made. Scientists try to increase the rate of photosynthesis to increase the edible **yield** of a crop.

Environmental conditions such as light intensity, carbon dioxide concentration, water supply and temperature affect the rate of photosynthesis.

### Light intensity

As shown in the graph photosynthesis increases when light gets brighter – but only up to a point.

When a certain light intensity is reached the rate of photosynthesis stays constant. It does not go any faster even if the light intensity continues to rise. This is because carbon dioxide concentration, water supply or temperature may be restricting the rate.

### PRACTICAL

#### Photosynthesis and light intensity

You can use this apparatus to measure the effects of light intensity on the rate of photosynthesis:

Cut a piece of pondweed about 5 cm in length.

Put a paperclip on the pondweed to stop it floating to the surface.

Put the lamp close to the plant and measure the distance between the plant and the lamp.

Count the number of bubbles released over 5 minutes. Repeat several times and calculate the average.

Repeat this procedure with the lamp at different distances from the plant.

The number of bubbles should decrease as the distance between the lamp and the plant increases.

When the lamp is close to the plant the light intensity is high. This gives the plant lots of energy so the rate of photosynthesis is high. As the lamp is moved further away the light intensity decreases, there is less energy for the plant and the rate of photosynthesis decreases.

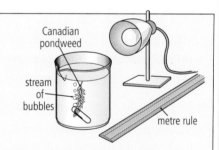

Canadian pondweed

stream of bubbles

metre rule

Many plants spread their leaves to catch as much light as they can.

Light that is too strong can damage the chloroplasts.

Some forest plants are adapted to grow in places with dim light such as under forest trees. These plants are called shade plants.

### Limiting factors

A **limiting factor** is something present in the environment in such short supply that it restricts life processes.

**Light intensity** influences the rate of photosynthesis. If the light intensity is low, it doesn't matter if the plant has lots of carbon dioxide and water and a warm temperature because there is a shortage of energy for photosynthesis and the rate cannot be very high. In this case, light intensity is the limiting factor for the rate of photosynthesis.

The only way to increase the rate is to increase the limiting factor – in this case, light intensity. Other limiting factors in photosynthesis are **carbon dioxide concentration** and **temperature**. But only *one* factor can limit the rate at any one time as it depends on which one is in the shortest supply.

There is usually enough water in plants so that it does not become a limiting factor. During dry conditions, plants reduce the quantity of water they lose to the atmosphere by closing their stomata. When stomata are closed no carbon dioxide can diffuse into the leaf which slows down the rate of photosynthesis.

## Temperature

Chemical reactions catalysed by enzymes increase with temperature. An increase in temperature increases the rate of photosynthesis until a certain temperature when the rate reaches a maximum and then decreases.

The maximum rate occurs at the **optimum temperature**. Plants from the tropics have higher optimum temperatures for photosynthesis than those from colder regions. The rate of photosynthesis decreases at higher temperatures because the **enzymes** in chloroplasts are denatured (see page 38).

### SUMMARY QUESTIONS

1 List the three main environmental limiting factors that may affect the rate of photosynthesis in a plant.

2 Suggest which factor would be limiting photosynthesis in each of the following. Give your reasons in each case:

   a  Plants growing on a high mountainside in the morning.

   b  Plants growing in a dense tropical forest at midday.

   c  A field of maize early on a very bright morning.

   d  The same field late in the afternoon.

3 Here are some results from the Practical on page 62

| distance from lamp (cm) | rate of photosynthesis (number of bubbles per minute) |
|---|---|
| 20 | 25 |
| 30 | 24 |
| 40 | 18 |
| 60 | 10 |
| 100 | 6 |

   a  Plot these results as a line graph.

   b  Explain the trend shown by the graph you have drawn.

   c  Explain why your graph does not look like the one opposite.

### EXAMINER SAYS...

The rate of photosynthesis is how much oxygen is produced in a period of time. See page 38 for rates of enzyme-catalysed reactions.

### PRACTICAL

**Effect of temperature on the rate of photosynthesis**

(Hint: Set up the apparatus opposite with water baths at different temperatures.)

Count the number of bubbles of gas produced by the pondweed at each temperature for 5 minutes.

Remember that other factors like light intensity and carbon dioxide concentration must be kept constant.

You should find that increasing the temperature of the pondweed increases the rate of photosynthesis, so producing more bubbles of gas. This should happen up to the optimum temperature for the pondweed. At higher temperatures the rate of photosynthesis will decrease.

### KEY POINTS

1 Increasing either light intensity or temperature increases the rate of photosynthesis up to a point where some other factor is limiting.

2 A limiting factor is something in such short supply that it restricts life processes. Limiting factors of photosynthesis are: light intensity, temperature and carbon dioxide concentration.

# Glasshouse production

## LEARNING OUTCOMES

• Describe the effect of carbon dioxide concentration on the rate of photosynthesis

• Explain the use of carbon dioxide enrichment, optimum light and optimum temperature in glasshouse systems

We have seen that light intensity and temperature influence the rate of photosynthesis in plants. Light intensity determines the energy available to photosynthesis and temperature influences the activity of enzymes in the chloroplasts. We will now deal with carbon dioxide concentration.

## Carbon dioxide

**Carbon dioxide** concentration is a limiting factor on the rate of photosynthesis. The higher the carbon dioxide concentration, the faster the rate of photosynthesis and the greater the crop yield. It is not possible to control the carbon dioxide concentration of crops grown outdoors. The air usually contains about 0.04% carbon dioxide.

In many countries, some crops are grown in glasshouses which give the growers the opportunity to control the factors that limit the rate of photosynthesis. Carbon dioxide is often added to the atmosphere within the glasshouse to increase the rate of photosynthesis, so increasing the growth of glasshouse crops and the final yields. This is known as carbon dioxide enrichment of the air.

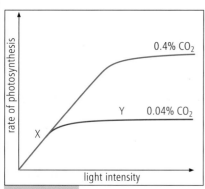

Figure 6.5.1

## PRACTICAL

**Plan an investigation into the effect of carbon dioxide on the rate of photosynthesis**

You could change the experiment on page 62 to find out the effects of changing the carbon dioxide concentration.

Adding sodium hydrogencarbonate to water increases the concentration of carbon dioxide as it dissolves in the water.

Other factors like light intensity and temperature must stay constant.

You should find that the plant produces more bubbles of gas as the carbon dioxide concentration increases. The rate of photosynthesis should increase up to a point and then remain constant because another factor becomes limiting.

### EXAMINER SAYS...

When you use a graph to answer a question, always move a ruler along the graph from left to right and follow the trends or patterns. Here you can rule lines on the graph to find the conditions when the rate starts to remain constant.

Look at the graph.

Light intensity is limiting the rate of photosynthesis at point X. Another factor is limiting the rate of photosynthesis at point Y. This could be carbon dioxide concentration because the rate increases if carbon dioxide concentration is increased from 0.04% to 0.4%. This is because there is more of this raw material available.

The **limiting factors** for the rate of photosynthesis are light intensity, temperature and carbon dioxide concentration.

# Glasshouse production

Growers try to improve the yield of their crops by giving them the best possible conditions for photosynthesis to take place.

Conditions inside a glasshouse allow plants to:

• grow earlier in the year
• grow in places where they would not normally grow well.

The following conditions inside glasshouses are controlled.

• **Temperature**
  Sunlight heats up the inside of the glasshouse.
  The glass stops a lot of this heat from escaping.
  Electric heaters are used in cold weather.
  Ventilator flaps are opened to cool the glasshouse on hot days.

• **Light**
  The glass lets in sunlight. Artificial lighting can be used to grow plants when light intensity gets too low. Blinds keep out very strong light.

• **Carbon dioxide**
  Growers can pump carbon dioxide into glasshouses to increase carbon dioxide concentration. They can also burn butane or natural gas which provides carbon dioxide and also heat to raise the temperature of glasshouses in cold weather.

• **Water**
  Many glasshouses have automatic watering systems using sprinklers and humidifiers which ensure plants always get enough water.

Glasshouses can control limiting factors.

Water misting of a glasshouse crop.

All these factors are monitored and controlled by computers so few staff are needed. Sensors for carbon dioxide concentration, humidity, light intensity and temperature detect changes in these limiting factors. Computers process data from the sensors and control all heating, ventilation, lighting and shading in the glasshouse.

## SUMMARY QUESTIONS

1 Explain what is meant by the term *limiting factor*. Use the process of photosynthesis to help explain your answer.

2 The graph shows the effect of increasing the carbon dioxide concentration on the rate of photosynthesis of a pondweed.

   a List two conditions that must be kept constant if this is to be a valid investigation.

   b How do you think the carbon dioxide concentration was increased?

   c Describe the trend shown by the graph.

   d Explain this trend.

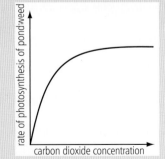

3 Explain how each of the following can be controlled in glasshouses to give optimum conditions for growth:

   a carbon dioxide concentration,

   b light intensity,        c temperature.

## KEY POINTS

1 Increasing the carbon dioxide concentration increases the rate of photosynthesis when no other factor is limiting.

2 Carbon dioxide concentration, light intensity, humidity and temperature are controlled in modern glasshouse systems to give optimum conditions. This ensures that the rate of photosynthesis is kept high so plants produce maximum yield.

A leaf has an ideal shape for photosynthesis.

The shape of a leaf makes it ideally adapted to carry out its functions of absorbing light for photosynthesis and allowing gases to diffuse into and out of the leaf tissues.

Leaves have:

- **a large surface area** – to absorb light rays
- **a thin shape** – so gases can diffuse in and out easily
- **many chloroplasts** – to absorb light for the reactions that take place in photosynthesis
- **veins** – to support the leaf surface and to carry water and ions to the leaf cells, and to take sucrose and amino acids away from the leaf to all other parts of the plant.

## Inside a leaf

To find out how a leaf works we can look at the structure of a typical leaf.

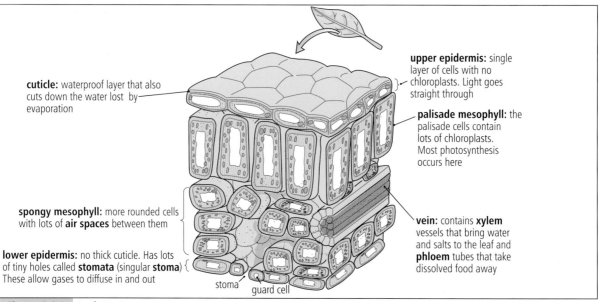

**cuticle:** waterproof layer that also cuts down the water lost by evaporation

**upper epidermis:** single layer of cells with no chloroplasts. Light goes straight through

**palisade mesophyll:** the palisade cells contain lots of chloroplasts. Most photosynthesis occurs here

**spongy mesophyll:** more rounded cells with lots of **air spaces** between them

**lower epidermis:** no thick cuticle. Has lots of tiny holes called **stomata** (singular **stoma**) These allow gases to diffuse in and out

stoma    guard cell

**vein:** contains **xylem** vessels that bring water and salts to the leaf and **phloem** tubes that take dissolved food away

**Figure 6.6.1**    Leaf structure.

## Stomata

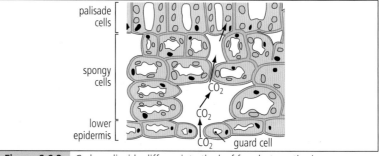

palisade cells

spongy cells

lower epidermis

$CO_2$

$CO_2$

$CO_2$    guard cell

**Figure 6.6.2**    Carbon dioxide diffuses into the leaf for photosynthesis.

Stomata are small pores (holes) in the epidermis that allow gases to diffuse in and out of the leaf. Stomata are usually in the lower epidermis, but some plants like water lilies have them in the upper epidermis.

In sunlight:

- carbon dioxide diffuses in for photosynthesis
- oxygen made in photosynthesis diffuses out
- water vapour diffuses out.

## Opening and closing

Stomata are opened and closed by **guard cells**.

Stomata usually open during the day. Water passes into the guard cells by **osmosis**. This makes them bend so the stoma opens.

Carbon dioxide diffuses into the leaf for photosynthesis and oxygen diffuses out. Water vapour also diffuses out.

At night the stomata close. Water passes out of the guard cells by osmosis and they straighten and move closer together so closing the stomata pores. The stomata also close in hot, dry weather to help prevent the plant wilting.

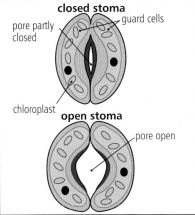

**Figure 6.6.3**  Closed stoma and open stoma.

### PRACTICAL

#### Looking at stomata

Paint a small square (1 cm × 1 cm) on the underside of a leaf with nail varnish. The nail varnish makes an imprint of the leaf surface.

Wait for the varnish to dry completely then peel it off. Put it on a slide with a drop of water and cover-slip.

Observe and draw two or three stomata using high power of the microscope. You can use this method to look at the upper epidermis of the same leaf and investigate the number and distribution of stomata on different leaves.

### SUMMARY QUESTIONS

1 Match each of the leaf parts on the left with their correct function on the right:

| | |
|---|---|
| stomata | carry water up from the stem |
| palisade mesophyll | allow gases to pass into and out of leaf |
| spongy mesophyll | contain chloroplasts for photosynthesis |
| cuticle | contain chloroplasts for photosynthesis |
| veins | prevent too much water being lost |

2 a  Which gas would pass into a leaf during daylight?

  b  Which gas passes out of a leaf during daylight?

3 Leaves have a large surface area to absorb light.

   Lay a leaf onto graph paper, draw around it and work out its area by counting the squares.

   Find out if leaves from the top and bottom of a plant have the same leaf area. Record your results and explain them.

### EXAMINER SAYS...

Revise osmosis on page 28 to understand how stomata open and close.

### KEY POINTS

1 The diagram of the internal structure of a leaf shows different tissues which each have important functions to carry out.

2 Stomata control the diffusion of gases into and out of a leaf.

This plant has magnesium deficiency.

Plants need more than light, carbon dioxide and water for healthy growth. They also need **mineral salts** (also called **plant nutrients**). Nutrients are absorbed from the soil in small quantities as ions by active transport in the roots (see page 32).

## Plant nutrients

Nutrients are needed for healthy growth of plants. They are used for a variety of purposes in plants. If these nutrients are lacking in the soil then plants do not grow well and show certain symptoms known as deficiency symptoms. Plants need **nitrate** ions to make amino acids which are used to make proteins. As proteins are required for growth, plants deficient in nitrate show poor growth.

**Magnesium** ions are absorbed by plants and used to make chlorophyll. Leaves of plants deficient in chlorophyll look yellow, a condition known as chlorosis. Plants need **phosphate** for making compounds such as DNA and for respiration. Deficiency symptoms are poor root growth and younger leaves turning purple rather than green.

**PRACTICAL**

### The effects of nutrients on growth

Some plants are grown in water culture to show that plants need different nutrients.

Set up some test-tubes as shown here.

Cover the tubes with black paper to prevent algae growing in the water.

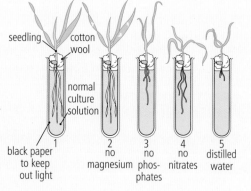

Each solution lacks a certain nutrient except test-tube 1 which has all of them.

Leave the apparatus in good light for 6 weeks.

After 6 weeks you could examine the colour and size of leaves.

You could measure length of stems and roots to compare growth.

## Fertilisers

If the soil does not contain enough nutrients farmers and growers may add more as **fertiliser** to replace the missing nutrients.

The graph shows the yield of wheat with different quantities of nitrate fertiliser (hectare is a unit of area).

The yield with no nitrogen fertiliser applied is 4 tonnes per hectare.

250 kg per hectare of fertiliser gives the maximum yield.

**NPK fertilisers** contain:

- nitrogen (N) (in the form of nitrate ions) for growth of leaves and stems
- phosphorus (P) (in the form of phosphate ions) for healthy roots
- potassium (K) (in the form of potassium ions) for healthy leaves and flowers.

The proportions of nitrogen, phosphorus and potassium (N:P:K) are shown on the fertiliser bag. This fertiliser is called 25:0:16 which means the fertiliser is rich in nitrogen and potassium but has no phosphate. This would be used for a soil that has plenty of phosphate.

## Natural or chemical?

Chemical or artificial fertilisers are used in huge quantities. They are easy to store and add to the land. They release their nutrients quickly but are short lasting.

The farmer knows exactly how much of each nutrient there is in the chemical fertiliser. The farmer has to be very careful about how much fertiliser is used and when.

Rain can wash fertiliser into rivers and streams where it causes water pollution because it provides nutrients for algae and water plants. (This is covered in Unit 19.)

Natural fertilisers include farmyard manure and composts. Some farmers prefer these because they add **humus** to the soil. Humus improves the structure of the soil. Natural fertiliser rots down and releases nutrients more slowly but over a longer period of time. The problem for the farmer is that the mass of each nutrient in the fertiliser is not known.

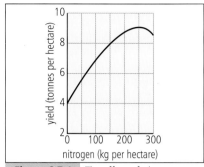

**Figure 6.7.1** The effect of nitrogen fertiliser on the yield of wheat.

**Figure 6.7.2** How much nitrogen, phosphorus and potassium does this fertiliser contain?

Modern farm machinery can spread chemical fertilisers efficiently.

---

### SUMMARY QUESTIONS

1  a  Explain why plants need mineral ions.
   b  State where plants obtain their mineral ions.
   c  Which mineral ion is needed for plants to make proteins?

2  a  Describe the likely appearance of a plant grown without a supply of nitrate ions.
   b  Describe the likely appearance of a plant grown without magnesium ions.

3  Explain each of the following:
   a  Farmers spread animal manure on their fields.
   b  If the same type of crop is grown in the same place every year, it will gradually grow less well and become stunted, with yellow leaves.
   c  If fertilisers get washed into ponds and lakes they cause algae and weeds to grow, polluting the water.

### KEY POINTS

1  Plant roots absorb nutrients including nitrate ions needed for healthy growth.

2  Nitrate ions are needed to make amino acids; magnesium ions are used by the plants to make chlorophyll.

3  If mineral ions are lacking, a plant develops deficiency symptoms.

1 Leaves have features that adapt them for their functions. Match the adaptations of leaves to their functions.

| large surface area | to allow gases to diffuse in and out of the leaf |
| green | contains chlorophyll to absorb light |
| veins | to trap as much light as possible |
| stomata | transport water and ions to leaf cells |
| thin | gases can diffuse easily to all the leaf cells |

2 Write definitions of the following:
(a) photosynthesis
(b) stomata
(c) fertiliser.

3 Write down the equation for photosynthesis in words. On the equation, identify the source of energy, raw materials, product and by-product.

4 State the function of chlorophyll.

5 Explain why plants require nutrients, such as nitrate ions and magnesium ions.

6 Explain how plants obtain the carbon dioxide and water they need for photosynthesis.

7 List four ways in which the sugars produced in photosynthesis are used by plants.

**Extension**

8 Write out a balanced chemical equation for photosynthesis. On the equation, identify the sources of energy, raw materials, product and by-product.

9 Define the term *limiting factor* and state the environmental factors that influence photosynthesis in plants.

10 Explain how environmental conditions in a large commercial glasshouse are kept at optimum levels for photosynthesis.

1 Photosynthesis occurs in palisade mesophyll cells. Which structure inside these cells carries out photosynthesis?

A chloroplast

B cytoplasm

C nucleus

D vacuole

*(Paper 1)* [1]

2 The raw materials for photosynthesis are:

A carbon dioxide and nitrate ions

B light energy and water

C light energy, carbon dioxide and water

D water and carbon dioxide

*(Paper 1)* [1]

3 Magnesium ions are used by plants for making:

A cellulose

B chlorophyll

C fats and oils

D proteins

*(Paper 1)* [1]

4 Which of the following represents the movement of gases through the open stomata of a leaf during the day?

| | gas into leaf | gas out of leaf |
|---|---|---|
| A | oxygen | carbon dioxide |
| B | water vapour | carbon dioxide |
| C | carbon dioxide | oxygen |
| D | oxygen | water vapour |

*(Paper 1)* [1]

5 The diagram on the next page shows a transverse section through a leaf as you would see it in a microscope.

(a) Name the tissues labelled **E, F, G** and **H**. *[4]*

(b) Describe the functions of the parts of the leaf labelled **I** and **J**. [3]

(c) Explain how cells in the tissues labelled **F** and **G** are adapted for photosynthesis. [3]

(d) Suggest the advantages of the large air spaces within the leaf. [2]

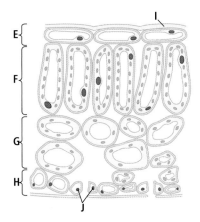

*(Paper 2)*

**6** Two plants, **K** and **L**, were placed in the dark for several days. They were then placed into the apparatus shown below in the light to find out if carbon dioxide is required for photosynthesis. **L** was provided with carbon dioxide.

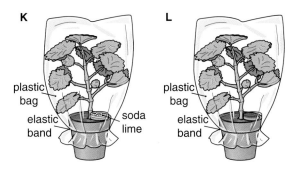

**(a)** Explain why the plants were put in the dark for several days. *[2]*

**(b)** Explain why the plants were well watered and kept in bright light. *[2]*

**(c)** Describe how you would show that plant **K** did not carry out any photosynthesis while inside the bag, but plant **L** did. *[4]*

**(d)** Explain why plant **L** was included. *[2]*

*(Paper 2)*

**7** A student investigated the effect of varying the light intensity on the rate of photosynthesis using the apparatus shown below.

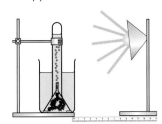

**(a)** State how the student would:

   **(i)** vary the light intensity; *[2]*

   **(ii)** determine the rate of photosynthesis; *[2]*

   **(iii)** maintain a constant temperature and constant carbon dioxide concentration throughout the investigation. *[4]*

**(b)** The graph below shows the student's results.

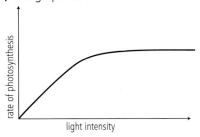

  Using the term *limiting factors*, explain the results shown in the graph. *[4]*

*(Paper 3)*

**8** Two groups of seedlings were grown in solutions that were deficient in two ions that plants need. Group **M** was grown without nitrate ions; group **N** was grown without magnesium ions. Group **O** received all the ions that plants require.

The results are shown in the table.

| group of seedlings | colour of leaves | growth |
|---|---|---|
| M | yellow (especially the lower leaves) | reduced growth but not as much as seedlings in group N |
| N | lower leaves – yellow upper leaves – pale green | severely reduced growth |
| O | green | normal growth |

**(a)** Explain the effects of the deficiencies of nitrate ions and magnesium ions as shown in the table. *[4]*

**(b)** Why was it necessary to include the seedlings in group **O**? *[2]*

*(Paper 3)*

# 7 Animal nutrition

## 7.1       A balanced diet

|  | energy used in a day (kJ) | |
| --- | --- | --- |
|  | male | female |
| 8-year-old | 8 500 | 8 500 |
| teenager, aged 14 | 12 500 | 9 700 |
| adult office worker | 11 000 | 9 800 |
| adult manual worker | 15 000 | 12 500 |
| pregnant woman |  | 10 000 |
| breast-feeding mother |  | 11 500 |

A **balanced diet** provides an adequate intake of the nutrients and energy needed to sustain the body and ensure good health and growth.

**Figure 7.1.1**    Which is the better-balanced meal?

A **nutrient** is a substance in food that provides benefit to the body. A balanced diet has these components:

carbohydrates, proteins, fats, vitamins, minerals, water, fibre

Each type of nutrient carries out one or more of three basic functions.

- **To provide energy** – this is mainly the role of carbohydrates and fats. Proteins are only used for energy if they are in excess of requirements for growth, development, repair and replacement.
- **To allow growth and repair** of body cells and tissues. Proteins in the diet provide a source of amino acids for cells to make their own proteins.
- **To regulate the body's metabolism** – these nutrients include vitamins and minerals that are needed in very small quantities in the diet.

Even if you are lying in bed and completely inactive you are still using energy to keep your heart beating, your lungs working and your body temperature constant. The chemical reactions in your body, such as those involved in growth and repair, are occurring and require energy.

The energy required for these body functions is the **basal metabolic rate (BMR)**. The BMR varies from person to person, but an adult requires about 7000 kJ per day. So even if you lie down and do very little you still need this energy.

## Diet depends on age, sex and activity

Children have a greater energy requirement than adults because they have a high basal metabolic rate (BMR).

A young child may weigh less than an adult but may have a higher BMR per kilogram per day because they are still growing. Young children also need more protein per unit of body mass because they are constantly developing and need to make new cells. Elderly people generally have lower energy and protein needs and have a lower BMR. However, they need to eat a balanced diet if they are to stay healthy. Women have a relatively higher fat content in their bodies than men. Fat is stored in fat tissue, for example under the skin. Fat tissue has a lower metabolic rate than muscle, so women generally have a lower energy requirement than men.

Women need extra nutrients when they are pregnant and breast-feeding (see page 191). Physical activity uses up energy and can increase the body's protein requirement when greater muscle development occurs. Body builders and people who take part in sports require extra protein in their diet for this reason.

Compare the daily energy requirements of the people in the table and try to explain the differences.

## Why can fat be bad for us?

Fat provides us with more energy per gram than carbohydrates or proteins. However, we should be aware that there are two main types of fat: **saturated fat** that comes from animals and **unsaturated fat** that comes from fish and plants.

Saturated fats in the diet may increase the concentration of **cholesterol** in our blood. Cholesterol is a chemical made in the liver and found in the blood. The quantity of cholesterol that we produce depends upon our diet as well as the genes that determine our metabolism which we inherit. High fat diets tend to increase the risk of producing more cholesterol and having a high concentration in the blood.

High concentrations of cholesterol in the blood are linked to a narrowing of the arteries (see page 106), an increased risk of developing high blood pressure and heart disease.

There are two types of unsaturated fat. Mono-unsaturated fats have little effect on blood cholesterol. Poly-unsaturated fats may help to reduce cholesterol concentrations which will help to reduce heart disease.

pregnant woman
10 000 kJ per day

teenage boy, 14 years
12 500 kJ per day

male manual worker
15 000 kJ per day

girl, 8 years
8 500 kJ per day

**Figure 7.1.3** Typical energy needs.

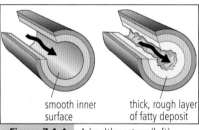

smooth inner surface

thick, rough layer of fatty deposit

**Figure 7.1.4** A healthy artery (left) and an artery with fat deposited in the wall.

## KEY POINTS

1 A balanced diet provides energy and nutrients (proteins, carbohydrates, fats, vitamins, minerals, water and fibre) in the correct quantities.

2 Requirements of the diet depend on a person's age, gender and how active they are.

3 Saturated fats increase blood cholesterol which is linked to narrowing of the arteries and heart disease.

## SUMMARY QUESTIONS

1 a What is meant by the term *balanced diet*?

  b State how the protein and energy requirements of the following will differ from those of a 16-year-old female who does not take much exercise:
    i an elderly person,   ii a 2-year-old child,
    iii a pregnant mother, iv a male athlete.

2 a What are the health risks associated with a diet high in fat?

  b Explain how a person may reduce the fat content of their diet. (You may find it useful to look at pages 49 and 74 before answering this question.)

# Balancing energy needs

**LEARNING OUTCOMES**

- State the reasons why some people put on weight
- Describe obesity and constipation as a result of malnutrition
- List the health risks associated with obesity
- Explain the role of roughage (fibre) in the diet

Many children do not eat this sort of meal at lunchtime!

Exercise helps fight heart disease and obesity.

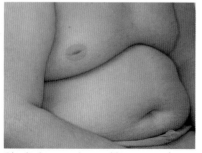

Obesity is a growing problem.

## Getting the balance right

The food you eat in a day should provide you with enough energy to get through that day.

## What happens if we eat too much?

If you eat more food than you need, your body stores the extra as fat.

Your **energy intake** is the energy you get in your food in a day in proteins, carbohydrates and fats.

Your **energy output** is the energy your body uses in a day. If energy intake is greater than energy output, then fat is stored in the body and body mass increases. We may run the risk of becoming overweight or even **obese**. Obesity is defined in the box on the next page. People with a low basal metabolic rate (BMR) are more likely to get overweight or obese than those with higher BMRs. It is likely that their diet contains fattening foods, such as high fat foods and refined foods with a lot of added sugar.

## Obesity

In rich, industrialised countries, like Britain and the USA, more people suffer from overeating than from eating too little. As we have seen, if a person takes in more energy in food than they use, then the excess is stored as fat. Taken to extremes, people can put on so much weight that they become obese.

Major causes of obesity include:

- high intake of fatty foods and refined foods containing a lot of added sugar
- too little exercise
- social and emotional stress, leading to 'comfort eating'.

People who are overweight and obese are much more likely than thinner people to have health problems such as heart disease (see page 106), high blood pressure, diabetes caused by high blood sugar (see page 130) and arthritis (worn joints).

## How could someone lose weight?

They could:

- eat less high-energy foods (lower their energy intake)
- take more exercise (increase their energy output).

A sensible approach to slimming should combine:

- a balanced diet with a lower intake of energy
- a gradual increase in exercise
- having an ideal, but achievable, target for weight reduction.

**Obesity**

There are two ways in which people can identify being obese:

- being 20% above the recommended weight for his or her height

- having a **body mass index (BMI)** greater than 30.

$$\text{body mass index} = \frac{\text{body mass (in kg)}}{\text{height (in metres)}^2}$$

A person with a BMI of less than 20 is underweight; between 25 and 30 is overweight; more than 30 is obese; more than 40 is severely obese. If your BMI is in the range of 20 to 24, then your body mass is in the acceptable range.

These calculations are for adults. The BMI is calculated in the same way for children but the interpretation is different.

**EXAMINER SAYS...**

You do not have to remember how to calculate the body mass index, but you should be aware that someone is classified as obese if their BMI is greater than 30.

## Constipation

**Roughage** or **fibre** is important for a healthy, balanced diet. It is indigestible but adds bulk to our food. This is important for keeping food moving down the alimentary canal. The muscles of the gut wall contract to squeeze the food along. Soft foods do not stimulate the muscles to contract as effectively as the harder, indigestible foods that form roughage. If the movement of food is slow it will result in **constipation** making it difficult to defecate.

A diet containing fruit and vegetables contains lots of roughage; these are the best foods to relieve constipation.

**EXAMINER SAYS...**

Malnutrition refers to diets that are not balanced because there is too little energy or too much energy, a shortage of certain nutrients or far too much of those nutrients. Constipation is a form of malnutrition as the diet is lacking in roughage.

**SUMMARY QUESTIONS**

1 Copy and complete the following using the words below:

**exercise   energy   sugar   obesity
high-energy   fat   fatty**

If you take in more _____ than you use, the excess is stored as _____ . Eating _____ foods and foods with added _____ over long periods of time can lead to _____. A person can lose weight by eating less _____ foods and taking more _____.

2 List four health problems that are linked to obesity.

3 Calculate the body mass index for the following people and name the BMI category in each case:

   a  a man 1.70 m in height with a body mass of 110 kg

   b  a woman 1.75 m in height with a body mass of 50 kg

   c  a man 1.85 m in height with a body mass of 75 kg.

4 a  State two good sources of roughage in the diet.

   b  Explain the effects of a lack of roughage in the diet.

**KEY POINTS**

1 Some people put on weight if their energy intake (in their food) is greater than their energy output (in exercise).

2 Obesity can be caused by a high intake of fatty foods and refined foods containing a lot of added sugar plus the effects of too little exercise.

3 A diet lacking in roughage (fibre) can lead to constipation.

# Starvation

### LEARNING OUTCOMES

- Describe the effects of starvation
- Discuss ways in which modern technology has resulted in increased food production
- Discuss the problems of world food supplies and the problems that contribute to famine

Symptoms of kwashiorkor:

oedema (swelling of the abdomen and legs)
sparse, dry hair
flaky skin
fat accumulation in liver.

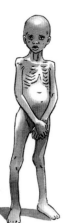

Symptoms of marasmus:

very low body mass
thin arms and legs
little muscle or fat
wizened, old-looking face.

**Figure 7.3.1** Typical symptoms of two forms of protein energy malnutrition.

People can survive for many weeks without food, provided they have water. This is because during periods of starvation, the body draws upon its stores of carbohydrate, fat and protein for energy, but there are no stores of water. During starvation the basal metabolic rate (BMR) is reduced. The body uses stored fat and then breaks down protein in the muscles to use as a source of energy. This leads to muscle wasting and an emaciated appearance.

Worldwide, the most common form of undernutrition is **protein energy malnutrition (PEM)**. As the term suggests, this is caused by a lack of dietary energy and protein. In its worst form it can lead to **kwashiorkor** or **marasmus**, which are terms to describe the appearance of children with PEM. These are two different ways in which the body responds to lack of food. In both conditions, children are underweight, though more so in marasmus. However, it is thought the children with marasmus have adapted better to lack of food and respond better when given food. The symptoms of these conditions are shown on the left.

In both cases, children are in danger and feeding should involve frequent servings of small quantities of food. This is because PEM causes cells of the pancreas and intestine to die, so fewer digestive enzymes are secreted and the surface area for absorption of digested food is reduced. During starvation, there are deficiencies of the protective vitamins; people are at risk of developing infectious diseases.

Dietary surveys of poor communities in developing nations have shown that protein, which should be used for the growth and repair of cells, has to be used as an energy source. This shows that children with these conditions are suffering from a lack of energy in the diet.

Children who develop the symptoms may be fed on tropical crops such as cassava and sweet potato; while having a high energy content, these are low in protein, so they need to be supplemented with other protein foods. Staple foods such as wheat and rice will satisfy energy intake and also provide enough protein.

## Increased food production

Modern technology has resulted in advances in agriculture over the past 60 years and improved food supplies in many parts of the world. These advances include:

- Arable farms use large **agricultural machines** to work very large fields. Examples are tractors and ploughs for preparing land for sowing seeds and combine harvesters for harvesting crops.
- **Chemical fertilisers** encourage the growth of crop plants, increasing the yield of the crop (see page 69).
- **Pesticides** kill pests like insects and nematodes that feed on crops (see page 5).

- **Herbicides** kill weeds that compete with crop plants for water, light and nutrients.
- **Selective breeding** has increased yield and made crops more resistant to drought and diseases (see page 220).
- **Genetic engineering** has transferred features, such as herbicide resistance, to crop plants from unrelated species (see page 221).

Extension

## World food supply

As the world's population has increased, the ability of the world's farmers to produce enough food has also increased. There is enough food in the world to feed everyone, but every year many people die from starvation and malnutrition.

Shortage of food is most often caused by politics, economics, wars and poverty. Many poorer countries produce enough food to feed their populations or have enough land to do so, but have to sell food or grow non-food cash-crops to gain foreign currency. There is poverty everywhere, even in the richest nations. Politics often means that these people do not receive help so their lives are put at risk.

Factors such as drought, flooding, pests and diseases may cause crops to fail, but famine is most often caused by a failure to supply food to those at risk of starvation. This may be because transport of food from areas where it is abundant to areas where there is a shortage has still not been able to solve the problem, and this may be the result of political pressures or war.

Even when conditions favour the growth of crops, an increasing human population means that there is not enough food to go round (see page 238).

**EXAMINER SAYS...**

In Paper 3, you may be expected to discuss these issues. You need to have about five or six different points to make about the problems of world food supplies and the factors that contribute to famines.

A cereal crop is harvested.

**SUMMARY QUESTIONS**

1 a  Explain the main causes of starvation in terms of an inadequate diet.
  b  What are the symptoms of:
    i  kwashiorkor and  ii  marasmus?
  c  Explain why treatment of these two conditions involves frequent servings of very small amounts of food.

2 Explain how each of the following has increased the world's food production:
  a  improved agricultural machinery,  b  artificial selection,
  c  use of fertilisers,  d  use of pesticides.

3 Explain how, despite an increase in global food production, starvation exists in parts of the world.

Extension

**KEY POINTS**

1  Starvation results in a very low body mass with lack of fat and muscle wasting, plus a lack of resistance to infections.

2  Improvements in agricultural technology, artificial selection and the use of chemical fertilisers and pesticides have resulted in an increase in the world's food production.

3  Famine can result from political problems, lack of food transport, drought, flooding and an ever increasing human population.

Extension

**Digestion** is the breakdown of large, insoluble food molecules into small, water-soluble food molecules so that they can be absorbed into the bloodstream. The large food molecules are starch, proteins and fats. Digestion occurs mechanically and chemically. This happens in the alimentary canal, or gut, which together with the liver and pancreas form your digestive system (see page 22).

**Mechanical digestion** is the breakdown of large pieces of food into smaller pieces of food without changing the food molecules. This starts in the mouth where chewing breaks down food into smaller pieces that can be swallowed. Muscular contractions of the stomach continue this process. In the small intestine large globules of fat are broken into smaller globules by emulsification by bile. There is more about mechanical digestion in the next few spreads.

**Chemical digestion** is the breakdown of the large food molecules into smaller molecules by the action of **enzymes**. This occurs in the mouth, stomach and small intestine. Mechanical digestion gives a larger surface area for the enzymes to work on.

## Chemical digestion

Before the body can use food that has been eaten, the food must be broken down into small molecules.

When the food has been digested, it is **absorbed** through the wall of the small intestine into the blood. Before the food molecules can go through the gut wall they must be dissolved. Large food molecules are insoluble; they will not dissolve therefore cannot get through the wall of the small intestine. On the other hand, small food molecules are soluble. They will dissolve so they can get through the wall of the small intestine and enter the blood and the lymph, which is another body fluid that absorbs and transports fat (see page 112).

There are three main types of enzyme in your alimentary canal:

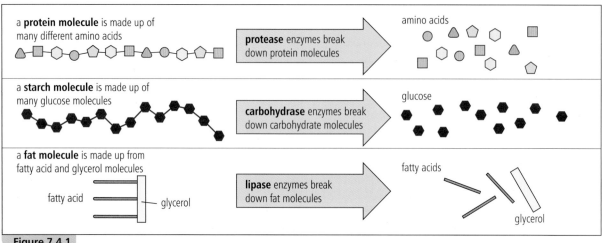

a **protein molecule** is made up of many different amino acids

**protease** enzymes break down protein molecules

amino acids

a **starch molecule** is made up of many glucose molecules

**carbohydrase** enzymes break down carbohydrate molecules

glucose

a **fat molecule** is made up from fatty acid and glycerol molecules

fatty acid — glycerol

**lipase** enzymes break down fat molecules

fatty acids

glycerol

Figure 7.4.1

# Chewing and swallowing

**Ingestion** is the taking of food and drink into the body through the mouth. When food enters the mouth, the incisor teeth and canine teeth bite it into chunks. The premolar and molar teeth grind these chunks of food into much smaller pieces. It is important to chew your food well as this makes digestion easier. The tongue mixes the food with **saliva** and the moistened food is chewed by the teeth. The food is then rolled into a ball or **bolus**.

The **salivary glands** make saliva, which contains:

- **mucus**, which is a slimy substance that lubricates the passage of the food bolus down the throat
- **amylase**, which is the enzyme that catalyses the breakdown of starch to maltose.

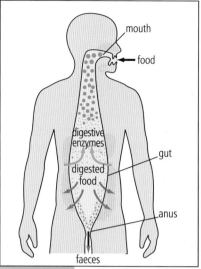

**Figure 7.4.2**  Digestion in the alimentary canal.

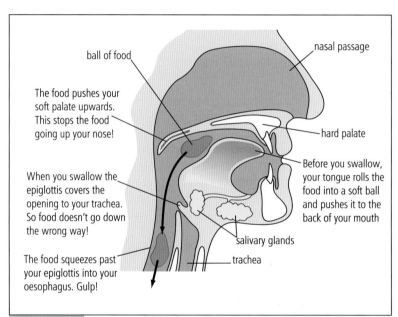

**Figure 7.4.3**  Events during swallowing.

**ball of food**

**nasal passage**

The food pushes your soft palate upwards. This stops the food going up your nose!

**hard palate**

Before you swallow, your tongue rolls the food into a soft ball and pushes it to the back of your mouth

When you swallow the epiglottis covers the opening to your trachea. So food doesn't go down the wrong way!

The food squeezes past your epiglottis into your oesophagus. Gulp!

**salivary glands**

**trachea**

## SUMMARY QUESTIONS

1. Name the enzymes and end-products involved in the chemical digestion of:
   a starch,    b protein,    c fat.

2. a  Explain why digestion is necessary.
   b  Explain the difference between mechanical digestion and chemical digestion.
   c  Outline what happens to food after it has been digested.

3. With reference to the following, describe the events that take place when food is chewed and swallowed:
   a  saliva,    b  mucus,    c  the tongue,    d  the epiglottis.

## KEY POINTS

1 Mechanical digestion is the physical breakdown of food particles to increase their surface area. Chemical digestion is the breakdown of large, insoluble food molecules into smaller, water-soluble molecules by the action of enzymes.

2 Amylase breaks down starch molecules to glucose molecules.

  Protease breaks down protein molecules to amino acids.

  Lipase breaks down fats to fatty acids and glycerol.

3 Food is chewed up by the teeth. It is then swallowed by the actions of the tongue, saliva, soft palate and epiglottis.

## LEARNING OUTCOMES

- Describe the structure and functions of human teeth
- State the causes of tooth decay and describe the proper care of teeth
- Describe how fluoride reduces tooth decay and explain arguments for and against fluoridation of drinking water supplies

A child usually has 20 milk teeth.

## EXAMINER SAYS...

Make sure that you can identify the different types of human teeth from photographs and diagrams and can state their functions in mechanical digestion.

The teeth carry out mechanical digestion when chewing food. This breaks down food into smaller pieces so making it easier to swallow. The surface area of food is increased so making it easier for enzymes to catalyse the reactions needed for chemical digestion.

Adult humans have 32 teeth, but not all of the teeth are the same. They have different shapes for performing different functions:

- incisors are chisel-shaped for biting and cutting
- canines are pointed for piercing and tearing
- premolars have uneven 'cusps' for grinding and chewing
- molars are like premolars and are for chewing up the food.

If you count how many of each type of tooth there is, you should find that there are:

8 incisors, 4 canines, 8 premolars, and 12 molars, which makes 32 teeth in all.

During our lives we have two sets of teeth. The first set, or **milk teeth**, are small teeth and there are only 8 molars as our jaws are small. Between the ages of 6 and 12 these teeth gradually fall out, to be replaced by our **permanent teeth**. The last of our permanent teeth will come through when we are at least 18, if at all! These are our back molars or **wisdom teeth**.

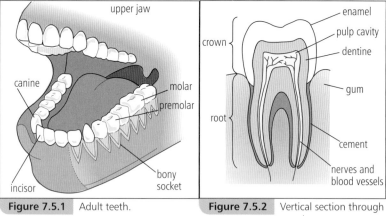

Figure 7.5.1   Adult teeth.

Figure 7.5.2   Vertical section through a molar.

**Enamel** forms the hard, outer layer of the crown of the tooth which is the part above the gum. Inside this is softer **dentine**, which is more like bone in structure. A layer of **cement** fixes the root of the tooth into a bony socket in the jaw. The root is the part that is below the gum.

The **pulp cavity** is a space in the tooth containing nerves and blood vessels.

## Healthy teeth and gums

Tooth decay is caused by bacteria in your mouth. They mix with saliva to form **plaque** which is a layer that sticks to your teeth and gums.

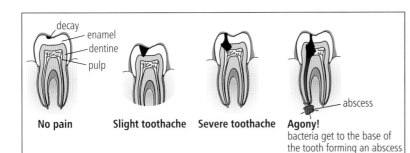

| decay |
| enamel |
| dentine |
| pulp |
| abscess |

| **No pain** | **Slight toothache** | **Severe toothache** | **Agony!**<br>bacteria get to the base of<br>the tooth forming an abscess |

**Figure 7.5.3**    Stages in tooth decay.

After a meal, sugary food may be left between your teeth. Bacteria in the plaque change the sugar into acid because they are respiring anaerobically. The acid can attack the enamel on the surface of a tooth and this starts off tooth decay. When the enamel is worn away acid will attack the dentine. If the cavity reaches the pulp cavity this will be very painful and cause severe toothache. The acid can also make your gums red and swollen.

Fluoride strengthens teeth by making the enamel more resistant to acid. In some places in the world, fluoride is put into the drinking water. This has helped to reduce the number of people with tooth decay. However, many people are opposed to this since they feel that they should be given the choice of whether to drink water with extra fluoride in it or not. Also the long-term effects of increased fluoride on the body are not known. Scientific data have shown that adding fluoride to drinking water results in a large decrease in tooth decay, especially in areas where natural fluoride levels from dissolved minerals in the water are low. Fluoride toothpaste is another option, but many people around the world cannot afford to buy this.

**Periodontal disease** can also occur if bacteria get into the space between the teeth. They can make the gums unhealthy. The bacteria can rot the fibres holding the teeth in position and make them fall out.

**EXAMINER SAYS…**

Note that fluoride strengthens the <u>enamel</u> of the teeth, giving them a hard exterior surface.

**KEY POINTS**

1 Incisors are for biting and cutting, canines for piercing and tearing, and premolars and molars are for grinding and chewing.

2 Tooth decay is caused by bacteria in plaque, which changes sugar to acid that attacks the enamel and dentine of the tooth.

3 Tooth decay can be avoided by regular brushing with a good toothbrush, avoiding sugary foods and visiting the dentist regularly.

4 Adding fluoride to drinking water reduces the incidence of tooth decay, but some people oppose this since it denies them choice and some long-term health effects are not known.

1 Copy and complete the following sentences using the words below:

**dentine   crown   mechanical   socket**
**root   bite   enamel   chew   bone**

The teeth are used to _____ and _____ your food. This is a type of _____ digestion. Each tooth consists of a _____ above the gum and a _____ which is fitted into a bony _____. The _____ is the hard, outer layer of the tooth; inside this is the softer _____ which is similar to _____.

2 **a**   Name the four main types of teeth.

  **b**   For each type in part **a**, describe its shape and its function.

  **c**   What is the difference between the milk teeth and the permanent teeth?

  **d**   Describe the stages of tooth decay.

  **e**   State three ways in which tooth decay can be prevented.

3 Explain why adding fluoride to drinking water is a controversial issue.

81

# The stomach and small intestine

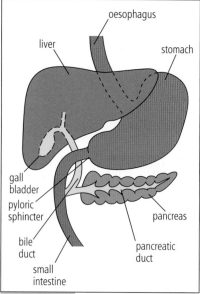

**Figure 7.6.2** Upper part of the digestive system.

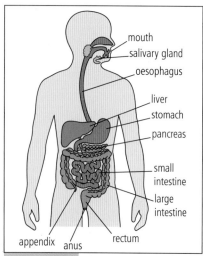

**Figure 7.6.3** The digestive system.

## The oesophagus

Food passes down the **oesophagus** from the mouth to the stomach. The oesophagus (also known as the gullet) has circular and longitudinal muscles in its wall.

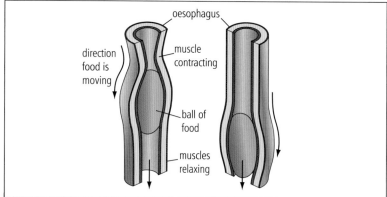

**Figure 7.6.1** Peristalsis in the oesophagus is a wave of contraction to pass food to the stomach.

The movement of food down the oesophagus occurs by a wave of muscular contraction called **peristalsis**. The circular muscles contract and the longitudinal muscles relax behind the food bolus to push it along. In front of the bolus the circular muscles relax and the longitudinal muscles contract to widen the oesophagus to allow the bolus of food to move along. Movement of food in the small and large intestines also occurs by peristalsis but to a lesser extent.

## The stomach

The stomach is a muscular bag that usually holds about 1 litre of food but can stretch to accommodate more. When food reaches the stomach a number of things happen to it.

The walls of the stomach make a digestive juice known as **gastric juice**. This contains the protease **pepsin** which starts the digestion of proteins to smaller molecules called polypeptides.

Gastric juices also contain **hydrochloric acid**, which kills any bacteria in the food. As a result the enzyme pepsin works in an acid pH of about 1.5 to 2.0. This mixture of food, gastric juice and hydrochloric acid is called **chyme**. The muscular walls of the stomach churn up the food making sure that it is mixed well with the juices. This muscular action is a type of mechanical digestion. After 2 to 3 hours of churning, the contents of the stomach are like a runny liquid.

A ring of muscle, called the **pyloric sphincter**, opens to let the food pass a little at a time into the **duodenum** which is the first part of the small intestine.

## The small intestine

The small intestine is not really so small as it is about 6 metres long; however its diameter is less than that of the large intestine. The first part, after the stomach, is the **duodenum** that leads into the **ileum**.

The **pancreas** is connected to the duodenum by the **pancreatic duct**. **Pancreatic juice** flows down the duct to meet food arriving from the stomach. Pancreatic juice contains:

- **amylase** – breaks down starch to maltose
- **trypsin** – a protease that breaks down proteins and polypeptides to peptides
- **lipase** – breaks down fats to fatty acids and glycerol.

These enzymes do not work well in an acidic environment, so pancreatic juice contains the alkali, sodium hydrogencarbonate. This neutralises the acidic food which enters the duodenum from the stomach.

**Bile** also enters the duodenum along a tube called the **bile duct**. Bile is a yellow-green fluid made in the **liver** and stored in the **gall bladder**.

Bile is alkaline and also neutralises acid which was added to the food in the stomach. This gives the best pH for enzymes in the small intestine to work.

Bile **emulsifies** fats by breaking down large globules of fats into smaller globules.

Cells lining the ileum make enzymes that complete the digestion of food. They break down maltose to glucose, peptides to amino acids and fats to fatty acids and glycerol. They also break down other molecules such as sucrose.

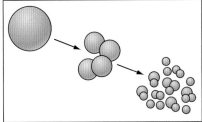

**Figure 7.6.4** Large globules of fat are emulsified to smaller globules of fat to increase their surface area.

**EXAMINER SAYS...**

Emulsification increases the surface area of fats for lipase enzymes to act upon. Emulsification is not a type of chemical digestion as the fat is not changed chemically.

### SUMMARY QUESTIONS

1 Match each part of the digestive system in the first column with its correct function in the second column:

| | |
|---|---|
| oesophagus | makes bile |
| stomach | moves food from the stomach to the ileum |
| liver | makes pancreatic juice |
| gall bladder | carries food to the stomach by peristalsis |
| pancreas | mixes food with gastric juice |
| duodenum | stores bile |

2 a State: i the components of bile, ii the organ where bile is produced, iii the organ where bile is stored.

  b Describe two ways in which bile aids the digestion of fats.

3 a How are conditions in the stomach different from the conditions in the small intestine?

  b State the composition of:

    i gastric juice

    ii pancreatic juice.

### KEY POINTS

1 Peristalsis involves a wave of muscular contractions that squeeze the food bolus, carrying it down the oesophagus to the stomach.

2 In the stomach, food is churned up and mixed with gastric juice and hydrochloric acid. This starts the digestion of protein.

3 Bile emulsifies fats in the duodenum. The smaller fat globules have a larger surface area upon which lipase can act.

4 Enzymes produced by the pancreas and the small intestine complete chemical digestion.

# Absorption and assimilation

- Define the terms *absorption* and *assimilation*
- Describe how the small intestine is adapted for efficient absorption of food
- Describe the role of the liver in assimilation

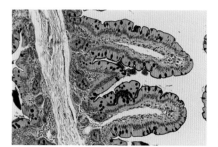

Villi increase the surface area of the small intestine.

## Absorption

**Absorption** is the movement of digested food molecules through the wall of the intestine into the blood or the lymph. Digested food includes simple sugars, amino acids, fatty acids and glycerol. These molecules pass through the wall of the small intestine either by diffusion or by active transport.

The small intestine is adapted for efficient absorption of food as it has:

- a very large surface area of about 9 square metres
- a thin lining (only one cell thick), so digested food can easily cross the wall into the blood and lymph.

It is possible to fit such a large surface area into such a small space because the small intestine is very long (at least 6 metres in an adult). It has a folded inner lining with millions of tiny, finger-like projections called **villi** (the singular of villi is **villus**).

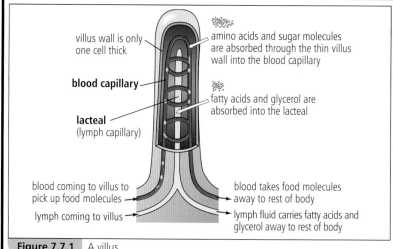

villus wall is only one cell thick

amino acids and sugar molecules are absorbed through the thin villus wall into the blood capillary

**blood capillary**

fatty acids and glycerol are absorbed into the lacteal

**lacteal** (lymph capillary)

blood coming to villus to pick up food molecules

lymph coming to villus

blood takes food molecules away to rest of body

lymph fluid carries fatty acids and glycerol away to rest of body

**Figure 7.7.1** A villus

The digested food reaches the capillaries and **lacteals** (lymph capillaries) in the villi. Absorbed food molecules are transported quickly to the liver by the **hepatic portal vein**. Fatty acids and glycerol are transported in the lymph. Movement of the gut empties the lacteal and the lymph moves slowly through lymphatic vessels, which are thin-walled like veins, eventually to enter into the blood near the heart. As a result fat does not enter the bloodstream too quickly (see page 112).

By the time the food gets to the **colon** there is not much useful food left. It is now mainly fibre, dead cells, bacteria and some water, as most of it has been absorbed in the small intestine.

The small intestine absorbs about 5–10 dm³ of water every day. As food passes along the colon, more water is absorbed into the blood: about 0.3–0.5 dm³ per day.

Extension

Extension

The solid waste or **faeces** are stored in the **rectum**. Eventually the faeces are egested through the **anus**. The passing out of indigestible food through the anus, in the form of faeces, is called **egestion**.

## Assimilation

**Assimilation** means that the food molecules that have been absorbed now become part of the cells or are used by the cells. The liver carries out a number of important functions as part of assimilation:

- stores glucose by removing it from the blood and storing it as glycogen. This helps to regulate the concentration of glucose in the blood (see page 131)
- uses amino acids to make proteins, such as those involved with blood clotting
- breaks down excess amino acids
- converts fatty acids and glycerol into fat which is stored around the body, e.g. under the skin
- produces cholesterol from fats (see page 73).

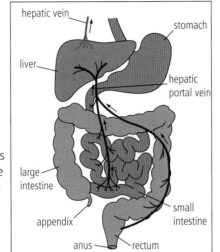

**Figure 7.7.2** The position of the hepatic portal vein.

Amino acids cannot be stored so the liver breaks down amino acids that are not required for making proteins. Each amino acid molecule is broken down into two by the process of **deamination**. One molecule is converted to carbohydrate or fat and used as a source of energy. The other molecule is ammonia ($NH_3$) which combines with carbon dioxide to form the excretory product **urea**. This is carried to the kidneys in the blood where it is filtered out and is excreted in urine (see page 134). The part of the amino acid molecule that contains nitrogen is known as the amino group – this is why the process is called deamination because this group is removed.

The liver breaks down toxins, for example drugs such as alcohol and paracetamol.

### SUMMARY QUESTIONS

1 a   State three ways in which the small intestine is adapted for absorption of digested food.
   b   Explain the role of each of the following:
      i   villi,   ii   a lacteal,   iii   the hepatic portal vein.
   c   What happens to food in the colon and rectum?

2 Explain as fully as possible the functions of the liver in assimilation.

3 Blood in the hepatic portal vein contains absorbed food. Explain how the composition of blood leaving the liver in the hepatic vein differs from that of blood entering in the hepatic portal vein.

4 Describe what happens during deamination.

**KEY POINTS**

1   Absorption is the movement of digested food molecules through the wall of the intestine into the blood and lymph.

2   Assimilation is the movement of digested food molecules into the cells of the body where they are used, becoming part of the cells.

3   The small intestine is adapted for absorption by being very long, having a folded inner lining with millions of tiny villi.

4   The liver stores glucose as glycogen, makes proteins, breaks down excess amino acids and converts fatty acids and glycerol back into fat for storage.

5   Deamination is the breakdown of excess amino acids in the liver to form ammonia, which is made into urea. The liver also breaks down toxins, such as alcohol.

1 (a) State the seven components of a human diet.

(b) List the three components of a balanced diet that provide energy.

2 State three functions of a balanced diet, other than providing energy.

3 Write definitions of the following:

(a) balanced diet

(b) malnutrition

(c) ingestion

(d) egestion.

4 Explain the importance of mechanical and chemical digestion.

5 Amylase, protease and lipase are three enzymes that are secreted into the alimentary canal.
For each enzyme, state where in the alimentary canal they are secreted, where they act and give their substrate and end-product(s).

6 Explain the difference between absorption and assimilation.

**Extension**

7 Explain why fluoride is added to the water supply in some parts of the world but not in others.

8 Describe the functions of capillaries and lacteals in the villi of the small intestine.

9 People who have a diet rich in protein may have an excess of amino acids in their bodies. Describe what happens to these amino acids.

1 The breakdown of large, insoluble food molecules into small, water-soluble molecules is:

A   absorption

B   digestion

C   egestion

D   ingestion

*(Paper 1)*                                         *[1]*

2 Which of the following is a correct description of the action of a protease?

A   breaks down fat into fatty acids and glycerol

B   breaks down protein into amino acids

C   breaks down starch into glucose

D   converts amino acids into proteins

*(Paper 1)*                                         *[1]*

3 The drawing shows a vertical section through an incisor tooth.

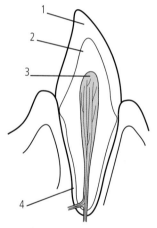

Which is the correct identification of the parts shown in the drawing above?

|   | 1 | 2 | 3 | 4 |
|---|---|---|---|---|
| A | cement | pulp | enamel | dentine |
| B | dentine | enamel | pulp | cement |
| C | enamel | dentine | pulp | cement |
| D | pulp | cement | dentine | enamel |

*(Paper 1)*                                         *[1]*

**4** The drawing shows part of the digestive system.

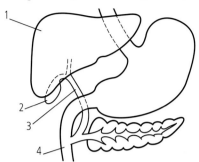

What is the function of the liquid produced by part 1, stored in part 2 and released into part 3?

**A** to digest proteins to amino acids

**B** to increase the surface area of fat droplets

**C** to acidify the contents of part 4

**D** to digest fats to fatty acids and glycerol

*(Paper 1)* [1]

**5** The liver performs an important function in the digestion and assimilation of food.

**(a)** Name the digestive juice secreted by the liver. [1]

**(b)** Explain what is meant by the term *assimilation*. [1]

**(c)** Describe how the liver is involved in the metabolism of **(i)** glucose, and **(ii)** amino acids. [6]

**(d)** Give one reason why fat is stored in the body. [1]

*(Paper 2)*

**6** Copy the diagram from question 4.

**(a)** On the diagram label the following: oesophagus, stomach, pancreas and duodenum. [4]

**(b)** Use arrows to show the direction taken by food as it passes through the parts of the alimentary canal on the diagram. [2]

**(c)** On the diagram use label lines and the following letters to show:

**E** the site of secretion of lipase

**F** site of storage of bile

**G** a place where physical digestion of fat occurs

**H** a part which has an acidic pH. [4]

*(Paper 2)*

**7** The diagram shows a villus.

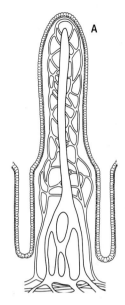

**(a)** Copy the drawing and label the capillaries and the lacteal. [2]

**(b)** State the parts of the alimentary canal where villi are located. [2]

**(c)** Describe the pathway taken by soluble food molecules from **A** on the diagram to the liver. [3]

**(d)** Name three substances that pass along the pathway you have described. [3]

*(Paper 3)*

**8 (a)** Write out and complete the following:

Excess amino acid molecules are not stored in the body. These amino acid molecules are taken up by the _____ and broken down. The _____ containing part of each amino acid molecule is removed and converted into _____. The rest of the molecule may be _____ to release _____. This breakdown of amino acids is called _____. [6]

**(b)** State two other substances that are broken down by the liver. [2]

*(Paper 3)*

# 8 Plant transport

## 8.1

# Transport systems

*Eucalyptus regnans* is the tallest flowering plant, growing up to 90 metres.

Most living organisms need a transport system. Only very small organisms, such as bacteria, protoctists and some worms, do not have transport systems. Their bodies are so small, or so flat, that they can rely on diffusion alone to obtain oxygen and remove carbon dioxide.

Vertebrates and flowering plants are large organisms and have transport systems to carry substances, such as food and water, throughout their bodies. These transport systems move fluids through tubes so that all of the fluid moves in the same direction within each tube. This type of transport is called **mass flow**.

Vertebrates have a circulatory system consisting of a pump (the heart) and blood vessels. Flowering plants have two separate transport systems: **xylem** and **phloem**.

## Xylem and phloem

Xylem and phloem are plant tissues composed of cells that are specialised for transport (see page 22). These tissues are found throughout the plant body in roots, stems and leaves.

Xylem tissue transports water and mineral ions. The roots absorb the water and mineral ions from the soil. These enter the xylem in the root and travel upwards in the stem to the leaves, flowers and fruits.

Transport in the xylem, unlike in the phloem, is in one direction only – from roots via stem to leaves.

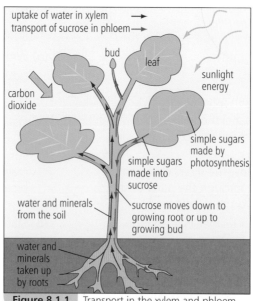

**Figure 8.1.1** Transport in the xylem and phloem.

Phloem tissue transports sucrose, amino acids and hormones throughout the plant. Sucrose is a soluble, complex sugar which is made especially for transporting energy. It is made in leaves with the sugars from photosynthesis and from starch in storage organs, such as swollen roots and stems.

Substances are transported in the phloem in two directions: downwards from leaves to roots and upwards from leaves to flowers, fruits and buds; also from storage organs to new stems and leaves. Hormones control cell division for growth of the stem, roots and leaves. They also control the growth of flowers and fruits (see page 154).

## Inside the root and stem

To find the transport tissues of roots and stems, we cut across them to give transverse sections.

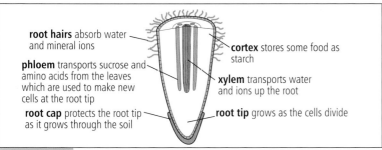

**root hairs** absorb water and mineral ions

**phloem** transports sucrose and amino acids from the leaves which are used to make new cells at the root tip

**root cap** protects the root tip as it grows through the soil

**cortex** stores some food as starch

**xylem** transports water and ions up the root

**root tip** grows as the cells divide

**Figure 8.1.2**    The internal structure of a root.

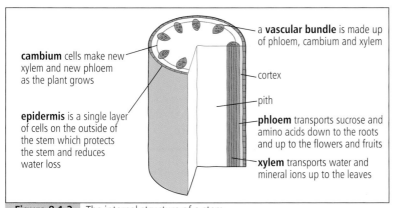

**cambium** cells make new xylem and new phloem as the plant grows

**epidermis** is a single layer of cells on the outside of the stem which protects the stem and reduces water loss

a **vascular bundle** is made up of phloem, cambium and xylem

cortex

pith

**phloem** transports sucrose and amino acids down to the roots and up to the flowers and fruits

**xylem** transports water and mineral ions up to the leaves

**Figure 8.1.3**    The internal structure of a stem.

This celery was left standing in a red dye for several hours. The red strands are the xylem vessels filled with dye.

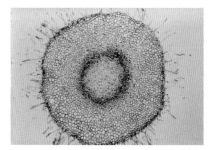

A transverse section of a root.

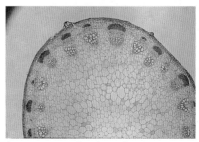

A transverse section through a young stem. Note the vascular bundles.

(see page 154).

## SUMMARY QUESTIONS

1 Copy and complete the following sentences, using the words below:

**leaves   sucrose   water   amino   blood vessels
mineral ions   fruits   heart   storage**

Vertebrates have a transport system made up of a _____ and _____. Flowering plants have two transport systems. Xylem tissue transports _____ and _____ up the stem from the roots to the _____, flowers and _____. Phloem tissue transports _____ and _____ acids from leaves to all parts of the plant, such as _____ organs.

2 Using the diagrams above, state the functions of each of the following tissues:

a  phloem,  b  xylem,  c  cambium,  d  epidermis,

e  root cap,   f  root cortex.

### KEY POINTS

1 Xylem vessels transport water and mineral ions from the roots up the stem to the leaves.

2 Phloem vessels transport sucrose, made in the leaves during photosynthesis and in storage organs, to other parts of the plant.

3 Xylem and phloem are distributed in a central core inside a root. Inside a stem they are organised into vascular bundles.

# Water uptake

- Identify root hairs as seen under the microscope and relate their structure to water uptake
- State the pathway taken by water through root, stem and leaf

## Water uptake by roots

The main functions of roots are to anchor the plant in the soil and to take up water and mineral ions. Just behind the root tip are small **root hairs**. Water passes into the root hairs by **osmosis**.

Soil water is a dilute solution of various solutes including mineral ions, such as nitrate and potassium. Root hairs have thin, permeable cell walls and provide a large surface area to absorb water. The cell sap in the root hair cells is a more concentrated solution than soil water. This is because root hair cells also absorb mineral ions and have other solutes such as sugars. The cell membrane is partially permeable so water diffuses from the soil into the root hair cells by osmosis.

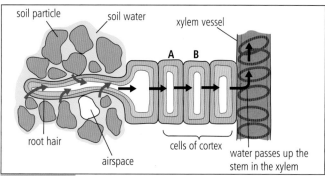

**Figure 8.2.1**    Absorption of water by a root.

Water then passes across the cortex of the root. Most of the water moves through the cell walls and in the spaces between the cells. Some moves from cell to cell. Water eventually reaches the xylem in the centre of the root. From here water moves up the xylem through the stem and to the leaves where it enters the spongy mesophyll cells. Much of the water enters the cell walls, evaporates to form water vapour and then diffuses through stomata to the atmosphere.

We describe the movement of water into a root hair, across the cortex and into a xylem vessel in terms of **water potential** (see page 28). Water passes *down* a **water potential gradient**, from a high water potential in the solution in the soil to a lower water potential in the root hair cell. Water in turn, passes from the root hair cell to a lower water potential in the cells of the cortex and eventually to an even lower water potential in the xylem vessel.

**Extension**

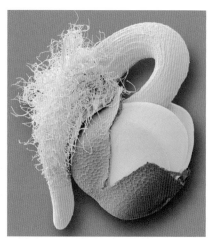

Root hairs of a germinating bean seed.

**PRACTICAL**

### Looking at root hairs

Look closely at a section of a young root with a hand lens and then with a microscope.

Look at the root hairs.

Root hairs are long and thin. You can also look at root hairs on a germinating seedling such as a bean or a radish.

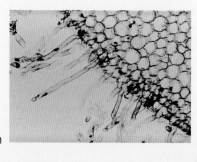

They have a large surface area through which water and mineral ions are absorbed.

**Extension**

Xylem vessels are like pipes as they are empty except for the water that fills them. Water is not *pushed* from the roots up to the leaves, instead it is *pulled* by the evaporation of water.

## Transmission pull

**Transpiration** is the evaporation of water from the leaves and the loss of water vapour to the atmosphere. Water vapour can diffuse out of the leaf when the stomata are open.

Water is 'pulled' up the xylem in the stem from the roots to the leaves by **transpiration pull**.

The water is used for photosynthesis and to stop the plant from wilting. As water is used up or lost from the leaves, more is sucked up from the xylem vessels, rather like water being sucked up a straw.

This mass flow of water up the xylem relies on two properties of water:

* **cohesion** – the water molecules tend to attract each other, sticking together
* **adhesion** – the water molecules also tend to stick to the inside of the xylem vessel.

So there is a continuous flow of water from the roots to the leaves. This movement of water up the xylem is called the **transpiration stream**.

**EXAMINER SAYS...**

Make sure that you write 'water vapour <u>diffuses</u> out of the leaf' and not 'water <u>goes out</u> of the leaf'.

**EXAMINER SAYS...**

When you are explaining how water moves in the xylem, always start with evaporation of water in the leaf that pulls the water from the roots.

## SUMMARY QUESTIONS

1 Copy and complete the following sentences using the words below:

**stomata osmosis large ions transpiration hair area**

Water passes into a root _____ cell by _____. Mineral _____ are also taken up. A root hair cell has a _____ surface _____ for taking up water and mineral ions. Water is lost from the leaves by _____. This is controlled by the opening and closing of the _____.

2 Look at the diagram of the root hair in the soil:

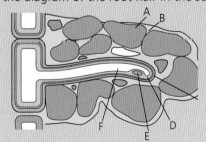

a Name the parts labelled A to F.
b Explain how water gets into a root hair cell from the soil.
c Give two other functions of root hair cells.

3 Explain, using the term *water potential*, how water passes into root hair cells, across the cells of the cortex, into the xylem vessels and up to the leaves, where it is lost to the atmosphere.

## KEY POINTS

1 Water enters a root hair cell by osmosis. It then passes across the cells of the root cortex by osmosis before passing into the xylem and then up the stem to the leaves.

2 Root hairs are well adapted for the absorption of water since they have thin cell walls and have a large surface area.

3 Loss of water from the leaves 'pulls' more water up the stem from the roots in the transpiration stream.

# Transpiration

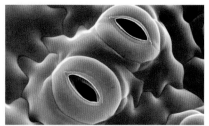

Two open stomata.

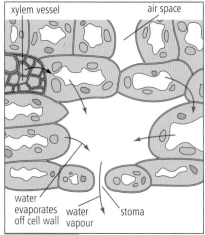

Figure 8.3.1   Loss of water vapour from a leaf.

xylem vessel     air space

water evaporates off cell wall    water vapour    stoma

Plants absorb large quantities of water from the soil. Much of this water passes into roots, moves up through stems and enters leaves where it is lost to the atmosphere as water vapour. If you look at a diagram of a leaf you will see that there are many air spaces inside. These are lined by mesophyll cells which have damp cell walls. Water evaporates from this huge internal surface so the air spaces become saturated with water vapour.

There is usually more water vapour in the air spaces than there is in the outside air, so water vapour diffuses through the stomata into the air. The water lost from the spongy mesophyll cells is replaced by more water from the xylem.

**Transpiration** is the term given to this evaporation inside the leaves and the diffusion of water vapour through stomata to the atmosphere.

## Wilting

More transpiration takes place during the day than at night because the stomata are open during the day and closed at night. The stomata open during the day so that carbon dioxide can diffuse into the leaf. Carbon dioxide is a raw material for photosynthesis and diffuses into chloroplasts in mesophyll cells.

The stomata close at night to reduce the volume of water lost by transpiration. They may also close in hot, dry conditions during the day as water lost in transpiration is not being replaced by water from the soil.

The stomata close up to reduce transpiration. If the plant still does not get enough water it will start to **wilt** (see above on the right). Its cells have lost so much water that they are no longer turgid or full of water. Turgid cells are firm and give the plant support. If the cells become flaccid then the plant becomes soft. The stem is no longer upright and the leaves droop.

Wilting is not a bad thing. The leaves move downwards so are out of the direct rays of the Sun so do not get as hot. When the temperature decreases and they can absorb more water than is lost by transpiration the leaves will recover.

# Factors affecting transpiration

Other factors affecting transpiration are environmental.

**Light** causes the stomata to open. As the light intensity increases the stomata open wider. The rate of transpiration increases up to a maximum that is determined by the conditions shown in the graphs.

**Humid** conditions decrease the rate of transpiration. The air contains a great many water molecules already, so there is not much difference between the concentration of water vapour in the leaf and outside. There is less transpiration because the concentration gradient for water vapour is less steep.

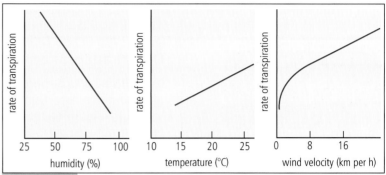

**Figure 8.3.2**

**Warm** conditions increase the rate of transpiration. Warm air can hold more water vapour.

**Windy** conditions increase the rate of transpiration. Water molecules are blown away from the leaf surface, so more water molecules diffuse out of the stomata.

## Measuring transpiration

It is not easy to measure the rate of transpiration but you can use a **potometer** to measure the **rate of water uptake**. The volume of water lost is slightly less than the volume of water taken in by the roots. This is because some of the water is used up in photosynthesis and in keeping cells turgid.

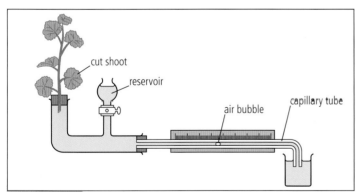

**Figure 8.3.3**    A potometer.

The potometer is filled by submerging it in water. It is set up as shown, making sure the stem in the stopper is air-tight. An air bubble is allowed to form in the capillary tube. The distance moved by the bubble is a measure of the rate of water uptake.

**SUMMARY QUESTIONS**

1 How you would set up a potometer to measure the rate of water uptake by a cut shoot? Explain how it works.

2 State and explain how each of the following conditions affects the rate of transpiration:

a   an increase in light intensity,

b   a decrease in temperature,

c   an increase in humidity.

# 8.4

# Adaptations of plants to different environments

Cacti store water in their swollen stems.

Spines provide some shade and protection from herbivores.

Water lilies, *Nymphaea sp.*

## Desert adaptations

All plants have to balance water uptake with water loss. It is important that they maintain the turgor in their cells, or they will wilt. Very high rates of transpiration can kill a plant if it cannot absorb enough water to prevent long-term wilting.

**Xerophytes** are plants are that are able to exist in conditions where water is scarce. Cacti are xerophytes that survive in hot, dry (arid) desert regions. Cacti reduce water loss and conserve water in the following ways.

• Their leaves are reduced to spines. This reduces the surface area of the leaf over which water can be lost.
• A thick, waxy cuticle covers the plant's surfaces and reduces transpiration.
• They have swollen stems containing water-storage tissue.
• They have a shallow, spreading root system to absorb quickly any water from rain and overnight condensation.
• Many cacti have a round, compact shape which reduces their surface area so there is less surface through which water can be lost.
• They have shiny surfaces which reflect heat and light.
• Their stomata are closed during the day to reduce water loss. They open their stomata at night to absorb the carbon dioxide which they store for use in photosynthesis during the day. Photosynthesis occurs in the outer layers of cells in their stems.

## Pond plants

**Hydrophytes** are plants that grow submerged or partially submerged in water. Living in water has both its costs and its benefits.

Buoyed up by water and with no need for water transport, floating plants save energy since they produce little or no xylem tissue.

Roots, if present, are for anchorage and since there is no need for the roots to absorb water or mineral ions, there are no root hairs. The leaves and stems of hydrophytes have little or no cuticle, since there is no need to conserve water.

The problem for hydrophytes is that carbon dioxide, which is needed for photosynthesis, diffuses through water much more slowly than it does through air. The same applies for oxygen, needed for plant respiration, since it is not very soluble in water. Therefore many hydrophytes have an extensive system of air spaces in their stems and leaves through which gases diffuse quickly. These air spaces provide buoyancy to keep the plants close to the light and are a reservoir of oxygen and carbon dioxide.

# Garden plants

Garden plants are grown for their colourful, scented flowers, for their subtle leaf colours, for shade and to provide an attractive environment. You should look in your locality and find some garden plants that are not xerophytes or hydrophytes and study their adaptations.

**Mesophytes** are terrestrial plants that usually have enough water and do not have such extreme adaptations to reduce water loss like those of xerophytes. Many garden plants are mesophytes, as gardeners can provide them with enough water even in parts of the world that might be dry for much of the year.

Coleus, *Solenostemon spp.*, brightly coloured garden plants.

## SUMMARY QUESTIONS

1 Make a list of four ways in which desert plants are able to reduce water loss and conserve water.

2 Explain each of the following statements about pond plants.

　a　They need little xylem in their stems and leaves.

　b　Their roots do not have root hairs.

　c　They have an extensive system of air spaces inside their stems and roots.

3 Freshwater aquatic plants are surrounded by a solution of a higher water potential than the cell sap in the cells of their stems and leaves.

　a　Explain how this is an advantage to the maintenance of turgor in the cells.

　b　What prevents these cells from bursting?

　c　Ions in the water are at a very low concentration. State the mechanism by which these ions are taken up by plants.

## KEY POINTS

1 Desert plants such as cacti have thick cuticles, leaves reduced to spines, swollen stems to store water and extensive root systems. Often their stomata close during the day and absorb carbon dioxide at night.

2 Pond plants do not need much transport tissue since they are buoyed up in water. They have extensive air spaces to store carbon dioxide and oxygen which diffuse very slowly in water.

3 Many garden plants do not experience these extremes of water supply and do not have extreme adaptations.

# Translocation

## LEARNING OUTCOMES

- Define the term *translocation*
- Describe the translocation of applied chemicals, such as systemic pesticides, throughout the plant
- Compare transpiration with translocation

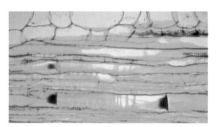

Phloem tubes are living tissues.

Food is made in the leaves by photosynthesis. The soluble products include sucrose, amino acids and fatty acids. These are carried to all parts of the plant in solution in the **phloem**. This transport is called **translocation** which means 'from place to place'.

The transport of food takes place from regions of production (the leaves) to the regions of storage or to regions where respiration or growth take place. The simple sugars produced by photosynthesis are converted in the leaves into sucrose. This is transported to parts of the plant where growth or storage occur to provide energy. Sucrose is:

- broken down by an enzyme to give simple sugars that are used in respiration
- changed to starch for storage in the root cortex and in seeds
- used to make cellulose for new cell walls at the growing root tip and shoot tip
- stored in some fruits to make them sweet and attract animals.

Leaves use the simple sugars from photosynthesis and nitrate ions to make amino acids. These are needed all over the plant to make proteins, especially where new cells are made in shoot and root tips. Leaves also make fatty acids that are stored in many seeds as oils and are also needed for the waxy cuticle on the upper surface of the leaves.

### DID YOU KNOW?

Maple syrup is prepared from phloem sap of maple trees. Farmers drill holes into the tree and insert tubes through which the sap flows and collects in buckets.

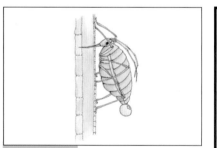

**Figure 8.5.1** Aphids are crop pests. They feed on phloem sap by using their piercing mouthparts.

## Translocation of systemic pesticides

Some farmers use **pesticides** to control pests and diseases, such as insects and fungi, that spoil crops and reduce yields. Organic farmers do not use chemical pesticides but use other methods such as encouraging natural predators of pests.

**Contact pesticides** kill the pests that they are sprayed onto. These may not always be effective because pests may be on the underside of leaves where the spray does not hit them. **Systemic pesticides** are a more effective alternative because they are sprayed on the crop plants which absorb them. The pesticides are translocated to all parts of the plant in the phloem. Any insect feeding on any part of the plant will ingest the pesticide with the plant tissue. After a while the insect will ingest enough to kill it. The same happens to fungi growing on or inside any part of a crop plant.

# Transpiration and translocation

In plant transport, the part of the plant where a substance begins its journey is called a **source**. The part where it ends its journey is a **sink**.

Water and ions are absorbed by roots (the source) and travel to leaves, flowers and fruits (the sinks). Xylem vessels are columns (or pipes) of dead, empty cells. The movement of water in xylem vessels is *passive*, since it relies upon the evaporation of water vapour from the leaves producing a tension in the xylem. This pulls up water from the roots to give the transpiration stream. Transpiration is greatest on hot, dry and windy days.

Translocation is an *active* process which occurs in phloem. The leaves are the source of food substances and the sinks are the respiring plant tissues, regions of growth (root and shoot tips) and regions of storage such as the root cortex and the seeds. Phloem tubes are living cells that contain some cytoplasm. Movement in the phloem requires active transport of sucrose at the source. Water enters the phloem tubes to build up a head of pressure that forces the phloem sap to the sinks. Translocation is most active on sunny, warm days when plants are producing increased levels of sugar.

Aphids spread diseases between plants caused by viruses when they feed on phloem. Systemic pesticides are used against aphids.

## SUMMARY QUESTIONS

1 a  Define the term *translocation*.

  b  What substances are translocated in the phloem?

  c  What are the materials transported in the phloem used for?

2 Draw a table to compare transpiration with translocation.

3 a  Explain how systemic pesticides work to kill pests.

  b  How is the action of systemic pesticides different from that of contact pesticides?

4 Substances are transported in plants from sources to sinks in the xylem and phloem.

| | substances transported | source of substances in the plant | sink for substances in the plant |
|---|---|---|---|
| transport in the xylem | | | |
| transport in the phloem (translocation) | | | |

  a  Copy and complete the table by giving two substances that are transported in each tissue and one source and one sink in each case.

  b  Explain how a root tuber can be a source and a sink at different times of the year.

## KEY POINTS

1 Translocation is the movement of sucrose and amino acids from the leaves to regions of respiration, growth and storage.

2 Systemic pesticides are effective since they are translocated around the plant to all the tissues that a pest may attack.

3 Transpiration is a passive process involving dead tissue. Translocation is an active process involving living tissue.

1 Define the following terms:
   (a) transpiration
   (b) translocation.

2 Describe the pathway taken by water as it travels from the soil through a plant to the atmosphere.

3 Describe what happens in a leaf to bring about the loss of water vapour to the atmosphere.

4 State the effects of increasing the following factors on the rate of water loss from plants:
   (a) light intensity
   (b) temperature
   (c) humidity.

5 Explain why most plants have higher rates of water loss during the day than at night.

6 Describe what happens in a plant when it wilts.

7 Describe the pathway taken by sucrose as it travels through a plant from the leaves.

8 A potometer was used to measure water uptake by a leafy shoot.

| conditions | time for water to move 10 cm (mins) |
|---|---|
| A  cool, moving air, in daylight | 2 |
| B  cool, still air, in daylight | 6 |
| C  warm, moving air, in daylight | 1 |
| D  warm, still air, in daylight | 3 |
| E  warm, still air, at night | 60 |

   (a) From the table, state three conditions which affect the rate of water movement through the plant.
   (b) Calculate the rate of water movement in millimetres per minute for condition A.
   (c) Give two ways in which the air around the shoot would be affected if it was covered with a transparent plastic bag.

**Extension**

9 Explain how root hairs are adapted for their functions (also see page 20).

10 Explain, using the term *water potential*, how water is transported to the tops of tall trees.

11 Define the terms *source* and *sink* as used in plant transport.

12 Explain how farmers make use of the phloem in pest control.

1 A sweet potato plant grows in a field in bright sunlight. Which option shows the correct movement of carbohydrate in the phloem?

| | type of carbohydrate | source of carbohydrate | destination |
|---|---|---|---|
| A | glucose | leaves | tubers |
| B | glucose | tubers | leaves |
| C | sucrose | leaves | tubers |
| D | sucrose | tubers | leaves |

*(Paper 1)*                                    [1]

2 Which of the following best describes the substances transported in the phloem and xylem?

| | phloem | xylem |
|---|---|---|
| A | amino acids and ions | sucrose and water |
| B | amino acids and sucrose | ions and water |
| C | sucrose and water | amino acids and ions |
| D | glucose and sucrose | ions and water |

*(Paper 1)*                                    [1]

3 Which is the correct pathway taken by a molecule of water as it moves through a plant?
   A   root cortex, xylem in root, xylem in stem, leaf mesophyll, atmosphere
   B   root hair cell, root cortex, xylem, leaf mesophyll cells, air spaces in mesophyll, stoma
   C   stoma, air spaces in leaf, xylem, root cortex, root hair cell
   D   xylem, root cortex, leaf mesophyll cell, stoma, atmosphere

*(Paper 1)*                                    [1]

4 A potted plant has wilted after being left without water for 6 days. Which combination of environmental conditions is likely to have caused it to wilt?

| | light intensity | humidity | air temperature |
|---|---|---|---|
| A | high | high | low |
| B | low | low | high |
| C | high | low | high |
| D | low | high | low |

*(Paper 1)*                                    [1]

5 The diagrams show transverse sections of **A** root, **B** stem and **C** leaf.

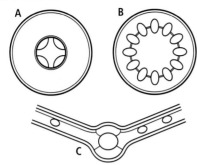

(a) Copy the diagrams and shade the areas that represent the positions of xylem and phloem in **A**, **B**. and **C**. [3]

(b) Copy and complete the table to compare the functions of xylem and phloem. The term *sap* refers to the liquid transported in these two tissues.

| feature | phloem | xylem |
|---|---|---|
| composition of the sap | | |
| direction of flow in the stem | | |
| destinations | | |

[6]

(c) Describe how you would discover the pathway taken by water as it travels through the parts of the plant that are above ground. [3]

*(Paper 2)*

6 The drawing shows a section through a leaf.

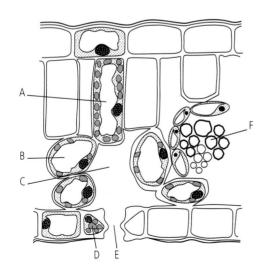

(a) Name **A** to **F**. [6]

(b) Use the diagram to explain how water is lost from leaves in transpiration. [5]

(c) A student found that the rate of transpiration of a potted plant changed over a 24-hour period.
Explain why the rate changed. [3]

*(Paper 2)*

7 A leafy shoot was cut from a plant and placed into a potometer (see diagram on page 93) which was placed on a balance. The table shows the rate of water uptake and the rate of transpiration by the leafy shoot during a hot, dry day.

| time (hours) | rate of water loss (grams per hour) | rate of water absorption (grams per hour) |
|---|---|---|
| midnight | 4 | 7 |
| 0300 | 6 | 9 |
| 0600 | 12 | 12 |
| 0900 | 18 | 14 |
| 1200 | 24 | 17 |
| 1500 | 22 | 19 |
| 1800 | 18 | 20 |
| 2100 | 8 | 14 |
| midnight | 6 | 10 |

(a) Plot a graph to show the data in the table. [5]

(b) Calculate the percentage change in the rate of water loss between 0600 hours and 1200 hours. Show your working. [2]

(c) Describe the changes in water loss and water absorption over the 24-hour period. [4]

(d) Explain how water moves from the cut end of the stem to the atmosphere. [4]

*(Paper 3)*

## 9.1     Circulation

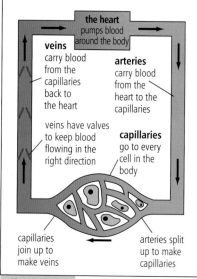

**Figure 9.1.1**   Circulation of blood around the body.

## The circulatory system

The blood, heart and blood vessels make up the circulatory system.

The circulatory system transports useful things like oxygen from the lungs to the cells and digested food from the small intestine to the cells. It also removes waste chemicals like carbon dioxide from cells to the lungs and other wastes from cells to the kidneys. The circulatory system also transports hormones, antibodies and blood proteins.

## Blood circulation

The **heart** is the pump which circulates the blood through the blood vessels.

Blood flows in **arteries** away from the heart to the different organs of the body. Blood flows back to the heart in **veins**. The smallest blood vessels that connect arteries to veins are **capillaries**. Cells are very close to capillaries so they receive a good supply of oxygen and food materials from these capillaries. This also enables them to have their carbon dioxide and other wastes removed efficiently.

The circulatory system allows a **one-way flow of blood** around the body. The heart pumps blood giving it pressure so that it flows inside arteries and this helps to maintain a one-way flow. This is good for getting blood to the capillaries, but high pressure blood will damage the delicate capillaries, so small muscular blood vessels known as **arterioles** reduce the pressure before the blood enters capillaries (you can find out more about arterioles on page 133). When blood leaves capillaries the blood pressure is even lower.

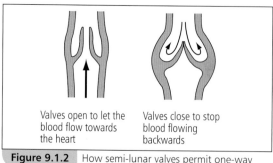

Valves open to let the blood flow towards the heart

Valves close to stop blood flowing backwards

**Figure 9.1.2**   How semi-lunar valves permit one-way flow of blood.

We have **valves** in our veins to make sure blood does not flow backwards away from the heart (see above). If this happened, blood would collect in veins, which would swell, preventing proper circulation. These valves are called **semi-lunar valves** as they consist of pockets that are half-moon in shape. Each valve has three of these pockets. The valves open when the pressure of the blood pushes against them, but they close when blood flows back to fill the pockets.

There are semi-lunar valves in the heart at the places where blood leaves the heart chambers to enter arteries. There are also valves between the chambers of the heart (see page 102).

## A double circulation

The heart is divided into two halves: *right* and *left*. The septum is a thick wall of muscle that separates the two halves of the heart. It stops blood in the right side of the heart mixing with blood in the left side.

Blood circulation has two functions.

- The *right side* of the heart pumps blood to the lungs and back to the heart again. The pressure required to force blood to the lungs is not very high since there is little resistance to flow in the lungs as they are a spongy tissue filled with air. Gas exchange occurs as blood flows through capillaries in the lungs. Blood absorbs oxygen and loses carbon dioxide. The blood that flows from the lungs is rich in oxygen and is called **oxygenated** blood. It is bright red in colour.

- The *left side* of the heart pumps blood to the rest of the body and back to the heart again. The pressure of blood leaving the left side is much greater than on the right side as there is much more resistance to flow than there is through the lungs. Gas exchange occurs as blood flows through capillaries in organs such as muscles, the gut, liver and kidneys. Oxygen leaves the blood and carbon dioxide enters. Blood that leaves capillaries and flows through veins contains less oxygen and is called **deoxygenated** blood. It is dark red in colour but is always shown as blue in diagrams like those on these pages.

The blood passes through the heart twice during one circuit around the body. That is why it is called a **double circulation**. You can confirm this by following the blood around the diagram on the right.

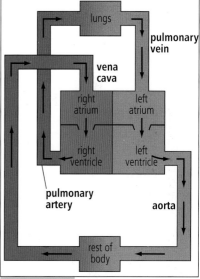

**Figure 9.1.3** Double circulation.

# The heart

## Heart structure

The human heart consists of two pumps lying side by side. The right side of the heart is one pump and the left side of the heart is another pump. The heart consists almost entirely of cardiac muscle tissue (see page 22).

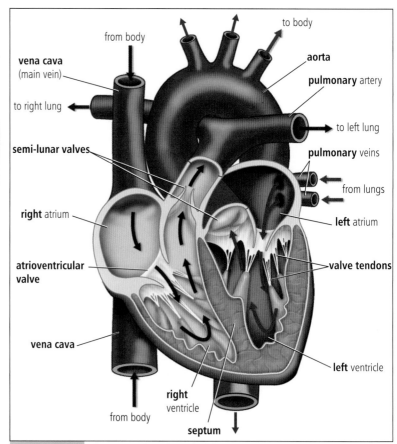

**Figure 9.2.1**   The arrows show how the blood moves through the heart.

The **septum** (wall of tissue) prevents deoxygenated blood on the right side mixing with oxygenated blood on the left side.

On each side of the heart there are two chambers. The upper chambers are called **atria** (singular **atrium**). Blood empties into them from veins. When the atria contract they pump blood into **ventricles**, which have much more muscular walls than the atria. When the ventricles contract they pump the blood out into arteries at higher pressure.

Between each atrium and ventricle is a **valve**. The valves prevent the blood flowing back into the right and left atrium when the right and left ventricles contract. The ventricles have more muscular walls than the atria because they have to pump the blood much further than the atria – either to the lungs or to the tissues of the body.

The left ventricle has a more muscular wall than the right ventricle because it has to pump blood around the body and has to overcome more resistance to flow.

## Heart action

The heart pumps blood when its muscles contract. When the muscles contract the chamber gets smaller and squeezes the blood out. After each chamber contracts it relaxes so it fills up with blood again.

The two sides of the heart work together. The atria contract and relax at the same time. The ventricles contract and relax at the same time.

**Diastole** is when the heart muscles are relaxed. Blood flows into the atria from the veins.

**Systole** is when the heart muscles contract.

- The atria contract and force blood into the ventricles. The valves between the atria and ventricles open due to the pressure of blood against them.
- Then the ventricles contract to force blood out into the arteries. The valves close to prevent blood flowing back into the atria.

The **right ventricle** pumps blood to the **lungs** in the **pulmonary artery**.

The **left ventricle** pumps blood to the rest of the body in the **aorta** (main artery).

Deoxygenated blood returns to the **right atrium** in the **vena cava** (main vein). Oxygenated blood returns to the **left atrium** in the pulmonary veins.

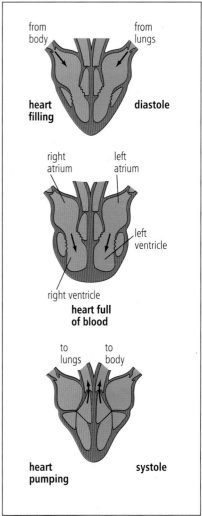

**Figure 9.2.2** The cardiac cycle – the changes that occur in the heart during one heartbeat.

## SUMMARY QUESTIONS

1 a  What are the two upper chambers of the heart called?
  b  What are the two lower chambers of the heart called?
  c  What is the function of the septum?

2 Explain each of the following statements.
  a  The atria have less muscular walls than the ventricles.
  b  The left ventricle has a much more muscular wall than the right ventricle.

3 In each of the following cases, which blood vessel carries:
  a  blood to the rest of the body
  b  blood from the lungs to the left atrium
  c  blood from the body to the right atrium
  d  blood to the lungs
  e  blood under the greatest pressure?

### KEY POINTS

1 The heart consists of two muscular pumps divided by a septum.
  Each side has two chambers: an atrium and a ventricle.

2 Ventricles contract to force blood into arteries; valves make sure that blood flows in one direction.

# 9.3 Blood vessels

## LEARNING OUTCOMES

- Name the main blood vessels to and from the heart, lungs, liver and kidney
- Describe the structure and function of arteries, veins and capillaries
- Explain how structure and function are related in arteries, veins and capillaries
- State and explain the effect of physical activity on pulse rate

Blood flows in arteries to all the organs of the body and flows away from them in veins. This table shows you some of the most important arteries and veins.

| Vessel | Organs | | | |
|---|---|---|---|---|
| | **Heart** | **Lungs** | **Liver** | **Kidneys** |
| bringing blood to organ | vena cava to right atrium; pulmonary vein to left atrium | pulmonary artery | hepatic artery; hepatic portal vein (see page 85) | renal artery (see page 135) |
| taking blood away from organ | pulmonary artery from right ventricle; aorta from left ventricle | pulmonary vein | hepatic vein (see page 85) | renal vein (see page 135) |

## Arteries

When your heart muscles contract they force the blood into the arteries at a high pressure. Arteries have quite a narrow space in the centre for the blood to flow along. Their walls have a thick layer of muscle and elastic fibres to withstand the pressure of the blood flowing through them. The elastic fibres in the walls of the arteries stretch and then recoil like a piece of elastic when you stretch it and then let it return to its original length. The recoil of elastic fibres helps to push blood along, so maintaining its pressure. As a result the pressure at the end of an artery where it enters an organ is only a little less than when it left the heart. Blood flows quickly through arteries.

## Veins

Veins have a wider space for blood to flow than arteries and are thinner, less muscular and have less elastic walls. The pressure inside **veins** is much lower than in arteries and blood flows slightly slower in veins than in arteries.

As the pressure of blood in the veins is very low, it is squeezed along by pressure from your body muscles and other surrounding organs. The flow of blood in veins is helped by **semi-lunar valves** that maintain a one-way flow of blood (see page 101).

## Capillaries

The arteries branch many times until the smallest branches form **capillaries**. It is estimated that there are over 80 000 km of these tiny vessels in the body to provide a huge surface area for exchange between blood and cells. Capillaries are very narrow; a red blood cell can only just squeeze through. Blood flows through capillaries very slowly (about 1 mm per second) giving time for exchange of substances with cells.

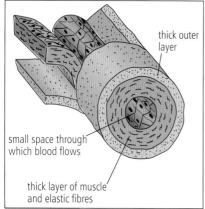

thick outer layer

small space through which blood flows

thick layer of muscle and elastic fibres

**Figure 9.3.1** An artery.

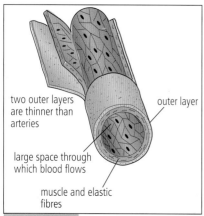

two outer layers are thinner than arteries

outer layer

large space through which blood flows

muscle and elastic fibres

**Figure 9.3.2** A vein.

Capillary walls are made of one layer of very thin cells which makes the diffusion distance very short. This makes it easy to supply oxygen and dissolved food substances and to remove carbon dioxide and other waste chemicals.

## The heart and exercise

During exercise, your muscles need more energy from respiration in order to contract. So the heart beats faster and arteries supplying muscles **dilate** (widen).

These changes increase the blood flow to muscles and result in:

• an increase in supply of oxygen and glucose
• an increase in removal of carbon dioxide.

You can detect the flow of blood through arteries as a 'pulse'. Each time the left ventricle beats, a wave passes along the arteries which you can feel. You can find your pulse by feeling an artery at your wrist. The number of pulses per minute is your **pulse rate** and this is the same as the heart rate.

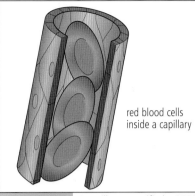

red blood cells inside a capillary

**Figure 9.3.3** A capillary magnified ×2500 (*the capillary is actually cylindrical, section removed to view red blood cells*).

### PRACTICAL

#### Investigating the effect of exercise on pulse rate

Sit still and get your partner to measure your pulse rate at rest.

Try doing step-ups for 1 minute (light exercise).

As soon as you have finished, sit down and count your pulse rate.

Wait until your pulse returns to the resting rate.

Now do step-ups as quickly as you can for 3 minutes (heavy exercise). Then count your pulse rate.

Remember that to make this a valid investigation you should have the same person doing the exercise, do the same type of exercise each time, rest for 5 minutes between each exercise or until your pulse returns to its resting rate.

You can also repeat the tests and calculate an average to make your results more reliable.

You can explain the results in terms of supplying substances to your muscles and removing their wastes.

### KEY POINTS

1 Arteries have thick muscular and elastic walls to withstand high blood pressure. Veins have much less muscle and elastic tissue and have thin walls. Blood pressure in veins is low.

2 Capillaries have walls that are one cell thick so that substances can pass easily in and out of the blood in body tissues.

3 Physical activity increases pulse rate, supplying the muscles with more oxygen and glucose and removing carbon dioxide quicker.

### SUMMARY QUESTIONS

1 Make a table to show the main differences between arteries and veins. Include three columns: feature, artery, vein.

2 In what ways are the capillaries well adapted for exchange of materials between the blood and body tissues?

3 a State what happens to pulse rate when a person exercises.
   b Explain how and why pulse rate changes with exercise.

# 9.4 Coronary heart disease (CHD)

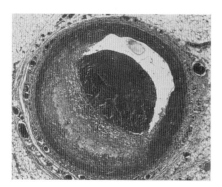

A coronary artery blocked by fatty deposits. A blood clot has formed to further narrow the artery. Compare with the healthy artery below.

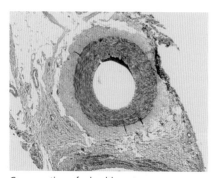

Cross-section of a healthy artery.

You need a healthy heart to pump blood around your body. Heart muscle needs glucose and oxygen to keep it contracting. These are transported to the heart in the **coronary arteries**. If these arteries get blocked then heart muscle could become starved of oxygen and die. This could cause a **heart attack**.

## Slowing the flow

Healthy arteries have a smooth lining, letting blood flow easily. However, **cholesterol**, which is made in the liver, can stick to their walls. This can narrow the artery and slow down the flow of blood. This condition is called **atherosclerosis**.

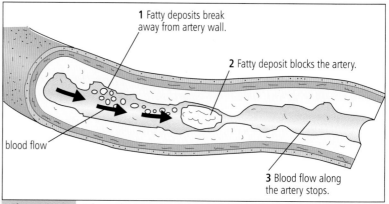

**1** Fatty deposits break away from artery wall.

**2** Fatty deposit blocks the artery.

blood flow

**3** Blood flow along the artery stops.

**Figure 9.4.1** Atherosclerosis.

The artery walls can become rough, which can cause the blood to clot and block the vessel. The blockage is called a **thrombosis**.

Narrowing of the coronary artery causes serious problems.

If the coronary artery gets partly blocked it can cause chest pains, especially if activity or emotion makes the heart work harder.

This is called **angina**. It is caused by not enough oxygen getting to the heart muscle.

Angina should act as a warning to the sufferer because it may lead to a heart attack.

A total blockage or thrombosis can cause a heart attack. When this happens, the supply of oxygen is cut off. It causes a severe pain in the chest and the affected part of the heart is damaged. The heart may stop beating altogether – this is called **cardiac arrest**. Death will follow unless the heart starts beating again within minutes.

## Risk factors for CHD

These are factors that are thought to increase the chances of getting CHD:

- **eating a diet with too much saturated (animal) fat**, which can increase the concentration of cholesterol in the blood (see page 73)
- **being over-weight**
- **smoking**
- **taking little or no exercise**
- **stress**.

People can do something about these risk factors by changing their way of life, but other risk factors cannot be avoided such as:

- **genes** inherited from parents – CHD tends to run in families. These genes control the metabolism of fat and cholesterol (see page 73)
- **age** – the chances of getting CHD increase with age
- **sex** – men are more likely to get CHD than women.

**Figure 9.4.2** Three activities that can put you at risk of heart disease.

## Avoiding CHD

- Take care of your diet.
  - Eat more poultry and fish – they are less fatty.
  - Cut down on fried foods.
  - Eat less red meat, which is rich in saturated fat.
  - Eat more fresh fruit and vegetables.
- Take some regular exercise.
- Do not smoke.

**EXAMINER SAYS...**

The coronary arteries branch from the base of the aorta just above the semi-lunar valves.

They transport oxygenated blood to the tissues of the atria and ventricles.

**SUMMARY QUESTIONS**

1 Define the following:
   a coronary heart disease, b thrombosis, c angina, d cardiac arrest.

2 a If the heart is full of blood, then why does it need its own blood supply?
   b How is the heart muscle supplied with oxygenated blood?
   c Why does the heart muscle need this oxygenated blood?

3 There are risk factors that can increase the chances of a person getting heart disease.
   a List some of the factors that cannot be controlled.
   b List some of the factors that can be controlled.
   c What advice would you give to a person recovering from a heart attack?

**KEY POINTS**

1 Coronary heart disease is caused by blockage of the coronary arteries that supply the heart with glucose and oxygen.

2 Risk factors which we cannot control are genes, age and sex. Avoidable risk factors include diet, stress, lack of exercise and smoking.

# Blood

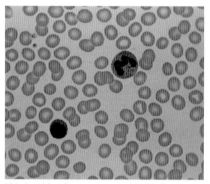

This is a blood smear seen with a light microscope.

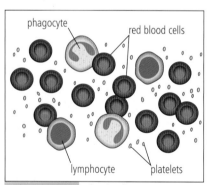

**Figure 9.5.2**   Blood cells.

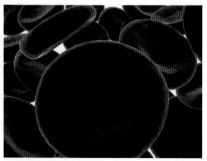

Red blood cells.

## Blood composition

You have about 5 litres of blood in your body. Blood is made of cells and cell fragments suspended in a yellow liquid called **plasma**. The red colour of blood is due to the pigment **haemoglobin** in red blood cells.

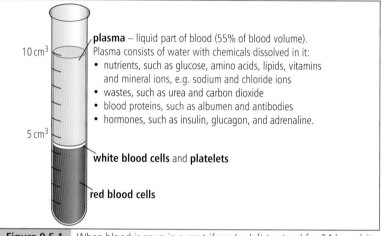

**Figure 9.5.1**   When blood is spun in a centrifuge (or left to stand for 24 hours) it separates into three layers.

## Blood cells

There are three main types of blood cell:

- **Red blood cells** have no nuclei.

  They look red because they have the red pigment haemoglobin.

- **White blood cells** have nuclei.

  There are two main types: **phagocytes** and **lymphocytes**.

  They look white when spun in a centrifuge. Under the microscope they are colourless as they do not have haemoglobin and do not transport oxygen.

- **Platelets** are tiny fragments of cells which cause blood to clot, for example when you cut yourself.

## Red blood cells

There are about 5 million red blood cells in every cubic millimetre (mm³) of blood.

They are made in the bone marrow.

The function of red blood cells is to carry oxygen.

Red blood cells are disc-shaped with the middle pushed in. They have a large surface area compared with their volume and this helps them to absorb oxygen.

The cytoplasm is full of haemoglobin. This is a special type of protein that contains iron. You must have enough iron in your diet to make enough haemoglobin for your red blood cells (see anaemia on page 49). As the cells have no nuclei this makes more space for haemoglobin.

Haemoglobin combines easily with oxygen in the lungs to form **oxyhaemoglobin**:

haemoglobin + oxygen $\longrightarrow$ oxyhaemoglobin

Look at the diagram below:

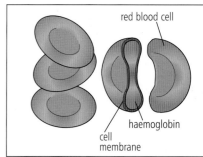

**Figure 9.5.3**  Red blood cells magnified ×2500.

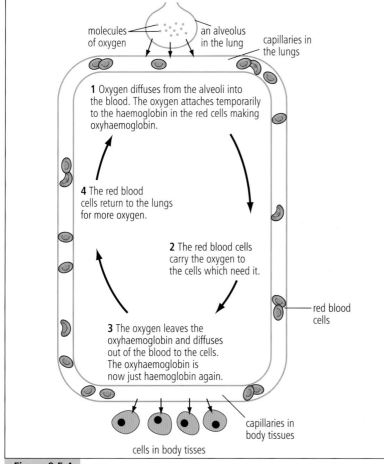

molecules of oxygen — an alveolus in the lung — capillaries in the lungs

**1** Oxygen diffuses from the alveoli into the blood. The oxygen attaches temporarily to the haemoglobin in the red cells making oxyhaemoglobin.

**4** The red blood cells return to the lungs for more oxygen.

**2** The red blood cells carry the oxygen to the cells which need it.

red blood cells

**3** The oxygen leaves the oxyhaemoglobin and diffuses out of the blood to the cells. The oxyhaemoglobin is now just haemoglobin again.

capillaries in body tissues

cells in body tisses

**Figure 9.5.4**

- Notice that oxyhaemoglobin forms while blood flows through capillaries in the alveoli in the lungs.
- Oxyhaemoglobin gives out oxygen as blood flows through capillaries in body tissues.

### KEY POINTS

**1** The main components of blood are plasma, red blood cells, white blood cells and platelets. Red and white blood cells are visible under the light microscope.

**2** Red blood cells contain haemoglobin which combines with oxygen to form oxyhaemoglobin.

### EXAMINER SAYS...

When asked to explain how a red blood cell is adapted to its function make sure you describe the feature, e.g. no nucleus, and then explain this, e.g. it makes more space for haemoglobin that carries oxygen.

### SUMMARY QUESTIONS

**1 a** List four chemicals found in the plasma.

 **b** Give three ways in which a red blood cell differs from a white blood cell.

 **c** Name the two main types of white blood cell.

**2 a** How is the red blood cell adapted for oxygen transport?

 **b i** What is haemoglobin?

 **ii** Where does it combine with oxygen and what molecule is formed?

# Blood in defence

## LEARNING OUTCOMES

- Describe how white blood cells such as lymphocytes and phagocytes protect the body from disease
- State the role of lymphocytes in immunity
- Describe the process of blood clotting

## EXAMINER SAYS...

When writing about white blood cells, make sure you use the names 'phagocytes' and 'lymphocytes' when you are describing their functions – do not call them 'white blood cells'.

## EXAMINER SAYS...

Like enzymes, antibodies are proteins with many different shapes. Enzymes have active sites that combine with their substrates. Similarly, each type of antibody has a binding site that combines with one type of pathogen.

## White blood cells

The white blood cells defend us against disease. There are far fewer of them than red blood cells.

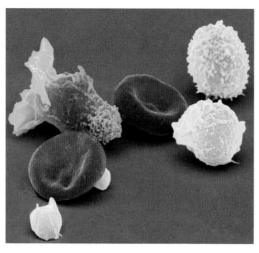

This image was taken with an electron microscope and then coloured with a computer program. You can see two red blood cells and three white blood cells. The image at the top of page 111 was taken in the same way. It shows a phagocyte ingesting a yeast cell.

They also look different. White blood cells are not disc-shaped. They do not have haemoglobin. They do have nuclei. Like red blood cells, the white blood cells are made in the bone marrow, but their function is to protect the body from any pathogens that enter the body.

## Phagocytes

These are white blood cells that ingest pathogens, such as bacteria.

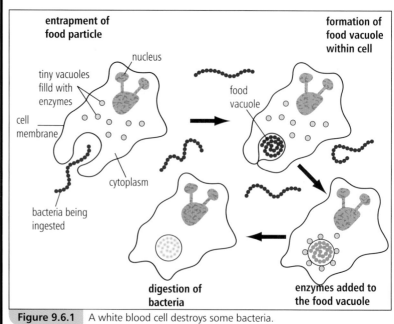

**Figure 9.6.1**   A white blood cell destroys some bacteria.

They surround the pathogens, ingest them and take them into food vacuoles. They then digest them by using enzymes and this kills them. The process is called **phagocytosis**.

When pathogens invade the body, phagocytes move towards them. They can squeeze through capillary walls.

Find out about tissue rejection on page 139.

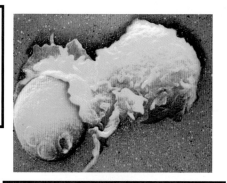

## Lymphocytes

Lymphocytes are a type of white blood cell. When a bacterium or virus enters the body the lymphocytes recognise that it is 'foreign' and should not be there. Lymphocytes then make proteins called **antibodies**.

Antibodies attack the pathogens in a number of ways:

* they make them stick together (agglutinate)
* they dissolve their cell membranes
* they neutralise the toxins (poisons) that some pathogens, such as some bacteria, produce.

There is a different type of antibody for each type of pathogen.

After you have had a disease, such as measles, lymphocytes are ready to produce more of the appropriate antibodies should the pathogen enter the body again. This makes you immune to that particular disease.

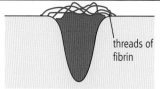

threads of fibrin

**1** The skin is cut and blood starts leaking out of the body. However there is a protein in the blood called **fibrinogen**. When **platelets** come in contact with air they turn the fibrinogen into threads of **fibrin**. The threads make a net over the cut.

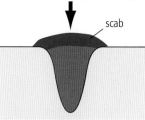

scab

**2** Red blood cells get caught in the net and make a blood clot which seals the cut. The clot dries to make a scab. New skin grows under the scab.

**Figure 9.6.2** Blood clotting.

## Blood clotting

When you cut yourself you bleed. Before long, platelets help the blood to thicken and the bleeding stops. The thickened blood has formed a **clot**. Without clotting, blood would be lost and pathogens would enter.

This is another way that the blood defends against disease.

**Platelets** are small fragments of cells. They are made in the bone marrow like the blood cells. When a blood vessel is damaged, platelets release substances to change the soluble protein **fibrinogen** in the plasma into the insoluble protein **fibrin**, which forms a meshwork of fibres. Red blood cells get trapped in these threads to make the clot. The clot hardens to make a scab which keeps the cut clean. With time the skin heals and the scab falls off.

### KEY POINTS

1 Phagocytes ingest pathogens and digest them using enzymes.

2 Lymphocytes make antibodies that protect against pathogens in the body.

3 After a person has had a disease, the lymphocytes remain to produce more antibodies for that pathogen if the disease is encountered again. This is called **immunity**.

4 Platelets help to convert fibrinogen to fibrin during blood clotting.

### SUMMARY QUESTIONS

1 a  State where white blood cells are made.

  b  Explain how lymphocytes act to defend the body from pathogens.

2 Explain how a person can become immune to an infectious disease like measles.

3 a  Explain, in detail, the role of platelets in the clotting of blood.

  b  What would happen if a person's blood did not clot when exposed to the air at a cut?

  c  Describe the process of phagocytosis.

# Lymph and tissue fluid

## Tissue fluid

When blood reaches body tissues, some of the constituents of the plasma move out through small gaps in the capillary walls to form the **tissue fluid** that surrounds the cells. White blood cells, which can change shape, are able to squeeze out of the capillaries through these gaps. Red blood cells stay in the blood. Tissue fluid 'bathes' the cells providing a stable environment for them.

Tissue fluid helps substances to diffuse into and out of cells. Useful substances like glucose and oxygen pass from tissue fluid into cells. Carbon dioxide and waste chemicals like urea pass out of cells into the tissue fluid. Most of the tissue fluid then passes back into the blood capillaries. Fluid is constantly flowing from the plasma and back into the plasma, but some of it drains into our lymphatic system.

## The lymphatic system

We all know about our blood circulatory system – we see blood when we cut ourselves, we can feel our heart beating and see our veins through the skin. Our other circulatory system – the lymphatic system – is not so obvious. But feel the glands beneath your lower jaw, think about adenoids and tonsils – these are the lymph nodes that are connected by lymphatic vessels. In Unit 7, page 84, you saw a lacteal in a villus. This is a thin-walled vessel that absorbs fat from the gut and is another part of the lymphatic system.

Not all of the tissue fluid returns to plasma in blood capillaries. About one-tenth of it enters a separate system of capillaries called **lymph capillaries**. Once inside these, the tissue fluid is called **lymph**.

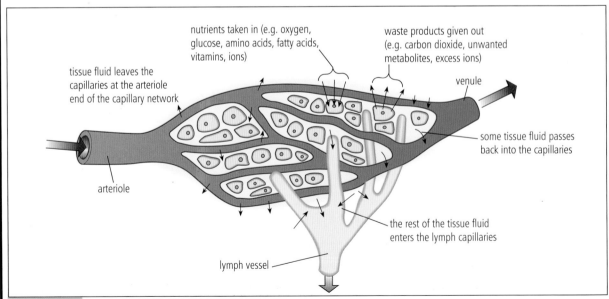

nutrients taken in (e.g. oxygen, glucose, amino acids, fatty acids, vitamins, ions)

waste products given out (e.g. carbon dioxide, unwanted metabolites, excess ions)

tissue fluid leaves the capillaries at the arteriole end of the capillary network

venule

arteriole

some tissue fluid passes back into the capillaries

the rest of the tissue fluid enters the lymph capillaries

lymph vessel

**Figure 9.7.1** The formation of tissue fluid and lymph.

Lymph capillaries have tiny valves that allow the tissue fluid to enter but will not let the lymph pass out again. They join up to form **lymph vessels**. These have a structure similar to veins; they are thin-walled and contain semi-lunar valves to make sure lymph flows in one direction.

The lymphatic system has no pump so the flow of lymph is slow. The contraction of surrounding muscles helps to make it flow.

**EXAMINER SAYS...**

Plasma, tissue fluid and lymph are three fluids that are very similar in composition, but occur in different places in the body. Read through the text carefully to find out where they are and remember!

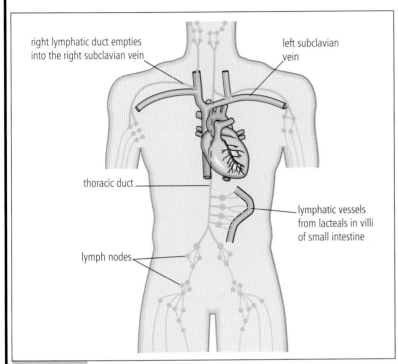

right lymphatic duct empties into the right subclavian vein

left subclavian vein

thoracic duct

lymphatic vessels from lacteals in villi of small intestine

lymph nodes

**Figure 9.7.2**   The lymphatic system.

Lymph flows from the tissues to the heart. The smaller lymph vessels join up to form two large lymph vessels which empty into the **subclavian veins**, under the collar bones. Here the lymph mixes with the blood before joining the **vena cava** just before it enters the heart.

At intervals along the length of the lymph vessels are **lymph nodes**. There are many **lymphocytes** in the nodes and during an infection they multiply by cell division and make antibodies. Some leave lymph nodes and circulate around the body in the blood, constantly patrolling for fresh invasions of pathogens. The lymphatic system is an important part of the body's immune system.

**KEY POINTS**

1 When tissue fluid enters the lymph capillaries it is termed *lymph*.

2 Lymph consists of plasma and white blood cells, but has no red blood cells or large plasma proteins.

3 The lymphatic system has a separate circulation which returns lymph to the blood.

4 Lymphocytes are in lymph nodes where they multiply during an infection and produce antibodies.

**SUMMARY QUESTIONS**

1 a   What is tissue fluid and what are its functions?
   b   What is lymph and what are its functions?

2 Explain, in as much detail as you can, why the flow of lymph is so slow and how the circulation is maintained.

3 What are lymph nodes, where are they found and what is their main function?

1 Sketch a simple diagram to show the human circulatory system. Use your diagram to define the following terms:

(a) circulatory system

(b) double circulation

(c) arteries, veins and capillaries.

2 Explain how the circulatory system ensures that blood flows in one direction.

3 Describe what happens within the heart during one heartbeat.

4 (a) What is the pulse?

(b) State and explain what happens to the pulse rate during and after exercise.

5 (a) People with CHD have blockages in one or more coronary arteries. Explain how these blockages are formed.

(b) State the risk factors of CHD and explain how people can reduce the chances of developing the disease.

6 (a) Draw diagrams to show transverse sections of an artery, a vein and a capillary.

(b) Use your diagrams to describe the differences between the structure of these blood vessels.

(c) State the functions of the three types of blood vessel.

7 List the components of blood and state a function of each.

**Extension**

8 Explain how the structure of arteries, veins and capillaries helps them carry out their functions.

9 Describe how:

(a) blood clots

(b) the immune system protects the body against disease

(c) tissue fluid is formed.

1 Which chamber of the heart pumps blood into the aorta?

A  left atrium

B  left ventricle

C  right atrium

D  right ventricle

(Paper 1) [1]

2 The plan diagram shows the human circulatory system. Which is the pulmonary artery?

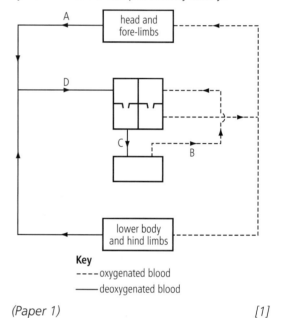

**Key**

---- oxygenated blood

—— deoxygenated blood

(Paper 1) [1]

3 Which is the correct pathway taken by blood flowing through the human circulatory system?

A  body ⟶ vena cava ⟶ left atrium ⟶ left ventricle ⟶ lungs

B  left ventricle ⟶ aorta ⟶ body ⟶ vena cava ⟶ right atrium

C  lungs ⟶ pulmonary artery ⟶ left atrium ⟶ left ventricle ⟶ aorta

D  right ventricle ⟶ aorta ⟶ lungs ⟶ body ⟶ right atrium

(Paper 1) [1]

**4** Which of the following shows the correct functions of the components of the blood?

|   | plasma | platelets | red blood cells |
|---|--------|-----------|-----------------|
| **A** | antibody formation | oxygen transport | clotting |
| **B** | clotting | antibody formation | oxygen transport |
| **C** | transport of water | clotting | oxygen transport |
| **D** | oxygen transport | clotting | antibody formation |

*(Paper 1)* [1]

**5** The diagram shows the heart.

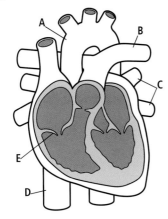

**(a) (i)** Name **A** to **E**. [5]

**(ii)** Give the letters from the diagram that indicate the blood vessels that contain oxygenated blood. [1]

**(b)** Describe what happens to blood as it flows through the capillaries in the lungs [4]

**(c)** Explain why blood flowing to the lungs is at a lower pressure than blood flowing to the rest of the body. [3]

*(Paper 2)*

**6** This is a drawing made of a blood smear as seen with a light microscope.

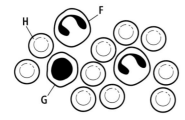

**(a) (i)** Name the cells **F**, **G** and **H**. [3]

**(ii)** State the functions of the cells **F** to **H**. [3]

**(b)** The magnification of the drawing is ×1100. Calculate the diameter of cell **H**. Show your working. [2]

**(c)** Some blood was spun in a centrifuge to separate the components. The diagram shows the results.

**(i)** Identify the cells that would be found in regions **K** and **L**. Give reasons for your answer. [3]

**(ii)** Name the fluid at **J** and describe its role in the body. [5]

*(Paper 2)*

**7 (a)** Copy and complete the table to compare arteries, veins and capillaries.

| feature | arteries | veins | capillaries |
|---------|----------|-------|-------------|
| relative thickness of wall | | thin | very thin |
| muscle tissue | | some | none |
| elastic tissue | | some | |
| direction of blood flow | heart to organs | | arteries to veins |

[5]

**(b)** Explain how the structure of an artery helps it to carry out its function. [3]

**(c)** Describe how substances are provided to muscle cells by capillaries. [4]

*(Paper 3)*

**8 (a)** The lymphatic system consists of lymphatic vessels and lymph nodes.

Describe the functions of **(i)** lymphatic vessels, and **(ii)** lymph nodes. [4]

**(b)** The immune system consists of phagocytes, lymphocytes and antibodies.

Explain how the immune system defends us against infection by bacterial pathogens. [5]

*(Paper 3)*

## 10.1 Respiration

Petrol burning in a dish.

### Aerobic respiration

When we burn a fuel such as petrol, oxygen is used up and carbon dioxide is made. The flame gives off a lot of light and heat.

Every cell in every living organism needs energy. A fuel used to provide energy in the cells is called glucose, but unlike burning petrol, the energy is released very gradually in a series of small, enzyme-controlled reactions. **Respiration** involves a number of chemical reactions that break down nutrient molecules, such as glucose, in living cells to release energy.

In **aerobic respiration** oxygen is used in the breakdown of glucose:

glucose + oxygen $\longrightarrow$ carbon dioxide + water + energy released

$$C_6H_{12}O_6 + 6O_2 \longrightarrow 6CO_2 + 6H_2O + \text{energy released}$$

*Extension*

Cells also respire fats and proteins to provide energy, but you only have to know about the respiration of glucose, which is a carbohydrate.

### Using energy

Your body needs energy for many different things. Energy is used in the following processes:

- muscle contraction
- cell division
- absorption of nutrients in the gut by active transport
- sending impulses along nerves
- protein synthesis for making enzymes, some hormones and antibodies
- making new cell membranes and cell structures like the nucleus during growth
- keeping the body temperature constant. Some of the energy released is in the form of heat.

Respiration takes place in *all* living cells *all of the time* because cells need a constant supply of energy to stay alive. In aerobic respiration, energy is released in tiny cell structures called **mitochondria**.

### Anaerobic respiration

It is possible to release energy from glucose without using oxygen. **Anaerobic respiration** is the release of relatively small amounts of energy from glucose in the *absence* of oxygen.

During hard, strenuous exercise not enough oxygen may reach the body muscles for aerobic respiration to supply all the energy the muscles need. Muscle tissue respires anaerobically to release energy.

The stages of respiration that occur in mitochondria do not happen without oxygen. As a result the glucose is not broken down to carbon dioxide and water, but to **lactic acid** instead:

glucose $\longrightarrow$ lactic acid + energy released

Extension

$$C_6H_{12}O_6 \longrightarrow 2C_3H_6O_3 + \text{energy released}$$

Extension

Other tissues, such as cardiac muscle in the heart, do not normally respire anaerobically as this would not release enough energy to keep the heart beating properly. Some bacteria also respire anaerobically to make lactic acid in the same way, for example those that we use to make yoghurt (see page 50).

Other microorganisms, such as yeast, respire anaerobically when oxygen is absent or in short supply in their surroundings, to make alcohol and carbon dioxide:

glucose $\longrightarrow$ alcohol + carbon dioxide + energy released

$$C_6H_{12}O_6 \longrightarrow 2C_2H_5OH + 2CO_2 + \text{energy released}$$

Plant roots respire anaerobically when land is flooded and soils become saturated with water so little or no oxygen is available.

Far less energy is released from each molecule of glucose in anaerobic respiration compared to aerobic respiration. This is because glucose is not completely broken down and a lot of energy remains stored in lactic acid and alcohol in the form of chemical bond energy. You can see this if you set alcohol alight. It burns like the petrol you can see opposite.

10.2

... w... of e... ...ows from ... ...gy to all the pr...ses in living organisms that need energy. You can add to the list opposite from other parts of this book.

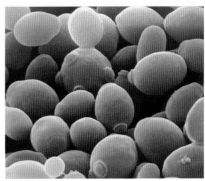
Yeast cells under an electron microscope.

## SUMMARY QUESTIONS

1 Copy and complete the following sentences using the words below:

**aerobic   glucose   oxygen   mitochondria
energy   carbon dioxide   cells**

Respiration takes place in all living _____. A fuel for respiration is _____. It is broken down to release _____. Also produced is water and the waste gas _____. When it takes place in the presence of _____ we call it _____ respiration.

These reactions take place in every living cell, inside tiny structures called _____.

2 a Write down the word equation for aerobic respiration.

   b Energy is released during aerobic respiration.
      Make a list of five processes that use this energy.

3 a Define the term *anaerobic respiration*.

   b Give two examples of anaerobic respiration.

   c Compare the energy released from a molecule of glucose during aerobic and anaerobic respiration.

Extension

4 Write balanced chemical equations for:
   a aerobic respiration, b anaerobic respiration in muscles,
   c anaerobic respiration in yeast.

### KEY POINTS

1 In aerobic respiration, glucose is broken down to release energy in the presence of oxygen, forming carbon dioxide and water.

2 In anaerobic respiration, glucose is broken down to release energy in the absence of oxygen, forming lactic acid in muscle tissue, or alcohol plus carbon dioxide in yeast and plants.

3 Far more energy is released from each molecule of glucose in aerobic than in anaerobic respiration.

# The gas exchange system

## Structure of the gas exchange system

We need to breathe air into our lungs in order to get oxygen. We breathe air out of our lungs to get rid of carbon dioxide. The lungs form part of the **gas exchange system**.

The lungs are spongy organs found inside the chest (**thorax**) and are surrounded and protected by the ribs and the sternum (breastbone). The **diaphragm** is a sheet of fibrous tissue and muscle that separates the thorax from the abdomen. Its movement up and down changes the volume of the lungs to move air when you breathe out and in.

Surrounding the lungs are two **pleural membranes** with fluid in between them. This slippery fluid prevents the lungs rubbing against the ribs. The **intercostal muscles** between the ribs move the ribs during breathing, especially during deep breathing.

Air enters the mouth or nose and passes through the throat to the **larynx** (voice-box). It then enters the **trachea** (windpipe), which connects the throat to the lungs. It branches to form two **bronchi** which enter each lung. These continue to divide to form many small **bronchioles**, which end in tiny air sacs called **alveoli**. It is here that gas exchange takes place.

The tubes through which air moves are often called airways.

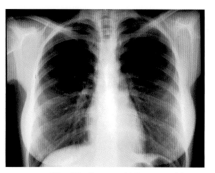

An X-ray of healthy lungs which appear black.

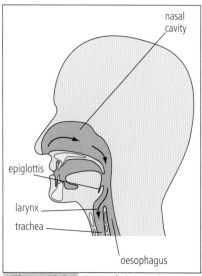

**Figure 10.2.1** Entry of air into the nose and trachea.

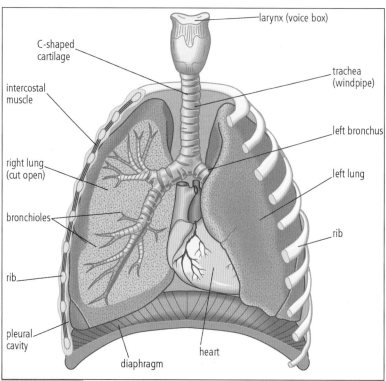

**Figure 10.2.2** The gas exchange system.

The larynx contains the vocal cords. When air passes over these you make sounds. You cannot breathe and swallow at the same time. This is because when you swallow, a flap called the **epiglottis** moves to cover the opening to your larynx. This stops any food from going down your trachea (see page 79). The trachea is kept open by C-shaped rings of cartilage. The 'arms' of the C are joined by muscle at the back of the trachea. The cartilage prevents the trachea from collapsing as you breathe in when the air pressure decreases.

## Deeper into the lungs

There is a very large number of alveoli in the lungs to give a huge surface area for diffusion (see page 26 to remind yourself about diffusion). Each alveolus is surrounded by a network of blood capillaries for efficient gas exchange into and out of the blood. The alveoli have thin walls made of a single layer of cells, so there is a short distance for diffusion. They are moist so oxygen dissolves in this watery fluid before diffusing through the walls into the blood.

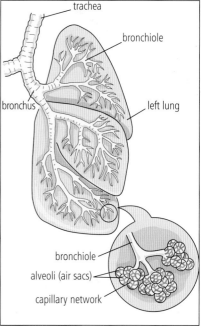

**Figure 10.2.3** Structure of a lung.

## SUMMARY QUESTIONS

1 Describe the route taken by inspired air (air we breathe in) from the nasal cavity to the alveoli in the lungs.

2 The diagram shows the human breathing system:

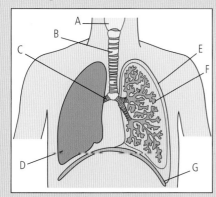

a   Name structures **A** to **G**.
b   Match parts **A** to **G** with these descriptions:
  i     sheet of muscle forming the floor of the thorax,
  ii    one of these enters each lung,
  iii   contains the vocal cords,
  iv    flexible tube kept open by rings of cartilage,
  v     where exchange of gases takes place,
  vi    slippery membranes,
  vii   an organ made of spongy tissue and found in the chest.

## EXAMINER SAYS...

Draw a simple diagram of the gas exchange system and label it. Add some notes to the labels explaining the functions of the different parts. By doing this you are <u>annotating</u> your diagram.

## KEY POINTS

1 Inspired air enters the larynx, which also contains the vocal cords.

2 The inspired air passes down the trachea, bronchi, bronchioles to the alveoli.

3 Gas exchange occurs between the air in the alveoli and the blood in the surrounding capillaries.

# Gas exchange

## Breathing out carbon dioxide

Carbon dioxide is a waste gas made in respiration. It can become toxic if it builds up in cells.

We breathe out in order to get rid of the carbon dioxide.

| gas | composition (%) | |
|---|---|---|
| | inspired air (breathing in) | expired air (breathing out) |
| oxygen | 21 | 16 |
| carbon dioxide | 0.04 | 4 |
| nitrogen | 78 | 78 |
| water vapour | variable | saturated |

The table shows that we breathe out more carbon dioxide than we breathe in.

The following practical demonstration confirms this.

### PRACTICAL

**Carbon dioxide in inspired and expired air**

Set up the apparatus as shown in the diagram and then breathe gently in and out of the mouthpiece several times.

- When you breathe in the air comes in through A.
- When you breathe out the air goes through B.
- The limewater turns cloudy first in B, showing that there is more carbon dioxide in expired air than in inspired air.

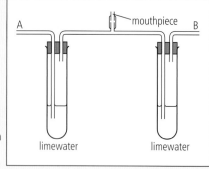

- The limewater in A will also go cloudy if you breathe through the apparatus long enough, showing there is a lower concentration of carbon dioxide in atmospheric (inspired) air.

## Gas exchange surfaces

Gas exchange surfaces, such as the gills of a fish and alveoli (air sacs) of a human, have features in common that adapt them for efficient exchange of oxygen and carbon dioxide:

- a very large surface area for the diffusion of gases
- moist surfaces so that gases can dissolve before diffusion

- thin walls (only one cell thick in each alveolus) so the gases do not have to diffuse very far
- a good blood supply so that lots of oxygen is removed quickly and lots of carbon dioxide is supplied quickly. This maintains the **concentration gradients** for these gases.

## Gas exchange at the alveolus

When inspired (breathed in) air reaches the alveoli (air sacs) it contains a lot of oxygen. Oxygen dissolves in the water lining each alveolus. It then diffuses through the wall of the alveolus and through the capillary wall into the blood. Although this involves diffusing through two cells, the distance is very small.

Each alveolus has a network of capillaries around it. Oxygen molecules from the alveolus diffuse into the red blood cells and

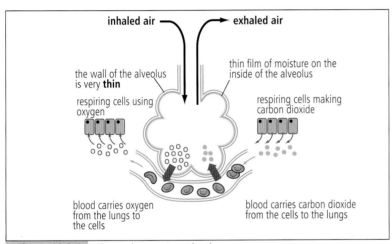

**Figure 10.3.1**    Gas exchange at an alveolus.

combine with haemoglobin. The blood cells can then transport this oxygen to the body tissues.

There is a lot of carbon dioxide in the capillary. It has been carried there from the respiring tissues in the blood plasma. It diffuses in the opposite direction, through the capillary wall across the alveolar wall into the space inside the alveolus. From here it is breathed out.

Alveoli are surrounded by elastic tissue. This stretches when you breathe in and recoils when you breathe out to help remove air from the lungs.

### KEY POINTS

1 There is more carbon dioxide in expired air than in inspired air.

2 Gas exchange surfaces are moist, thin, have a large surface area and a good blood supply.

3 Alveoli are well adapted for gas exchange as they have these features and are surrounded by many capillaries.

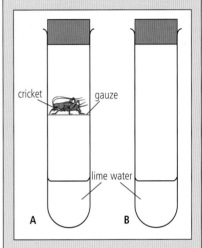

# 10.4 Breathing

## PRACTICAL

### A model of the chest

Obtain a model like the one in the diagram. The rubber sheet represents the diaphragm.

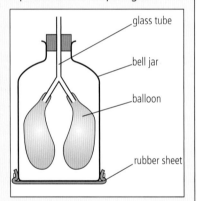

Pull the rubber sheet down and then push it up.

Do this a few times and watch what happens to the balloons.

This model shows how movement of the diaphragm changes the volume and pressure in the thorax represented by the bell jar. As the diaphragm contracts and moves downwards, the lungs inflate as a result of an increase in volume and decrease in pressure in the space around the balloons.

When you breathe it feels as if the lungs are expanding to push your ribs outwards. This is not so. When you breathe in, movements of your diaphragm and ribcage move the chest cavity and pull on the lungs so they occupy a larger volume. This decreases the air pressure inside the lungs to below the pressure of atmospheric air so that air moves in through your nose and/or mouth.

When you breathe out, the diaphragm and intercostal muscles relax and this causes the chest cavity to decrease in volume. The air pressure in the lungs increases to above atmospheric pressure so air is forced out. You can do this just by movement of your diaphragm alone (try breathing without moving your ribs).

This is fine for quiet breathing, but during deep breathing and when you exercise the intercostal muscles contract to move the ribs. (Intercostal means between the ribs.) There are two layers of these: the external muscles that are closer to the skin and the internal muscles that are deeper into the chest wall. The diaphragm is made of tough fibrous tissue in the centre and strong muscles that connect to the backbone, the lower ribs and the sternum (breastbone).

## Inspiration (breathing in)

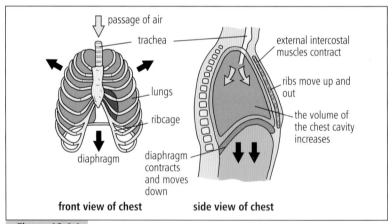

**Figure 10.4.1**

- The external intercostal muscles *contract* and the internal intercostals muscles *relax*, raising the ribs upwards and outwards.
- At the same time, the diaphragm contracts and flattens.
- Both of these actions *increase* the volume inside the thorax, causing the pressure inside the thorax to *decrease*.
- Since atmospheric pressure is greater, air moves *into* the lungs and they inflate.

## Expiration (breathing out)

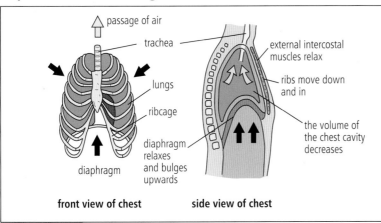

**Figure 10.4.2**

- The internal intercostal muscles *contract* and the external intercostal muscles *relax*.

- This lowers the ribs downwards and inwards.

- The muscle in the diaphragm *relaxes* and it bulges up due to pressure from the organs below, for example the liver and stomach, and contraction of the abdominal muscles.

- Both of these actions *decrease* the volume inside the thorax, causing the pressure inside the thorax to *increase*.

- Elastic recoil of the alveoli helps to force air *out* of the lungs.

## Cleaning the air

As you breathe in through your nose, air is warmed and moistened by evaporation of water from the lining. Hairs inside the nose filter the air, removing particles and some pathogens.

The trachea, bronchi and bronchioles are lined with ciliated epithelial cells and mucus-secreting cells. Dust particles and pathogens become trapped in the slimy mucus. The **cilia** beat to carry a stream of mucus up to your nose and throat, removing the particles and pathogens which you then swallow.

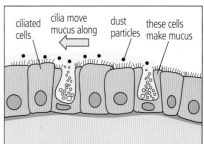

**Figure 10.4.3** Mucus-secreting cells and ciliated epithelial cells keep the lungs free of dust and pathogens.

### SUMMARY QUESTIONS

1 Describe what happens to each of the following when a person breathes in:

    a  the intercostal muscles, **b** the ribs, **c** the diaphragm, **d** the volume inside the thorax, **e** the pressure inside the thorax.

2 Look at the model of the chest in the Practical, opposite.

    a  Which part of the model represents:

      i  the lungs,  ii  the diaphragm,  iii  the ribs?

    b  Make some criticisms of the model as a way of representing the changes that occur during breathing.

3 Explain the role of mucus and cilia in keeping the air passages free from dust particles and pathogens.

### KEY POINTS

1 Inspiration and expiration occur due to changes of volume and pressure in the thorax.

2 The internal intercostal muscles, external intercostal muscles and the diaphragm control these changes during ventilation.

3 Mucus traps dust particles and pathogens in the air and cilia beat to remove mucus from the airways.

# Rate and depth of breathing

## LEARNING OUTCOMES

- Investigate and describe the effects of physical exercise on the rate and depth of breathing

- Describe how the effects of exercise increase carbon dioxide concentration and lower pH in the tissues and how this affects the rate and depth of breathing

Performing step-ups.

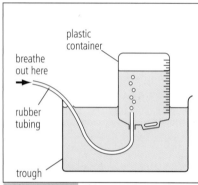

**Figure 10.5.1** This apparatus can be used to measure your vital capacity (see top of next page).

## Breathing and exercise

At rest you probably take between 12 and 16 breaths per minute. When you exercise this breathing rate changes.

### PRACTICAL

**An investigation into the effects of exercise on breathing rate**

You can measure your breathing rate by counting the number of times that you breathe out in a minute.

You could record your results in a table like this:

|  | breathing rate (breaths per minute) | | |
|---|---|---|---|
|  | at rest | light exercise | heavy exercise |
| 1 |  |  |  |
| 2 |  |  |  |
| 3 |  |  |  |
| average = |  |  |  |

- Try doing step-ups for 1 minute (light exercise).
- As soon as you have finished, sit down and count your breathing rate.
- Wait until your breathing rate returns to its resting value.
- Now try doing step-ups as quickly as you can for 3 minutes (heavy exercise).
- Then count your breathing rate when you have finished.
- You will notice that your breathing rate and depth of breathing change after doing exercise.
- Repeat this twice and calculate averages.

The rate and depth of breathing increase with exercise. When they are working hard, your muscles need more oxygen for respiration. They also produce more carbon dioxide in respiration.

Increasing the rate and depth of breathing gets more oxygen into the blood and gets rid of more carbon dioxide from the blood. Muscles continue to respire quite fast after exercise finishes. They still need a good supply of oxygen and they still have carbon dioxide to be removed. Your pulse rate remains high after exercise because your heart is beating fast to deliver plenty of blood to your muscles so they gain this extra oxygen and have their carbon dioxide removed.

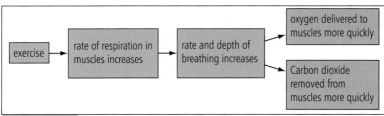

**Figure 10.5.2** The effect of exercising on breathing.

## Depth of breathing

An adult can take in about 5 litres of air in their deepest breath. This is their **vital capacity** – the maximum volume of air that is breathed out after breathing in as much air as possible. At rest, about half a litre of air is breathed in and out. During exercise approximately four and a half litres of extra air can be taken in during a deep breath.

## Control of breathing

You don't think about your breathing – most of the time it just happens. So what makes you breathe faster and deeper when you exercise? The brain has a special part for controlling breathing. When you exercise the tissues respire more quickly and make *more carbon dioxide* which *lowers* the *pH* in the tissues and the blood (i.e. they become more acidic). They may also make lactic acid which does the same (see page 116).

Your brain detects this rise in carbon dioxide and the lowering of the pH of the blood reaching it. The brain sends nerve impulses to the diaphragm and to the intercostal muscles so they contract faster and further to increase the rate and depth of breathing. By breathing deeper and more rapidly, you lower the concentration of carbon dioxide in the blood and this raises the blood pH back to normal. In turn this has the same effect on the tissues because the blood flows through them. This is an example of **homeostasis** – see page 130.

### SUMMARY QUESTIONS

1 Describe what happens to each of the following when you exercise:

   a   the rate of breathing,      b   the depth of breathing.

2 Describe what happens to each of the following when you exercise:

   a   the concentration of carbon dioxide in the tissues,

   b   the pH in the tissues.

3 a   Explain how the brain monitors and controls the rate of breathing when you exercise.

   b   Explain what happens to the following when you exercise:

      i     the intercostal muscles,      ii   the diaphragm,

      iii   the heart rate?

### KEY POINTS

1 Exercise increases both the rate and depth of breathing.

2 An increase in the concentration of carbon dioxide and a lowering of pH in the blood reaching the brain triggers these changes in breathing.

Extension

## LEARNING OUTCOMES

- State the word equation for anaerobic respiration in muscles during hard exercise
- State the word equation for anaerobic respiration in yeast
- Describe the effect of lactic acid in muscles during exercise
- Describe the role of anaerobic respiration in yeast during brewing and breadmaking

## Muscles without oxygen

Your muscles need oxygen and glucose to respire aerobically. These are brought to your muscles by your blood system. During vigorous exercise your heart and lungs cannot get enough oxygen to your muscles quickly enough. When this happens your muscles start to carry out **anaerobic respiration**.

Glucose is broken down to **lactic acid** when there is not enough oxygen:

$$\text{glucose} \longrightarrow \text{lactic acid} + \text{energy released}$$

### Lactic acid

Lactic acid can slowly poison your muscles and cause cramp, so it must be removed from the body. We carry on breathing faster and deeper *after* vigorous exercise.

The extra oxygen breaks down the lactic acid. This extra oxygen is called the **oxygen debt**.

Our oxygen debt builds up after we exercise hard. It has to be 'paid back' straight away.

Sprinters build up lactic acid in their muscles. They often hold their breath during a 100 metre race. Afterwards they need about 7 dm³ of oxygen to get rid of the lactic acid. They breathe deeply after the race in order to 'repay their oxygen debt'; their heart rate remains high after the race to deliver lots of blood to the muscles to remove the lactic acid they have made.

Anaerobic respiration releases less energy for every molecule of glucose than aerobic respiration.

This athlete is repaying her oxygen debt by breathing deeply after her training.

|  | energy released (kJ per gram of glucose) |
|---|---|
| aerobic respiration | 16.1 |
| fermentation by yeast | 1.2 |
| anaerobic respiration in muscle | 0.8 |

Without oxygen, glucose is only partly broken down into alcohol or lactic acid. A lot of energy remains in the molecules of alcohol and lactic acid.

## Brewing and breadmaking

Many microbes can respire successfully without oxygen. Yeast can respire with or without oxygen.

When it respires without oxygen (anaerobically) it is called **fermentation**:

$$\text{glucose} \longrightarrow \text{alcohol} + \text{carbon dioxide} + \text{energy released}$$

Yeast is used in brewing and in breadmaking.

## Brewing

In beer production, barley grains are the source of the sugar.

In a process called **malting**, these grains are allowed to germinate for a few days. During this time, enzymes break down the starch in the grains into a sugar called **maltose** (see page 40). This sugar is dissolved in water to give a brown liquid called **wort**.

Next, in a process called **mashing**, yeast is added to the wort and fermentation begins. To give beer its characteristic bitter flavour, the flowers of a plant are added. These are called hops and come from the hop plant, *Humulus lupulus*.

Most beer is brewed on an industrial scale in large copper vats. Brewers also use computer technology to carefully monitor and adjust conditions in the vats.

## Breadmaking

Baking is another example of using yeast to help produce a food. Bread is made from **dough**, a mixture of flour, water, salt, sugar and yeast. This mixture is kept at a warm temperature. The yeast starts to ferment the sugar, producing carbon dioxide gas and alcohol.

Bubbles of gas are trapped inside the dough and make it rise. When the bread is baked in a hot oven the bubbles of gas make the bread 'light' in texture. The heat causes the alcohol to evaporate, leaving behind the traditional taste of bread.

Checking the brewing process in large copper vats.

Yeast made carbon dioxide which caused the dough to rise and give these loaves their light texture.

### SUMMARY QUESTIONS

1 Explain the importance of anaerobic respiration in yeast in the following industries:

   a   brewing,        b   bread making.

2 Describe and explain the differences between the amount of energy released in aerobic and anaerobic respiration. (See the table opposite for some figures to use in your answer.)

Extension

3 The table below shows the units of lactic acid produced in the leg muscles of an athlete during a race:

| time (minutes) | 0 | 10 | 20 | 30 | 40 | 50 | 60 | 70 | 80 |
|---|---|---|---|---|---|---|---|---|---|
| units of lactic acid | 0 | 1 | 7 | 12 | 9 | 6 | 3 | 1 | 1 |

   a   Draw a graph using the data.

   b   When did the lactic acid reach a maximum?

   c   Explain why the muscles produced lactic acid.

   d   Explain why the muscles produced less lactic acid towards the end of the race.

4 Explain why we carry on breathing heavily after we finish a session of hard exercise.

### KEY POINTS

1 In the absence of oxygen, yeast and exercising muscles carry out anaerobic respiration.

2 The build up of lactic acid in muscles during hard exercise produces an *oxygen debt* that has to be paid back by breathing in extra oxygen.

3 Anaerobic respiration of yeast has an important role to play in both brewing and breadmaking.

Extension

1 Define the following terms:
   (a) respiration
   (b) aerobic respiration
   (c) anaerobic respiration.

2 Explain the difference between respiration and breathing.

3 List seven ways in which energy is used in the human body.

4 Write out word equations for:
   (a) aerobic respiration
   (b) anaerobic respiration in yeast
   (c) anaerobic respiration in muscle tissue.

5 Describe how we make use of anaerobic respiration in yeast in brewing and breadmaking.

6 List the ways in which alveoli in the lungs are adapted for efficient gas exchange between air and blood.

7 Explain how you would investigate the effect of exercise on your breathing.

8 Look at the following table:

| activity | volume of each breath (cm³) | number of breaths taken per minute |
|---|---|---|
| rest | 500 | 18 |
| 20 step-ups per minute | 750 | 25 |
| 50 step-ups per minute | 1200 | 34 |

   (a) Describe and explain what happens to the volume of each breath with increased exercise.
   (b) Describe and explain what happens to the number of breaths taken per minute with increased exercise.

9 Write out the chemical equations for the types of respiration listed in question 4.

10 Explain why sprinters may not breathe at all during their race, but breathe very deeply at the end of it.

11 Describe the movements that occur to ventilate the lungs during a period of deep breathing.

12 Explain how the brain controls breathing during and after exercise.

1 Which process does *not* require energy from respiration?
   A   diffusion of oxygen across the alveolar wall
   B   contraction of muscle during exercise
   C   passage of nerve impulses
   D   synthesis of protein molecules

   *(Paper 1)* [1]

2 During fermentation, yeast cells produce:
   A   alcohol
   B   carbon dioxide and alcohol
   C   lactic acid
   D   lactic acid and carbon dioxide

   *(Paper 1)* [1]

3 The diagram shows apparatus to investigate the production of carbon dioxide during respiration of insects. What would you expect to see in tubes **A** and **B** 5 minutes after setting up the apparatus?

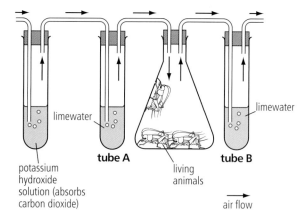

limewater

tube A

tube B

limewater

potassium hydroxide solution (absorbs carbon dioxide)

living animals

air flow

|   | tube A | tube B |
|---|---|---|
| A | cloudy | cloudy |
| B | cloudy | no change |
| C | no change | cloudy |
| D | no change | no change |

   *(Paper 1)* [1]

4 What are the features of a gas exchange surface?
   A   thick-walled, large surface area, many capillaries
   B   thick-walled, small surface area, few capillaries

**C** thin-walled, large surface area, many capillaries

**D** thin-walled, small surface area, few capillaries

*(Paper 1)* [1]

**5** Copy and complete the table with ticks and crosses. The first row has been completed for you.

| feature | photosynthesis | respiration |
|---|---|---|
| occurs only in plant cells | ✓ | ✗ |
| produces oxygen | | |
| consists of a series of enzyme-catalysed reactions | | |
| produces carbon dioxide | | |
| releases energy | | |
| takes place all the time (night and day) | | |

*(Paper 2)* [5]

**6 (a)** Write out and complete the word equation for aerobic respiration:

_____ + oxygen ⟶ _____ + _____ + _____ [4]

A student set up the apparatus shown below to find the rate of respiration of crickets.

The student took several readings from the apparatus. After each reading the clip was opened for several minutes before being sealed again.

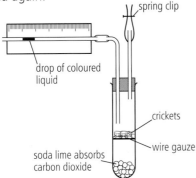

spring clip

drop of coloured liquid

crickets

soda lime absorbs carbon dioxide

wire gauze

**(b)** State the direction in which the coloured drop will move as the crickets respire in the apparatus. Explain your answer. [3]

**(c)** Explain why the clip is opened after taking the readings. [2]

**(d)** State one factor that should be kept constant during the investigation. [1]

*(Paper 2)*

**7** The diagram shows the human breathing system:

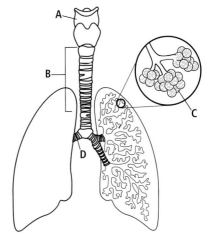

A

B

C

D

**(a) (i)** Name **A** to **D**. [4]

**(ii)** State the functions of each structure **A** to **D**. [4]

**(b)** Explain how you would show that expired air has a different concentration of carbon dioxide compared with atmospheric air. Give full practical details. [5]

*(Paper 2)*

**8** The diagram shows the ribs and muscles of the thorax from the side.

**(a)** Name **A** to **C**. [3]

**(b) (i)** Describe how the structures shown bring about breathing movements during inspiration and expiration. [5]

**(ii)** Explain how the movements you describe cause air to move into and out of the lungs. [5]

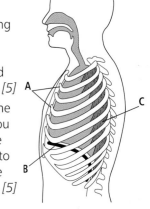

A

B

C

*(Paper 3)*

## 11.1 Controlling conditions in the body

### LEARNING OUTCOMES

- Define the term *homeostasis*
- Explain the concept of negative feedback
- Describe the control of blood glucose concentration

### EXAMINER SAYS...

Although we say that homeostasis is maintaining <u>constant</u> conditions in the body, they do change slightly all the time. It is more precise to say that homeostasis maintains <u>nearly constant</u> conditions or keeps them <u>within narrow limits</u>.

### Controlling conditions

During metabolism, many chemical reactions occur inside the body. In cells, some molecules are built up, such as proteins, and some are broken down, such as glycogen. Enzymes control these reactions and work best when conditions, such as temperature, pH and concentration of water, are kept suitable and constant. See Unit 4 to see how temperature and pH influence enzyme activity.

Any slight change in the conditions in the body can slow down or stop enzymes from working. **Homeostasis** is the maintenance of constant internal conditions in the body, so that enzymes control metabolism efficiently.

The brain has overall control of our body processes. The control of body temperature is an example of homeostasis.

In humans, the normal temperature of the blood is 37 °C. When blood reaching the brain is warmer than this temperature it sends impulses along nerves to the skin to promote heat loss. For example, our sweat glands produce sweat and this helps us to cool down, returning body temperature to normal.

When we feel cold our blood temperature falls below 37 °C. Then the brain will stimulate the production of more heat in the muscles by shivering and by increasing the rate of respiration in the liver. It also stimulates the body to conserve heat by decreasing the production of sweat by sweat glands.

### Negative feedback

The control of body temperature is an example of **negative feedback**. This is the same sort of control system as in an oven to keep the temperature constant at the pre-set temperature. Negative feedback acts to ensure that the actual temperature is as close to the pre-set temperature as possible. In our body, if the temperature increases above or below the normal 37 °C, then it responds by taking actions that will bring it back to normal. There are also control systems for blood glucose concentration, the water content of the blood, blood pH and the oxygen and carbon dioxide concentrations of the blood.

### Controlling blood glucose

Cells need glucose for energy and therefore need a constant supply from the blood.

When you eat a high carbohydrate meal your blood glucose concentration can increase by a factor of 20. However, it does not stay high because cells in the **pancreas** detect the high glucose

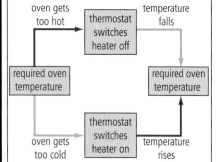

**Figure 11.1.1** Controlling the temperature of an oven is an example of negative feedback.

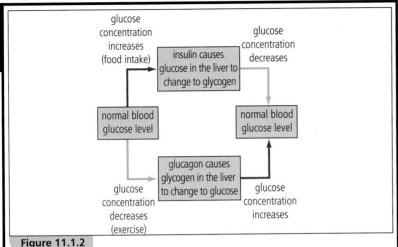

Figure 11.1.2

concentration in the blood. These cells secrete the **hormone** called **insulin** into the blood. Insulin stimulates liver cells to convert glucose into the storage compound **glycogen** (see page 44). This stimulates the liver cells to absorb lots of glucose from the blood so the concentration decreases and returns to normal.

When you run a race or carry out some other type of exercise, your muscles take up lots of glucose from the blood to provide the energy you need. Your blood glucose concentration decreases, but it does not keep decreasing. Other cells in the pancreas detect this decrease and secrete the hormone **glucagon** into the blood. Glucagon stimulates liver cells to break down glycogen to glucose, which diffuses into the blood so the blood glucose concentration increases to normal.

Blood glucose concentration is controlled by the pancreas, which *monitors* the blood glucose concentration and releases hormones to instruct liver cells to remove glucose molecules from the blood or add more.

This is an example of negative feedback because the pancreas:

• makes insulin to stimulate a decrease in blood glucose concentration, or
• makes glucagon to stimulate an increase in blood glucose concentration

to make sure the concentration stays within limits and does not increase or decrease too much.

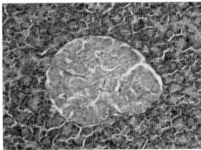

The tissue in the centre of this photo of the pancreas secretes insulin and glucagon.

**KEY POINTS**

1 Homeostasis is the maintenance of constant internal conditions, such as body temperature

2 Homeostasis involves negative feedback. It operates to maintain constant conditions of glucose, water, carbon dioxide and oxygen in the blood as well as its pH.

3 The pancreas controls the concentration of glucose in the blood by producing the hormones insulin and glucagon which stimulate the liver.

**SUMMARY QUESTIONS**

1 a  Define the term *homeostasis*.

  b  Explain why is it important that conditions in cells are kept constant.

2 a  Explain the term *negative feedback* using temperature regulation as an example.

  b  Explain the roles of the pancreas and the liver in maintaining a constant blood glucose concentration.

# Controlling body temperature

**EXAMINER SAYS...**

We produce heat in respiration and by shivering; we lose heat to our surroundings, e.g. by evaporation when we sweat; we conserve heat, e.g. by having fat beneath the skin.

Polar bears have a thick layer of insulating fat to conserve their body heat.

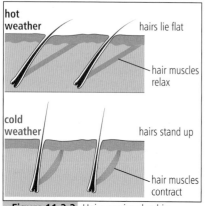

**Figure 11.2.2** Hairs are involved in maintaining body temperature.

Birds and mammals maintain a constant body temperature. They are very successful animals as they can live in cold environments as well as hot ones and be active at night as well as during the day. The skin provides ways to adjust the body temperature in different conditions.

## The skin

The skin is the largest organ in the body and has several important functions:

• protects the body from damage
• stops pathogens from entering
• prevents too much water loss
• detects changes in temperature
• detects pressure (touch) and pain
• loses heat by conduction, convection, radiation and evaporation.

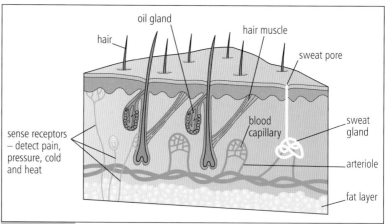

**Figure 11.2.1** The structure of human skin.

Many of the structures in the diagram help in controlling body temperature. We lose and absorb heat through our skin – mostly by radiation. We use our skin for heat loss when we are hot and to conserve heat when we are cold.

Mammals have fur or hair, which traps a layer of air close to the skin. Air is a poor conductor of heat. So air pockets in the fur reduce the loss of heat to the atmosphere by keeping convection currents of air away from the warm surface of the skin. When it is cold, hair muscles *contract* so that hairs stand erect to trap a thick layer of air so reducing heat loss.

When it is hot, hair muscles *relax* so that hairs lie flat. Less air is trapped close to the skin so more heat can be lost as convection currents flow closer to the surface of the skin.

Mammals also have a layer of fatty tissue beneath their skin, which is a good insulator as it does not conduct heat well. Mammals that live in cold environments have very thick layers of fat.

## Controlling body temperature

No matter what the weather is like, your body temperature stays at 37 °C unless you have a fever.

The **hypothalamus** in the brain monitors the temperature of the blood running through it. Nerves bring information to the brain about the temperature of the skin.

### In the heat

The hypothalamus detects an increase in the temperature of the blood flowing through it. Temperature sensors in the skin are stimulated by the high temperature of our surroundings and send information to the brain. The hypothalamus sends nerve impulses to structures in the skin.

- **Arterioles** (small blood vessels) widen to allow an increase in blood flow through capillaries just beneath the skin surface. This process is called **vasodilation**. More heat is lost to the surroundings by convection and radiation.
- **Sweat glands** in the skin produce lots of sweat. The sweat on the skin's surface evaporates and this cools the body.

### In the cold

Temperature sensors in the skin are stimulated and give an early warning about possible loss of heat to the surroundings. The hypothalamus detects a decrease in the temperature of the blood flowing through it. It reacts to this information by sending nerve impulses to structures in the skin.

- **Arterioles** near to the surface of the skin become narrower to reduce the blood flow through capillaries near the surface of the skin. This is called **vasoconstriction**. Less heat is lost by radiation.
- **Sweat glands** stop producing sweat.

We may also need to increase heat production if conserving heat is not successful at keeping the body temperature normal. The hypothalamus stimulates:

- **Shivering** by the muscles which start to contract spontaneously and release heat from respiration. Blood flows through the muscles and is warmed by this heat.

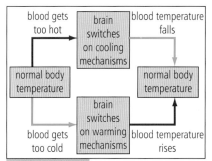

**Figure 11.2.3**

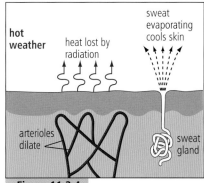

**Figure 11.2.4**

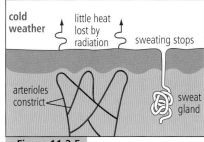

**Figure 11.2.5**

### SUMMARY QUESTIONS

1 Explain how the hypothalamus controls body temperature.

2 Describe what happens in the skin:
   a to lose heat when we are hot,
   b to conserve heat when we are cold.

3 How do we produce heat in the body if we are cold?

4 Explain how fur and fat tissue beneath the skin help in temperature control in cold environments.

# Excretion

Excretion is the process of removing toxic materials, waste products of metabolism and substances in excess of requirements.

## Excretory products

Humans have two main excretory products.

- **Carbon dioxide** is made in body tissues during respiration. It is transported to the lungs in the blood plasma. Here, it diffuses out of the blood into the air in the alveoli and is breathed out (see page 121).
- **Urea** is made in the liver from excess amino acids. It is carried to the kidneys in the plasma where it is filtered out and leaves the body dissolved in the form of urine.

## Role of the liver in excretion

When you eat proteins, they are digested to amino acids in the alimentary canal and transported to the liver. Your body cannot store excess amino acids so they are broken down in the liver into two parts. One of these parts is made into urea.

**LEARNING OUTCOMES**

- Define the term *excretion*
- Name the excretory organs and excretory products
- Describe the structure of the urinary system
- List the functions of the liver

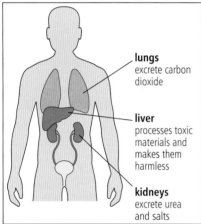

**Figure 11.3.1** The excretory organs.

- lungs
  excrete carbon dioxide
- liver
  processes toxic materials and makes them harmless
- kidneys
  excrete urea and salts

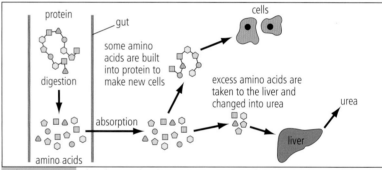

**Figure 11.3.2** This shows what happens to amino acids in the body.

protein — gut — cells
some amino acids are built into protein to make new cells
digestion
amino acids
absorption
excess amino acids are taken to the liver and changed into urea
urea
liver

## Other liver functions

The liver carries out over 200 different functions including:

- storing excess glucose as insoluble glycogen
- making bile which helps to emulsify fats (see page 83)
- breaking down hormones after they have circulated in the blood for a while
- breaking down harmful substances like alcohol and drugs (see page 85).

## The kidneys

Your kidneys are at the top of your abdominal cavity just underneath the diaphragm. They are protected by the backbone, lower ribcage and the fat that surrounds them.

**EXAMINER SAYS...**

Do not confuse 'excretion' with 'egestion'. Substances that are <u>excreted</u> are produced by body cells in metabolism. Substances that are <u>egested</u> have been eaten and have passed through the alimentary canal without being digested and absorbed into the bloodstream. Fibre is an example.

Waste chemicals like urea diffuse from cells into the blood and are transported to the kidneys. Blood enters the kidneys through the **renal arteries**. Inside each kidney is a complex network of filtering units called kidney tubules. As the blood flows through these units small molecules, such as glucose, salts, water and urea, are forced out of the blood plasma to form a fluid known as filtrate. As the filtrate passes along the tubule the useful substances (glucose and salts) are reabsorbed into the blood. However, the volume of water reabsorbed depends on the body's water content. If you are dehydrated (short of water) perhaps because you have been sweating a lot, then the kidneys will take back as much as they can so you produce concentrated urine and conserve water. If not, they will reabsorb less water and you will produce dilute urine.

**EXAMINER SAYS...**

<u>Urine</u> is a body fluid that consists of waste substances dissolved in water. It is yellow because one of the waste substances is a yellow pigment. <u>Urea</u> is a colourless compound that dissolves in water, in blood plasma and in urine.

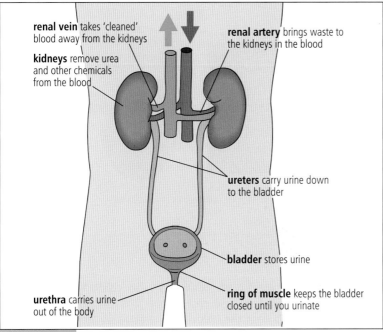

renal vein takes 'cleaned' blood away from the kidneys

renal artery brings waste to the kidneys in the blood

kidneys remove urea and other chemicals from the blood

ureters carry urine down to the bladder

bladder stores urine

urethra carries urine out of the body

ring of muscle keeps the bladder closed until you urinate

**Figure 11.3.3** The urinary system.

**DID YOU KNOW?**

Each kidney has a million tubules when you are born, but the number decreases with age.

At the end of each tubule the urine is released and flows into the **ureter** and to the **bladder** where it is stored. From here it leaves the body, at intervals, through a shorter tube called the **urethra**. The **renal vein** carries blood with a low concentration of waste chemicals away from the kidney.

**KEY POINTS**

1 Excretion is the removal from the body of waste chemicals made in tissues during metabolism.

2 Excretory products include carbon dioxide and urea.

3 The kidneys filter materials out of the blood, take back useful substances into the blood, e.g. glucose, control the quantity of water lost in the urine and excrete urea in the urine.

**SUMMARY QUESTIONS**

1 Match each structure **A** to **E** in the urinary system with one of the functions **1** to **5**.

  **A** renal artery  **1** stores urine.

  **B** ureter     **2** filters urea and other waste chemicals out of the blood.

  **C** kidney    **3** carries blood with a high concentration of urea.

  **D** bladder   **4** carries urine down to the bladder.

  **E** renal vein  **5** carries blood with a low concentration of urea.

2 List five functions of the liver.

# 11.4     Kidney function

## DID YOU KNOW?

People on survival courses are taught to assess their level of dehydration by looking at the colour of their urine. The darker yellow the urine, the more dehydrated the person.

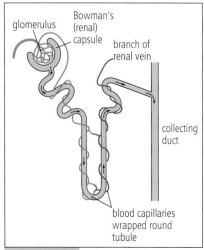

**Figure 11.4.1**   Kidney tubule.

## Inside the kidneys

If you cut open a kidney lengthways, you can see three areas:

**cortex** – a brown outer area

**medulla** – a reddish inner area

**pelvis** – a white area.

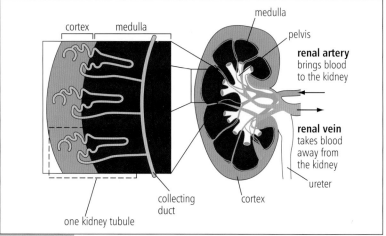

**Figure 11.4.1**   A vertical section of a kidney (right hand side). Detailed view of part of the kidney (left hand side).

Inside each kidney are thousands of tiny tubes called **kidney tubules** which you can only see with a microscope. The function of the kidney tubules is to filter the blood and remove waste chemicals and determine how much water is excreted. The filtering is carried out in the cortex. The waste chemicals and excess water are removed from the body in the urine which flows from the kidneys down the ureter and is stored in the bladder.

## Structure of a kidney tubule

Blood containing waste chemicals flows into the kidney in the renal artery. Inside the kidney, the renal artery branches many times to give smaller arteries. Each of these small arteries supplies blood to a closely packed group of capillaries called a **glomerulus**. After filtration, blood flows out of the glomerulus into another small artery. Blood then flows in capillaries around the rest of the tubule which joins to form the renal vein.

The diagram shows that the tubule forms a loop which goes deep into the medulla and back to the cortex. The end of the kidney tubule drains into a **collecting duct** which goes through the medulla and empties into the pelvis. Urine collects in the pelvis and then flows into the ureter.

# Filtration and reabsorption

Look at the diagram opposite of how a kidney tubule works.

The kidneys are close to the heart so the blood pressure in the renal artery is high. You can see that the blood vessel entering the glomerulus is wider than the one leaving it which causes pressure to increase inside the glomerulus so that blood is filtered. Small molecules, including water, leave the blood plasma so that less blood leaves the glomerulus than enters it.

The lining of the capillaries is like a net with tiny holes in it. Blood cells and large molecules, like blood proteins, are too big to pass through the capillary lining and so stay in the blood. Small molecules, like urea, glucose, salts and water, pass out of the glomerulus and into the Bowman's capsule which is a space where the filtrate collects.

All the glucose, some salts and much of the water are needed by the body. They are **reabsorbed** into the blood from the kidney tubule. What is left is urea and excess salts dissolved in water. As this fluid flows on through the tubule, some more water may be reabsorbed if the body is low in water. The fluid that enters the collecting ducts is urine. It flows down the collecting duct and then to the ureter and the bladder. The blood, with a lower concentration of waste chemicals, leaves the kidney in the renal vein.

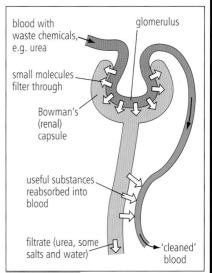

**Figure 11.4.3** Filtration and reabsorption.

## SUMMARY QUESTIONS

1 Sketch a vertical section of a kidney and label:

  a cortex, b medulla, c renal artery, d renal vein, e ureter.

2 Describe what happens in kidney tubules to form urine.

3 The table shows the concentrations of five substances in three body fluids.

| substance | concentration (g per dm³) | | |
|---|---|---|---|
| | blood in renal artery | filtrate in kidney tubule | urine |
| urea | 0.2 | 0.2 | 20.0 |
| glucose | 0.9 | 0.9 | 0.0 |
| amino acids | 0.05 | 0.05 | 0.0 |
| salts | 8.0 | 8.0 | 16.5 |
| protein | 82 | 0 | 0 |

Use the information in the table to:

a state the substances that pass from the blood into the kidney tubule,

b explain how the substances you have named pass into the kidney tubule,

c state the substances that are reabsorbed into the blood from the kidney tubule and explain why they are reabsorbed,

d explain the results for protein.

## EXAMINER SAYS...

Reabsorption of glucose and salts occurs by diffusion and active transport. Water is reabsorbed by osmosis. Expect to explain reabsorption in the kidney by referring to these processes (see pages 26 and 28).

## KEY POINTS

1 The renal capsule filters the blood removing urea, salts, glucose and water.

2 The useful materials such as glucose, some salts and most of the water are reabsorbed into the blood capillaries along the tubule.

3 Urine, consisting of urea, some salts and water passes out of the kidneys, along the ureters, to be stored in the bladder until urination.

# Kidney dialysis and kidney transplants

## LEARNING OUTCOMES

- Describe the process of dialysis and explain how it controls the concentration of glucose, urea and protein in the blood
- Describe how a kidney dialysis machine works
- Describe the advantages and disadvantages of kidney transplants compared with dialysis

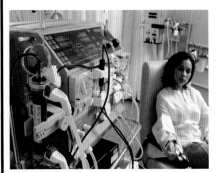

Dialysis machine.

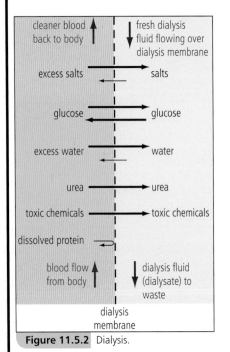

Figure 11.5.2 Dialysis.

## The kidney dialysis machine

A person can survive on one kidney. However, if both kidneys become diseased or damaged, it can be fatal unless a medical procedure known as **kidney dialysis** is available. A common indicator that the kidney is damaged is the presence of protein in the urine. This happens when the renal capsules are damaged so that large molecules of protein pass out of blood plasma into the filtrate.

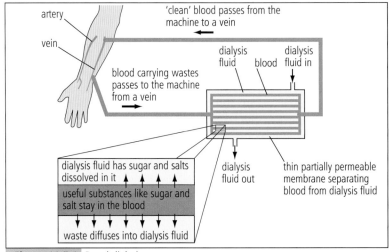

Figure 11.5.1 Renal dialysis.

This is what happens when someone has dialysis treatment.

- A tube is connected to one of the patient's veins.
- The blood flows along the tube and into the machine.
- Inside the machine the blood is pumped over the surface of a dialysis membrane, which separates the patient's blood and the dialysis fluid.
- Urea diffuses out of the blood, across the dialysis membrane and into the dialysis fluid.
- The dialysis fluid already has glucose and salts in it, so there will be no overall loss of glucose and salts from the blood by diffusion into the fluid.
- Urea and other waste chemicals leave the machine in the dialysis fluid.
- The patient's 'cleaner' blood passes back into the vein.

The patient has to use the dialysis machine for several hours, two or three times a week. This may involve attending a special ward in hospital or it can be done at home. Between visits to the dialysis ward of the hospital, patients eat a restricted diet without too much protein and salt. If they eat too much protein, they will produce too much urea which becomes toxic and would mean more frequent dialysis treatment.

## Dialysis

Dialysis involves the separation of two solutions by a partially permeable membrane. This **dialysis membrane** has tiny pores in it which allow water and small solutes to diffuse through, but not larger molecules such as proteins. In the case of kidney dialysis the blood is pumped over the surface of a dialysis membrane which contains a fluid (the **dialysate**) which has the normal concentrations of salts and glucose and is the same water potential as normal plasma.

During dialysis, solute molecules such as salts and glucose diffuse through the membrane. As the dialysis fluid has the same water potential as normal blood plasma, the concentrations of solutes, such as blood proteins, reach equilibrium and are restored to normal. Excess salts, urea and other toxic chemicals are not present in the dialysis fluid, so they diffuse out of the blood and across the membrane into the dialysate.

## Kidney transplants

A person with failed kidneys may have a kidney transplant. This involves replacing the diseased kidney with a healthy one from a donor. A donor may be a close relative or friend or someone who has just died.

Before a kidney transplant is carried out the blood type and tissue type of donor and recipient (the person receiving the kidney) must be matched. Blood typing is the same as for blood transfusion. Tissue typing reduces the chances that the recipient's immune system will attack the new kidney and reject it. To reduce the chances of rejection occuring, drugs are given to the patient after the operation to suppress the immune system. They remain on these for life, which means they are more likely to catch certain infections and to have those infections for longer.

Also to prevent rejection, the bone marrow of the patient is treated with radiation to stop white blood cell production for a period after the operation.

After recovering from the operation the patient is able to lead a normal life, including a normal diet, and does not need to have dialysis treatment in hospital or at home. Transplants replace all the functions of a kidney, not just some of them as with dialysis. Kidneys continuously remove urea from the blood rather than at intervals. They also make a hormone that stimulates red blood cell production in bone marrow. However, it is difficult to find a donor kidney that is a suitable match and there is always the danger of tissue rejection. Some wealthy people have resorted to paying healthy, poor people to donate them a kidney.

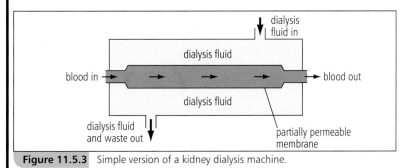

**Figure 11.5.3** Simple version of a kidney dialysis machine.

### KEY POINTS

1 A dialysis membrane allows small molecules to pass through pores but prevents large molecules from diffusing through.

2 During kidney dialysis urea and some salts pass out of the blood into the dialysis fluid. There is no net diffusion of glucose, since it is in the same concentration in the blood and the dialysis fluid.

3 Kidney transplants avoid the inconvenience of dialysis, but there may be problems in finding a suitable donor and there is always the risk of tissue rejection.

### SUMMARY QUESTIONS

1 Explain why the presence of protein in the urine may indicate kidney damage.

2 Figure 11.5.3 shows a simple version of a kidney dialysis machine.

   The patient's blood is kept separate from the dialysis fluid by a partially permeable membrane.

   a Name the process by which urea passes from the blood into the dialysis fluid.

   b Explain how concentrations of salts, glucose and proteins are returned to normal while on dialysis.

3 Make a table to show the advantages and disadvantages of kidney dialysis and kidney transplants.

1 Define the following terms:

(a) homeostasis

(b) toxin

(c) metabolic waste

(d) excretion.

2 Explain how arterioles control the flow of blood through capillaries.

3 Explain how the skin is involved with controlling body temperature.

4 Describe the role of the brain in temperature control.

5 Name the main excretory organs of the body.

6 List the main excretory products of the body.

7 Explain how excretion differs from egestion.

8 What happens to excess amino acids in the liver?

9 List the parts of the urinary system and state the function of each.

10 State four functions of the liver in excretion.

11 Explain why temperature control is an example of negative feedback.

12 Draw a flow diagram to show how the glucose concentration in the blood is controlled. Include the roles of the pancreas and liver in your diagram.

13 Outline the roles of the kidney in removing metabolic waste and maintaining the glucose and salt concentration of the blood and its water potential.

14 Explain how the composition of the blood is regulated by kidney dialysis.

1 Which substances are found in the urine of a healthy person?

A glucose and proteins

B glucose and water

C proteins and salts

D salts and water

(Paper 1) [1]

2 Which organ is *not* part of the urinary system?

A bladder

B kidney

C liver

D ureter

(Paper 1) [1]

3 Which occur when in a hot environment?

|   | arterioles in the skin | sweat glands | hair erector muscles |
|---|---|---|---|
| A | constrict | active | relax |
| B | constrict | not active | contract |
| C | dilate | active | relax |
| D | dilate | active | contract |

(Paper 1) [1]

4 Which is *not* an excretory function of the liver?

A breakdown of alcohol

B deamination

C production of urea

D protein synthesis

(Paper 1) [1]

5 The diagram shows the urinary system and its blood supply.

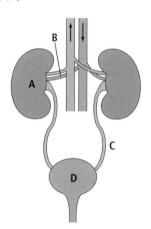

**(a) (i)** Name parts **A** to **D**. [4]

**(ii)** State the functions of structures **A** to **D**. [4]

**b) (i)** The following is a list of components of the blood. Identify those that are found in the urine of healthy people.

**blood proteins, urea, glucose, platelets, red blood cells, salts, water** [1]

**(ii)** Explain why some components of the blood are present in the urine and others are not. [3]

*(Paper 2)*

**6** The diagram shows the human skin in two different environmental conditions.

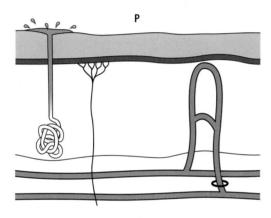

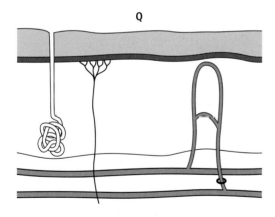

**(a) (i)** Describe how the skin in **P** differs from the skin in **Q**. [4]

**(ii)** State the environmental conditions in **P** and **Q**. [2]

**(b)** Suggest the advantages of maintaining a constant internal temperature. [2]

*(Paper 2)*

**7 (a)** Copy and complete the flow chart that shows part of the control of the concentration of glucose in the blood.

increase in blood glucose concentration
↓
detected by ......
↓
insulin secreted
↓
liver cells respond by ...... [2]

**(b)** Write out a similar flow chart to show the body's response to a decrease in blood glucose concentration. [3]

**(c)** Explain the principle of negative feedback, using the control of glucose in the blood as an example. [5]

*(Paper 3)*

**8 (a)** Describe how urea is formed from excess amino acids in the liver. [4]

**(b)** The graph shows the concentration of urea in the blood of a person who suffered from kidney failure following an accident.

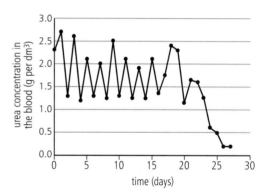

**(i)** State the highest concentration of urea and the number of the day on which it occurred. [2]

**(ii)** How many times did the person receive dialysis? Give a reason for your answer. [2]

**(iii)** Explain why the urea concentration decreased towards the end of the period shown in the graph. [4]

*(Paper 3)*

## 12.1     Nervous control in humans

### LEARNING OUTCOMES

- Describe the structure of the nervous system
- Distinguish between voluntary and involuntary actions

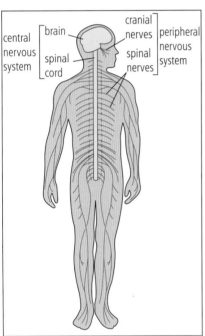

**Figure 12.1.1** The main parts of the human nervous system.

### EXAMINER SAYS...

Nerve cells transmit impulses, not 'signals' or 'messages'. Never write these words in an examination answer about the nervous system.

All living organisms are sensitive to changes in their environment. The changes in daylight, wind speed, temperature, movement, availability of food that they detect are called **stimuli** (singular: stimulus). **Receptors** are the cells that detect the stimuli, for example cells in your taste buds detect chemicals in your food. **Effectors** are the organs, such as glands and muscles, that bring about responses. Glands secrete useful substances and muscles contract to bring about movement. The actions they take as a result are called **responses**.

Animals have nervous systems which at their simplest are networks of specialised nerve cells, as in jellyfish and sea anemones. At their most complex, they are organs with powerful processing skills, such as the human brain. Two organ systems are involved – the sensory system for detecting changes in our environment and the nervous system for coordinating our responses and initiating actions. Here we discuss the nervous system. You will find information about the sensory system on page 148.

### Human nervous system

The human nervous system consists of two parts: the **central nervous system** (CNS) and the **peripheral nervous system** (PNS). The central nervous system is made up of only two organs: the **brain** and the **spinal cord**. The brain is protected by the skull and the spinal cord is protected by the vertebral column.

The central nervous system is connected to different parts of the body by nerves that make up the peripheral nervous system. **Cranial nerves** and **spinal nerves** are in pairs on either side of the brain and spinal cord respectively. Cranial nerves link the brain with all the organs in the head and also some in the thorax and abdomen. Spinal nerves link the brain to the arms, thorax, abdomen and legs. Spinal nerves leave the spinal cord in pairs through spaces between the vertebrae.

Each nerve is made up of lots of nerve cells or **neurones** surrounded by a protective fibrous tube. Nerves are visible to the naked eye, but you need microscopes to see neurones. Neurones transmit information in the form of nerve impulses which are like pulses of electricity passing along a wire.

Voluntary actions are under conscious control and involve the brain in decision making. A footballer carries out a voluntary action when he or she kicks a ball. Turning over the pages of a book is an example of a voluntary action. These actions are under the conscious control of the brain.

## Involuntary and voluntary actions

We make two types of action. Some happen automatically without us having to think about them. These are **involuntary actions** that occur unconsciously. Swallowing, blinking, breathing and the beating of the heart are four such actions that we are not conscious of most of the time, but we can choose to control occasionally. Movement of food in the ileum (see page 82) and of urine in the ureter (see page 135) are other involuntary actions you have studied that we can't control by thinking about them. **Voluntary actions** are those we choose to make and the decisions to make them occur in our brains.

When a person sits down on a sharp object such as a pin without realising it there is a very quick, automatic response that the person does not need to think about.

This is an example of a **simple reflex** which is an involuntary action.

The stimulus is the pin and the receptors are pain sensors in the skin. The effectors are the muscles in the legs that cause the person to get up quickly.

The sequence of events is:

stimulus ⟶ receptor ⟶ coordinator ⟶ effector ⟶ response

The **coordinator** is the part of the body that connects information about the stimulus to the effector. This always happens inside the central nervous system to allow connections with other parts of the body and for the brain to be aware of stimuli. Inside the spinal cord, neurones from pain receptors connect with neurones to the muscles. Some reflexes involve the brain as we will see in the section on the eye (see page 149).

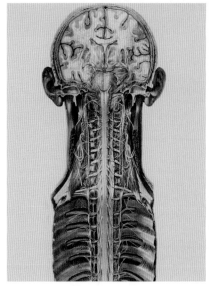

Front view of the top part of the nervous system.

### EXAMINER SAYS...

You can see more about the neurones that control simple reflexes on page 145. They are arranged into reflex arcs involving peripheral nerves and the CNS. All responses are coordinated through the CNS.

### SUMMARY QUESTIONS

1 Copy and complete the following sentences using the words below:

**cranial   peripheral   spinal   neurones   central**

The brain and spinal cord make up the _____ nervous system. All the nerves of the body make up the _____ nervous system. _____ nerves are connected to the brain and _____ nerves are connected to the spinal cord. The nervous system is composed of many specialised cells known as _____.

2 a Put the following words into the correct sequence:

**coordinator   stimulus   effector   receptor   response**

b Define each of the above words.

3 a Explain the difference between an involuntary action and a voluntary action.

b Give two examples of involuntary actions.

c Give two examples of voluntary actions.

### KEY POINTS

1 The human nervous system is made up of the central nervous system (brain and spinal cord) and the peripheral nervous system (cranial and spinal nerves).

2 Neurones or nerve cells transmit nerve impulses.

3 Some actions are involuntary (not under conscious control). Other actions are voluntary and involve conscious control by the brain.

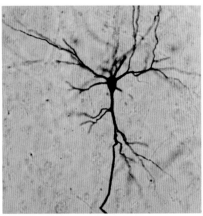

This neurone has a long axon.

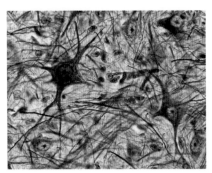

Neurones in the brain. Notice the cell bodies with their nuclei.

## Neurones

Neurones are highly specialised cells. Their structure allows them to transmit information as nerve impulses over long distances. The cell body contains the nucleus and almost all of the cytoplasm, but there are thin extensions of cytoplasm that may be quite short or extend a long way through the body.

**Sensory neurones** transmit impulses from sense organs to the brain and spinal cord.

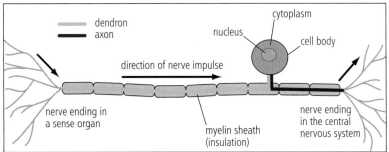

**Figure 12.2.1** A sensory neurone.

**Motor neurones** transmit impulses away from the brain and spinal cord to effector organs – muscles and glands.

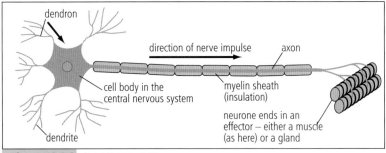

**Figure 12.2.2** A motor neurone.

The diagrams above show the sensory and motor neurones surrounded by insulation. This insulation is known as **myelin**, formed by separate cells that grow around the neurones to form a layer rich in fat. This insulation makes impulses travel very quickly. Some myelinated neurones, which are used in our fast reflexes, transmit impulses at 100 metres per second.

A third type of neurone is the **relay neurone**. These are short and pass on impulses from sensory neurones to motor neurones inside the brain and spinal cord.

When any two neurones meet, they do not actually touch each other. There is a tiny gap between them called a **synapse**. When an impulse reaches a synapse a **chemical transmitter substance** is released from the first neurone. It diffuses across the synapse and triggers off an impulse in the second neurone. Since the chemical transmitter is only produced on one side of the synapse, it ensures that impulses travel in one direction through the nervous system. Many drugs produce their effects by acting at synapses (see page 158).

## Reflex arcs

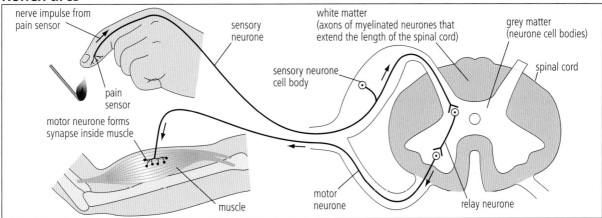

**Figure 12.2.3**

If you touch a hot object, you remove your hand very quickly and automatically without thinking. This is an example of a simple reflex. Your brain receives impulses about the pain but not until you have already moved your hand. If you relied on the brain to make a decision you would be burnt in the time it took for the impulses to travel to the brain and back.

Look at the diagram above and trace the pathway of the impulse along the neurones.
This pathway is called a **reflex arc**.

The **stimulus** in the example is the hot flame. The **receptor** is the heat sensor in the skin. When it is stimulated the heat sensor generates an impulse.

The impulse travels to the spinal cord along a **sensory neurone**.

Inside the grey matter of the spinal cord the impulse passes across a synapse to a **relay neurone**. The relay neurone passes the impulse across a second synapse to a **motor neurone**.

The motor neurone transmits the impulse to a muscle in the arm. The muscle is the **effector** and it contracts to remove the hand from the hot object. This action is the **response**.

Many reflexes are protective; they happen very quickly, so you do not harm yourself.

### SUMMARY QUESTIONS

1 Copy and complete the sentences using the words below:

**synapse     grey     arc     relay     motor
sensory     effectors     transmitter**

In a reflex _____ nerve impulses are transmitted to the spinal cord by _____ neurones. Inside the _____ matter of the spinal cord the impulses are passed on to _____ neurones. The impulses leave the spinal cord along _____ neurones to go to _____. There is a gap between two neurones called a _____ where chemical _____ substances are released to pass the impulse to the next neurone.

2 Look at the diagram of the motor neurone:
   a  Name the parts labelled **A** to **D**.
   b  Give the functions of parts **B**, **C** and **D**.

3 a  Define each of the following:
      i    synapse
      ii   chemical transmitter substance
      iii  myelin     iv   relay neurone.
   b  Explain the function of **i – iv** in the nervous system.

### KEY POINTS

1  A reflex arc is made up of three types of neurone: a sensory neurone, a relay neurone and a motor neurone.

2  Reflex actions are rapid, automatic and often protective.

Doctors test reflexes to see if the nervous system is working correctly or not. Here a doctor is testing a baby's grasping reflex.

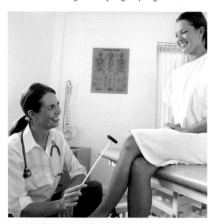

Testing the knee jerk reflex.

A light shone into the eye should stimulate the pupil to constrict. The pupil reflex is described on page 149.

## Reflex actions

We have seen that reflex actions are fast and automatic. Most are protective, such as pulling your hand away from a hot object, blinking when dust gets into your eye and coughing when food starts to enter the trachea (windpipe) instead of the oesophagus (see page 119).

Doctors test reflexes to gain information about the nervous system.

## Reaction time

Lots of sportsmen and sportswomen need fast reflexes. Sports like tennis, fencing and cricket all need quick reactions. The time it takes to react to a stimulus is known as the **reaction time**.

**PRACTICAL**

### Measuring your reaction time

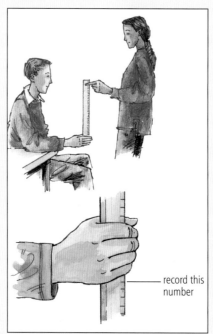

record this number

You can measure your reaction time with a falling ruler.

Place your arm on the bench as in the diagram.

Your partner holds the ruler with zero next to your little finger, but not touching it.

When your partner decides to let the ruler go, try to catch it as quickly as possible.

Read off the scale next to your little finger. Try the test 10 times.

Record your results in a table.

Now repeat the test but with the ruler touching your hand. Your reaction time should improve with practice.

Now try the other hand and compare all your results with other people's results.

## Antagonistic muscles

The muscles that are attached to our skeleton are known as skeletal muscles. They provide the force needed to move bones at joints. Muscles are attached to bones by **tendons**. The bones at a joint are held together by **ligaments**.

Both tendons and ligaments are made of tough fibrous tissue. Tendons do not stretch so that all the force of the muscle contraction is transferred to the bone. Ligaments have some elastic tissue in them and may stretch a little. The most elastic ligaments are those that you can feel at the back of your neck that are attached to your skull.

Joints allow movement to take place. They are lubricated with a special, oily fluid and are protected by tough ligaments. The joint at the elbow allows movement in one plane (up and down) like a hinge and is called a hinge joint.

When a muscle **contracts** it gets shorter. When a muscle is not contracting it **relaxes** and is pulled back to its original length by the contraction of another muscle because muscles cannot *push*, they can only pull. Muscles like the **biceps** and **triceps** in the arm work in pairs. When one contracts, the other relaxes. They form an **antagonistic pair** of muscles.

When you pick up a book from a table, nerves from your brain and spinal cord transmit impulses to the muscles in your arm. They cause your biceps to contract and your triceps to relax. As your biceps shortens it pulls on the tendon that pulls up your lower arm. Your arm bends at the hinge joint at the elbow.

When you put the book back onto the table your triceps contracts and your biceps relaxes to straighten or extend your arm.

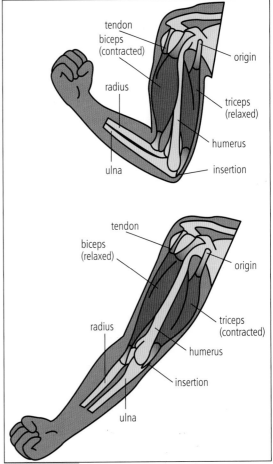

**Figure 12.3.2** The arm bends when the biceps contracts and pulls on the radius and the arm extends when the triceps pulls on the ulna. The origin and insertion are places where muscles are attached to bones by tendons.

### KEY POINTS

1 Reflex actions are rapid, automatic and usually protective.

2 Reaction time is the time it takes to respond to a stimulus.

3 Antagonistic pairs of muscles bring about movement at joints; when one muscle contracts, the other muscle relaxes.

### SUMMARY QUESTIONS

1 a What is meant by the term *reflex action*?

2 a State the function of each of the following:
   i tendon, ii ligament, iii joint.

   b State what happens to the following muscles when the arm is straightened:
   i biceps, ii triceps.

   c Explain the term *antagonistic muscles*.

### EXAMINER SAYS...

Antagonistic means to 'work against'. Some hormones work against each other as they have opposite effects. For example, adrenaline stimulates an increase in blood glucose concentration, whereas insulin stimulates a decrease.

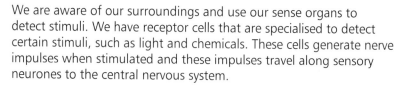

Musicians use a variety of their senses when performing.

We are aware of our surroundings and use our sense organs to detect stimuli. We have receptor cells that are specialised to detect certain stimuli, such as light and chemicals. These cells generate nerve impulses when stimulated and these impulses travel along sensory neurones to the central nervous system.

Some receptors are found concentrated in groups in certain organs. The eye and the ear have receptors arranged in special tissues. They also have other tissues to modify the information from the environment before it reaches the receptors. In the eye there are structures for focusing light rays; in the ear there are structures for amplifying sound.

**Sense organs** are groups of receptor cells that respond to specific stimuli.

- The eyes respond to light rays and give us our sense of sight.
- The nose responds to chemicals in the air and gives us our sense of smell.
- The tongue responds to chemicals in our food and drink and gives us our sense of taste.
- The ears respond to sound vibrations and give us our sense of hearing. The ear also detects movement and position of the body, so provides information about our balance.
- The skin responds to pressure and gives us our sense of touch. It also detects pain and temperature (see pages 130 and 132).

## Eye structure

Your eye sits inside a socket in the skull and is moved about by three pairs of eye muscles as you can see in the diagram.

At the front of the eye is the transparent **cornea**, through which light enters the eye. Light then passes through the **pupil**, which is a hole in the centre of the pigmented **iris**, through the lens to the **retina** at the back of the eye. The retina is the tissue with light-sensitive receptor cells.

At the very front of the eye is the **conjunctiva**. This is a delicate, transparent layer, which provides protection. It is kept moist by the tear glands that make the tears that wash your eye clean every time you blink. Tears also contain **lysozyme**, an enzyme that kills bacteria.

In humans, the eyes are set side by side at the front of the head as opposed to at the side, like a rabbit. What you see in front of you is called your visual field. As the eyes are a few centimetres apart, each eye views the same visual field but from a slightly different angle. Just try shutting your eyes alternately to experience this. The two fields of view overlap to give stereoscopic vision which gives us the ability to judge distances accurately. Stereoscopic vision is an essential adaptation for tree-dwelling animals, such as monkeys, and predators, such as lions and tigers, which must judge distances accurately to survive.

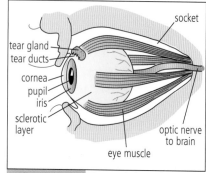

**Figure 12.4.1** The eye in its socket.

## The pupil reflex

If you look in the mirror you will see that there are muscles in your iris. The role of the iris and pupil is to regulate the intensity of light that reaches the sensitive retina. The **circular muscles** are arranged around the pupil. The **radial muscles** run outwards from the pupil like the spokes in a wheel.

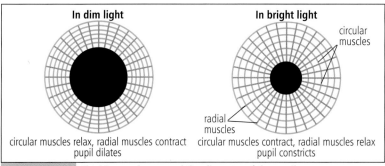

**In dim light**

circular muscles relax, radial muscles contract
pupil dilates

**In bright light**

circular muscles

radial muscles

circular muscles contract, radial muscles relax
pupil constricts

**Figure 12.4.2** The iris muscles control the diameter of the pupil.

In *dim light* the circular muscles **relax** and the radial muscles **contract**. This **dilates** (widens) the pupil and so more light is able to reach the retina.

In *bright light* the circular muscles **contract** and the radial muscles **relax**. This **constricts** (narrows) the pupil and so less light reaches the retina to avoid damage.

This is another example of a simple reflex arc. The retina is stimulated by the intensity of light reaching it. It sends impulses along sensory neurones in the optic nerve which connect with motor neurones in the brain. Impulses pass along the motor neurones to the iris muscles which contract or relax to alter the size of the pupil. This protective reflex makes sure that the retina is not damaged by bright light, but receives enough light when it is not so bright.

**EXAMINER SAYS...**

The sensory system also has receptors inside the body for detecting changes in things like blood temperature and the tension in our muscles. This information helps with homeostasis (see Unit 11) and in controlling our balance and posture.

**EXAMINER SAYS...**

Here is a way to remember this: the three C's: circular, contract, constrict.

### SUMMARY QUESTIONS

1 Name the stimuli that each of the following sense organs respond to:
   a ears, b skin, c eyes, d tongue, e nose.

2 Give the name of the part of the eye which carries out each of the following functions:
   a controls the intensity of light entering the eye
   b protects the front of the eye
   c secretes the enzyme lysozyme
   d allows light to pass through the iris.

3 a State what happens to each of the following in bright light:
   i circular muscles of the iris, ii radial muscles of the iris,
   iii the size of the pupil.
   b State what happens to each of the above in dim light.
   c Explain how the pupil reflex is controlled.
   d Suggest why doctors shine a light in people's eyes when they are unconscious.

### KEY POINTS

1 Sense organs are groups of receptor cells that respond to specific stimuli: light, sound, touch, temperature and chemicals.

2 The pupil reflex involves the coordination of radial muscles and circular muscles in the iris to control the intensity of light entering the eye through the pupil.

**LEARNING OUTCOMES**

- Describe the structure and function of the eye including accommodation
- Distinguish between rods and cones, in terms of function and distribution

## Inner structure of the eye

The eye is a complex organ which is composed of different tissues, such as fibrous tissue, muscle tissue, sensory tissue and blood. Each tissue has a function to help with the detection of light. The diagram shows you the structures in the eye and their functions.

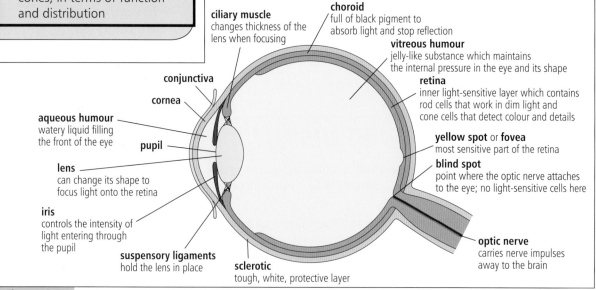

**ciliary muscle**
changes thickness of the lens when focusing

**conjunctiva**

**cornea**

**aqueous humour**
watery liquid filling the front of the eye

**pupil**

**lens**
can change its shape to focus light onto the retina

**iris**
controls the intensity of light entering through the pupil

**suspensory ligaments**
hold the lens in place

**sclerotic**
tough, white, protective layer

**choroid**
full of black pigment to absorb light and stop reflection

**vitreous humour**
jelly-like substance which maintains the internal pressure in the eye and its shape

**retina**
inner light-sensitive layer which contains rod cells that work in dim light and cone cells that detect colour and details

**yellow spot** or **fovea**
most sensitive part of the retina

**blind spot**
point where the optic nerve attaches to the eye; no light-sensitive cells here

**optic nerve**
carries nerve impulses away to the brain

**Figure 12.5.1**

**EXAMINER SAYS...**

In Unit 2 we dealt with cells, tissues, organs and organ systems. The eye is a very good example of an organ where you can identify tissues (e.g. muscle tissue) and cells (e.g. rod and cone cells). The eye is part of an organ system: the sensory system.

## Rods and cones

Light enters the eye through the transparent cornea, it then passes through the lens and is focused on the retina. In the retina there are cells which are sensitive to light called **rods** and **cones**.

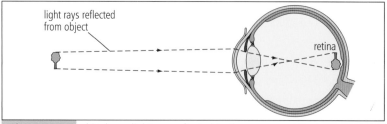

light rays reflected from object

retina

**Figure 12.5.2** This shows light rays refracted by the cornea and the lens.

Rod cells are responsible for night vision and respond to light of low intensity. They are located mainly around the periphery of the retina.

Cone cells are responsible for colour vision and only respond to light of high intensity. We have most of our cones in the **fovea** where the light from the centre of the visual field is focused. When light stimulates rods and cones, they send impulses to the brain along the optic nerve. The brain interprets these impulses to make a picture. Notice that the image on the retina is inverted (upside down) because of the way the light rays reflected from top and bottom of an object enter the eye and cross over behind the lens. Information about this inverted image goes to the brain where it is interpreted the right way up. We learn to do this in the first few months of life.

## Accommodation

Accommodation is the term used to describe the changes that occur in the eye when focusing on far and near objects. As light enters the eye it must be refracted (bent) so that we can see the image clearly. We call this focusing. About 60% of the refraction of the light rays is done by the cornea and the rest is done by the lens. The lens is surrounded by elastic tissue which can be stretched and can recoil. The shape of the lens is controlled by the **ciliary muscles**.

If you are looking at a distant object:

- the ciliary muscles relax,
- the pressure inside the eye pulls the suspensory ligaments tight (or taut) so the lens is pulled into an **elliptical** (thin) shape. Light rays are refracted as they pass through the lens and focused on the retina. The distant object is in focus.

If you are looking at a near object:

- the ciliary muscles contract to counteract the pressure inside the eye,
- the suspensory ligaments are not pulled and become slack so the elastic tissue around the lens recoils so the lens becomes more **spherical** (fatter). Light rays are refracted more than they were when looking at the distant object. The near object is in focus.

The control of the shape of the lens by the ciliary muscles is another simple reflex. This too is protective – if you cannot see where you are going clearly you will damage yourself.

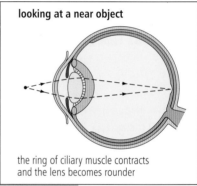

looking at a distant object

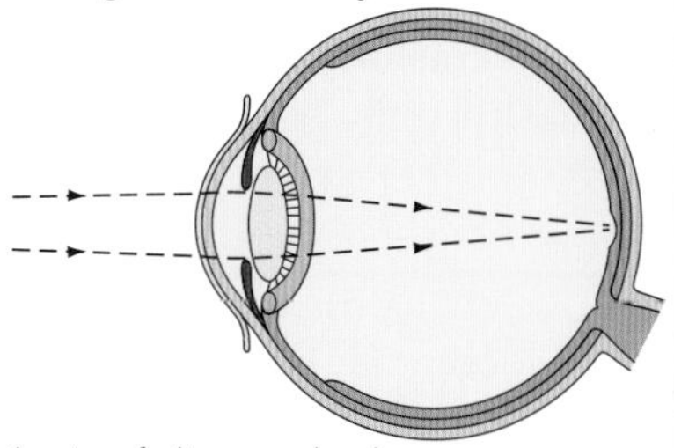

the ring of ciliary muscle relaxes and the lens is pulled into a thin shape

**Figure 12.5.3**

looking at a near object

the ring of ciliary muscle contracts and the lens becomes rounder

**Figure 12.5.4**

## SUMMARY QUESTIONS

1 Give the name in each case for the part of the eye that:
   a is sensitive to light
   b controls the intensity of light entering the eye
   c forms the tough, white, outer layer of the eye
   e forms the jelly-like substance that gives the eye its shape
   f transmits nerve impulses to the brain
   g prevents reflection in the eye
   h controls the shape of the lens.

2 a Explain what happens to each of the following when the eye views a distant object:
     i the ciliary muscles, ii the suspensory ligaments,
     iii the shape of the lens.
   b Explain what happens to each of these structures when the eye views a near object.

3 Describe the distribution of rods and cones in the retina and explain their functions.

### KEY POINTS

1 The ciliary muscles, suspensory ligaments and the lens are all involved in accommodation (focusing) in the eye.

2 In the retina, rod cells are distributed around the periphery and respond to light of low intensity. Cone cells respond to high light intensity and detect colour. The fovea is made entirely of cones.

## LEARNING OUTCOMES

- Define the term *hormone*
- State the role of adrenaline in control of body metabolism
- Compare the nervous system with the endocrine system
- Discuss the use of hormones in food production

## EXAMINER SAYS...

The term 'secretion' means that cells make a substance that is useful for the body and release it into the blood or some other part of the body, e.g. the gut. Do not confuse secretion with 'excretion', which is the removal of metabolic waste (see page 134).

Adrenaline is released during times of excitement, fear or stress.

## The endocrine system

A **hormone** is a chemical produced by an **endocrine gland** and transported in the blood. Endocrine means that the gland produces hormones that are secreted into the bloodstream rather than into a duct. Hormones travel throughout the body but only certain organs or tissues recognise each hormone and respond to it. These are referred to as target organs.

Hormones coordinate the activities of the body but in a different way to the nervous system. Hormones can affect the rate of metabolism, growth and development. After they have performed their function they are broken down by the liver.

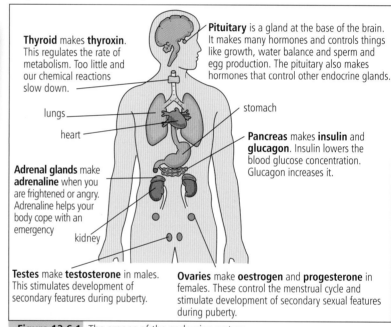

**Thyroid** makes **thyroxin**. This regulates the rate of metabolism. Too little and our chemical reactions slow down.

**Pituitary** is a gland at the base of the brain. It makes many hormones and controls things like growth, water balance and sperm and egg production. The pituitary also makes hormones that control other endocrine glands.

lungs

heart

stomach

**Pancreas** makes **insulin** and **glucagon**. Insulin lowers the blood glucose concentration. Glucagon increases it.

**Adrenal glands** make **adrenaline** when you are frightened or angry. Adrenaline helps your body cope with an emergency

kidney

**Testes** make **testosterone** in males. This stimulates development of secondary features during puberty.

**Ovaries** make **oestrogen** and **progesterone** in females. These control the menstrual cycle and stimulate development of secondary sexual features during puberty.

**Figure 12.6.1** The organs of the endocrine system.

## Adrenaline

Adrenaline is produced by the adrenal glands which are located above the kidneys. Adrenaline helps the body prepare for action by stimulating the following.

- Liver cells to convert glycogen to glucose, which diffuses into the blood. This makes more glucose reach the muscles as a source of energy for the rapid contractions needed for sudden action.
- The heart rate to increase so that more glucose and oxygen are delivered to the muscles for energy release.
- Dilation (widening) of the airways so more air reaches the alveoli in the lungs for more gas exchange.
- Vasodilation of arterioles in the brain and muscles, so more glucose and oxygen are delivered to these organs.
- Vasoconstriction of arterioles in the gut and other organs, allowing blood to be diverted to the muscles.

## Comparing the endocrine and nervous systems

The endocrine system and the nervous system act to control and coordinate the activities of the body. The table below compares the ways in which they work.

| feature | nervous system | endocrine system |
|---------|---------------|------------------|
| structures | nerves | glands containing secretory cells |
| forms of information | electrical impulses | hormones (chemicals) |
| pathways | along neurones | in the blood |
| speed of information transfer | fast | slow |
| duration of effects | short-lived, e.g. muscle contracts for a short time | usually slow and longer lasting (some are rapid, e.g. response to adrenaline) |
| target area | localised – only the area immediately at the end of a neurone | whole tissue or organ; some hormones affect the whole body |
| response | muscle contraction or secretion by glands | many responses, e.g. conversion of glucose to glycogen, protein synthesis, rate of respiration |

## Hormones in food production

Farmers in some countries use hormones to increase the growth rate of their animals or their ability to produce certain products like milk. **Bovine somatotropin (BST)** is a protein hormone produced by cattle. If dairy cows are given extra quantities of this hormone, they produce up to 20% more milk. Farmers can use this hormone to increase the milk yield of their herd and so increase profits. They may also be able to reduce the size of their herd so cutting down costs.

There are, however, concerns about the use of BST in cattle.

• Some people are worried about drinking milk from BST-treated cows. There should not be a risk to most consumers since only tiny quantities of BST get into milk and are digested into amino acids in the gut.

• There are animal welfare concerns as some cows treated with BST have become infertile. BST-treated cows are more likely to get **mastitis** (an inflammation of the udders) due to the abnormally large quantities of milk produced.

• There is a surplus of milk in some parts of the world. The European Union (EU) imposed a milk quota to prevent farmers from producing too much milk, but with rising demand from India and China this is being scrapped. The EU banned the use of BST in 1994. It is also banned in New Zealand, but is used by dairy farmers in the USA.

### EXAMINER SAYS...

Setting out tables in this way ensures you make direct comparisons between the two systems, as here, or whatever else you choose to compare.

### KEY POINTS

1 Hormones are chemicals, produced by endocrine glands that circulate through the blood and alter the activity of target organs.

2 Adrenaline stimulates the liver, heart, lungs and arterioles in muscles and gut during stress and emergencies.

3 Bovine somatotropin is a hormone that is used to increase milk production in cattle.

### SUMMARY QUESTIONS

1 What is meant by the following terms:
a endocrine system, b hormone, c target organ?

2 Discuss the use of BST to increase milk production, pointing out its advantages and possible disadvantages.

# Tropic responses

## LEARNING OUTCOMES

- Define the terms *geotropism* and *phototropism*
- Explain the chemical control of plant growth by auxins
- Explain the effect of synthetic plant hormones used as weedkillers

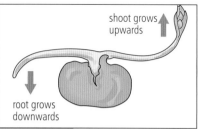

**Figure 12.7.1** Which way is up?

## EXAMINER SAYS...

*A seed germinates. A root and then a shoot appear. Which way is up? Geotropic responses ensure the survival of the seedling as it establishes itself in competition with other plants nearby.*

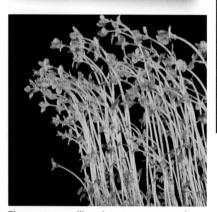

These cress seedlings have grown towards the light.

## Tropisms

Plants respond to stimuli such as light and gravity. Different parts of the plant either grow towards or away from the different stimuli. These growth responses are much slower than the responses coordinated by the nervous systems in animals. They are called **tropisms**.

## Geotropism

Whichever way a seed is planted, the root always grows downwards in the direction of gravity. The shoot always grows upwards against the direction of gravity.

A growth response to gravity is called a **geotropism**.

Roots are **positively geotropic** because they grow in the same direction as the stimulus, gravity. They grow downwards into the soil to absorb water and mineral ions.

Shoots, on the other hand, are **negatively geotropic**. They will always grow in the opposite direction to the direction of gravity. This ensures that shoots grow upwards getting the leaves into sunlight.

## Auxin

A plant hormone called **auxin** controls this growth. Auxin in shoots stimulates growth by causing the cells to elongate, but in roots auxin inhibits growth by slowing down cell elongation.

If a seedling is put on its side the auxin builds up on the lower side of the shoot and root. In the shoot the auxin builds up on the lower side and stimulates the cells there to elongate and therefore to grow more on the lower side. This causes the shoot to bend upwards.

In the root the auxin also builds up on the lower side. But auxin slows down growth in a root by inhibiting cell elongation. As a result, cells on the upper side of the root elongate more than those on the lower side so the root bends downwards.

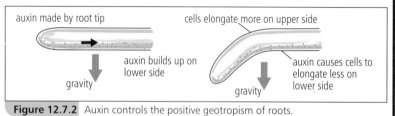

**Figure 12.7.2** Auxin controls the positive geotropism of roots.

## Phototropism

The cress seedlings in the photo have been put in a window for some time and their shoots have grown towards the light.

This sort of growth response is called a **phototropism**. Because shoots grow *towards* the light they are **positively phototropic**.

The advantage of this tropic response is that the leaves expose the maximum surface area to the light. They can then absorb light more efficiently for photosynthesis.

Extension

This response is again controlled by auxin made by the shoot tip. When a shoot only receives light from one side most auxin is found on the shaded side. The auxin stimulates the cells on the shaded side to elongate more than the cells on the illuminated side. The shoot grows more on the shaded side and bends towards the light. Roots are not sensitive to light.

Extension

**EXAMINER SAYS...**

Cells become longer, or elongate, when they absorb water by osmosis. The vacuole swells increasing the turgor pressure inside the cell which causes the cell wall to stretch. Auxins work by making it easier for the walls to stretch.

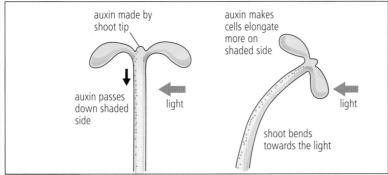

auxin made by shoot tip

auxin makes cells elongate more on shaded side

auxin passes down shaded side

light

light

shoot bends towards the light

**Figure 12.7.3** Auxin controls the positive phototropism of shoots.

## Synthetic plant hormones

Synthetic auxins are very effective as **selective weedkillers**. Important cereal crops like wheat and barley are narrow leaved (monocotyledonous) whereas most of the weeds that compete with them for water, nutrients and light are broad leaved (dicotyledonous). Herbicides like 2,4-D are sprayed on the crop but tend to run off the leaves of the cereal plants because they are thin and point upwards. The weedkillers are more likely to be absorbed by the broad-leaved weeds.

The auxins increase the growth rate of the affected weeds, possibly by increasing the rate of cell division. The weeds cannot provide enough food from photosynthesis to maintain this rate of growth and soon die.

This plant has been sprayed with a hormone weedkiller that has made it grow in a twisted fashion, causing it to die.

**KEY POINTS**

1 A geotropism is a growth response to the stimulus of gravity. Roots are positively geotropic and shoots are negatively geotropic.

2 A phototropism is a growth response to the stimulus of light. Shoots are positively phototropic and grow towards the light.

Extension

3 Auxins are plant hormones that control growth. Synthetic auxins are used as weedkillers by making the weeds grow too fast.

**SUMMARY QUESTIONS**

1 Define each of the following:

a a tropic response, b phototropism, c geotropism.

2 State what growth response will happen in each of the following.

a Some seedlings are placed in a window, in sunlight for 6 hours.

b Some germinating seeds are placed with their roots lying horizontally for a few hours.

Extension

3 Explain the observed growth responses in question **2** in terms of the action of auxin.

4 Explain how synthetic auxins are able to act as weedkillers.

1 Name the two parts of the human nervous system.

2 (a) Make a simple sketch to show the outline shapes of a motor neurone, a sensory neurone and a relay neurone.

(b) State the functions of the three neurones you have drawn.

3 (a) Give an example of a simple reflex action.

(b) Explain the term *reflex arc* by reference to the following:

stimulus, sensory cell, sensory neurone, relay neurone, motor neurone, effector and response.

(c) Explain the roles of simple reflexes in our survival.

4 Define the following terms:

(a) coordination

(b) sense organ

(c) antagonistic.

5 (a) Name the two muscles that move the forearm.

(b) Explain how these muscles bring about movement of the forearm.

6 Which hormone:

(a) prepares the body for emergency action

(b) reduces the concentration of glucose in the blood

(c) controls the rate of chemical reactions in the body

(d) is produced in the testes

(e) is produced in the ovaries?

7 State four ways in which coordination by the nervous system differs from coordination by hormones.

**Extension**

8 What is the difference between a voluntary action and an involuntary action?

9 Make a table to compare rods and cones from the eye.

10 Explain how hormones are used in food production.

11 Describe and explain the roles of auxins in the control of plant growth.

1 In which pathway do nerve impulses travel in a spinal reflex?

A effector $\longrightarrow$ sensory neurone $\longrightarrow$ relay neurone $\longrightarrow$ sensory cell $\longrightarrow$ motor neurone

B motor neurone $\longrightarrow$ relay neurone $\longrightarrow$ sensory neurone $\longrightarrow$ effector

C sensory cell $\longrightarrow$ sensory neurone $\longrightarrow$ effector $\longrightarrow$ relay neurone $\longrightarrow$ motor neurone

D sensory cell $\longrightarrow$ sensory neurone $\longrightarrow$ relay neurone $\longrightarrow$ motor neurone $\longrightarrow$ effector

*(Paper 1)* [1]

2 Where are relay neurones situated?

A effector

B spinal cord

C spinal nerve

D receptor

*(Paper 1)* [1]

3 The diagram shows an arm being lowered. What causes this movement?

A Biceps muscle contracts, triceps muscle contracts.

B Biceps muscle relaxes, triceps muscle contracts.

C Triceps muscle relaxes, biceps muscle contracts.

D Triceps muscle relaxes, biceps muscle relaxes.

*(Paper 1)* [1]

4 The diagram shows the response of a plant shoot to receiving light from one side only. Which statement explains how this response is controlled?

**A**   Auxins stimulate a geotropic response.

**B**   Auxins stimulate a phototropic response.

**C**   Auxins stimulate cells on the side closest to the light to grow faster than the cells on the opposite side.

**D**   Auxins stimulate cells on the side away from the light to grow faster than the cells on the opposite side.   *[1]*

*(Paper 1)*

**5** The diagram shows a vertical section of the eye.
*[3]*

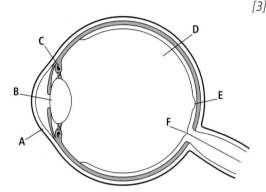

**(a)** Name **A** to **F**.   *[6]*

**(b)** Explain why the eye is a sense organ.   *[2]*

**(c)** A person walks from a dark room into a brightly lit place.

   **(i)**   Describe the change that you would see in the person's pupils.   *[1]*

   **(ii)**  Explain how the change you described in **(i)** is coordinated.   *[5]*

**(d)** A person looks at an object in the distance and then looks down to focus on a book.

   Describe the changes that would occur in the eyes to focus on the book.   *[3]*

*(Paper 2)*

**6** The diagram shows a reflex arc. The arm moves in response to touching the pin.

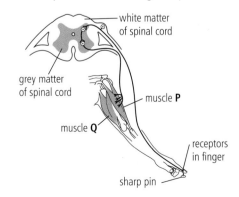

**(a)** State two other stimuli detected by receptors in the skin.   *[2]*

**(b)**  An impulse takes 0.02 seconds to pass from the finger tip to the spinal cord. This is a distance of 1.4 metres. Calculate the speed of the impulse. Show your working.   *[2]*

**(c)** Name the muscles, **P** and **Q**.   *[2]*

**(d)** Describe what happens in this reflex arc after the person puts their finger on the pin until the arm moves in response.   *[6]*

*(Paper 2)*

**7** A scientist investigated the distribution of rods and cones across the retina of a mammal as shown in the diagram. The graph shows the distribution of cones in the retina.

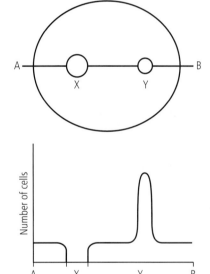

**(a)** Name the parts of the retina **X** and **Y**. Give reasons for your answers.   *[4]*

**(b)** Copy the graph and show on it the distribution of rods in the retina.   *[3]*

**(c)  (i)**   State an involuntary action involving the eye.   *[1]*

   **(ii)**  Explain how the control of an involuntary action differs from the control of a voluntary action.   *[3]*

**(d)** Explain the advantages to an animal of having two coordination systems: the nervous system and the endocrine system.   *[3]*

*(Paper 3)*

# 13 Drugs

## 13.1 Drugs and how they work

### LEARNING OUTCOMES

- Define the term *drug*
- Describe the use of antibiotics in the treatment of bacterial infection

*Extension*

- Explain why antibiotics kill bacteria but not viruses

### What are drugs?

A drug is any substance that is taken into the body that alters or influences chemical reactions in the body.

There are several different types of drug. Some are the active ingredients of medicines and are used to treat and cure people of disease. Others are mood-enhancing and alter sensory perception. Aspirin, paracetamol, morphine and antibiotics are medical drugs designed to suppress pain, counteract the symptoms of 'flu, soothe muscular pain or kill pathogenic bacteria. Alcohol, nicotine and caffeine are socially acceptable drugs that people take for their pleasurable effects, to help them relax or concentrate.

Drugs that tend to be illegal because of their more severe effects are sometimes called **recreational drugs**. Hallucinogens, like Lysergic Acid Diethylamide or LSD, cause psychedelic visions for the drug user. Stimulants, like cocaine, ecstasy and amphetamines are all mood-enhancing drugs which give the user a short-lived feeling of wellbeing and energy. Heroin, although it affects the body in a different way, also gives a feeling of wellbeing.

Drugs act in various ways upon the human body. Some drugs, such as nicotine and heroin, interfere with the way that the nervous system works and these are often abused by people. Many of the mood-enhancing drugs, such as heroin and nicotine, act at synapses in the nervous system and change the way in which neurones send impulses. They do this by combining with protein molecules on the cell membranes of the neurones.

Drugs are broken down in the body by enzymes and the products are excreted. The breakdown products can be detected in the urine, and this is why urine tests are carried out to see if people have been taking drugs. Sportspeople and car drivers who have been in accidents are routinely tested for drugs.

Many drugs have the potential to be **addictive**. If the body comes to rely on the drug a person can become addicted and feel the need to take it regularly. In many countries some or all of the non-medicinal drugs are illegal and possession or dealing in them results in severe punishment.

The body's metabolism may become used to the drug. The liver may produce more enzymes to break it down so that the dose of the drug has to increase to have the effect that the user first experienced. In the case of heroin, synapses may produce more target molecules and if these do not combine with heroin this leads to an increase in the feeling of pain.

### EXAMINER SAYS...

There are many ways to define the term 'drug'. Learn the definition at the top of this page, which covers all the types of drugs we describe, so you can write it from memory.

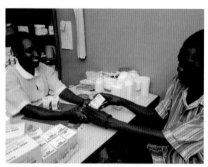

Many medical drugs are dangerous if taken in an uncontrolled way and are available only on prescription from a doctor.

This is how drug **tolerance** develops and it means that people take more of the drug to achieve the same effect. The person has become **dependent** on the drug and cannot survive without it. When people stop taking the drug they may experience **withdrawal symptoms** which can vary from nausea to severe cramp. This makes giving up the drug very difficult.

## Antibiotics

The use of drugs to treat disease is called chemotherapy. **Antibiotics** are a group of chemicals made by microorganisms (bacteria and fungi) that are used in chemotherapy as they kill pathogens or stop their growth. Many antibiotics are synthesised artificially, as that is a more reliable way to obtain sufficient supply and to make them more effective or reduce their side effects.

Antibiotics are prescribed to treat and cure human and animal diseases caused by bacteria and fungi. Penicillin was the first antibiotic to be discovered and mass-produced. Penicillin acts on bacteria by inhibiting cell wall formation, leading to a breakdown of the cell wall and the leakage of cell contents. There are now many penicillins, each of which acts on bacteria slightly differently. There are other groups of antibiotics such as tetracyclines, polymyxins and sulfa drugs.

Some antibiotics act on only a few species of bacteria and are known as **narrow-spectrum** antibiotics. Others, such as tetracycline, affect many species and are known as **broad-spectrum**. Doctors have to know which antibiotic to prescribe for a particular disease. A big problem with antibiotics is that many bacteria have become resistant to them (see page 219).

(see page 219).

**EXAMINER SAYS...**

There are dangers in overusing antibiotics and you may be questioned about these. You will learn about these dangers in Unit 17.

*Extension*

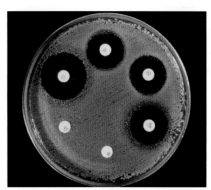

Before prescribing, a doctor may ask for a sensitivity test to be carried out in a hospital laboratory to find out which antibiotic to use against the pathogen that has infected a patient. The white discs on this agar plate contain different antibiotics. Here four antibiotics would be effective because they have killed the bacteria, whereas two would not.

*Extension*

Antibiotics are effective against bacteria and the few fungi that infect us. Viruses are not cells. They do not carry out their own metabolism but rely entirely on the cells of their host for their reproduction. This means that to control viruses we would have to use antibiotics that inhibit our own metabolism and that is not possible. There are anti-viral drugs available, but they work differently to antibiotics.

**KEY POINTS**

1 A drug is a substance taken into the body, which alters or influences chemical reactions in the body.

2 Antibiotics destroy pathogens by disrupting cell wall formation, inhibiting protein synthesis and metabolism in the pathogen cell.

3 Antibiotics cannot kill viruses since they have no cell wall and live inside host cells, taking over their metabolic processes.

*Extension*

**SUMMARY QUESTIONS**

1  a  Define the term *drug*.
   b  Name two drugs that are used as medicines.
   c  Name two mood-enhancing drugs.
   d  Name two drugs that can be harmful but are not illegal in many countries.

2 Explain how antibiotics act to kill pathogens like bacteria and fungi.

3 Explain why antibiotics can kill bacteria but not viruses.

*Extension*

# Heroin

- Describe the effects of the abuse of heroin
- Describe the problems of addiction to heroin, severe withdrawal symptoms and problems such as crime and HIV infection

**EXAMINER SAYS...**

Heroin and alcohol are both depressants. You should use this term when writing about their effects on the body.

**EXAMINER SAYS...**

You should be able to apply these ideas of tolerance and dependence to heroin and alcohol.

## Biology of heroin

Morphine and codeine are two compounds extracted from opium poppies and used as painkillers in medicine. **Heroin** is a compound modified from morphine. Heroin only has limited medical uses as it is highly addictive and so is rarely used.

Heroin is a powerful **depressant** that slows down the nervous system. The molecular structure of heroin is similar to one of the body's own painkillers, known as a natural opiate, which slows down impulses along neurones transferring information from pain receptors to the brain. When people take heroin for the first time they usually feel a warm rush and a feeling of contentment and intense happiness. This state is known as **euphoria**.

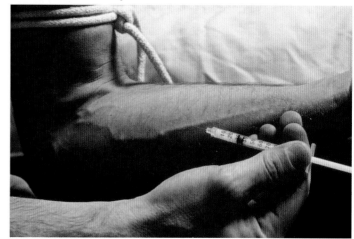

An addict injecting heroin into a vein.

## Addiction to heroin

Heroin becomes part of the body's metabolism and the body quickly gets used to the drug. This includes the nerve cells where it has its effect. More painkillers are needed to prevent them sending impulses to the brain. But the body does not produce more of its own natural painkillers. The feeling of pain becomes unbearable and addicts have to take heroin to reduce the pain. This is how the body develops a **tolerance** to the drug, and it has to be taken in ever greater quantities in order to feel euphoria or just to deaden the pain.

People who start taking heroin want to repeat the feelings they first experienced, but they quickly get 'hooked' or addicted as they are dependent on the drug. This can happen within a matter of 2 to 3 weeks of use.

Heroin is taken by smoking, sniffing or injecting it into a vein. Injecting is highly dangerous as veins can collapse and tissues surrounding injection points start to die, giving the condition known as gangrene. Long-term addicts can run out of suitable places to inject it. Some addicts share needles and syringes. The danger associated with this is the transmission of the human immunodeficiency virus (HIV) and the virus that causes hepatitis (see page 198).

## Social problems

Heroin addiction is a serious problem for many countries. The drug often dominates the lives of addicts and they think only about how they can get their next 'fix'. The drug can be expensive, which drives many people to turn to crime in order to fund their habit. It can often become difficult to keep a job and addiction often leads to family breakdown and homelessness. Addicts tend to shun friends and families, preferring the company of other addicts, and so they become isolated from society.

Heroin is produced in Afghanistan, which is the largest producer of heroin in the world, and the Golden Triangle (Laos, Vietnam, Burma and Thailand). It is then trafficked illegally into Europe, North America and elsewhere. Networks of criminal gangs help process and smuggle the drugs into developed countries and distribute drugs to drug dealers who sell it on the streets. Most of the heroin-producing countries have harsh penalties, such as life imprisonment and the death penalty, to stop trafficking. A user who stops taking the drug experiences very unpleasant **withdrawal symptoms**. These can include sleeplessness and hallucinations (imagining terrible things are happening to them), muscle cramps, sweating, vomiting and nausea. These symptoms are often known as cold turkey. There have been two cases of people in the UK contracting necrotising fasciitis – a flesh-eating disease – from bacteria in Afghan heroin.

A great deal of will power and support from others is needed to overcome heroin addiction. Often the only way to overcome the habit is to go into **rehabilitation**. This may involve staying in a treatment centre. In some countries addicts are given another drug, methadone, which gives some of the same effects as heroin. The treatment consists of gradually reducing the dose. Different countries have different approaches to treating heroin addiction. For example, in Malaysia, military style rehabilitation is mandatory. In the UK, both heroin and methadone can be prescribed for users in an attempt to get them off the drug. In countries like Russia, however, methadone is illegal.

Drugs are often the cause of many people becoming involved with crime. Support for drug addicts who want to give up their habit is available in rehabilitation centres.

Heroin addiction is a serious form of addition, but far more people put their lives at risk from nicotine addiction.

## KEY POINTS

1 Heroin is a highly addictive depressant. While the user experiences a feeling of euphoria, tolerance and dependence develop, resulting in addiction.

2 Heroin addicts may turn to crime to obtain money for their next dose. Shared needles have resulted in the spread of hepatitis and HIV amongst addicts who inject heroin.

## SUMMARY QUESTIONS

1 Define each of the following in relation to drug use:

   a tolerance, b dependence,

   c addiction, d rehabilitation.

2 a Why is heroin described as a highly addictive, depressant drug?

   b If a heroin addict stops taking the drug, describe what happens to them.

3 Heroin addiction can lead to crime, social and family problems and the spread of viral diseases.

   Explain how these consequences can affect society in a negative way.

| type of drink | volume (cm³) | alcohol by volume (%) | units |
|---|---|---|---|
| alcopop | 400 | 5 | 2 |
| extra strong lager | 500 | 8 | 4 |
| cider (glass) | 500 | 4 | 2 |
| cocktail | 125 | 40 | 5 |
| wine | 175 | 12.5 | 2.2 |
| spirit (vodka) and mixer | 35 | 40 | 1.4 |

alcopop    extra strong lager    cider

cocktail    wine    spirit and mixer

**Figure 13.3.1**

## Biology of alcohol

Alcohol is a socially acceptable drug in many countries in the world. In some, its supply and consumption are very tightly regulated and in others it is banned entirely.

When alcohol is consumed, it is absorbed into the blood very quickly since it is a small molecule that does not need to be digested. It is also soluble in cell membranes, so it is absorbed very quickly through the wall of the stomach and small intestine. The presence of food in the stomach slows down its absorption.

Alcohol gets distributed throughout the body in the blood. Some is lost through the lungs and the kidneys. It is absorbed by liver cells and broken down by enzymes so that its concentration in the blood decreases gradually. This breakdown happens more quickly in men than in women because men have more of these enzymes and their enzymes tend to be more active. They also have more water and less fat in their bodies than women, which tends to cause the concentration of alcohol in the blood to decrease more quickly.

Like heroin, alcohol is a depressant. It affects the brain by slowing down the transmission of nerve impulses. In small quantities, this has the effect of removing inhibitions so people find it easier to socialise with others. With larger quantities this lack of inhibitions leads to loss of coordination, judgment and control of fine movements. Unlike heroin, alcohol does not lead to addiction as quickly if at all. Many people drink alcohol in small to moderate quantities throughout their lives without becoming addicted.

The alcohol content of drinks is measured in units. One unit is 8 grams of alcohol which is the quantity broken down in the liver in an hour. The UK government recommends that men should not drink more than 3 to 4 units a day and women 2 to 3 (but see page 190 for advice about drinking during pregnancy).

The blood alcohol concentration (BAC) is measured in milligrams of alcohol per 100 cm³ of blood. The table on the next page shows you the effects of increasing BAC on behaviour.

## Addiction

Some people become dependent upon alcohol and are sometimes referred to as alcoholics. They develop a tolerance as more enzymes that metabolise alcohol are made in the liver. They therefore need to take greater quantities of alcohol to get the same effect. They feel tense and irritable and find it hard to cope with everyday problems without a drink. Alcoholics can cause their families pain and misery. They can become aggressive after drinking and spend a lot of money on drink.

| units of alcohol | | blood alcohol concentration (mg per 100 cm³ blood) | effects of alcohol on behaviour |
|---|---|---|---|
| men | women | | |
| 1½–3 | ½–2 | 20–50 | reduced tension, relaxed feeling, increase in confidence |
| 3–5 | 2–3 | 50–80 | euphoria, impaired judgment, loss of fine motor control, loss of inhibitions |
| 5–8 | 3–5 | 80–120 | slurred speech, impaired coordination, walking in a staggered way, slow reaction times |
| 8–15 | 5–10 | 120–260 | loss of control of voluntary actions, loss of balance, erratic behaviour, signs of emotion and aggression |
| 15–26 | 10–15 | 260–400 | total loss of coordination, difficulty remaining upright, extreme confusion |
| >26 | >15 | >400 | coma, depression of breathing control centres in the brain, death |

### Social problems

The misuse of alcohol is a factor in crime, family disputes, marital breakdown, child neglect and abuse, absenteeism from work, vandalism, assault and violent crime including murder. In some countries the damage done by alcohol is considerable and often difficult for governments to measure.

Alcohol and other drugs are involved in many road accidents. Alcohol has adverse effects on people's concentration while at the same time making them feel more confident. In some countries it is against the law to drink alcohol and then drive a vehicle or operate machinery. In most of Europe the legal limit of alcohol in the blood is 50 mg per 100 cm³. There are severe penalties for driving with more than the legal limit.

Alcohol and other drugs are thought to be the cause of many road accidents. Alcohol slows reaction times so it takes longer to respond to stimuli, such as traffic lights.

### Long-term effects of alcohol

Drinking large quantities of alcohol over a number of years can have serious effects on health. It can lead to stomach ulcers, heart disease and brain damage. The liver is the part of the body that breaks down alcohol. Drinking large quantities of alcohol impedes metabolism in the liver so that fat is stored and builds up. This condition is known as fatty liver. If this continues the liver tissue is damaged and replaced by fibrous scar tissue.

If heavy drinking continues then the liver becomes full of nodules. This is the condition known as **cirrhosis**. The liver becomes less able to carry out its job of removing the toxins from the blood. This condition is not reversible and is fatal unless the person stops drinking. Long-term alcohol consumption also leads to brain damage with changes in personality and behaviour.

### KEY POINTS

1 Alcohol is a depressant and if taken in excess, it can lengthen reaction times and bring about a lack of self-control in a person.

2 Long-term effects of alcohol abuse include cirrhosis of the liver and brain damage.

### SUMMARY QUESTIONS

1 a Describe how alcohol reaches the brain after it is drunk.

b What effects does alcohol have on the brain?

c Explain why a person who has drunk alcohol should not drive.

2 a What are the long-term effects of alcohol on the body?

b Summarise the effects of alcohol on society and discuss the banning of its use.

# Smoking and health

**EXAMINER SAYS...**

The chemicals in tobacco smoke have effects on the heart and circulatory system as well as on the gas exchange system. You may be asked about this in questions on transport in humans.

People who smoke large numbers of cigarettes every day have a high risk of dying from a smoking-related disease.

Tobacco plants make nicotine as a way to protect against insect attack. It is a natural pesticide. Nicotine happens to have a molecular structure that allows it to interact with our nervous system and so fits the definition of the term drug. Smoking has been linked with many diseases. It is a direct cause of lung diseases, including lung cancer, and is implicated in other cancers and in heart disease.

## Biology of tobacco smoke

**Nicotine** is absorbed very quickly through the alveoli to enter the bloodstream. Like heroin it is a drug that interacts with nerve cells at synapses. But unlike heroin it is a stimulant, not a depressant. Nicotine makes the heart beat faster and narrows the arterioles, which increases the blood pressure. It also increases the stickiness of blood platelets that promote blood clotting.

**Tar** is the black sticky material that collects in the lungs as smoke cools. It does not pass into the bloodstream. Tar irritates the lining of the airways and stimulates them to produce more mucus. This tends to accumulate because the cilia which normally help to remove mucus are damaged by smoking, resulting in narrowing of the airways. Smokers cough to make this material move to the back of the throat giving rise to 'smoker's cough'. There are about 4000 different chemical compounds in tar. Some of these can cause cancer and are described as **carcinogenic**.

**Carbon monoxide** is a poisonous gas. It is absorbed by haemoglobin in red blood cells. It combines permanently with haemoglobin so reduces the volume of oxygen that blood can carry by as much as 10%. This puts an added strain on the heart that may already be beating harder and faster in response to nicotine. At a time when it needs more oxygen for its respiration, there is less delivered by the blood as it flows through the coronary arteries to supply heart muscle. If a woman smokes during pregnancy there may not be enough oxygen in the blood for the fetus to develop properly. Due to this the baby may have a smaller birth weight and is sometimes premature (see page 190).

**Smoke particles** are small burnt fragments of tobacco. They accumulate in lung tissue and stimulate the body's defence system to remove them.

## Diseases caused by smoking

### Chronic bronchitis and emphysema

The effect of hot tobacco smoke on the airways is to reduce the efficiency with which they keep the lungs clean. Tobacco smoke irritates the lining of the airways. Mucus-secreting cells produce more mucus in response, but cilia on the cells lining the air passages stop beating. This means that mucus and the dust, dirt and bacteria that stick to it are not removed from the lungs. It accumulates and bacteria multiply. This stimulates the body's immune system to send phagocytes to the places where this happens – particularly the bronchi where particles settle out of the air.

You can see why this happens if you look at a diagram of the lungs (see page 118). There is almost a right-angle bend at the base of the trachea. The bronchi become blocked as there is less space for air to flow. Large amounts of **phlegm** (a mixture of mucus, bacteria and white blood cells) are produced, which people attempt to cough up. This condition is **chronic bronchitis**. Chronic means long term. People with this condition find it difficult to move air into and out of their lungs as the bronchi are partly blocked.

Particles, bacteria and tar reach the alveoli. Phagocytes digest a pathway through the lining of the alveoli to reach them. Eventually this weakens the walls of the alveoli so much that they break down and burst, reducing the surface area for gas exchange. This condition is **emphysema**, which leaves people gasping for breath as they cannot absorb enough oxygen or remove carbon dioxide efficiently. Many long-term smokers have both these conditions.

### Lung cancer

Ninety percent of cases of lung cancer occur in people who smoke or who have smoked. The cause of lung cancer is the carcinogens in tar. These substances promote changes in the DNA of cells lining the airways. The cells grow and divide out of control. This growth is very slow but eventually may form a small group of cells known as a **tumour**. If this is not discovered, it may grow to occupy a large area of the lung and block airways and blood vessels. Worse still a part of the tumour may break off and spread into other organs.

### Heart disease

Tobacco smoke increases the chances that fat will deposit in the walls of arteries. As nicotine increases the chance that blood will clot, there is an increased risk of developing coronary heart disease (see page 106). Blocked arteries reduce the supply of oxygen to the heart and this damages the heart muscle.

EXAMINER SAYS...

You should revise the way in which mucus and cilia keep the lungs clean before reading this section, see page 123. You can expect questions on how they work and what happens to them in the lungs of a smoker.

A small cancerous tumour between alveoli in the lungs.

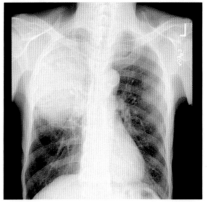

X-ray showing a cancer in the right lung. Compare with the X-ray on page 118.

### SUMMARY QUESTIONS

1 Define the following words:

   a nicotine, b tar, c carbon monoxide, d carcinogen.

2 Explain how cigarette smoking is linked to an increased risk of developing:

   a lung cancer, b bronchitis, c heart disease.

3 a What is the function of the alveolus (air sac)?

   b Describe two ways in which a healthy alveolus is adapted to carry out its function.

   c Describe what happens to alveoli in people who develop emphysema.

   d Explain how emphysema affects the functioning of the lungs.

### KEY POINTS

1 Tobacco smoke consists of nicotine, tar, carbon monoxide and smoke particles.

2 Smoking is associated with diseases such as bronchitis, emphysema, heart disease and lung cancer.

1 Write definitions of the following terms:
  (a) drug
  (b) drug tolerance
  (c) antibiotic
  (d) addiction.

2 Heroin and alcohol are both depressants. Explain the meaning of the term *depressant*.

3 (a) Describe briefly the effects of heroin on the body.
  (b) Describe the problems for the individual and for society when a person becomes addicted to heroin.
  (c) When someone dependent on heroin stops taking the drug they may experience severe effects. Name the term given to these effects.

4 (a) Describe the effects on the body as the alcohol content of the blood increases.
  (b) Explain the dangers of drinking alcohol and then driving a motor car.
  (c) Describe the effects on the liver of excessive consumption of alcohol.

5 The gas exchange system consists of the trachea (windpipe), bronchi and lungs. Tobacco smoke has serious effects on the gas exchange system.
  (a) Describe the effects of tobacco smoke on the gas exchange system of someone who has only been smoking for a few years.
  (b) (i) Name three diseases of the gas exchange system that are associated with long-term smoking.
      (ii) For each disease that you have named in (i), describe the effects on the tissues of the gas exchange system.

6 Describe how antibiotics are used to treat disease.

7 Explain why antibiotics are not used for the treatment of viral diseases.

Extension

1 The best definition of the term *drug* is:
  A any substance taken into the body that influences chemical reactions in the body
  B any substance that affects the nervous system
  C substances that are taken to treat disease
  D substances that may become addictive

*(Paper 1)*                                    [1]

2 The drug in tobacco smoke is:
  A carbon dioxide
  B carbon monoxide
  C nicotine
  D tar

*(Paper 1)*                                    [1]

3 Which of the following is *not* related to the taking of heroin?
  A The drug is a stimulant.
  B The drug is addictive.
  C Not taking the drug may lead to severe withdrawal symptoms.
  D The drug is a depressant.

*(Paper 1)*                                    [1]

4 Which component in tobacco smoke is the cause of lung cancer?
  A carbon dioxide
  B carbon monoxide
  C nicotine
  D tar

*(Paper 1)*                                    [1]

5 Drugs may be classified as useful and harmful drugs.
  (a) Explain why antibiotics are classified as (i) drugs, and (ii) useful drugs.    [4]
  (b) (i) Name one drug that is classified as a harmful drug.    [1]
      (ii) Explain briefly why the drug you have named is classified as a harmful drug.

*(Paper 2)*                                    [2]

6 People who inject drugs, such as heroin, are known as injecting drug users. The table shows the number of injecting drug users who were diagnosed as HIV+ between 2002 to 2006 in the countries of the World Health Organization's European region.

| year | number of injecting drug users diagnosed as HIV+ |
|------|---------------------------------------------------|
| 2002 | 29 139 |
| 2003 | 22 351 |
| 2004 | 21 272 |
| 2005 | 21 982 |
| 2006 | 24 102 |

Source: WHO

(a) Describe the trend shown in the table. *[4]*

(b) Calculate the percentage change in the number of injecting drug users diagnosed as HIV+ between 2002 and 2006. *[2]*

(c) Explain how people who take heroin are likely to become infected with HIV. *[2]*

*(Paper 2)*

**7** The graph shows the number of deaths in the UK in which alcohol was the major cause between 1991 and 2006. The death rates are shown as number of deaths per 100 000 men and per 100 000 women.

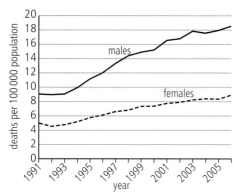

Source: Office of National Statistics. Crown Copyright material is reproduced with the permission of the Controller, Office of Public Sector Information (OPSI)

(a) Use the graph to describe the trends in deaths in which alcohol was the major cause. *[3]*

(b) Calculate the percentage increase in death rates for men between 1991 and 2006. *[2]*

(c) Cirrhosis of the liver is often caused by heavy consumption of alcohol. The number of cases of cirrhosis has increased in the UK, especially among young people. Explain how you would find out if the increase in the number of cases of cirrhosis is likely to be due to an increase in alcohol consumption. *[2]*

(d) Explain why driving a motor car under the influence of alcohol is dangerous. *[3]*

*(Paper 2)*

**8** The graph shows the number of cigarettes

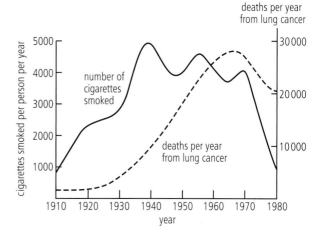

smoked by men each year in the UK from 1910 to 1980. The dotted line shows the number of deaths of men from lung cancer over the same period.

(a) State the year in which there was:
   (i) the highest consumption of cigarettes, and
   (ii) the highest number of deaths from lung cancer. *[2]*

(b) Describe what happened to:
   (i) cigarette consumption, and
   (ii) deaths from lung cancer over the period shown by the graph. *[5]*

(c) Discuss whether the graph provides any evidence to support the idea that smoking causes lung cancer. *[3]*

*(Paper 2)*

**9** In many countries antibiotics are only available on prescription from a doctor.

(a) Explain why antibiotics are prescribed. *[2]*

(b) Under what circumstances should antibiotics *not* be prescribed? *[1]*

(c) Discuss the dangers of overusing antibiotics. *[4]*

*(Paper 3)*

# 14 Reproduction in plants

## 14.1

# Asexual and sexual reproduction

### LEARNING OUTCOMES

- Define *asexual* and *sexual* *reproduction*
- Describe asexual reproduction in bacteria, spore formation in fungi and tuber formation in potatoes
- Discuss the advantages and disadvantages of asexual and sexual reproduction

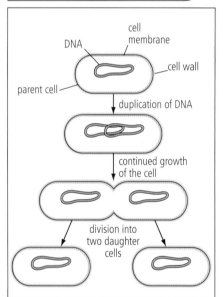

**Figure 14.1.1** Binary fission in bacteria. Each new bacterial cell is genetically identical to each other and to the parent cell.

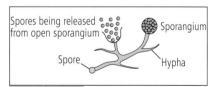

**Figure 14.1.2** Spores are produced by the pin mould inside sporangia.

**Reproduction** means producing new living organisms. Animals and plants reproduce to make new individuals of the same species. There are two types of reproduction: **asexual** and **sexual reproduction**.

## Asexual reproduction

In asexual reproduction there is only *one* parent. All the offspring are identical to the parent as they inherit exactly the same genetic information. They are genetically identical to the parent, which means there is little variation amongst the offspring. Any variation is due to the effect of the environment, for example the availability of nutrients and water determine how well organisms grow. Bacteria, fungi and plants reproduce asexually.

Bacteria are microscopic organisms made up of one cell. They do not have a nucleus, but a loop of DNA. When bacteria reproduce asexually the DNA loop is copied so that there is some for each new cell. You can find some information about how DNA is copied on page 204. The bacterial cell divides into two by making a new cell wall. This type of asexual reproduction is called **binary fission**, because the parent cell splits into two.

Pin mould is a fungus which grows on bread (see page 11). It reproduces asexually by making **spores**. These are small and light, like specks of dust, and they float through the air. When a spore lands on a damp surface, it splits open and a thread grows out. This thread or **hypha**, grows over the surface of bread forming a dense network of threads called a **mycelium**. Eventually short hyphae grow upwards and produce spore cases or **sporangia** at their tips. Inside each sporangium hundreds of new spores are formed asexually by division of the nuclei. Each nucleus gains a small quantity of cytoplasm and a protective spore case. When ready, the sporangia break open and the spores are dispersed.

Potatoes reproduce asexually by means of **stem tubers**, which are swollen underground stems that grow from the parent plant. Sucrose is transported in the phloem from the leaves into these underground stems that swell as they convert the sucrose into starch. The parent plant dies at the end of the growing season leaving the tubers in the ground to survive over the winter. However, farmers dig them up and sell them. Some are kept as 'seed' potatoes to plant the next year. All the tubers produced from one parent plant are genetically identical. When they start regrowing, new shoots and roots emerge from the growing points of the potato known as 'eyes'.

## Sexual reproduction

In sexual reproduction there are two parents. The parents have **sex organs**. The sex organs make sex cells or **gametes**. In animals the male gametes are **sperm cells**. In flowering plants the male gametes are nuclei inside **pollen grains**. In animals the female gametes are **egg cells**. In flowering plants the female gametes are inside structures called **ovules**. During sexual reproduction the gametes fuse together at **fertilisation**. The fertilised egg or **zygote** divides to form an **embryo** which may grow into a new individual plant.

At fertilisation, half the genetic material comes from the male gamete and half of it comes from the female gamete. The nuclei in the gametes are called **haploid** nuclei as they contain one set of chromosomes. A zygote has a nucleus that contains two sets of chromosomes – one from each gamete. This is known as a **diploid** nucleus.

Unlike asexual reproduction, the offspring produced are not genetically identical to the parents. Each zygote receives half its genes from its male parent and half from its female parent. This means that sexual reproduction brings about **variation** in the offspring.

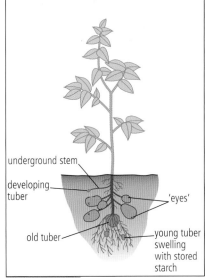

**Figure 14.1.3** The potato plant reproduces asexually by producing tubers, as well as sexually with flowers.

## Advantages and disadvantages of asexual reproduction in plants

An advantage of asexual reproduction is that it is fast. Organisms can reproduce rapidly to spread and colonise areas where the parent plants grow. Plants grow more rapidly from tubers than from seeds.

If left in the ground, potato tubers grow into new plants in the same place as the parent, but compete with each other for resources. Seeds produced in sexual reproduction are dispersed to new areas where there may not be as much competition. However, many seeds land in unsuitable places for growth so many are wasted.

There is very little, if any, variation as a result of asexual methods of reproduction. This can be a disadvantage if these individuals are affected by a certain disease. Since they are all genetically identical, none may have resistance to the disease and they may all be killed. If environmental conditions change, it is unlikely that there will be individuals with features adapted to the new conditions. Sexual reproduction gives rise to variation. Many individuals may not be as well adapted to the existing conditions as their parents, but may be well adapted if the environment changes. If there is plenty of variation, species are better able to survive and evolve.

### SUMMARY QUESTIONS

1 Explain each of the following:
   a gamete, b fertilisation, c zygote, d embryo.

2 Describe each of these examples of asexual reproduction:
   a binary fission in bacteria, b spore production in fungi,
   c tuber formation in potatoes.

3 Make a table to compare the advantages and disadvantages of asexual reproduction and sexual reproduction in plants.

### KEY POINTS

1 Asexual reproduction results in the production of genetically identical offspring from one parent.

2 Sexual reproduction involves the fusion of male and female nuclei to form a zygote, producing offspring that are genetically different from each other and their parents.

3 Binary fission in bacteria, spore production in fungi and tuber formation in potatoes are all examples of asexual reproduction.

4 Asexual reproduction may produce many individuals rapidly, but it does not result in variation of offspring as in sexual reproduction.

# Flower structure

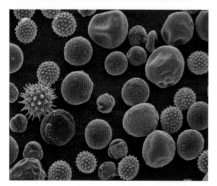

The spiky pollen grains are from insect-pollinated flowers and the smooth grains are from wind-pollinated flowers.

The Titan arum from Sumatra in Indonesia produces a smell of rotting flesh to attract flies – the flies jump in, slide down the sticky walls and are covered in pollen; after a few days the walls of the plant change, allowing the flies to climb out to visit another flower of the same species.

Flowering plants carry out sexual reproduction by producing flowers, which have male and female parts. The male parts make pollen grains to carry male gametes to the female parts. The transfer of pollen grains is **pollination**. Female gametes are deep inside the female part and pollen grains grow a tube to reach them. Each pollen tube delivers a male gamete so it can fuse with the female gamete to form a **zygote**. Fusion of male and female gametes is **fertilisation**.

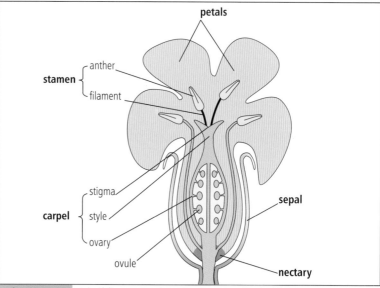

**Figure 14.2.1** A half flower drawing of an insect-pollinated flower.

Flowers vary in structure depending upon their method of pollination.

## Insect-pollinated flowers

Flower parts are often arranged in rings attached to the end of a swollen flower stalk. The sepals form the outer ring and the carpels form the inner ring.

- Sepals are leaf-like structures that protect the flower when it is a bud.
- Petals are brightly coloured and scented. Many have a nectary at the base, which makes sugary nectar. Visiting insects land on the petals to feed on nectar.
- Stamens are the male sex organs. Each one is made up of two parts: the anther, where the pollen is made, and the filament, a stalk which holds the anther. In this flower there are four stamens (eight in the full flower).
- Carpels are the female sex organs. Each carpel is made up of a stigma, a style and an ovary.
- The ovules are inside the ovary. Each ovule has a female gamete – the egg cell.

Pollen grains land on the sticky stigma during pollination. In this flower there is one carpel in the middle of the flower.

## Wind-pollinated flowers

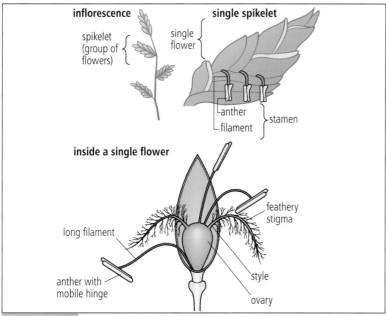

**Figure 14.2.2** This species of rye grass is an example of a wind-pollinated flower.

Grasses and cereals are all pollinated by the wind. Rye grass, *Lolium perenne*, has many features typical of a wind-pollinated flower. The flowers are small, green and inconspicuous compared with insect-pollinated flowers. They have no scent and no nectar.

The anthers hang outside the flower so the wind can blow away the large quantities of small, smooth and light pollen that they produce. The feathery stigmas are also positioned outside the flower. They act like a net, providing a large surface area for catching pollen grains that get blown into them. Wind-pollination can waste a lot of pollen, which is why the anthers produce so much. But the fact that plants such as grasses and cereals grow close to one another means that pollen is more likely to be transferred.

### KEY POINTS

1 Insect-pollinated flowers have sepals to protect the flower in the bud and bright petals to attract insects. The stamens consist of anthers and filaments. Each carpel is made up of a stigma, style and ovary.

2 Wind-pollinated flowers are inconspicuous, with feathery stigmas and anthers that hang outside the flower.

3 Wind-pollinated flowers produce large quantities of light, smooth pollen that is easily carried on the wind. Insect-pollinated flowers produce smaller quantities of sticky and spiky pollen that attach to insects.

### SUMMARY QUESTIONS

1 Copy and complete the following sentences using the words below (you may use some more than once):

**carpels      pollen      stigma**
**anther      ovary      stamens**

The male parts of a flower are called the _____. Each is made up of an _____ and a filament. The _____ grains are made inside the _____. The female parts of a flower are called the _____. Each is made up of a _____, style and _____.

# Pollination

## LEARNING OUTCOMES

- Define the term *pollination*
- Name the agents of pollination
- Compare the different structural adaptations of insect-pollinated and wind-pollinated flowers
- Distinguish between self-pollination and cross-pollination and discuss their significance

Honey bee with pollen on its legs.

## EXAMINER SAYS...

When you look at insect-pollinated flowers with a hand lens, identify how their structure helps them to be pollinated by insects. In an examination you may have to do this for a flower you have not seen before.

**Pollination** is the transfer of pollen grains from the anther to a stigma of a plant of the same species. Pollination may be carried out by insects or by the wind, and flowers are adapted to one of these methods. Insects and wind are two agents of pollination; there are others such as birds and bats.

When an anther is ripe, it splits open along its length and releases the pollen so that pollination can occur. Pollination is needed in order to bring the male gamete (inside a pollen grain) near to the female gamete so that **fertilisation** can occur.

## Insect pollination

Look at the diagram of the flower below. It has a number of adaptations for insect pollination.

The flower is pollinated by bees, which land on the petals. Bees have long tongues and are able to reach the nectaries at the base of the petals.

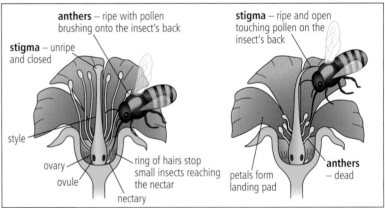

anthers – ripe with pollen brushing onto the insect's back

stigma – ripe and open touching pollen on the insect's back

stigma – unripe and closed

style

ovary

ovule

ring of hairs stop small insects reaching the nectar

nectary

petals form landing pad

anthers – dead

**Figure 14.3.1** A bee transfers pollen from one flower to another of the same species.

The bees feed upon the sugary nectar made in the nectaries. The anthers are positioned in such a way that sticky pollen from them will brush against the bee's back as it pushes its head down to the base of the petals. When the bee enters another flower, it brushes some of the pollen against the ripe stigma and pollination is achieved.

## Wind pollination

Look at the picture of wind pollination on the next page. The anthers hang outside the flower so that they release their pollen when the wind blows them.

The stigmas are feathery and are also found outside the flower, where they act as a net to catch pollen grains in the air. Wind-pollinated flowers have light, smooth pollen grains which can easily be carried by the wind to another flower. The anthers produce many pollen grains so that some, by chance, will land on the stigma of a flower of the same species. Most of the pollen produced will be lost.

| feature | insect-pollinated flowers | wind-pollinated flowers |
|---|---|---|
| petals | present – colourful and scented to attract insects | absent or very small and difficult to see |
| nectaries | present – make nectar which is a sugary liquid food for pollinating insects | absent |
| stamens | present – usually with short filaments; anthers attached firmly to filaments; inside the flower for insects to rub against | long filaments so anthers hang outside the flower; anthers loosely attached to the filaments so pollen is easily blown away |
| pollen | small quantities of sticky, spiky pollen grains that stick easily to insects' bodies | large quantities of smooth, light pollen that can easily be carried by the wind |
| carpels | sticky, small stigmas usually inside the flower for insects to rub against | large, feathery stigmas to catch pollen grains in the air |

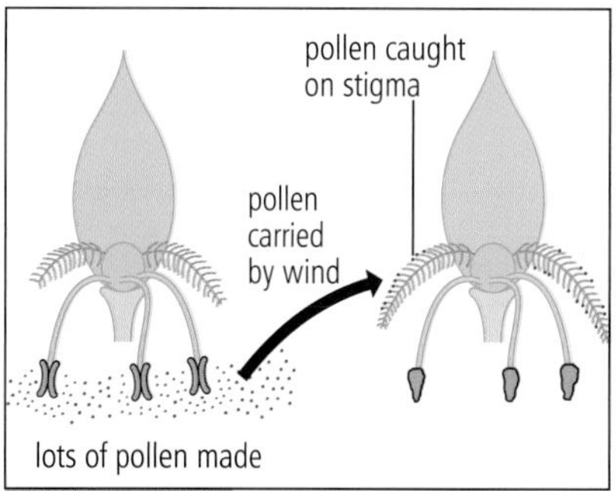

**Figure 14.3.2** Wind pollination.

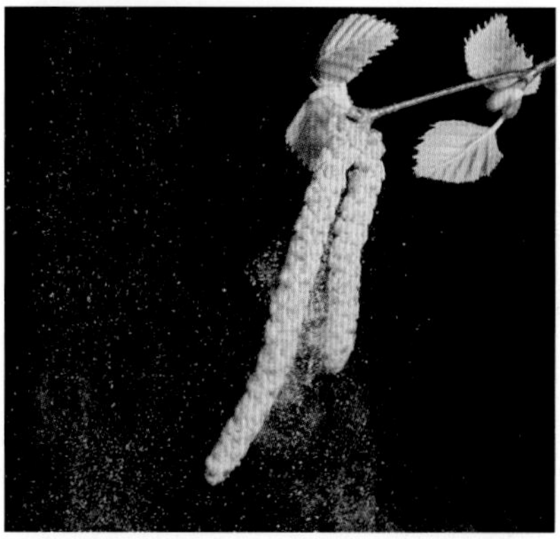
Hazel catkins release pollen to be carried by the wind.

Extension

## Pollination and variation

**Self-pollination** occurs when pollen is transferred from the anther to a stigma of the same flower or to a different flower but on the same plant. **Cross-pollination** occurs when pollen is transferred to a stigma of another plant of the same species. Cross-pollination is of a greater benefit to a species of plant, since it ensures exchange of genetic material between different plants and results in greater **variation** upon which **natural selection** can operate (see Unit 17). Self-pollination results in much less variation, since genetic material is not exchanged with different plants but with the same one. However, self-pollination is an advantage if there are no pollinating insects, and for plants growing in isolation from others of the same species.

### KEY POINTS

1 Pollination is the transfer of pollen grains from the anther of the male part of the flower to the stigma of the female part of the flower.

2 Insect-pollinated flowers have bright petals, scent and nectar. Wind-pollinated flowers are inconspicuous with feathery stigmas and anthers that hang outside the flower.

Extension

3 Self-pollination involves the transfer of pollen from the anthers to the stigma of the same flower. Cross-pollination involves the transfer of pollen from the anthers of one flower to the stigma of another flower on a different plant of the same species.

### SUMMARY QUESTIONS

1 a Give two ways in which pollen from insect-pollinated flowers is different to the pollen from wind-pollinated flowers.

b Write down three other differences between insect-pollinated and wind-pollinated flowers.

Extension

2 a What is the difference between self-pollination and cross-pollination?

b State the advantages of cross-pollination over self-pollination.

# Fertilisation and seed formation

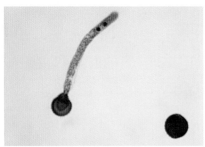

A pollen grain and a germinated pollen grain (left) with its pollen tube and male gamete nuclei.

Scanning electron micrograph of pollen grains and pollen tubes of lily, *Lilium* sp.

## Fertilisation

Fertilisation in flowering plants follows pollination.

Pollination is complete when the pollen grains land on the female stigma. The pollen nucleus must now be transferred to the egg cell inside the ovule, which is inside the ovary.

If pollen grains land on a ripe stigma they start to grow, each forming a **pollen tube** which grows down the style to the ovary. As it grows, it gets nutrition from the tissues of the style and carries the male gamete nucleus with it. The first pollen tube reaches the ovary. It enters the ovule through a small hole – the **micropyle**. The male gamete nucleus then fuses with the egg cell nucleus. This is fertilisation in which a zygote is formed by fusion of the two nuclei.

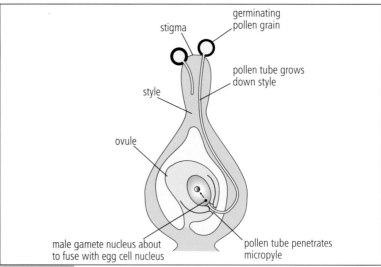

**Figure 14.4.1** Fertilisation occurs within the ovule.

The zygote divides and grows into the embryo. The ovule forms the seed with the embryo inside it.

The ovary forms the fruit with the seeds inside it.

**PRACTICAL**

### Growing pollen tubes

Find some flowers with anthers covered in pollen. Lily flowers are suitable.

Cut some small squares of damp Visking (dialysis) tubing and transfer them to filter paper soaked in a nutrient solution rich in sucrose. Use a paintbrush to transfer some pollen grains from the anthers to the squares of dialysis tubing. Leave in a covered Petri dish for 24 to 48 hours. Remove the squares carefully with a pair of forceps, put on a microscope slide and observe.

# Seed formation

After fertilisation, many of the parts of the flower are not needed any more, so the sepals, petals and stamens wither and fall off. They have completed their functions.

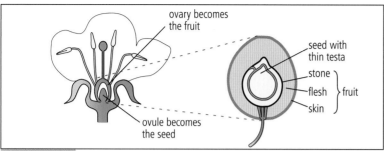

**Figure 14.4.2** How a plum flower grows into a plum fruit.

Each ovule grows to form a seed. Each seed is made up of:

• the embryo

• a food store

• a seed coat or testa.

The ovary forms the **fruit**.

## PRACTICAL

### Looking at seed structure

Cut open a bean seed. The **testa** (seed coat) is a tough, protective layer which prevents the embryo from being damaged and stops the entry of bacteria and fungi.

Radicle and plumule are embryonic structures that will grow into the root and shoot during germination.

The **micropyle** is a small hole in the testa which allows water to enter so that the enzymes can be activated.

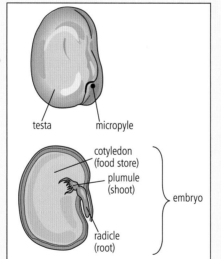

Cotyledons contain a store of starch and protein that will be broken down by enzymes to provide soluble food as the embryo grows into a new plant.

⚠ **Safety:** sharp cutting instruments

## DID YOU KNOW?

In 1993 a magnolia tree flowered for the first time. It had grown from a seed found in an ancient Japanese tomb built 2300 years ago!

> Remember what happens after fertilisation: the zygote develops into an embryo, the ovule develops into a seed and the ovary wall becomes a fruit.

## KEY POINTS

**1** Pollen grains that land on the stigma produce a pollen tube that grows down the style to an ovule in the ovary.

**2** Fertilisation occurs when the male gamete nucleus from the pollen tube fuses with the egg cell nucleus inside an ovule.

**3** A fertilised egg grows into an embryo inside an ovule which now forms the seed. The ovary forms the fruit containing many seeds.

**4** A seed is made up of an outer testa, the embryo (made up of the radicle and plumule) and the cotyledons (food store).

## SUMMARY QUESTIONS

**1 a** Explain briefly how fertilisation occurs in flowering plants.

**b** What happens to each of the following after fertilisation:

i petals, ii ovule,
iii ovary?

**2** State the function of each of the following:

a testa, b radicle,
c plumule, d cotyledons,
e micropyle.

# Fruits and seeds

**LEARNING OUTCOMES**

- State that seed and fruit dispersal, by wind and by animals, provides a means of colonising new areas
- Describe examples of dispersal by wind and animals

This is where the tomato was attached to the rest of the plant; you can also see the sepals

There is a tiny scar here where the style was attached

Inside of fruit contains xylem and phloem that supply the seed

**Figure 14.5.1** A tomato is a fruit.

The seed pods of this flame tree crack open and eject their seeds. This is an example of self-dispersal.

After fertilisation, the zygote grows into an embryo and the ovule becomes a seed which develops a testa to protect the embryo. Food is transported into the seed by phloem tissue and is stored as starch, protein and fat.

The embryo develops two cotyledons (seed leaves), a plumule and a radicle. Water is transported out of the seed so it becomes very dry. This loss of water decreases the mass of the seed making it easier to travel a greater distance. Also as it is dry, chemical reactions occur very slowly.

At this stage, many seeds become **dormant**, which means they do not grow any more until some environmental factor stimulates them. Seeds may remain in this state of **dormancy** for many years, even for two thousand years in the case of a date palm found in Israel.

While the seeds are forming, the ovary swells into a fruit to protect the seeds. The wall of the fruit is called the **pericarp** (which means 'around the carpel'). Some of these are fleshy, such as citrus fruits, papaya and tomatoes. Others are dry and may be quite hard, such as fruits of poppies, oaks, poincianas and cocklebur. The structure of the fruit is related to the way in which its seeds are dispersed.

## Dispersal of fruits and seeds

The function of the fruit is to spread the seeds. This is called **dispersal**, which can occur by animals or by the wind. Dispersal helps plants colonise new areas and avoids them all growing close together and competing for resources. Animals can move to find new places to live, but plants are stationary, so dispersal is important to their survival.

Some fruits disperse their own seeds by throwing them out.

### Dispersal by the wind

**Figure 14.5.2** Wind dispersal. Poppy fruits have tiny seeds that are shaken out when the wind blows.

Fruits and seeds dispersed by the wind do not weigh very much. Some, like the poppy, have tiny seeds that are shaken out of the fruit. In others, the pericarp grows into 'wings' or 'hairs' to help them stay in the air for some time so they are carried away from the parent plant.

### Investigation to see how seeds fall

You can investigate the effect of different shapes and sizes of fruits on dispersal. Collect some examples of fruits and seeds that are dispersed by the wind. Release them from a known height and time how long it takes them to reach the ground. Then you can make some models of fruits and seeds with paper or card. You can change the length of the wings and investigate what effect this has on the time spent in the air.

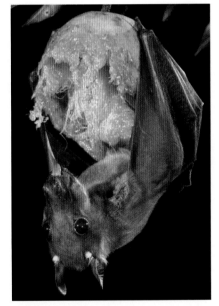

A fruit of the spinning top cone bush is blown away from the parent plant in the wind.

### Animal dispersal

Fleshy fruits are brightly coloured to attract animals, such as birds, monkeys and bats. Tough seed coats protect the seeds from digestion by enzymes in the guts of these animals. The seeds are egested in the faeces, usually miles away from the parent plant.

The fruits of cocklebur are covered with stiff, hooked spines, which catch onto animal fur or onto our clothes. They can be carried a long distance before they drop off or more likely are pulled or scratched off.

Nuts are fruits which contain a single seed. Rodents, such as squirrels and chipmunks, collect nuts to eat them somewhere safe or to store them by burying them in the ground. They either drop some of them or forget where they buried them so the seeds germinate at a distance from the parent plant. Hazelnuts, acorns from oak trees and chestnuts are examples of fruits that get dispersed in this way.

1 Fruits and seeds are dispersed by the wind or by animals, as a means of colonising new areas.

2 Without dispersal, new plants would be too crowded, competing for space, light, water and nutrients.

Animal dispersal. An epauletted fruit bat eats a mango.

1 Define the following:

a i fruit, ii a seed.

b Give two functions of a fruit.

2 a Give two different ways in which fruits and seeds may be dispersed, giving two examples of each.

b Explain how each fruit you have given in **a** is adapted to its method of dispersal.

3 Explain the advantage of fruit and seed dispersal to flowering plants.

A cocklebur fruit stuck in the fur of a racoon.

# Growth and development

## Germination

Germination is when the embryo begins to grow. The first sign that germination is happening is the appearance of the **radicle** from the seed. The radicle is the embryo's root.

The process of germination starts before this. At the start of germination the seed absorbs water through the micropyle. Embryos have very little water inside them when they are dispersed and water is needed for chemical reactions to take place. Enzymes like amylase, protease and lipase become active when the water content increases.

Amylase breaks down stored starch to soluble sugars, protease breaks down stored protein to soluble amino acids and lipase breaks down oils to fatty acids and glycerol. Sugars are used in respiration to provide energy for growth and to make cellulose for cell walls. Amino acids are used to make proteins for new cells. Oils also provide energy for the seedlings.

After the radicle has appeared, the **plumule** starts to grow upwards towards light. When it reaches the light its growth slows and the first leaves spread out to absorb light and photosynthesise. The seedling continues to use the stored food until its own leaves are able to make enough food by photosynthesis for all its needs. It is then no longer dependent on the food stores provided by the parent plant.

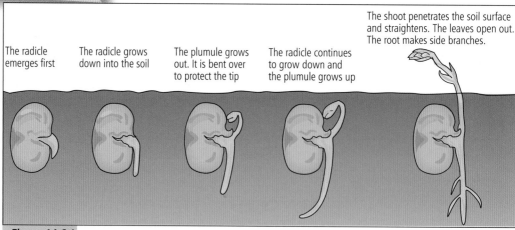

The radicle emerges first

The radicle grows down into the soil

The plumule grows out. It is bent over to protect the tip

The radicle continues to grow down and the plumule grows up

The shoot penetrates the soil surface and straightens. The leaves open out. The root makes side branches.

Figure 14.6.1

## Conditions for germination

Three conditions are needed for seeds to germinate:

- Water is needed for seeds to swell. This swelling breaks the testas of some seeds. Cells absorb water, develop vacuoles and expand. Cell expansion makes the radicle grow out through the testa. Water is also needed to dissolve the soluble products made by enzymes from the food stores. Water also activates these enzymes.
- Oxygen is needed for aerobic respiration to provide the embryo with energy.
- A suitably warm temperature is needed so that enzymes can work efficiently.

## Conditions for germination

You can investigate the conditions necessary for germination with mung beans. Set up the tubes as shown and leave them for a week, checking them every day to see if germination has started.

Only the seeds in **A** have all the conditions needed for germination.

| | A | B | C | D |
|---|---|---|---|---|
| damp cotton wool | ✓ | ✓ | ✗ | ✓ |
| oxygen absorber | ✗ | ✓ | ✗ | ✗ |
| temperature | warm | warm | warm | cold |

## Growth

Animals and plants are multicellular (many celled) organisms. When they grow, their cells increase in size as they make new cytoplasm. But cells cannot increase in size too much as it becomes impossible for them to gain enough oxygen by diffusion to respire. When cells reach a certain size they divide into two. In animals, cell division and growth take place all over the body – although there may be places where it is concentrated such as at the ends of bones. In plants, cell division and growth take place at the **root tips** and the **shoot tips** to give growth in length. It also occurs in the stem and root to give growth in width to provide support to the growing plant.

Growth can be measured by finding the **wet mass** of a plant. If you measure the growth of the mung bean seedlings by weighing them every day you will find that their mass increases. But much of this mass is water and the quantity of water in plants can vary for reasons other than the effects of growth. So an increase in size may only be temporary as it depends on the water. The water content of a plant depends on how much is available to absorb and how much is lost by transpiration.

A better way to measure growth is to remove the water by heating the plant material. This is done by heating for a certain period of time in an oven and weighing. The plant material is then heated again and weighed again. This continues until two readings are the same, indicating that all the water has been removed. This is now the **dry mass** and is a measurement of all the materials that the plant has made, for example protein, cellulose and plant oils. Dry mass is not used for animals, since it involves killing the organism you are measuring. Animal tissue does not vary so much in its water content so it is not so important to take dry mass measurements.

Growth is defined as a permanent increase in size and dry mass of an organism, by an increase in cell number or cell size or both.

As plants and animals grow the new cells produced by cell division become specialised to carry out different functions. Tissues and organs develop so that plants and animals become more complex as they grow. This increase in complexity is known as **development**. In plants, cells produced by cell division change into xylem vessels, phloem tubes, mesophyll cells and epidermal cells among others.

1 Germinating seeds require water, oxygen and a suitably warm temperature for growth and development.

2 Growth is a permanent increase in size and dry mass by an increase in cell number or cell size or both.

3 As they grow, the cells of an organism become specialised and the organism becomes more complex. This is termed development.

1 Define each of the following terms:
   a growth, b development,
   c dormancy.

2 Describe the stages in the germination of a broad bean seed.

3 A scientist measured the changes in dry mass during the germination of bean seeds.

   Explain: a how this would be done, and b the advantage of measuring changes in dry mass rather than in wet mass.

4 a State the three environmental conditions that affect the germination of seeds.

   b In each case in part **a**, explain how the condition affects germination.

   c Explain why the seeds in tubes **B**, **C** and **D** in the Practical box above did not germinate.

1 Match the parts of a flower (left) with their functions (right).

sepals     make pollen grains
petals     provide protection for flower in the bud
anthers    pollen grains land here
stigmas    contain ovules
ovaries    landing site for pollinating insects

2 Describe how:
(a) a potato plant produces stem tubers
(b) bacteria reproduce asexually
(c) fungi produce spores.

3 Write definitions of the following terms:
(a) asexual reproduction
(b) sexual reproduction
(c) pollination.

4 What are the similarities and differences between pollen from wind-pollinated flowers and insect-pollinated flowers?

5 Describe how insect-pollinated flowers and wind-pollinated flowers are adapted to their forms of pollination.

6 (a) Distinguish between pollination and fertilisation.
(b) Describe how the male gamete is delivered to the female gamete in a flowering plant.

7 Describe the changes that occur in a flower after fertilisation to:
(a) petals, sepals and anthers
(b) zygote, ovule and ovary.

8 (a) In each case give the names of *two* plants that have their seeds dispersed by:
(i) wind, and (ii) animals.
(b) What is the advantage of seed dispersal to a plant?

**Extension**

9 Flowering plants, such as potato plants, reproduce both asexually and sexually.
(a) Make a table that lists the advantages and disadvantages of asexual reproduction to a flowering plant.
(b) List the advantages and disadvantages of sexual reproduction for flowering plants.

1 The drawing shows a half flower. Which is the correct identification of the labels **1** to **4**?

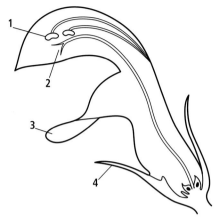

|   | 1 | 2 | 3 | 4 |
|---|---|---|---|---|
| A | anther | stigma | petal | sepal |
| B | petal | stigma | sepal | anther |
| C | sepal | petal | anther | stigma |
| D | stigma | anther | sepal | petal |

*(Paper 1)* [1]

2 Which shows the correct functions of an insect-pollinated flower?

| A | anthers produce pollen grains | carpels contain ovules | sepals provide landing site for insects |
|---|---|---|---|
| B | sepals attract insects | anthers produce pollen grains | carpels contain ovules |
| C | stigmas receive pollen grains | ovaries contain ovules | anthers produce pollen grains |
| D | petals protect a flower in the bud | stigmas are site of pollination | anthers produce ovules |

*(Paper 1)* [1]

3 The following four processes occur during sexual reproduction in flowering plants.
1 Pollen grain lands on the stigma.
2 The male gamete fuses with the female gamete.

**3** The male gamete travels down the pollen tube.

**4** The pollen tube grows out from the pollen grain.

In which order do these processes occur?

**A** 3, 4, 1, 2

**B** 4, 3, 2, 1

**C** 1, 4, 3, 2

**D** 4, 2, 1, 3

*(Paper 1)* [1]

**4** Which of the following does *not* occur following fertilisation in flowering plants?

**A** The stigma opens and becomes ripe.

**B** The ovary increases in size to accommodate the seeds.

**C** The ovule becomes the seed.

**D** The zygote changes into the embryo.

*(Paper 1)* [1]

**5** The drawing shows a half flower of hibiscus.

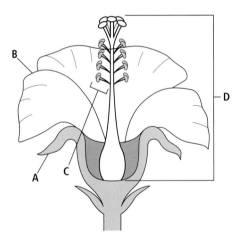

**(a)** Name the parts of the flower labelled **A** to **D**. [4]

**(b)** State the functions of parts **A** to **D**. [4]

**(c) (i)** State how this flower is pollinated. [1]

**(ii)** Describe the adaptations to the type of pollination you have given in part **(i)** that are visible in the drawing. [4]

*(Paper 2)*

**6** The drawing shows a grass flower:

**(a)** Name the parts of the flower labelled **A** to **D**. [4]

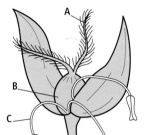

**(b)** List the ways in which this flower differs from the flower in question 5. [5]

**(c)** Describe the adaptations that this flower shows for pollination. [4]

*(Paper 2)*

**7** The drawing shows a section of a carpel from a flowering plant after pollination.

**(a)** Name the parts labelled **A** to **D**. [4]

**(b)** Use the diagram to describe how fertilisation occurs. [3]

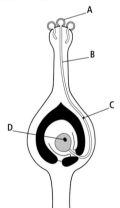

*(Paper 2)*

**8 (a)** Describe how the stigmas of insect-pollinated flowers and wind-pollinated flowers are adapted to their functions in receiving pollen. [4]

**(b)** Define the terms self-pollination and cross-pollination. [3]

**(c)** Some plant species rely almost entirely on self-pollination. Discuss the advantages and disadvantages for these species of relying on self-pollination rather than cross-pollination. [5]

*(Paper 3)*

## 15.1    The male reproductive system

### LEARNING OUTCOMES

- Identify on diagrams the parts of the male reproductive system and state their functions
- Compare male and female gametes

The **testes** are the male sex organs. They produce the male gametes or **spermatozoa** – a word that is usually abbreviated to **sperm** or sperm cells. The testes also make the male hormone **testosterone**. This stimulates changes in a boy's body as he develops into an adult during puberty. This happens between about 10 and 16 years of age.

The testes are located inside a sac called the **scrotum** which hangs outside the body. This keeps the testes at a cooler temperature as sperm cells need a temperature cooler than 37 °C to develop properly and be stored. After puberty, the testes produce sperm cells constantly which are stored in small tubules just outside the testes where they mature. A much wider tube called the **sperm duct** connects these tubules to the urethra. The **prostate gland** and other glands secrete fluids in which the sperm cells can swim. The prostate secretes mucus and other glands secrete sugars which sperm cells use as a source of energy for their respiration. Sperm cells and the fluid together form **semen**, also known as seminal fluid.

The two sperm ducts join with the urethra, which runs down the centre of the **penis**. The urethra also carries urine out of the body from the bladder, but urine and semen never pass down the urethra at the same time. A ring of muscle around the urethra contracts to prevent the loss of any urine from the bladder during sexual intercourse.

### Male and female gametes

**Gametes** are sex cells. The male gamete is called the **sperm** and the female gamete is called the **ovum** or **egg**. The sperm cell is a specialised cell that is adapted for swimming. It is designed to carry

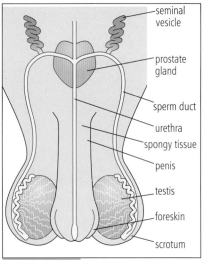

**Figure 15.1.1** Male reproductive system: front view.

seminal vesicle
prostate gland
sperm duct
urethra
spongy tissue
penis
testis
foreskin
scrotum

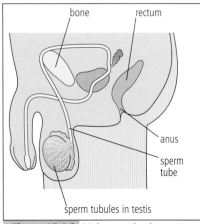

**Figure 15.1.2** Male reproductive system: side view.

bone
rectum
anus
sperm tube
sperm tubules in testis

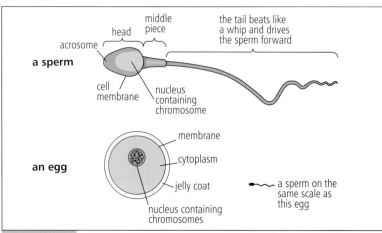

**Figure 15.1.3** Structure of a human sperm (top) and an egg (bottom).

**a sperm**
head
middle piece
acrosome
the tail beats like a whip and drives the sperm forward
cell membrane
nucleus containing chromosome

**an egg**
membrane
cytoplasm
jelly coat
a sperm on the same scale as this egg
nucleus containing chromosomes

genetic information from the male parent to the egg of the female parent. The nucleus contains the father's chromosomes. An egg is much bigger than a sperm because it provides the food store that supports the embryo after fertilisation. Its nucleus contains the mother's chromosomes. Gametes contain half the number of chromosomes as body cells. They are described as haploid cells. Body cells have the normal number of chromosomes and are described as diploid.

An egg is fertilised by a sperm cell. The cell membrane of the sperm cell fuses with the egg cell membrane. The sperm nucleus moves through the cytoplasm of the egg and the two nuclei fuse together to form a **zygote** (fertilised egg).

EXAMINER SAYS...

Egg cells and sperm cells are specialised cells adapted for their functions. Make sure you can state their key features and explain how these adapt them for their functions.

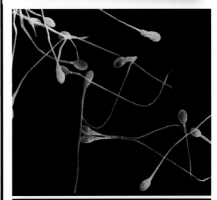

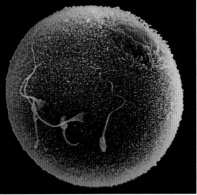

Human sperm (top) and sperm fertilising an egg.

**Extension**

## Comparing male and female gametes

| feature | sperm cell | egg cell |
|---|---|---|
| size | small | much larger than sperm cell |
| movement | swims using tail that lashes from side to side | does not move itself – is moved along the oviduct by cilia and peristalsis |
| food store | has very little – uses sugar in seminal fluid for respiration | protein and fat in cytoplasm – enough to last until implantation in uterus |
| number of chromosomes | 23 (haploid number) | 23 (haploid number) |
| number produced | millions constantly produced (after puberty) often throughout life | one a month after puberty until menopause, except when pregnant or taking the contraceptive pill |

Each sperm cell has **mitochondria**, which releases energy to power swimming by the tail. The **acrosome** contains enzymes that are released during fertilisation. These enzymes digest a pathway through the jelly coat surrounding the egg.

### SUMMARY QUESTIONS

1 Copy and complete the following sentences using the words below:

**semen   urethra   testes   ejaculation   prostate
sperm cells   penis   sperm duct   scrotum**

The male gametes are called _____ and are made in the male sex organs or _____ which are contained within a sac called the _____. A tube called the _____ carries the sperm away from each testis. The _____ gland adds fluid to the sperm cells to form _____. During an _____ the semen passes along the _____ and out of the erect _____.

**Extension**

2 a   Give three differences between sperm cells and egg cells.

b   Explain how sperm cells and egg cells are adapted for their functions.

### KEY POINTS

1 The male reproductive organs consist of the testes, scrotum, sperm ducts, prostate gland, urethra and penis.

2 The sperm cells are much smaller than the female egg cell. They are produced in huge numbers and are able to swim using a tail.

**Extension**

# The female reproductive system

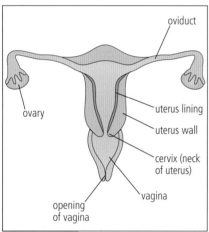

**Figure 15.2.1** Female reproductive system: front view.

**Ovaries** are female sex organs that produce the female gametes called **ova** or **eggs**. The ovaries also make the female hormones **oestrogen** and **progesterone**, which starts to happen between 10 and 15 years of age during puberty.

Oestrogen stimulates the development of the sex organs and secondary sexual characteristics in a girl's body as she starts to develop into an adult. Progesterone prepares the uterus so that it is ready to receive an embryo in the case of a pregnancy.

The ovaries are attached to the inside of the abdomen just below the kidneys. After puberty an egg is released from an ovary about every 28 days. The ovaries tend to release an egg (or eggs) on alternate months. The egg passes out of the ovary and into the funnel-shaped openings of the oviduct in a process called ovulation. The egg moves slowly down the oviduct towards the **uterus** (womb).

If sperm cells are present in the oviduct the egg will be fertilised. If the egg is not fertilised it will die after about a day. If the egg is fertilised it will divide to form an embryo which may attach itself to the lining of the uterus where it develops into a fetus.

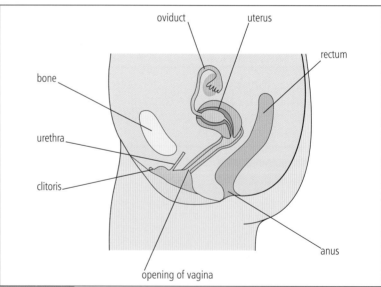

**Figure 15.2.2** Female reproductive system: side view.

The lower end of the uterus has a ring of muscle called the **cervix**. It leads to a muscular tube called the **vagina** that opens to the outside of the body. Above the opening of the vagina is the opening of the **urethra** through which urine from the bladder passes out. Above the urethra is the sensitive **clitoris**. The outer opening of the vagina is called the **vulva**. The vagina is sometimes known as the birth canal, as it is through here that a baby passes at birth.

## Sexual intercourse

During sexual intercourse males and females stimulate each other. Blood is pumped into special spongy tissue in the penis so that it becomes erect. The erect penis is placed into the vagina during sexual intercourse. Fluid made by the walls of the vagina lubricates movements of the penis within the vagina. This movement stimulates the penis and contractions begin in the sperm ducts to move sperm cells from the tubules around the testes towards the penis. As they flow, secretions from the glands including the prostate gland are added to form semen or seminal fluid. Contractions of the urethra move the seminal fluid through the penis into the vagina. This is an **ejaculation** and at this time the man experiences feelings of pleasure called an **orgasm**. Repeated movements of the erect penis against the clitoris or against the vagina walls may also produce orgasms for the woman.

Each ejaculation contains between 2 to 5 cm³ of semen with up to 500 million sperm cells.

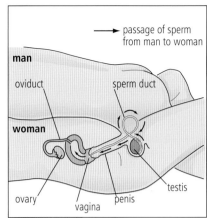

**Figure 15.2.3** Sexual intercourse.

### SUMMARY QUESTIONS

1 Copy out the list of organs on the left and match each organ with its correct function from the list on the right.

| | |
|---|---|
| ovary | carries urine out of the body |
| vagina | a ring of muscle at the opening of the uterus |
| oviduct | receives the penis during sexual intercourse |
| cervix | carries the egg from the ovary |
| uterus | produces eggs and female hormones |
| urethra | the place where a fetus develops |

2 Look at the diagram of the female reproductive system below:

a Name the parts labelled **A** to **G**.

b Where on the diagram do each of the following take place:

   i the production of oestrogen

   ii fertilisation

   iii development of an embryo

   iv the passage of the baby during birth?

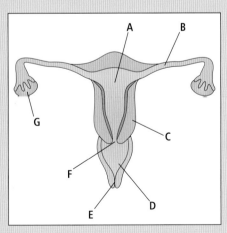

3 Some women's oviducts can get blocked. Explain why a woman with blocked oviducts would be unable to have a baby, whereas a woman with only one blocked oviduct may be able to have a baby.

### EXAMINER SAYS...

Always make sure you answer the question and do not give more information than is necessary. For example, if you are asked to describe sexual intercourse in humans there is no need to describe the sperm cells moving through the cervix to the uterus and then to the oviduct. These events happen after sexual intercourse.

### KEY POINTS

1 The female reproductive system consists of the ovaries, oviducts, uterus, cervix and vagina.

2 During sexual intercourse the male's semen is transferred into the vagina of the female.

# Fertilisation and implantation

- Describe fertilisation in humans
- Describe the early development of the zygote to form a ball of cells that is implanted into the uterus wall

## Human fertilisation

There are millions of sperm in the man's semen. If one of them is to meet an egg it must swim from the vagina to the oviduct – the muscular tube that links the ovary to the uterus.

After intercourse, sperm cells swim through the mucus in the cervix into the uterus and then all the way to the oviduct. Many sperm cells do not survive this difficult journey, which is why so many sperm cells are produced – to increase the chance of some of them reaching the oviduct.

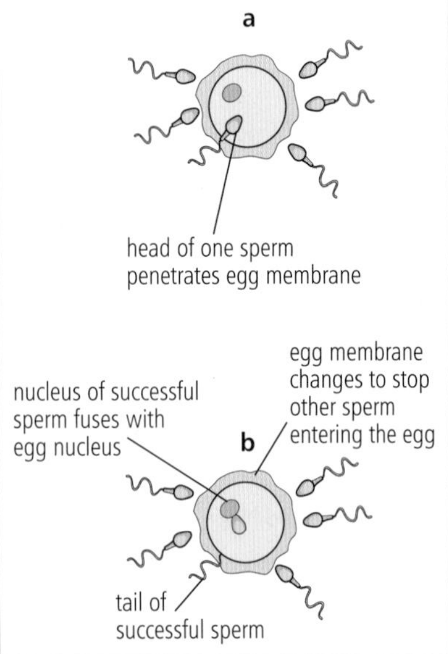

a

head of one sperm penetrates egg membrane

nucleus of successful sperm fuses with egg nucleus

egg membrane changes to stop other sperm entering the egg

b

tail of successful sperm

**Figure 15.3.2** Events at fertilisation.

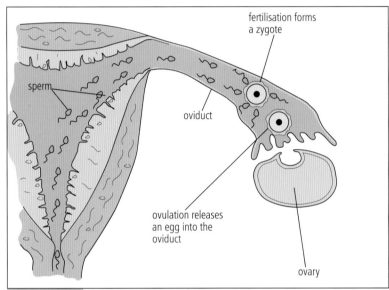

fertilisation forms a zygote

sperm

oviduct

ovulation releases an egg into the oviduct

ovary

**Figure 15.3.1** Ovulation and fertilisation.

If there is an egg in the oviduct, a sperm cell may succeed in penetrating it. Enzymes released by the acrosome on the head of the sperm digest a pathway through the jelly coat surrounding the egg.

After the sperm membrane has fused with the egg membrane the nucleus enters the egg cytoplasm and the tail is left outside. The sperm nucleus fuses with the egg nucleus to form the zygote nucleus which is diploid as it contains two sets of chromosomes – one from the mother and one from the father. The zygote nucleus now contains 46 chromosomes and these start being copied in readiness for the first cell division which occurs shortly after fertilisation.

A membrane immediately forms around the fertilised egg or zygote. This stops other sperm cells from entering so only *one* sperm is able to fertilise the egg. If there is no egg in the oviduct, no fertilisation can take place. However, the sperm can stay alive for 2 or 3 days. So if intercourse happened just before ovulation, the sperm can fertilise an egg if it is released during this time.

# Implantation

Fertilisation takes place in the oviduct. After this the fertilised egg or **zygote** begins to divide. It divides once to form a two-celled embryo. Then it continues to divide to give four cells and then eight, but after a while this cycle of divisions becomes less regular. Some cells continue to divide while others stop or slow down the rate at which they divide. After a few hours the embryo is a hollow ball of cells. It moves down the oviduct, pushed along by peristaltic contractions of the oviduct and the beating of the ciliated epithelial cells lining the oviduct.

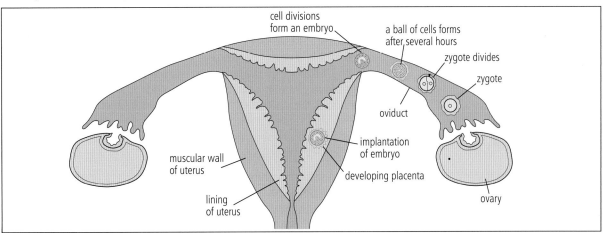

**Figure 15.3.3** Implantation of the embryo.

It may take a number of days for the embryo to reach the uterus. The embryo embeds into the soft lining of the uterus. This is called **implantation**. The uterus lining has thickened in preparation and contains numerous blood vessels. The embryo obtains food and oxygen from these blood vessels by diffusion. Carbon dioxide and chemical wastes diffuse out in the opposite direction.

## SUMMARY QUESTIONS

1 Copy and complete the following sentences using the words below:

   **zygote sexual ovaries implants uterus**
   **sperm cells vagina fertilisation weeks embryo**

   Sperm cells enter the _____ of the female during _____ intercourse. The sperm cells swim through the cervix and up through the _____ and then enter the oviduct. An egg is made in one of the _____ about every four _____. The egg passes into the oviduct where _____ may take place if _____ are present. The fertilised egg or _____ divides to form an _____ which passes down to the uterus where it _____ in the lining of the uterus.

2 a  How many sperm cells are needed to fertilise an egg?

   b  Why does a membrane form around the egg after fertilisation?

3 State the number of chromosomes in the nuclei of the following human cells:

   a  an egg, b  a sperm cell, c  a zygote.

## KEY POINTS

1 Fertilisation occurs when a sperm cell fuses with an egg in the oviduct of the female.

2 For fertilisation to occur, ovulation must have taken place and a sperm cell must have reached the oviduct.

3 The zygote divides to form a ball of cells called the embryo, which passes down the oviduct and implants in the lining of the uterus.

## The placenta

After implantation, part of the embryo grows into finger-like projections or **villi** that penetrate the lining of the uterus. They are surrounded by blood vessels which supply nutrients and oxygen. This structure continues to grow to form the **placenta** which is all formed from embryonic tissue.

The placenta is disc-shaped and has many villi surrounded by blood spaces in the uterus. The villi give the placenta a very large surface area for diffusion. In the placenta, the blood of the fetus flows close to the blood of the mother but they do not mix. The mother's blood flows under high pressure and this would damage the delicate blood vessels of the fetus if they did mix. If the mother and fetus have different blood groups then the fetal blood would clot if the mother's blood flowed into its blood vessels.

There is a very thin lining of cells between the fetal blood and maternal blood. This allows food molecules and oxygen to diffuse easily from the mother's blood into the blood of the fetus. Carbon dioxide and waste products diffuse easily from the blood of the fetus into the mother's blood.

**EXAMINER SAYS...**

Once all the organs have formed and the embryo has features that are recognisably human, it is known as a fetus.

**EXAMINER SAYS...**

The placenta is the gas exchange surface for the fetus. It is also where dissolved food substances are absorbed. This is why it has the same features as the lung and the small intestine: a large surface area and a short distance for diffusion. Since the exchanges are between fetal and maternal blood there are <u>two</u> good blood supplies to maintain concentration gradients (see page 26).

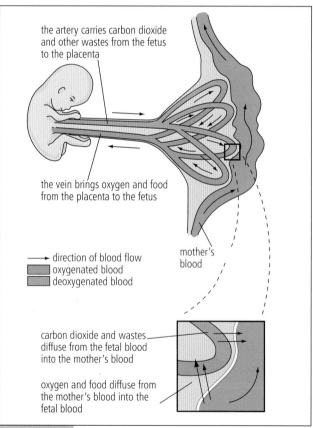

the artery carries carbon dioxide and other wastes from the fetus to the placenta

the vein brings oxygen and food from the placenta to the fetus

→ direction of blood flow
oxygenated blood
deoxygenated blood

mother's blood

carbon dioxide and wastes diffuse from the fetal blood into the mother's blood

oxygen and food diffuse from the mother's blood into the fetal blood

**Figure 15.4.1** The role of the placenta.

The fetus obtains all its food from its mother. This includes glucose, amino acids, fats, mineral ions, vitamins and water. The fetus produces some urea which diffuses into the mother's blood to be excreted through her kidneys.

The **umbilical cord** joins the fetus to the placenta. The cord contains an artery and a vein that carry the fetal blood to the placenta and back again.

## Pregnancy

Pregnancy is the period of time between fertilisation and birth, which in humans is 9 months. This period of time is called the **gestation period**.

Extension
The fetus becomes surrounded by a membrane called the **amnion** or **amniotic sac** which contains **amniotic fluid**. This fluid supports the fetus and protects it from mechanical damage.

At about 4 weeks the heart is beating. By 8 weeks it has a face, limbs and fingers and toes. The mother feels the fetus start to kick after about 16 weeks.

Even though the womb is a sterile environment, the fetus is still susceptible to disease. Rubella (German measles) is caused by a virus that can get across the placenta and harm the fetus. This is why all young women should be vaccinated against rubella before they become pregnant. Young men should also be vaccinated since they can act as a reservoir of infection for the disease.

The HIV virus that causes AIDS may cross the placenta, so a baby may be born HIV positive if the mother is infected with the virus. However, with careful management during pregnancy a mother who is HIV+ can give birth to a child who does not carry the virus.

### KEY POINTS

1 The placenta has a large surface area for gas exchange and diffusion of food and waste between fetal blood and mother's blood.

Extension
2 The amnion and amniotic fluid protect the fetus from mechanical damage in the uterus.

### SUMMARY QUESTIONS

1 a How is the fetus connected to the placenta?

  b List two substances that pass from the mother's blood to the fetal blood and two substances that pass in the opposite direction.

2 Describe two ways in which the structure of the placenta helps efficient diffusion to take place between fetal blood and the mother's blood.

3 What is meant by the term *gestation period*? How long does it last in humans?

Extension
4 What are the functions of the amnion and amniotic fluid?

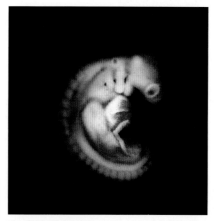
The fetus at 26 days.

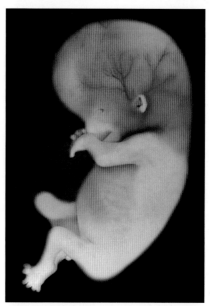
The fetus at 8 weeks.

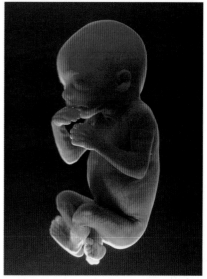
The fetus at 5 months.

# Ante-natal care and birth

## LEARNING OUTCOMES

- Describe the ante-natal care of pregnant women
- Describe the processes involved in labour and birth
- Describe the advantages and disadvantages of breast milk and formula milk

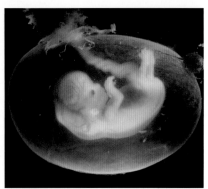

A fetus inside the amnion at 7 to 8 weeks of pregnancy.

## Ante-natal care

Ante-natal care, or care before birth, is vital for the health of the fetus while it is in the womb. The mother also needs to make sure that she provides the right nutrition and protection for the fetus during the pregnancy.

It is important that the mother has a balanced diet during this time so the fetus obtains all the nutrients it needs for growth and development. Particularly important are vitamins and minerals, such as iron and calcium. A pregnant woman will need to ensure that she gets adequate quantities of:

- **calcium**, as the bones of the fetus are growing
- **iron**, so that her body can make the extra red blood cells needed to carry oxygen to the fetus. Her growing fetus is also making red blood cells. They both need the extra iron in the diet to make more haemoglobin, the substance in red blood cells that carries oxygen
- **carbohydrate**, so that the pregnant mother has enough energy to move her heavier body around
- **protein**, to provide the amino acids that they both need to make new tissues. The mother makes muscle tissue in the uterus in preparation for birth. The fetus is also growing and developing and therefore making many new cells.

The mother should not smoke since nicotine and carbon monoxide cross the placenta and can result in **premature** or **underweight** babies. She should drink no alcohol, or very small quantities, as alcohol also crosses the placenta and can cause a variety of effects including birth defects and mental retardation. Drugs, such as heroin, cross the placenta so some babies are born with an addiction to heroin.

## Birth

A normal pregnancy takes about 9 months. In some cases babies are born prematurely, perhaps because there has been a problem during pregnancy. An early breaking of the membrane (amnion) around the fetus is the most common reason.

A few weeks before birth the fetus usually turns over inside the uterus. This positions its head above the cervix. Hormones released by the fetus and the build up of pressure in the uterus stimulate hormonal changes in the mother. A hormone, oxytocin, is released from her pituitary gland that stimulates the muscles of the uterus to contract. The mother starts to feel small contractions of the uterus wall. This is the beginning of **labour**.

These contractions become stronger and more frequent. Stronger contractions slowly stretch the opening of the cervix and the amnion breaks, allowing the amniotic fluid to escape.

The muscles of the uterus wall now contract very strongly and start to push the baby towards the cervix. The cervix widens or dilates and

**Figure 15.5.1** Position of the baby just before birth.

Diagram labels: the amniotic cavity fills the uterus; placenta; umbilical cord; fetus (50 cm); uterus; cervix; vagina the baby's head is pushed through the vagina. This part of the birth takes place quite quickly. As soon as it is born the baby breathes for the first time. It is important that the baby has airways clear of mucus and can breathe easily.

The umbilical cord is tied and cut just above the point where it attaches to the baby. The remains of the cord heal to form the baby's navel. After a few minutes the placenta comes away from the uterus wall. It is pushed out of the vagina as the **afterbirth**.

The process of labour with the muscular contractions of the uterus is painful for the mother. She can help the process by gentle exercises of the body before labour and by breathing in a special way during labour. Pain-killing drugs can also be given to ease the pain during birth. These may be given by an epidural. This involves inserting a catheter (tube) into the space between the spine and the spinal cord. The drugs prevent the transmission of impulses from pain receptors to the brain.

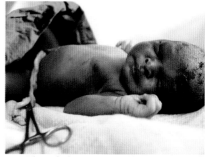
A newborn baby with its umbilical cord.

## Breastfeeding

**Extension**

During her pregnancy the glands in the mother's breasts will enlarge. This is so that soon after birth she is able to produce milk.

Breast milk contains **antibodies** which pass to the baby and give it passive immunity to the diseases that the mother has had recently. **Passive immunity** means that the child has the mother's antibodies in the blood, but is unable to produce them itself. The antibodies remain in the child's blood while it is breastfed and for a short time afterwards. Breastfeeding also enables a close bond to form between mother and baby that is beneficial to both.

Medical research has shown that breastfeeding is beneficial to both children and mothers. Children who are breastfed are less likely to develop certain diseases such as childhood cancers and diabetes. Mothers are less likely to develop cancers of breast, womb and ovaries.

Some women are not able to breastfeed their babies or they find it difficult or embarrassing. They therefore rely on bottle-feeding. Formula milk may be more convenient, but since it comes in powdered form it needs to be mixed with water under sterile conditions. In some places women may not be able to do this, with the risk of babies getting infections from non-sterile milk or bottles. Formula milk also costs money, whereas breast milk does not.

### KEY POINTS

1 During labour the muscles in the uterus wall contract.

2 At birth, the baby passes out of the vagina and takes its first breath. The umbilical cord is tied and cut. The placenta detaches from the uterus and passes out as the afterbirth.

3 Ante-natal care involves the mother having enough calcium, iron, carbohydrate and protein in her diet. She should avoid smoking, drugs and alcohol.

4 Breast milk has advantages over formula milk, notably that it contains antibodies that protect the baby from common infections.

**Extension**

### SUMMARY QUESTIONS

1 Describe what happens to each of the following during the birth of a baby:
  a the muscles in the uterus wall, b the cervix,
  c the amnion and amniotic fluid, d the placenta.

2 Make a table to show the advantages and disadvantages of breastfeeding and bottle-feeding.

**Extension**

## LEARNING OUTCOMES

- Describe the menstrual cycle in terms of changes in the uterus and ovaries
- Explain the role of hormones in controlling the menstrual cycle

One change that happens in girls at puberty is that they start to have periods. This usually happens when a girl is between 10 and 15 years old but can happen earlier. During a period, the lining of the uterus breaks down and blood and cells pass out of the vagina. This is called **menstruation**. When this happens for the first time, it shows a girl has had her first menstrual cycle.

## Stages in the menstrual cycle

Girls are born with a very large number of potential egg cells in their ovaries. They do not produce any more during their lifetime. Each potential egg is surrounded by a small group of cells and together they form a **follicle**. There are thousands of these follicles in each ovary.

At puberty, some of the follicles start to develop. This development involves the egg dividing by meiosis which reduces the number of chromosomes in the nucleus by half. The cytoplasm fills with stored food. Each month one or a few follicles start to develop. This is stimulated by hormones released by the pituitary gland (see page 152).

A follicle starts to develop in the ovary at the beginning of the cycle as menstruation finishes. As the follicle grows it enlarges and fills with fluid and moves towards the edge of the ovary. After 2 weeks, the follicle bursts releasing the egg, some follicle cells and the fluid into the oviduct. This is called **ovulation**. The follicle cells left behind in the ovary form the **yellow body** which remains for the next 2 weeks. If implantation does not occur, it will then decrease in size. If implantation occurs it remains active during pregnancy.

While the egg is developing in the ovary the lining of the uterus starts to thicken. In the week after ovulation it has a thick lining of blood vessels and glands. If fertilisation occurs, the fertilised egg divides to form a ball of cells which **implants** into the thick uterus lining and the woman becomes pregnant.

If fertilisation does not occur, the egg dies and passes out of the vagina and the yellow body in the ovary breaks down. The thick lining of the uterus breaks down and is lost during menstruation. The cycle now begins again.

If a pregnancy does occur, the embryo releases a hormone that stimulates the yellow body to remain active which in turn stimulates the lining of the uterus to continue to thicken. This supplies the embryo with food and oxygen as it continues its development. It also ensures that menstruation will not occur.

Between the ages of 45 and 55 years a woman's periods stop as her menstrual cycles have stopped. This is called the **menopause**.

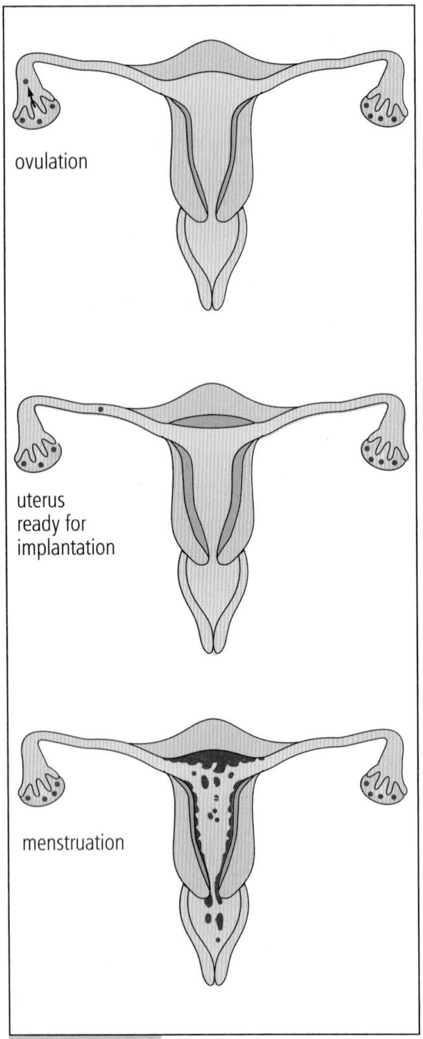

**Figure 15.6.1** During the menstrual cycle the activities of the ovaries and the uterus are synchronised.

# Control of the menstrual cycle

Hormones from the **pituitary gland** control the cycle.

A pituitary hormone called **follicle stimulating hormone (FSH)** starts the cycle by stimulating a follicle to develop. The egg cell starts to divide inside the follicle and increase in size. Cells in the follicle start to secrete **oestrogen** into the bloodstream.

Oestrogen causes the lining of the uterus to thicken in preparation to receive a fertilised egg and prevents any more eggs developing. Oestrogen passes to the pituitary gland in the blood and stops it from making any more FSH.

Instead it stimulates the production of another pituitary hormone called **luteinising hormone** (**LH**). LH travels to the ovary in the blood, stimulating it to release an egg (ovulation) and stimulating the remaining follicle cells to form a yellow body.

The yellow body starts to make the hormone **progesterone**. This makes the uterus lining thicken even more and prevents it breaking down. Both oestrogen and progesterone are needed to prepare the lining of the uterus for implantation of the fertilised egg.

If pregnancy occurs, these two hormones continue to be produced. They make sure that the lining of the uterus stays thick and they stop the woman's menstrual cycle starting again.

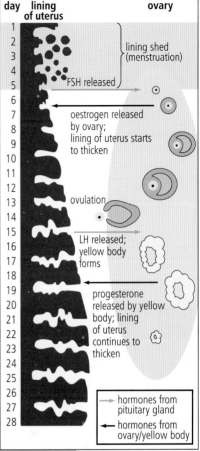

**Figure 15.6.2** Hormonal control of the menstrual cycle.

## KEY POINTS

1 During a menstrual cycle a follicle develops inside the ovary and the lining of the uterus thickens. If implantation does not occur, the lining of uterus and vagina break down. This is menstruation.

2 The pituitary hormone FSH stimulates the development of a follicle inside the ovary and the secretion of oestrogen.

3 Oestrogen stimulates the thickening of the uterus lining, inhibits FSH production and causes the pituitary to release LH.

4 LH stimulates ovulation and the formation of the yellow body from the remains of the follicle. The yellow body secretes progesterone which maintains the lining of the uterus.

## EXAMINER SAYS...

The menstrual cycle and its control are quite difficult to learn. Remember that the hormones are produced so the events happen in a sequence. The lining of the uterus has to be ready to receive an embryo. The activities of the ovaries and uterus are synchronised so they happen at the right times.

## SUMMARY QUESTIONS

1 Explain the meaning of the following terms:
   a  menstruation, b  ovulation, c  implantation.

2 Draw a timeline to show the changes that occur in the ovary and in the uterus during a menstrual cycle.

3 a  Name four hormones involved in coordinating the menstrual cycle and state where they are secreted.

   b  Describe the roles of these hormones in controlling the menstrual cycle.

## Puberty and adolescence

You are born with a complete set of sex organs. But they only become active later in life. Between the ages of about 10 and 14, the testes start to make sperm and follicles start to develop in the ovaries. This time of development in your life is called **puberty**.

Girls usually develop earlier than boys. The actual age of puberty varies from person to person. The changes that take place are all controlled by **hormones**. At the beginning of puberty the **pituitary gland** at the base of the brain starts to make hormones that stimulate the testes and the ovaries.

These make the sex organs active. The sex organs start to produce sex hormones which develop our **secondary sexual characteristics**.

### Puberty in boys

The testes start making **testosterone**, which stimulates:

- the growth of the male sex organs
- the testes to make sperm cells
- growth of hair on the face
- the deepening of the voice
- development of muscles in the body.

### Puberty in girls

The ovaries start making **oestrogen**, which stimulates:

- the growth of female sex organs
- the start of the first menstrual cycle and the first period
- growth of hair on parts of the body
- growth and development of breasts
- widening of the hips.

A person becomes an **adolescent** when puberty starts. Adolescence finishes when you stop growing at about 18 years of age. Adolescence can be an emotional time. Hormones can bring about mood changes and increase sexual urges.

A group of adolescents.

## Fertility drugs

Some couples want to have children but cannot because the man or woman is infertile. Couples are regarded as being infertile if they have had regular, unprotected sexual intercourse for 12 months without the woman becoming pregnant.

Often the cause of infertility in women is that the ovaries do not release eggs. This may be due to a lack of FSH production by the pituitary. Treatment for this type of infertility may involve regular injections of a fertility drug containing FSH. The FSH stimulates the ovaries to release eggs.

Other treatments involve tablets that make the pituitary insensitive to oestrogen. Remember that oestrogen inhibits the production of FSH. So if the effect of oestrogen on the pituitary is blocked by the drug, then the pituitary continues to release FSH and ovulation occurs.

Unfortunately fertility treatment does not always work for a variety of reasons that may not be easy for doctors to discover. On the other hand, it can work too well; too many eggs may be released, resulting in twins, triplets, quadruplets or even more!

Some couples cannot have children because the man is infertile. This may be because he does not produce enough sperm or there are problems with ejaculation. It is possible that semen may be collected from the man and placed via a fine plastic tube into the woman's uterus. The process is called **artificial insemination** (AI).

If the man does not produce enough sperm for this, or if the sperm are defective, then a **donor** may provide a sample of semen for AI. Artificial insemination by donor can lead to problems later in life because the child's father is not the *biological* father who probably remains unknown.

It is also possible to take the nucleus from a defective sperm cell and inject it into an egg. The zygote is then cultured for several days so it grows into an embryo and is then transferred into the woman in the hope that it implants in the uterus.

A couple with triplets resulting from fertility treatment.

## SUMMARY QUESTIONS

1 Explain the role of the pituitary gland, the testes and the ovaries in the development and regulation of secondary sexual characteristics in males and females at puberty.

2 a List the effects that testosterone has on the body of a boy at puberty.

   b List the effects that oestrogen has on the body of a girl at puberty.

3 a Explain how fertility drugs can increase the chance of a pregnancy in infertile women.

   b Explain how artificial insemination can help bring about a pregnancy when the man is infertile.

   c Discuss the social implications of the use of each of the above techniques.

## KEY POINTS

1 Testosterone stimulates the changes in secondary sexual characteristics that occur in males during puberty.

2 Oestrogen stimulates the changes in secondary sexual characteristics that occur in females during puberty.

3 Infertile females can take fertility drugs containing FSH to stimulate the release of eggs and increase the chances of pregnancy.

4 If the male is infertile, couples may opt for artificial insemination where donor sperm are used to fertilise a woman's fertile eggs.

# Methods of birth control

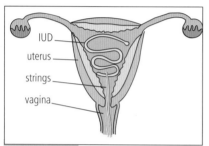

**Figure 15.8.1** Intra-uterine device.

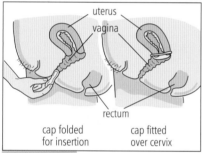

**Figure 15.8.2** Cap.

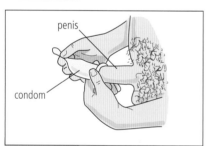

**Figure 15.8.3** Condom.

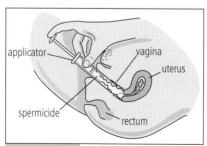

**Figure 15.8.4** Spermicide.

Birth control lets couples decide whether or not to have children and if so, how many. To prevent pregnancy, the method of birth control should either:

- stop the sperm from reaching the egg
- stop the eggs from being made, or
- stop the fertilised egg from implanting and developing in the uterus.

## Mechanical methods

The **IUD** (**Intra-Uterine Device**) is a small plastic device that is wrapped in copper or contains hormones. It is fitted inside the woman's uterus and it is thought to work by preventing sperm passing through the uterus. It may also prevent an embryo from implanting in the uterus should conception occur.

Some IUDs contain progesterone that is released slowly and causes the mucus in the cervix to become thick and sticky, making it unlikely that sperm will swim through.

The **cap** or **diaphragm** is a rubber dome. The woman places it over her cervix before intercourse. It prevents the man's sperm from entering the uterus. It should be used with sperm-killing cream or foam.

The **condom** is a thin rubber tube. It is rolled over the man's erect penis before intercourse. It stops the sperm from entering the woman's body. It also gives protection against sexually transmitted diseases. It is the most common form of birth control and is easy to use.

A **femidom** is the female equivalent of a condom and is inserted into the vagina.

## Chemical methods

'**The pill**' is an oral contraceptive as it is taken by mouth. There are different types of pill available. They contain the hormones oestrogen and progesterone in varying concentrations. There are also progesterone-only pills. These work by preventing the ovary releasing eggs. (They do this by inhibiting the production of FSH by the pituitary.) As a result, no eggs mature to be released by the ovaries and so pregnancy cannot occur. The woman has to take a pill every day.

For many couples the pill is a very reliable and convenient method of contraception. Drawbacks are that failure to take the pill regularly can result in a pregnancy. The side effects are sore breasts, weight gain, depression and painful periods – each pill has its own set of side effects. In a very small number of women, the pill can be the cause of heart and circulation problems.

**Spermicides** are chemicals that kill sperm. They are sold as foam, cream or jelly. The woman puts the cream into her vagina before intercourse. Spermicides are not very effective on their own and should be used with another method such as the cap or the condom.

## Natural methods

Some couples may not be able to use the methods described here or they may have religious or moral objections to using contraception. To avoid becoming pregnant they may abstain from having sex at times when fertilisation is most likely to happen. They may use the **rhythm method**. This relies on determining when ovulation is most likely to occur and abstaining from sex in the days just before and just after that date. A woman keeps a record of when she has her periods and then predicts each month when ovulation should occur. This is about 2 weeks after having her period. This is not a very reliable method, especially in women who do not have regular periods.

A better method is to follow changes in symptoms associated with ovulation. For example, checking for the increase in body temperature and changes in cervical mucus which becomes wetter and less sticky just before ovulation. This symptoms-based method is more effective. It is useful for people who do not have access to family planning clinics and the other methods of contraception described here.

## Surgical methods

A sperm duct is also known as a vas deferens. The operation to cut them is a **vasectomy** and is a minor operation for a man. His sperm tubes are cut and tied. The operation is not usually reversible, so the man must be sure that he does not want any more children. The man can still ejaculate but there are no sperm in the semen, just fluid.

**Sterilisation** is a minor operation for a woman. Her oviducts are cut and blocked. The operation is not reversible, so the woman must be sure that she does not want any more children.

**Figure 15.8.5** Calendar for rhythm method.

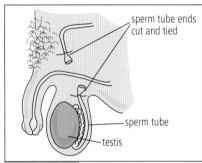

**Figure 15.8.6** Vasectomy.

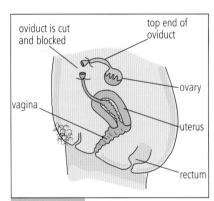

**Figure 15.8.7** Sterilisation.

### KEY POINTS

1 Mechanical methods include the condom, diaphragm and IUD.

2 Chemical methods include the pill and spermicides.

3 Methods of birth control can be natural (abstinence, rhythm method).

4 Surgical methods involve vasectomy and female sterilisation.

### SUMMARY QUESTIONS

1 a What is meant by the term *contraception*?

 b Under what circumstances would a couple choose to use birth control methods?

2 Explain how the following birth control methods work:

 a cap or diaphragm, b condom, c spermicides,

 d vasectomy.

3 a Explain how oral contraceptives ('the pill') act to prevent pregnancy.

 b What are the disadvantages associated with this form of birth control?

# Sexually transmitted diseases

Extension

## LEARNING OUTCOMES

- Describe the methods of transmission of HIV and the ways in which HIV/AIDS can be prevented from spreading
- Describe how HIV affects the immune system
- Describe the symptoms, signs, effects and treatment of gonorrhoea

## Human immunodeficiency virus (HIV)

The **human immunodeficiency virus** (**HIV**) is a human pathogen that was first identified in the early 1980s. Like all viruses it is composed of a few genes and a protein coat. It enters human cells and uses the cell to make more viruses which then enter even more cells.

HIV infection may lead to the development of **Acquired Immunodeficiency Syndrome** or **AIDS**. If someone has been infected with HIV they are described as being HIV positive (HIV+).
The virus weakens the body's immune system. It is easier for a person who is HIV+ to be infected by other diseases, such as TB and pneumonia. People who do not have HIV are described as HIV negative (HIV–).

## HIV and lymphocytes

HIV attacks and destroys an important type of lymphocyte that coordinates the immune system. During an infection these T lymphocytes stimulate other lymphocytes to produce antibodies. During an HIV infection the number of T lymphocytes decreases and so fewer antibodies are produced every time there is another infection. This means that HIV+ people develop diseases, as well as cancers, that form because the immune system does not recognise and destroy them.

Extension

### EXAMINER SAYS...

AIDS is not a disease; it is a collection of diseases which result from a weakening of the immune system. This is what the word 'syndrome' means. Often the term HIV/AIDS is used.

The early symptoms of AIDS are very much like flu, with swollen glands and a high temperature. Later, symptoms might include weight loss, various types of cancer and a decrease in brain function. Not all HIV+ people develop AIDS. Some people remain HIV+, but without any symptoms at all.

### How is HIV transmitted?

HIV is transmitted in the blood and semen. The virus can pass from one person to another during unprotected sexual intercourse.

Either partner may infect the other. The virus can also be passed via hypodermic needles contaminated with infected blood. In this way, HIV has spread very quickly amongst drug addicts.

Unborn babies are also at risk from HIV. This is because the virus can pass across the placenta to the fetus. Even more likely is its passage from the mother's blood to the baby's blood at birth when the two bloodstreams come into close contact. HIV can also be transmitted in breast milk. Blood used for transfusions is another way in which HIV has been transmitted.

### How can AIDS be prevented?

Although there is no cure for AIDS and as yet no vaccine for HIV, there are treatments. These involve taking anti-viral drugs, some of which prevent the virus multiplying inside the body's cells. Antibiotics do not work against viruses, but people with AIDS take them to treat bacterial and fungal infections that they have.

Since HIV infection cannot be cured, it is important to prevent the transmission of the virus. Methods to reduce its spread include:

A health worker treating a patient with AIDS in Cambodia.

- the use of condoms during sexual intercourse
- free needle exchange schemes to reduce the use of shared needles amongst drug users
- careful screening of donated blood used for transfusions.

## Gonorrhoea – a sexually transmitted disease

Unlike HIV, **gonorrhoea** is *only* transmitted during sexual intercourse. Gonorrhoea is caused by *Neisseria gonorrhoea*, a small, spherical bacterium. It can only survive inside the moist lining of the male or female reproductive tracts. If the bacteria are present in either the vagina of a woman or the urethra of a man, the infection can be transmitted from one to the other during sexual intercourse.

The first symptoms of the disease appear between 2 to 7 days after infection. In a man, the bacteria multiply within the urethra, producing an unpleasant discharge and pain when urinating. Sores develop on the penis. There may be long-term damage to the urinary and reproductive systems if the disease is not treated effectively.

In a woman, the bacteria multiply in the cervix and to a lesser extent inside the vagina. A discharge is once again produced, but this may well go unnoticed by the woman. The woman does not experience the same pain that men do at this time. Consequently, most men will know that they have gonorrhoea from their early symptoms, whereas many women will not realise that they have the infection. Again if not treated there may be long-term damage to the urinary and reproductive systems.

Gonorrhoea may cause sterility in both men and women if it is not treated. Gonorrhoea can be treated effectively by antibiotics. However, as with many diseases, prevention is better than cure. The following steps can be taken to prevent infection.

- Have only one partner; if both partners are disease-free then infection is not possible.
- If the man uses a condom then the bacteria cannot pass through it from one person to another.

If a person is diagnosed with gonorrhoea, then all sexual contacts should be traced, warned and treated with antibiotics to stop the spread of the disease.

### SUMMARY QUESTIONS

1 a  What is the difference between AIDS and HIV?

  b  What sort of organism causes gonorrhoea?

  c  Why can gonorrhoea be treated by antibiotics whereas HIV cannot be?

2 a  Describe the signs, symptoms and effects of gonorrhoea.

  b  Explain how the spread of the disease can be prevented.

3 a  State the ways in which HIV is transmitted.

  b  State the measures that can be taken to reduce the spread of HIV infection.

4 Describe the effect of HIV on the immune system and explain how HIV infection leads to the development of AIDS.

*Extension*

### KEY POINTS

1 HIV is a virus that infects cells in the immune system. It is transmitted in the semen or in the blood. With time HIV infection may lead to a collection of diseases which is known as AIDS.

2 The spread of HIV can be reduced by men using condoms during sexual intercourse, by reducing the use of shared needles between drug users and by careful screening of donated blood used in transfusions.

3 HIV destroys lymphocytes leading to a weakening of the immune system. This makes people susceptible to many diseases, such as TB.

4 Gonorrhoea is a bacterial disease which is spread during sexual intercourse with an infected partner. It can be prevented by having just one uninfected partner or by using condoms. Its spread is controlled by tracing and treating any sexual contacts of an infected person.

*Extension*

1 State the functions of the following structures in reproduction:

   testes, scrotum, sperm ducts, prostate gland, urethra, penis.

2 State the functions of the following structures in reproduction:

   ovary, oviduct, uterus, cervix, vagina.

3 Describe and explain the methods of birth control that are taken by men and women.

4 Outline the changes that occur to the ovary and uterus during one menstrual cycle.

5 Make a flow chart to show the stages that occur in human reproduction starting with the formation of gametes and ending with birth.

6 Describe the functions of the placenta and umbilical cord during pregnancy.

7 Explain the precautions that a woman should take during her pregnancy for the benefit of her health and that of her fetus.

**Extension**

8 Draw diagrams to show the parts of a sperm cell and an egg cell. Annotate your diagrams to explain how sperm cells and egg cells are adapted for their functions.

9 Make a flow diagram to show how the activities of the ovaries and uterus are controlled by hormones during the menstrual cycle and pregnancy.

10 Explain how a fetus is protected in the uterus.

11 What are the effects of HIV on the immune system?

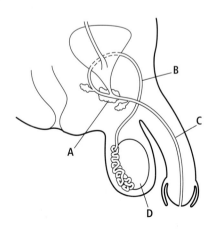

1 In a life cycle of a mammal, which describes the egg, sperm cell and zygote?

|   | egg | sperm | zygote |
|---|-----|-------|--------|
| A | diploid | diploid | haploid |
| B | diploid | haploid | diploid |
| C | haploid | diploid | haploid |
| D | haploid | haploid | diploid |

(Paper 1)                    [1]

2 The diagram shows the female reproductive system. Which identifies the places where the events occur?

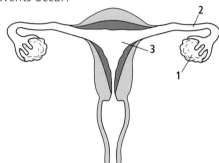

|   | 1 | 2 | 3 |
|---|---|---|---|
| A | fertilisation | implantation | ovulation |
| B | implantation | ovulation | fertilisation |
| C | ovulation | production of eggs | fertilisation |
| D | production of eggs | fertilisation | implantation |

(Paper 1)                    [1]

3 The diagram left shows the male reproductive system. Where are gametes produced?

(Paper 1)                    [1]

4 The diagram below shows the changes that occur to the uterus during the menstrual cycle.

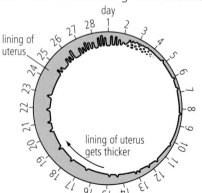

Which shows the times in days when the events during the cycle occur?

| | ovulation is likely to occur | menstruation occurs | uterus lining gets thicker |
|---|---|---|---|
| A | 10–27 | 25–28 | 4–10 |
| B | 13–15 | 1–4 | 6–25 |
| C | 22–25 | 1–4 | 7–14 |
| D | 10–27 | 13–15 | 25–28 |

*(Paper 1)* [1]

**5** The diagram shows a fetus in the womb just before birth. [3]

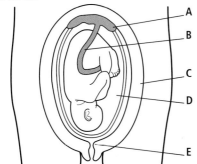

(a) Name **A** to **E**. [5]

(b) Describe the changes that happen to the structures **A** to **E** during birth. You may use the letters rather than the names in your answer. [3]

*(Paper 2)*

**6** The table shows methods of birth control, an explanation of how they work and measures of their reliability.

| method | how the method works | number of women who get pregnant in a year | percentage reliability |
|---|---|---|---|
| condom | | 2 in 100 | |
| contraceptive pill ('the pill') | | fewer than 1 in 100 | more than 99 |
| diaphragm or cap | | 4 to 8 in 100 | 92 to 96 |
| vasectomy | | 1 in 1000 | 99.9 |

(a) Copy and complete the table. [5]

(b) Explain why most methods of birth control do not protect against the transmission of sexually transmitted diseases. [3]

(c) State two ways in which the human immunodeficiency virus (HIV) is transmitted other than by sexual intercourse. [2]

*(Paper 2)*

**7** Clomiphene is a drug that is used to treat infertility in women. It works to cause an increase in production of FSH from the pituitary gland.

(a) Explain how a deficiency in FSH causes a woman to be infertile. [2]

(b) Outline the social issues involved with fertility treatment. [4]

(c) Describe the roles of oestrogen and progesterone in pregnancy. [3]

*(Paper 3)*

**8** The graph shows the number of cases of gonorrhoea in the USA per 100 000 people between 1996 and 2006.

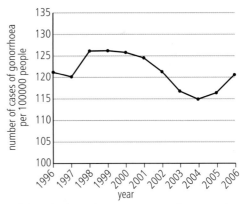

(a) Calculate the percentage decrease in the number of cases of gonorrhoea per 100 000 in the USA between 2001 and 2004. Show your working. [2]

(b) Describe the pattern of cases of gonorrhoea as shown in the graph. [3]

(c) Describe two symptoms of gonorrhoea in men. [2]

(d) Outline methods that health authorities can use to reduce the number of cases of sexually transmitted diseases such as gonorrhoea. [4]

(e) Explain why people who are HIV positive are more at risk from infectious diseases than people who are HIV negative. [3]

*(Paper 3)*

## 16.1

# Chromosomes, genes and DNA

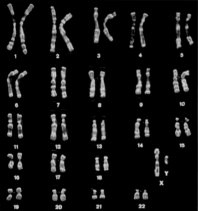

People who belong to the same family often resemble each other – sometimes quite closely. In the case of identical twins, very closely. Characteristics or traits such as physical appearance, personality and capabilities at such things as sport and music, often run in families. We say that someone has inherited features from their parents.

The transfer or transmission of these features from one generation to the next is called **inheritance**. The characteristics are controlled by genes which are like coded instructions. The study of inheritance is known as **genetics**.

In Units 14 and 15 we looked at how new generations of flowering plants and humans are produced. Genes from one generation are transmitted to the next in the gametes. At fertilisation, the gametes fuse to form a zygote which contains the genetic information from both parents. A new individual grows from the zygote – half of its genetic information comes from its male parent and half from its female parent.

## Chromosomes

We cannot see genes through a light microscope, but we can see **chromosomes**. Most cells have nuclei containing chromosomes. The first step in visualising the genetic information that we inherit is to look at these chromosomes.

Chromosomes are visible through a microscope during cell division. The photograph shows the chromosomes of a human white blood cell specially prepared so that they can be counted and analysed.

There are 46 chromosomes in the nucleus of a human cell. This is called the **diploid number**. The chromosomes are different shapes and sizes. They can be sorted into pairs based on their size and shape. In the photograph a human male's chromosomes are sorted into 23 pairs. In each pair, one of the chromosomes has been inherited from the male parent and one from the female.

You can see that each of the chromosomes in the photo on the left is double stranded. They have two strands joined together usually at the centre, but not always. The diagram at the top of the next page shows the two strands of one chromosome in two different colours.

If we could unravel a chromosome, it would form an extremely long thread. That thread is made up of a long chain molecule called **DNA** which stands for **deoxyribonucleic acid**. The DNA is wound around molecules of protein. During cell division the DNA and protein are packed very tightly together and the chromosomes are coiled up. At other times they are uncoiled so the cell can use the information in the DNA.

## What is a gene?

Genes are lengths of the DNA that you can see in the diagram below. Each chromosome has many genes along its length although the actual number depends on its length. You can see that some of our chromosomes are much longer than others; these chromosomes have large numbers of genes.

Each gene is a unit of inheritance in that it codes for a specific protein. It is a chemical code that the cell interprets as an instruction to make a protein molecule. You know about several proteins – haemoglobin, amylase and lipase for example. There is a gene for each of these proteins and many more. Humans have between 20 000 to 25 000 different genes. The proteins produced by cells influence how the body works and what it looks like. Some features that genes control are influenced by the environment. Your height is determined by both genes you inherit and your environment – for example by your diet and how much exercise you take. Other genes are not affected by the environment. Your blood group is determined by a gene and the environment has no affect on this at all.

**Figure 16.1.1** A double-stranded chromosome.

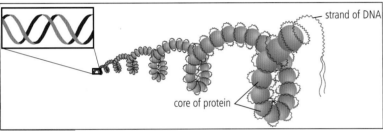

strand of DNA

core of protein

**Figure 16.1.2** The arrangement of DNA in a chromosome.

### SUMMARY QUESTIONS

1 Copy and complete the following sentences using the words below:

**chromosomes DNA genes genetic information gametes nuclei resemble**

Offspring _____ their parents because of the _____ passed on to them in the _____ (sex cells) from which they developed.

This information is contained in the thread-like structures called _____ that are inside the _____ of most cells. These threads are made of proteins and _____. The information is found in small units called _____.

2 a Define the terms *gene* and *chromosome*.

   b Name three human proteins.

   c Write a few sentences to explain the relationship between the following:

   nucleus, chromosome, gene, protein.

3 a What is meant by the *diploid number*?

   b State the diploid numbers of three non-human species.

### KEY POINTS

1 Inheritance is the transfer of genetic information from generation to generation.

2 A chromosome is a thread of DNA made up of genes.

3 A gene is a length of DNA that codes for a protein.

# Mitosis and meiosis

New cells are produced by the division of old ones. In the photograph you can see the fertilised egg of a sea urchin in the process of dividing into two **daughter cells**. Before the cell divides, the nucleus must divide. As the nucleus is finishing its division into two, the cytoplasm divides. In animal cells a constriction occurs between the two nuclei to divide the cell into two. In plants a new cell wall is formed between the nuclei.

There are two ways in which nuclei divide.

• **Mitosis** is the type of nuclear division that occurs during growth and asexual reproduction. The daughter cells are genetically identical.

• **Meiosis** occurs in sex organs to form gametes. The daughter cells are not genetically identical.

## Mitosis

Before a cell can divide, new copies of the genetic information in the DNA of the chromosomes must be made. This is a very reliable process in which exact copies are made. This copying process occurs *before* the nucleus divides. While it is going on the DNA in the chromosomes is uncoiled and arranged very loosely in the nucleus. You cannot see chromosomes in the nuclei when this is going on.

The new copy of DNA of each chromosome is attached to the original copy. As mitosis begins, the DNA coils up so that each chromosome becomes thicker. They become visible under the microscope when a suitable staining technique is used.

During mitosis the two copies separate so each new cell gets a copy of each chromosome. The diagram shows what happens to one chromosome.

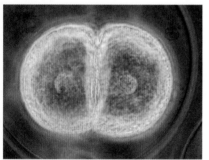

A zygote of a sea urchin has just divided in two by mitosis.

Some cells continually divide all through your life. These are **stem cells** like those in your bone marrow that continually produce red blood cells and phagocytes. They are copying chromosomes and then separating them in cycle after cycle of cell growth, followed by mitosis and cell division.

As a result of **mitosis**, each daughter cell has the same chromosome number as the original parent cell. As the chromosomes have been copied by a reliable system, they are genetically identical to one another and to the parent cell. If they were genetically different they would be rejected by the body's immune system.

Mitosis occurs in the following processes:

• **growth** – in animals this happens all over the body, in plants it happens in special growing areas such as the tips of stems and roots

• **repair** of wounds – your skin cells divide by mitosis to repair damaged tissues and wounds

• **replacement** of cells that wear out and die, such as red blood cells which only live for a short time

• **asexual reproduction** – this occurs in fungi and in plants, but is rare in the animal kingdom. There are some examples of asexual reproduction on page 168.

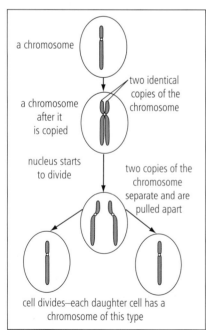

a chromosome

a chromosome after it is copied

two identical copies of the chromosome

nucleus starts to divide

two copies of the chromosome separate and are pulled apart

cell divides—each daughter cell has a chromosome of this type

**Figure 16.2.1** This is what happens to each chromosome when cells divide by mitosis.

# Meiosis

If human sperm cells and egg cells both had 46 chromosomes the zygote formed at fertilisation would have 92 chromosomes. If this continued generation after generation the number of chromosomes in the nuclei would double every generation. This does not happen. Instead the number remains at 46. This is because there is a different sort of nuclear division in the life cycle involved in producing gametes. This type of nuclear division is **meiosis**.

Meiosis halves the number of chromosomes so egg cells and sperm cells only have 23 chromosomes each. The zygote has 46 chromosomes, 23 from the mother, in the egg, and 23 from the father, in the sperm. In sexual reproduction the number of chromosomes stays constant from generation to generation.

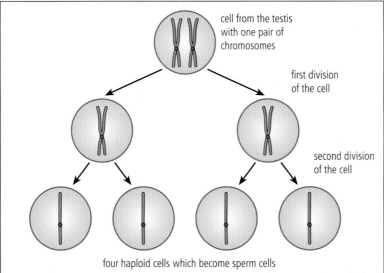

**Figure 16.2.3** This shows what happens to one pair of chromosomes during meiosis. There are two divisions of the cell to give four cells. Each of these has one chromosome so the number has been halved.

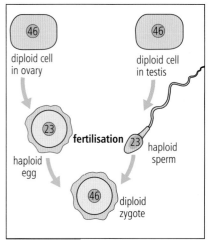

**Figure 16.2.2** The number of chromosomes in the gametes is called the **haploid number**. The number in a zygote is the diploid number.

Meiosis occurs in sex organs in humans – the ovaries and testes. In flowering plants meiosis occurs in anthers and in the ovules.

In meiosis the daughter cells are not identical. They are genetically different and this contributes to genetic variation that provides the raw material for selection, and allows organisms to evolve in response to changing environments.

## SUMMARY QUESTIONS

1 a   How many pairs of chromosomes are there in the nucleus of a human body cell?

   b   State the number of chromosomes in these human cells:

   i   an egg cell,        ii   a sperm cell,

   iii   a zygote,        iv   a red blood cell.

2 a   State three ways in which meiosis differs from mitosis.

   b   Explain the advantage of genetic variation among gametes.

## KEY POINTS

1 Mitosis produces daughter cells that are genetically identical and have the same number of chromosomes as the parent cell.

2 Meiosis is involved in gamete production in sex organs. It produces a halving of chromosome number in cells from the diploid to the haploid number.

3 Meiosis results in genetic variation so, unlike mitosis, the cells are not genetically identical.

# Genes and chromosomes

## Sex determination

Your chromosomes determine which sex you are. In humans there are 46 chromosomes and these occur in 23 pairs. In females all 46 chromosomes can be matched together into pairs. This is done by taking images of the chromosomes and matching them for size and shape. In males there are two chromosomes that are not alike. They are known as the X and Y chromosomes. Females have two X chromosomes and males have an X chromosome and a Y chromosome (see page 202).

In the diagram on the left you can see how sex chromosomes in the gametes determine the sex of individuals. Remember that the number of chromosomes is halved in meiosis so a gamete can only have one of the sex chromosomes. In sperm production this means that half get a Y and half get an X chromosome. All egg cells contain an X chromosome.

At fertilisation, the egg may fuse with either a sperm with an X chromosome or a sperm with a Y chromosome. Since there are equal numbers of sperm with the X chromosome and sperm with the Y chromosome, there is an equal chance of the zygote inheriting XX or XY and the child being female or male.

## Genes and alleles

A gene is a length of DNA that is the code for making a protein molecule. Each gene is always located in the same place on one of the chromosomes. Each species has its own genes and every individual from the same species has the same genes. However, genes vary between individuals within each species. The different versions of each gene are known as **alleles**. There may be two alleles of a gene (see below), usually there are many more (see page 210).

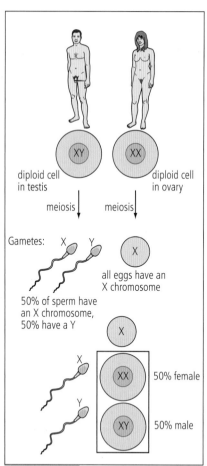

**Figure 16.2.2** The diagram only shows the inheritance of the sex chromosomes, X and Y. Do not forget that each of the gametes (egg and sperm) contain 22 other chromosomes to give the haploid number of 23.

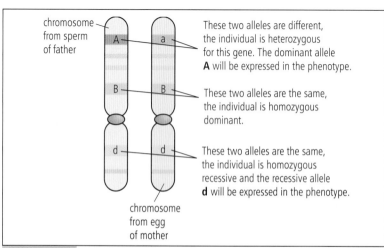

**Figure 16.3.2** This shows three genes that are on the same chromosome.

Diagram labels:
chromosome from sperm of father

A — These two alleles are different, the individual is heterozygous for this gene. The dominant allele **A** will be expressed in the phenotype.

B — These two alleles are the same, the individual is homozygous dominant.

d — These two alleles are the same, the individual is homozygous recessive and the recessive allele **d** will be expressed in the phenotype.

chromosome from egg of mother

In the diagram, you can see three genes on one pair of chromosomes. You can also see the alleles **A/a**, **B/B** and **d/d**.

Sometimes an organism gains two copies of the same allele so there is only one type of instruction to use during growth, development or metabolism. But many organisms contain two different alleles. If an allele is expressed and affects the appearance of the individual, it is said to be a **dominant allele**. If it is not, then it is said to be a **recessive allele**.

In the 1850s, Gregor Mendel investigated inheritance in pea plants. He noticed that amongst garden pea plants one variety grew to be tall while another remained short, or dwarf. He used pea plants that always bred true – from generation to generation they were either tall plants or dwarf plants.

When he cross-bred these two varieties, all the next generation were tall. None of them were dwarf. But when this new generation of pea plants self-pollinated and produced seeds, the next generation consisted of many tall plants and some dwarf. He reasoned that dwarfness had been passed on although it had 'skipped' a generation. He did not know anything about genes and DNA, but he used his knowledge of algebra to give letters to represent what he called 'factors' that controlled height.

Using modern terminology there is a gene that controls height in pea plants. This gene has two alleles.

Let **T** represent the allele for tall, and let **t** represent the allele for dwarf. A capital letter is used for the dominant allele and a lower case letter for the recessive allele.

The **genotype** of an organism is the alleles it has. So the genotype of a pea plant could be **TT**, **Tt** or **tt**. If the two alleles are the same, **TT** and **tt**, the plant is **homozygous**. They can be **homozygous dominant** (**TT**) or **homozygous recessive** (**tt**). Individuals are **heterozygous** if they have two alleles that are different, for example **Tt**.

The **phenotype** is the way the alleles are expressed in an individual. It refers to all the aspects of an organism's biology except its genes. We will apply the term to one feature of an organism, for example height in pea plants. The genotypes **TT** and **Tt** result in plants with the tall phenotype, whereas the genotype **tt** results in dwarf plants.

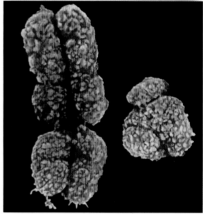

An X chromosome on the left and a Y chromosome on the right photographed in an electron microscope.

**KEY POINTS**

1 Sex is determined in humans by the sex chromosomes, X and Y. Females are XX and males are XY.

2 An allele is a version of a gene. Most genes have many alleles.

3 The genotype is the genetic makeup of an organism; the phenotype is all the features of an organism other than its genotype.

4 A dominant allele is always expressed in the phenotype.

5 A recessive allele is only expressed when no dominant allele is present.

6 A homozygous individual has two identical alleles of a gene and a heterozygous individual has two different alleles of a gene.

**SUMMARY QUESTIONS**

1 Chromosomes occur in pairs in all cells except the gametes. Explain why they are not in pairs in gametes.

2 a What are alleles?

  b Explain what is meant by the terms *dominant allele* and *recessive allele*.

3 Explain each of the following genetic terms:

  a homozygous,    b heterozygous,

  c genotype,    d phenotype.

# Monohybrid inheritance

**EXAMINER SAYS...**

When you write out genetic diagrams like these on this page, make them simple – homozygous organisms only make gametes of one genotype so only write this once in the diagram.

**Monohybrid inheritance** concerns the inheritance of a *single* characteristic, such as plant height or flower colour.

It involves the inheritance of the alleles of one gene. We will use the example of Mendel's peas.

There is one gene for height in pea plants. The gene for plant height has two alleles: tall, **T**, and dwarf, **t**.

There are three possible genotypes for plant height:

**TT** = homozygous tall

**Tt** = heterozygous tall

**tt** = homozygous dwarf.

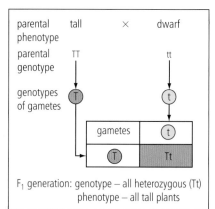

F₁ generation: genotype – all heterozygous (Tt)
phenotype – all tall plants

**Figure 16.4.1**

## The parental cross

The genetic diagram above shows a cross between a homozygous tall plant, **TT**, and a homozygous dwarf plant, **tt**. These represent the pure breeding plants that Mendel used in his crosses. This is called the parental cross.

As a result of meiosis, all the gametes from the tall plant contain the dominant allele, **T**, and all the gametes from the dwarf plant contain the recessive allele, **t**. When fertilisation occurs, the new plants receive one dominant allele and one recessive allele so will be heterozygous and all have the genotype, **Tt**. Their phenotype will be tall, because the allele, **T**, is dominant to the recessive allele, **t**.

The first generation is known as the F₁ generation, and in this particular genetic cross, all the plants in the F₁ generation are heterozygous tall (**Tt**).

## Crossing the F₁ generation (3:1 ratio)

The F₁ plants are allowed to self-pollinate (see genetic diagram, left). When meiosis occurs half of the gametes of *each* plant will have the dominant allele, **T**, and half will have the recessive allele, **t**.

This time when fertilisation occurs, there are three possible combinations of alleles in the **F₂**, or second generation:

**TT** (homozygous tall)

**Tt** (heterozygous tall)

**tt** (homozygous dwarf).

Amongst this generation ¼ (or 25%) will be homozygous tall; ½ (or 50%) will be heterozygous and therefore tall; ¼ (or 25%) will be homozygous dwarf. Since the phenotypes of TT and Tt are the same, ¾ of the F₂ plants will be tall and ¼ will be dwarf. This can also be written as 3 tall : 1 dwarf.

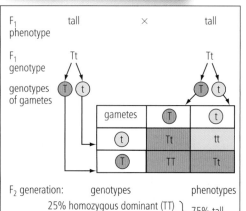

**Figure 16.4.2**

## A test cross

If you look at the last two crosses, you will see that the recessive allele is not expressed in the $F_1$ generation but is expressed in the $F_2$ generation. This means that we do not know the genotype of a tall plant just by looking at it because plants with genotypes **TT** and **Tt** have the same phenotype. We do know the genotype of a dwarf plant because it can only be **tt**.

A test cross is used to determine the genotype of an individual to find out whether it is homozygous or heterozygous (see genetic diagrams below).

If our tall plant is homozygous (**TT**), then crossing it with a dwarf plant (**tt**) gives all tall plants (**Tt**). If, however, our tall plant is heterozygous (**Tt**), then crossing it with a dwarf plant (**tt**) will give half tall plants (**Tt**) and half dwarf plants (**tt**) in a ratio of 1:1.

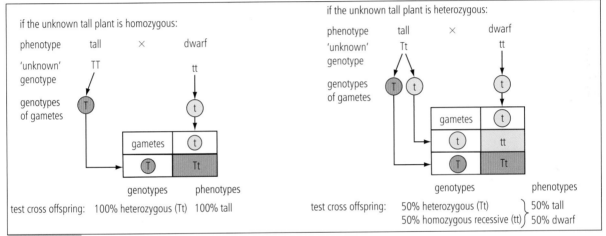

**Figure 16.4.3**

## SUMMARY QUESTIONS

1 Complete these sentences by choosing the correct word from inside the brackets.

   a  A pea plant with a tall (genotype/phenotype) could have the (genotype/phenotype) **TT** or **Tt**.

   b  A tall pea plant with genotype **TT** is (homozygous/heterozygous) dominant.

   c  A tall pea plant with genotype **Tt** is (homozygous/heterozygous).

   d  A dwarf pea plant with genotype **tt** is (homozygous/heterozygous) recessive.

2 Fruit flies have a gene that determines the length of their wings.

   a  Using the symbols **W** = long wing and **w** = short wing, answer the following:

      i   state the genotype of a fruit fly which is heterozygous for this characteristic,

      ii  give the genotypes of its gametes.

   b  A fruit fly heterozygous for wing length is mated with one which is homozygous for short wing. Use a genetic diagram to predict the proportions of each wing-type in their offspring.

# 16.5

# Codominance

## Codominance

Up to now the examples that we have looked at involve alleles that are either dominant or recessive. The recessive allele is not expressed in the phenotype of individuals with the heterozygous genotype. Sometimes, however, *both* alleles are expressed and neither is dominant.

So the phenotype is a mixture of the effects of each allele.

This condition is known as **codominance** and the alleles are called codominant alleles. The four o'clock plant can have red flowers or white flowers. Flower colour is determined by one gene. However, if you cross homozygous red-flowered plants with homozygous white-flowered plants, the offspring are all pink. The two parents produce heterozygous offspring (the $F_1$ generation) in which both alleles are expressed to give pink – an intermediate colour.

You can see in the diagram what happens when the pink plants are pollinated amongst themselves. There are red-, pink- and white-flowered plants in the $F_2$ generation in a ratio of 25%: 50%: 25% or 1:2:1. Notice that the ratio of the phenotypes is the same as the ratio of the genotypes when the alleles are codominant.

Notice also that each allele is represented as a capital letter, so red flower = $C^R$ and white flower = $C^W$. This shows that neither allele is recessive and that they both exert an equal effect on the phenotype.

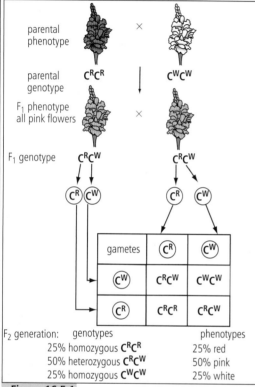

parental phenotype ×

parental genotype $C^RC^R$ $C^WC^W$

$F_1$ phenotype all pink flowers ×

$F_1$ genotype $C^RC^W$ $C^RC^W$

$C^R$ $C^W$ $C^R$ $C^W$

| gametes | $C^R$ | $C^W$ |
|---|---|---|
| $C^W$ | $C^RC^W$ | $C^WC^W$ |
| $C^R$ | $C^RC^R$ | $C^RC^W$ |

$F_2$ generation:    genotypes                        phenotypes
25% homozygous $C^RC^R$          25% red
50% heterozygous $C^RC^W$        50% pink
25% homozygous $C^WC^W$          25% white

**Figure 16.5.1**

## Multiple alleles

So far, we have looked at examples where a gene has only two alternative alleles. There are examples where a gene may have three or more alleles.

The four groups of the human ABO blood group system are determined by one gene, **I**, with three different alleles: $I^A$, $I^B$ and $I^O$.

The alleles $I^A$ and $I^B$ are codominant and code for slightly different molecules on

| Genotype | Blood group |
|---|---|
| $I^AI^A$ | A |
| $I^AI^O$ | A |
| $I^BI^B$ | B |
| $I^BI^O$ | B |
| $I^AI^B$ | AB |
| $I^OI^O$ | O |

the surface of red blood cells. The allele $I^O$ is recessive to both $I^A$ and $I^B$ and does not code for one of these molecules.

Look at the table. You can see the possible genotypes for each blood group. Remember any person can only have two alleles as we are all diploid.

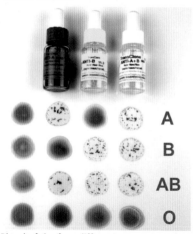

A

B

AB

O

Blood of the four different groups tested with anti-sera A (blue), anti-sera B (yellow) and anti-sera A and B (white). Red blood cells clump together if the anti-sera reacts with the A or B molecules on their surfaces.

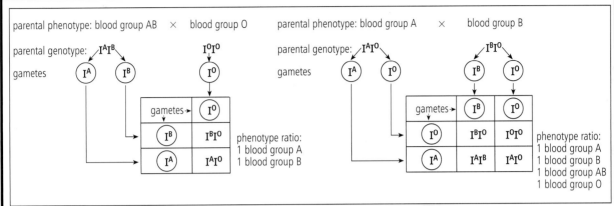

Figure 16.5.2

Look at the genetic diagrams. Two parents have blood groups AB and O. The children will have blood groups A or B. None of them will have the same blood group as their parents.

Two parents have blood groups A and B. They could have children with all four blood groups – A, B, AB and O.

## SUMMARY QUESTIONS

1 There are red-flowered, white-flowered and pink-flowered varieties of the four o'clock plant (see photo on right). The results of a number of crosses between the varieties are shown in the table. Explain the results of each cross.

| crosses | number of plants of each colour | | |
|---|---|---|---|
| | red | pink | white |
| red × pink | 126 | 131 | |
| white × pink | | 92 | 88 |
| red × white | | 115 | |
| pink × pink | 39 | 83 | 43 |

2 Use a genetic diagram to work out the possible blood groups of the offspring where the father is heterozygous for blood group A and the mother is blood group O.

3 The inheritance of coat colour in some cattle is an example of codominance. If a homozygous red cow is crossed with a homozygous white bull, all the calves have coats with a colour known as 'roan'.

The allele $R^R$ causes red hairs to be produced and the allele $R^W$ causes white hairs. Heterozygous cattle have coats that are a mixture of red and white hairs giving roan.

Use genetic diagrams to show the genotypes and phenotypes of the offspring in the following crosses:

a a roan bull and a roan cow,

b a roan bull and a red cow,

c a roan bull and a white cow.

### EXAMINER SAYS...

The ABO blood group system is an example of codominance and also of discontinuous variation (see page 215). You can expect to be asked about both topics in the same question.

### KEY POINTS

1 Codominance occurs when both alleles are expressed in the phenotype, as neither is dominant over the other.

2 The inheritance of ABO blood groups involves three alleles: $I^A$, $I^B$ and $I^o$.

1 Explain what is meant by the term *inheritance*.

2 Draw a diagram to show a pair of chromosomes. Use your diagram to explain the meanings of the following terms: *chromosome*, *gene* and *allele*.

3 Draw a diagram to show how haploid gametes are formed in meiosis and how these cells form a diploid cell at fertilisation. Use your diagram to explain the meanings of the terms *haploid* and *diploid*.

4 Draw a diagram to show how the sex chromosomes are inherited. Use your diagram to explain why the sex ratio in the human population is approximately 1:1.

5 Describe the importance of **(a)** mitosis, and **(b)** meiosis in the life cycle of a diploid organism.

6 Make a table to compare mitosis with meiosis. You should include when they take place in the life cycle of flowering plants and humans, the structures in which they occur, the types of cell produced and whether the cells are diploid or haploid.

7 Draw a genetic diagram to show how height is inherited in pea plants. Use your diagram to explain the meaning of the following terms: *gene*, *allele*, *genotype*, *homozygous*, *heterozygous*, $F_1$ *generation*, $F_2$ *generation* and *phenotype*.

**Extension**

8 The gene that controls blood type in humans has three alleles: $I^A$, $I^B$ and $I^O$. Use a genetic diagram to show how a man and a woman may have four children each with a different blood group.

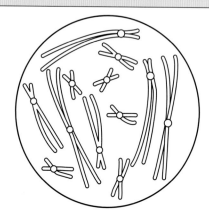

1 Which explains the advantage of meiosis occurring in a life cycle?

A Meiosis allows sexual reproduction to occur.

B Meiosis produces four times as many cells as mitosis.

C Meiosis produces haploid gametes.

D Meiosis produces sperm and eggs.

*(Paper 1)* [1]

2 Which feature is controlled only by a gene and not influenced by the environment?

A blood group

B concentration of glucose in the blood

C heart disease

D lung cancer

*(Paper 1)* [1]

3 A recessive allele:

A causes a harmful feature

B is never expressed in the phenotype

C is not expressed when in a genotype with a dominant allele

D produces the same phenotype when homozygous as when heterozygous

*(Paper 1)* [1]

4 What are the sex chromosomes in a man and his sperm cells that will give rise to male offspring?

|   | man | sperm cells |
|---|-----|-------------|
| A | XX | X |
| B | XX | Y |
| C | XY | X |
| D | XY | Y |

*(Paper 1)* [1]

5 The diagram on the left shows a nucleus with chromosomes.

**(a) (i)** State the number of chromosomes in the nucleus. [1]

**(ii)** State the number of pairs of chromosomes in the nucleus. [1]

**(iii)** How many chromosomes will be in the daughter cells when the nucleus divides by mitosis and by meiosis? [2]

**(iv)** Explain how the nuclei of the daughter cells produced in mitosis and meiosis would differ other than by having different chromosome numbers. *[1]*

**(b)** State three roles of mitosis in mammals. *[3]*

**(c)** In cats, short hair, **H**, is dominant over long hair, **h**. A male cat with long hair was crossed with a female cat with short hair. The female gave birth to 15 kittens in four different litters. Seven of the kittens had short hair and eight had long hair.

Use a genetic diagram to explain the results of this cross. *[5]*

*(Paper 2)*

**6** The diagram shows a family tree for the rare inherited condition known as brachydactyly in which people have short fingers and toes.

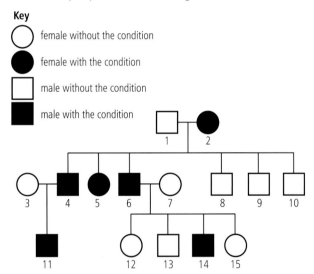

**Key**
- ◯ female without the condition
- ● female with the condition
- ☐ male without the condition
- ■ male with the condition

**(a)** Brachydactyly is caused by a dominant allele. Give the evidence from the family tree that supports this statement. Refer to the people shown in the tree by the numbers. *[3]*

**(b)** What are the chances of parents 3 and 4 having another child with this condition? Draw a genetic diagram to explain your answer. *[3]*

*(Paper 2)*

**7** In tabby cats the pattern of stripes in the coat is controlled by a gene. The allele for parallel stripes (**T**) is dominant to the allele (**t**) for blotched pattern.

parallel · · · · · · · blotched

**(a)** Use genetic diagrams to predict the proportions of cats with different coat patterns in the next generation in the following crosses:

**(i)** homozygous dominant × homozygous recessive, *[4]*

**(ii)** heterozygous × homozygous recessive. *[4]*

**(b)** Explain why it is possible to state the genotype of a tabby cat with blotched stripes, but not one with parallel stripes. *[3]*

**(c)** Explain why male and female tabby cats with blotched stripes cannot produce a kitten with parallel stripes. *[2]*

**(d)** Use the example of inheritance in this question to explain the terms *gene* and *allele*. *[3]*

*(Paper 2)*

**8 (a)** Define the term *inheritance*. *[1]*

**(b)** Explain how you would use a test cross to find the genotype of an organism that could either be homozygous dominant or heterozygous. *[5]*

The four o'clock plant, *Mirabilis jalapa*, has a red-flowered variety and a white-flowered variety. When these are cross-bred the offspring have pink flowers.

**(c) (i)** Explain why this is so. *[3]*

**(ii)** Show, by means of a genetic diagram, the result of cross breeding the pink-flowered plants among themselves. *[5]*

**(d)** Plants with pink flowers were crossed with plants with red flowers. The seeds were collected and grown. When they flowered 64 plants were of the pink variety and 78 of the red variety.

**(i)** Use a genetic diagram to explain these results. *[5]*

**(ii)** Explain why there were no white-flowered plants among the offspring in this cross. *[3]*

*(Paper 3)*

Although we show a lot of variation, we are all one species.

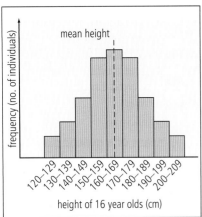

**Figure 17.1.1** Frequency histograms are drawn to present data on continuous variation.

## Types of variation

All humans have many features in common as we are all members of the same **species**. Now think about the similarities and differences between ourselves and monkeys and apes. We have many features in common, but there are significant differences which we use to categorise animals into different species. In Biology, the term variation means:

- differences between species – we use these when constructing keys
- differences within a species.

It is differences *within* a species that we are concerned with in this unit. Although we all belong to the same species, there are many differences between us – even between identical twins. Some people are taller or heavier, others have different coloured hair, skin and eyes. There is considerable variation between individuals of the same species. This variation occurs in what we can see and in the many features we cannot see, such as protein molecules like haemoglobin.

There are two types of variation within a species:

- continuous variation
- discontinuous variation.

### Continuous variation

If you measured the heights of all the pupils in your year group you would find a range of heights from the shortest to the tallest. If you divide the class into groups (170 cm to 179 cm, etc.) you can plot a frequency histogram. It is likely that the mean height will be in the middle of the range and correspond to the group with the largest number of people. This type of distribution is called a normal distribution.

This type of variation is called **continuous variation** because there is a continuous range of heights from shortest to tallest. There are many genes that contribute to your overall height. But other factors such as the quantity and quality of the food you eat and the amount of exercise you take influence your height. Also people go through their growth spurts at different ages and this will influence the results you get from your class.

Other features that you can measure also show this type of variation. Try measuring the length of your index finger or your hand span. You can collect data from the whole class and plot as frequency histograms.

Continuous variation also occurs in plants. You can measure the lengths of leaves or stems and you will get the same results – a range between two extremes with many intermediates in between. There are no clear divisions between the intermediates.

## Discontinuous variation

Look at people's ears and compare them with the photographs. Some people have attached ear lobes. Other people's ear lobes are free and not attached. This is an example of **discontinuous variation**.

Discontinuous variation is caused by genes alone and results in a limited number of distinct phenotypes with no intermediates. There is no range of intermediates between attached and not attached. If you collect data about a feature showing this type of variation, you plot it as a bar chart (see question 7 on page 223).

Another example of discontinuous variation is the human ABO blood group system. Everyone has an ABO blood group – it is either A, B, AB or O. There are no intermediates. Some flowering plant species have flowers of distinctly different colours. This is another example.

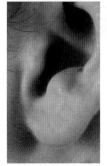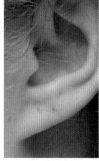

Unattached (left) and attached ear lobes.

## Inheritance versus environment

Identical twins develop from the same embryo and are genetically identical. However, they are different in many ways. These differences will have come about because they developed slightly differently in the womb and have been exposed to different environmental influences. Identical twins separated at birth, or shortly afterwards, and brought up apart often show striking similarities. These are often to do with personality, which shows the influence that genes have on us.

The effect of environmental factors can be investigated with plants. The bottom photograph shows the plant sometimes called the Mexican hat plant. It reproduces asexually to make lots of tiny plantlets all around its leaves. You can detach these and grow them in pots and keep them under different conditions. Any variation shown will be because of **environmental** factors.

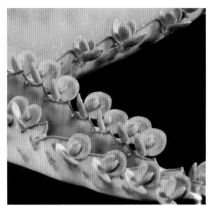

These plantlets grow on the leaves of the Mexican hat plant. They are genetically identical.

### KEY POINTS

1 Continuous variation is influenced by genes and the environment resulting in a range of phenotypes, e.g. height in humans.

2 Discontinuous variation is caused by genes alone and results in a limited number of distinct phenotypes, e.g. A, B, AB and O blood groups in humans.

### SUMMARY QUESTIONS

1 a  Distinguish between continuous and discontinuous variation.

 b  Give three examples of continuous variation.

 c  Give three examples of discontinuous variation.

2 Describe how you would investigate the effect of an environmental factor on the growth of plants that all share the same genotype. Give full practical details that ensure you have designed a valid investigation.

**EXAMINER SAYS...**

When examiners use the words 'distinguish between' in a question they want you to give the differences between two things. Here they could ask you to distinguish between the two types of variation.

# Mutations

## LEARNING OUTCOMES

- Define the term *mutation*
- Describe Down's syndrome as an example of mutation
- Describe the possible effects of radiation and certain chemicals on the rate of mutations
- Describe sickle cell anaemia as an example of mutation

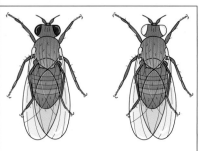

**Figure 17.2.1** As no eye pigment is produced this fly has white eyes.

Down's syndrome is the result of a chromosome mutation.

Albinos occur in many species. These are wallabies; the one on the left is albino.

A **mutation** is a change in a gene or a chromosome that may cause a change in a phenotypic characteristic. Often this change can be harmful, but some mutations are beneficial and some have no effect at all.

## Gene mutations

One of the first mutations studied was in the fruit fly. The normal eye colour of fruit flies is red, but a **mutant** form with white eyes was discovered. A gene controlling eye colour had changed. This was due to a change in the DNA so that the gene no longer coded for the production of the red pigment.

A similar example occurs in **albinos**. A gene controls production of the skin, hair and eye pigment **melanin**, which protects the skin and eyes from ultra-violet light. The gene can mutate to a form that does not produce melanin. It is a recessive allele and homozygous recessive individuals are albino. Gene mutations are the cause of many human genetic diseases. Sickle cell anaemia is an example.

## Chromosome mutations

**Down's syndrome** is caused by a **chromosome mutation**. The most common cause of this is a mutation that occurs during meiosis when an egg cell is formed in the ovary.

The mutation occurs when two of the chromosomes do not separate properly. Instead of the egg having 23 chromosomes there is an extra chromosome, giving a total of 24. This usually happens with chromosome number 21 (see the human chromosomes on page 202). If this egg is fertilised the baby will have 47 chromosomes, one more than normal. Down's syndrome affects about 1 in 1000 babies worldwide.

## Causes of mutations

Gene mutations are the only way in which new genetic material is produced. They are caused by damage to DNA or by a failure in the copying process that occurs before nuclear division. They occur naturally at random, but the rate at which they occur is increased by exposure to radiation and some chemicals. Ultra-violet radiation, X-rays and gamma rays are the most damaging. The greater the dose of radiation, the greater the chance of mutation. Benzpyrene in cigarette smoke is a cause of mutations (see page 165).

If mutations occur in body cells they may affect the individual. For example they may lead to cancers, as happened after the atomic bombs were dropped in Japan in 1945 and the nuclear power station at Chernobyl in the Soviet Union exploded in 1986. It is only mutations that occur in gamete-forming cells, or gametes themselves, that are important in the long term. This is because these mutations can be inherited and provide new forms of variation.

## Sickle cell anaemia – an inherited disease of the blood

The blood at the top shows normal red blood cells. The blood at the bottom is from a person with sickle cell anaemia (SCA). These red blood cells are in the shape of a sickle. (A sickle is a C-shaped tool for cutting plants like grasses and cereals.) These cells have abnormal haemoglobin which makes it difficult for the red blood cells to carry oxygen. This inherited disease is most common in West, Central and East Africa.

SCA is the result of an allele that causes the production of the abnormal form of haemoglobin. People with SCA only produce this abnormal form as they are homozygous for this allele. The abnormal form of haemoglobin is not very good at transporting oxygen, which causes severe problems. The allele is common among people from areas where malaria is common. This is because people who are heterozygous have both the normal and abnormal forms of haemoglobin and do not usually have a problem with transport of oxygen, but they do have a resistance to malaria as the parasite that causes this disease cannot enter their red cells. The genetic diagram shows that children of parents who are both heterozygous have a 1 in 4 chance of suffering from SCA.

Note that alleles are shown as for co-dominance (see page 210) since both of them are expressed in the red blood cells of heterozygous people.

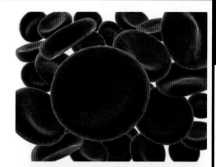
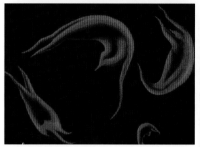

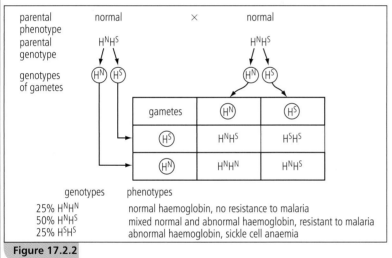

| parental phenotype | normal | × | normal |
| --- | --- | --- | --- |

genotypes
25% $H^NH^N$ — normal haemoglobin, no resistance to malaria
50% $H^NH^S$ — mixed normal and abnormal haemoglobin, resistant to malaria
25% $H^SH^S$ — abnormal haemoglobin, sickle cell anaemia

**Figure 17.2.2**

**KEY POINTS**

1 A mutation is a change in a gene or to the number of chromosomes.

2 Down's syndrome is caused by an extra chromosome 21.

3 Ionising radiation and some chemicals increase the mutation rate.

4 Sickle cell anaemia is a genetic disease caused by an allele of the gene for haemoglobin.

**SUMMARY QUESTIONS**

1 A mutation occurring during meiosis can have a serious effect on a future child.

   a What is a mutation?

   b Name one condition caused by a chromosome mutation occurring during meiosis.

   c Explain how this type of mutation could have occurred and given rise to a child showing the condition.

2 a What is the cause of sickle cell anaemia?

   b Describe the effects on the body of sickle cell anaemia.

   c Explain why the allele is found most commonly in groups of people who live in certain parts of Africa.

Charles Darwin as a young man.

Sockeye salmon.

Vultures and a hyaena compete for a dead gnu.

Natural selection is the process by which organisms that are well adapted to their environment have a greater chance to breed and pass on their genes to the next generation than those that are less well adapted. The process may be summarised as follows.

## Variation

**Variation** is the term used to describe all the differences that exist within a species. Gene mutation is the only way in which completely new genetic material is produced. Some mutations may give an advantage to the individual that expresses them. An example is having good camouflage to avoid being seen by a predator. But variation is also produced by sexual reproduction between two individuals.

During meiosis, the alleles of different genes are 'shuffled' to give new combinations in the gametes. At fertilisation, when the gametes fuse, alleles from the two different individuals are combined within the same nucleus. Gene mutation, meiosis and fertilisation give rise to variation between individuals in every generation.

## Over-population

These sockeye salmon return from the Pacific Ocean to rivers in British Colombia where they hatched in order to breed. The females produce millions of eggs, many of which are fertilised. We see the same in other species, for example a poppy plant releases over 15 000 seeds a year. Yet, in spite of this huge over-production of eggs and seeds, populations of animal and plant species remain fairly stable (see page 236).

Populations remain stable because, in the case of sockeye salmon, most of the eggs are eaten by predators as are many of the young that hatch from the eggs. Many young salmon die from disease and starvation. Similarly, many poppy seeds may be eaten by birds; others may land in places where they cannot grow as there is no soil or water. Production of large numbers of eggs and seeds ensures that enough offspring make it into the early stages of life to maintain the population from year to year.

## Competition

Among the organisms that survive the early stages of life there is competition for resources. Plants compete for space, light, water and nutrients. Animals compete for food, water, space (territories) and mates. This is referred to by biologists as the '**struggle for existence**' (see page 237).

## Differential survival

Competition leads to the survival of some individuals but not others. Those that survive compete successfully, as they have features that help them gain the resources they need. Competition is fiercest between individuals of the same species as they have the same structures and ways to get those resources. Individuals of different species also compete, but often the competition is not as fierce. For example, one species may feed at night and the other in the day time, or they have slightly different foods in their diets. Survival of some individuals rather than others is called **differential survival**.

## Adaptation

The organisms that survive this struggle are the best adapted individuals to their particular environmental circumstances. They have features that help them to do so. They may be well camouflaged, have rapid growth so they get established quickly or have other inherited features that help them to survive. It is the alleles that they have inherited from their parents that will help them to do this. The individuals that are well adapted will breed and pass on their characteristics to their offspring.

## Evolution

If the environment does not change, then natural selection maintains populations or organisms so they do not change much over time. Individuals at the extremes of the range of variation do not survive as they are not well adapted. For example, female sparrows with very long or very short wings do not survive to breed as they are often killed during stormy weather.

However, when the environment changes individuals with features that help them survive the changed conditions are at an advantage. They may now compete successfully, survive and breed. Natural selection will bring about a change to a species over time. Thus selection is the mechanism by which evolution occurs – an idea first proposed by Charles Darwin in 1859.

## Antibiotic resistance

Antibiotics are chemicals that kill bacteria or inhibit their growth. Soon after the introduction of antibiotics in the 1940s, some bacteria developed a resistance to their effects.

When bacteria are exposed to an antibiotic, such as penicillin, most are killed. However, there may be some individual bacteria that have a mutation giving them resistance to the antibiotic. The bacteria may be able to produce an enzyme that breaks down the antibiotic. These individuals survive and now have more resources available as all their competitors – the non-resistant bacteria – have died. The resistant bacteria survive to reproduce and pass on the gene for resistance to their offspring. This is an example of natural selection.

Humans have been responsible for the change in the environment by introducing antibiotics, but we have not consciously chosen the bacteria which are resistant to antibiotics. There is a constant search for new antibiotics as bacteria develop resistance to existing ones.

1 There is variation between individuals of the same species.

2 There is a 'struggle for existence' due to competition, predation and disease.

3 Only well adapted individuals survive to breed and pass on their genes to their offspring.

1 Explain the following terms in the context of natural selection: variation, over-production, competition, struggle for existence, adaptation to environment.

2 a Antibiotics are prescribed for bacterial diseases. Explain why people are told to take all the antibiotics that they are given rather than stopping when they feel better.

  b Why do drug companies invest in finding new antibiotics?

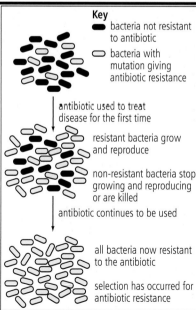

**Figure 17.3.1** Selection for antibiotic resistance.

Key
- bacteria not resistant to antibiotic
- bacteria with mutation giving antibiotic resistance

antibiotic used to treat disease for the first time

resistant bacteria grow and reproduce

non-resistant bacteria stop growing and reproducing or are killed

antibiotic continues to be used

all bacteria now resistant to the antibiotic

selection has occurred for antibiotic resistance

Ankole longhorn (top) and Zebu are breeds of cattle well adapted to conditions in Africa such as shortages of water.

Merino sheep.

## Artificial selection

People have grown crops and kept animals for at least ten thousand years. Over that time they have kept seed from one year to another and have bred their livestock. Domesticated plants and animals have changed considerably over that time due to this **artificial selection**. These changes have happened in this way:

1 Humans choose a feature or features of an animal or plant to improve, e.g. fast growth, short stems (so less straw), docile (not fierce) nature, high yield, disease resistance, resistance to drought.

2 Animals or plants showing these features are bred to produce the next generation.

3 The offspring are checked to find those that show an improvement in the desired feature or features. These are kept for breeding the next generation.

4 This process of **selective breeding** continues for many generations.

Commercial farmers want to increase the yields of their crops and animals. They want to improve features of economic importance to maximise their profits. Plant breeders have increased the yield of grain in cereal crops such as rice, wheat and maize. Animal breeders have increased the milk yield in dairy cattle, and meat quantity and quality in beef cattle. Breeders of dogs and growers of ornamental plants are looking to improve other non-economic features, such as appearance.

This is called *artificial* selection as it is humans who are the selective agent, not the environment as it is with *natural* selection. Humans decide which feature to improve and which individuals survive to breed and pass on their genes.

Merino sheep have been selectively bred for their wool. They have been particularly successful since being introduced to Australia and New Zealand from Europe.

The danger of selective breeding is that there may be too much inbreeding between closely related individuals. This may result in harmful recessive alleles being passed on to the descendants and a reduction in variation. Many breeds of dog suffer from the effects of inbreeding, e.g. failure of the hip joint to develop properly leading to lameness.

(a) These ewes from a flock of sheep have thick wool. They are mated with this ram who also has a thick coat

(b) to give these offspring – some of whom have thick wool

(c) but these sheep have thicker wool and are selected to breed the next generation

**Figure 17.4.1** Artificial selection in sheep.

## Genetic engineering

A gene is a section of DNA that codes for the production of a specific protein. **Genetic engineering** is the transfer of a gene from the DNA of one species to the DNA of another species. This is a process that can never be achieved by artificial selection, because only in rare cases will one species breed with another. Genetic engineering allows transfer of genes between totally unrelated species, for example from humans to bacteria and from bacteria to plants.

## Industrial production of insulin

Diabetics cannot control the concentration of glucose in their blood. In some cases this is because they do not make the hormone insulin, which is a protein. The treatment for this is daily injections of the hormone. The only source of insulin used to be pigs and cattle slaughtered for the meat trade. In the 1970s it was thought that demand for insulin from increasing numbers of diabetics worldwide would be too great for the supply from animals. Also there were concerns that diseases could be transferred from animals to humans by using such material. In the late 1970s, the gene for human insulin was isolated and transferred into bacteria. This made it possible to make a synthetic form of human insulin on a large scale, giving a cheap, reliable supply.

- The gene that codes for the production of insulin is identified.
- **Restriction endonuclease enzyme** cuts the human DNA to remove the gene from the rest of the DNA.
- A circular piece of DNA (**plasmid**) is removed from a bacterium.
- The same restriction endonuclease cuts open the plasmid.
- The human insulin-making gene is put into the plasmid with the aid of another type of enzyme called a **ligase**.
- The plasmid is placed back into the bacterium.
- The bacterium now has the gene to code for insulin.
- The bacteria multiply very rapidly inside an industrial fermenter and produce insulin.

Genetic engineering makes it possible to make insulin quickly and cheaply on a large scale. Animal insulin is also available for diabetics to use and is just as safe.

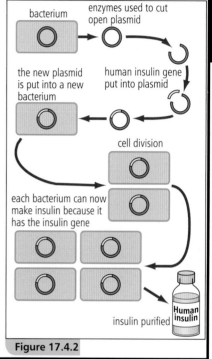

**Figure 17.4.2**

### KEY POINTS

1 Artificial selection has produced new varieties of animals and plants with increased economic importance.

2 Examples of these are high-yielding crops, cattle that produce more milk or better meat and sheep that produce more wool.

3 Genetic engineering involves taking a gene from one species and putting it into another species.

4 The human insulin gene can be transferred into a bacterial plasmid. The bacteria grow to produce lots of human insulin.

### SUMMARY QUESTIONS

1 State the useful features that are improved by breeders in the following:
   a   race horses, b   sheep,
   c   cereal crops, e.g. wheat, rice or maize.

2 Describe the procedure that a farmer would take to improve the milk yield of a herd of cows.

3 List the stages that show how the insulin gene was removed from a human cell and grown in a bacterial cell.

1 Define the term *variation*.

2 (a) Give three examples of continuous variation.

(b) Use one of the examples to explain what is meant by this type of variation.

3 (a) Give three examples of discontinuous variation.

(b) Use one of the examples to explain what is meant by this type of variation.

4 Define the term *mutation*.

5 Explain the difference between gene mutation and chromosome mutation.

6 'Mutation provides the raw material for selection.' Explain this statement.

7 State two factors that increase the rate of mutation.

8 Explain the difference between artificial selection and natural selection.

9 Define the term *genetic engineering*.

10 Explain the roles of competition and adaptation in natural selection.

**Extension**

11 (a) Describe the effects of sickle cell anaemia (SCA).

(b) Use a genetic diagram to show how two people free of SCA can have children with this condition.

(c) Explain the link between the distribution of SCA in the world's population and the distribution of malaria.

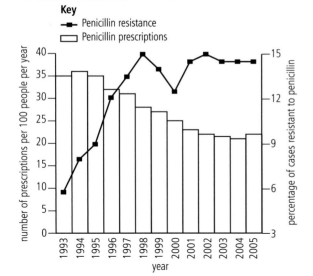

Key
— Penicillin resistance
□ Penicillin prescriptions

1 Variation is more likely to arise amongst organisms that reproduce by:

A self fertilisation

B cross fertilisation

C vegetative reproduction

D binary fission

*(Paper 1)* [1]

2 Which correctly identifies the causes of continuous and discontinuous variation?

| | continuous variation | discontinuous variation |
|---|---|---|
| A | environmental factors only | genes only |
| B | genes and environmental factors | genes only |
| C | genes only | environmental factors only |
| D | genes only | genes and environmental factors |

*(Paper 1)* [1]

3 Individuals of a species of flightless sand-burrowing beetle range in colour from pale brown to almost black. The beetles have the same colour as the sand in which they live. The reason for this is likely to be:

A Beetles are well camouflaged so that predators cannot see them.

B Beetles change colour to match their surroundings.

C Beetles are subject to artificial selection.

D Dark beetles absorb more heat.

*(Paper 1)* [1]

4 In order to transfer a feature from one species to another it is necessary to transfer:

A a chromosome

B a gene

C a genotype

D a nucleus

*(Paper 1)* [1]

**5 (a)** Match each of the following terms with the correct definition on the right:

| | |
|---|---|
| mutation | outward appearance of an organism |
| variation | genetic constitution of an organism |
| selection | range of forms found in a species |
| phenotype | change in DNA |
| genotype | organisms best adapted to their environment survive and breed |

*[5]*

**(b)** Describe the cause of Down's syndrome. *[2]*

*(Paper 2)*

**6** The distance between the outstretched thumb and little finger is the handspan. A group of students measured their handspans. The data is shown in the table.

| handspan (mm) | number of students | frequency (%) |
|---|---|---|
| 160–69 | 7 | 4.7 |
| 170–79 | 12 | 8.0 |
| 180–89 | 25 | 16.7 |
| 190–99 | 45 | 30.0 |
| 200–09 | 34 | |
| 210–19 | 19 | 12.7 |
| 220–29 | 8 | 5.3 |
| Total | 150 | 100.0 |

**(a) (i)** Calculate the percentage of students who had a handspan measurement between 200 and 209 mm. *[1]*

**(ii)** State the range in the handspan measurements. *[1]*

**(b)** Draw a frequency histogram of the results shown in the table. *[5]*

**(c) (i)** State the type of variation shown in your graph. *[1]*

**(ii)** Explain your answer to part **(i)**. *[2]*

*(Paper 2)*

**7** Surveys were carried out in Pakistan and New Zealand to find the percentage of the population in the different blood groups of the ABO blood group system.

The results are shown in the table.

| country | percentage of people in the sample in each blood group | | | |
|---|---|---|---|---|
| | **A** | **B** | **AB** | **O** |
| Pakistan | 31.0 | 36.2 | 7.7 | 25.1 |
| New Zealand | 35.5 | 8.8 | 2.6 | 53.1 |

**(a)** Draw a bar chart to show the data. *[5]*

**(b) (i)** What type of variation is shown by the data? *[1]*

**(ii)** Explain your answer to part **(i)**. *[2]*

**(c)** A couple are blood group B. They have a child who is blood group O. Use a genetic diagram to explain how this is possible. *[5]*

**(d)** Before a kidney transplant operation may be carried out, the blood groups of the donor and recipient must be checked. Explain why it is important to do this. *[3]*

*(Paper 3)*

**8** The bacterium *Streptococcus pneumoniae* is a pathogen that causes bronchitis, sinusitis, ear infections and pneumonia. Before treatment doctors use an antibiotic sensitivity test to find the most effective antibiotic to use. The graph on page 222 shows the changes in the percentage of cases that were resistant to the antibiotic penicillin between 1993 and 2005 in Canada. It also shows the changes in the number of prescriptions for penicillin over the same time period.

**(a)** Use the graph to describe trends in:

**(i)** penicillin resistance, *[3]*

**(ii)** the number of prescriptions for penicillin. *[2]*

**(b)** Explain how bacteria, such as *S. pneumoniae*, become resistant to penicillin. *[5]*

**(c)** Suggest ways in which it is possible to reduce the number of cases of antibiotic resistance. *[3]*

Bacteria have been genetically engineered to produce human insulin.

**(d)** Define the term *genetic engineering*. *[2]*

**(e)** Explain the advantage of producing human insulin in bacteria. *[2]*

**(f)** State two ways in which genetic engineering differs from artificial selection. *[2]*

*(Paper 3)*

## 18.1 Food chains and food webs

EXAMINER SAYS...

Make sure you realise that energy flows through an ecosystem and is not recycled. It is easy to say 'the energy cycle' or 'energy is recycled', but it doesn't happen, as you will see.

Sunlight is the source of energy for all living things in this ecosystem.

A **habitat** is a place where an organism lives. A group of organisms of the same species living in the same habitat at the same time is a **population**. All the populations of all the species in an area form a **community**. The community and all the physical factors that influence it is known as an **ecosystem**.

When biologists talk about ecosystems they refer to the community and all non-living components of that place, including physical factors such as light, water, pH and temperature. Ecosystems provide habitats for all the organisms that live in them. An ecosystem may be as small as a pond or as large as the ocean. Here we are looking at the flow of energy and recycling of nutrients to organisms in ecosystems.

### Communities

Living organisms can be placed into groups based on similar features. However, when looking at a community of living things, it is often more useful to group them according to the way that they feed. Living organisms can be divided up into those that make their own food and those that cannot.

**Producers** make their own food from simple raw materials, such as carbon dioxide and water. Green plants use light as a source of energy to make sugars from carbon dioxide and water by photosynthesis. Some bacteria are also producers and they are either photosynthetic or obtain their energy from simple chemical reactions. Some of the bacteria involved in recycling nitrogen obtain their energy from reactions involving compounds of nitrogen (see page 233).

Producers make energy available for all the other members of the community in the form of energy-rich carbon compounds, such as carbohydrates, fats and proteins. Sunlight is the ultimate source of energy for almost all food chains. The major exceptions are the vent communities in the deep ocean that rely on chemical energy rather than light energy.

**Consumers** obtain their energy by eating other organisms, either plants or animals or both. All animals are consumers. They cannot make their own food, so they have to eat (consume) it. Herbivores are primary consumers as they eat the producers. Carnivores are secondary consumers and they eat herbivores.

**Decomposers** are fungi and bacteria that feed on dead and decaying material (see page 11 for details of how they feed).

Each of these feeding groups is a **trophic level**. (The word *trophic* comes from a Greek word meaning 'to feed'.) You can put each organism in an ecosystem into a trophic level as you will see in these food chains.

## Food chains

Food chains show what living organisms feed on in a community. They show the flow of food and energy from one organism to the next. Look at this food chain from an East African ecosystem.

The arrows show the direction in which energy in food is transferred from one organism to the next. This food chain tells us that the gazelle eats grass and that the lion eats the gazelle. Notice that the food chain always begins with a producer, often a green plant. This can include parts of a plant, such as seeds, fruits or even dead leaves.

Food chains not only show the flow of food, they also show the flow of energy. Producers gain their energy from the Sun, so an *energy chain* would look like this:

Sun $\longrightarrow$ producers $\longrightarrow$ primary consumers $\longrightarrow$ secondary consumers

But we do not include the Sun in food chains, as it is not a 'food'. Food chains start with producers.

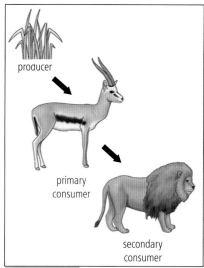

**Figure 18.1.1** A food chain.

Energy flows to decomposers, but they are rarely included in these simple food chains.

## Food webs

In most communities, animals will eat more than one type of living organism. A food web gives a more complete picture of the feeding relationships in an ecosystem.

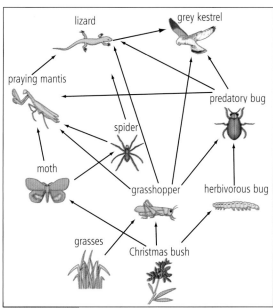

**Figure 18.1.2** A food web for a West African forest ecosystem.

### SUMMARY QUESTIONS

1 Look at the food web for the woodland ecosystem above:
  a Give one example from the food web of each of the following:
    i a producer, ii a primary consumer,
    iii a secondary consumer.
  b Name the carnivores in the food web.
  c Draw a food chain with four trophic levels. Indicate the trophic levels on the food chain.
  d If all the spiders were killed by disease, what do you think would happen to the numbers of moths and plants?
  e Explain why all the food chains in the woodland ecosystem begin with green plants.

# Pyramids of numbers and biomass

**LEARNING OUTCOMES**

- Draw, describe and interpret pyramids of numbers and pyramids of biomass
- Compare pyramids of numbers and pyramids of biomass

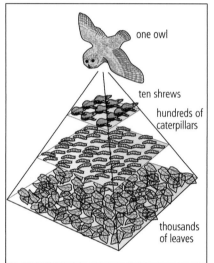

**Figure 18.2.1** This shows the producers and consumers that support an owl for several days.

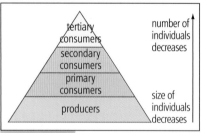

**Figure 18.2.3** Pyramids of numbers and biomass show these trends.

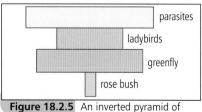

**Figure 18.2.5** An inverted pyramid of numbers.

## Pyramids of numbers

Food chains and food webs show feeding relationships in a community, but they do not show *how many* living organisms are involved. For instance, grasshoppers feed on many grasses and other plants and many grasshoppers and lizards are eaten by grey kestrels. Food chains and food webs do not show this.

Look at Figure 18.2.1. There are far more plants than caterpillars because each caterpillar eats leaves from many plants. There are far fewer owls than shrews because each owl eats many shrews.

Look at the numbers in this food chain:

plants 600 ⟶ caterpillars 100 ⟶ mice 10 ⟶ owl 1

This information can be shown in a **pyramid of numbers**. The area of each box in the pyramid shows roughly how many living organisms there are at each trophic level.

The producers are the first level, herbivores are the second level and carnivores are the third. Notice that there are fewer primary consumers than producers. There are also fewer secondary consumers than primary consumers. But secondary consumers are bigger than primary consumers as they have to eat them!

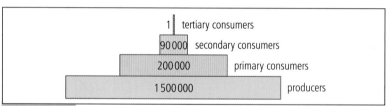

**Figure 18.2.2** Pyramid of numbers for a grassland community in 0.1 hectare.

A problem with pyramids of numbers is that they do not take into account the **size** of organisms at each trophic level.

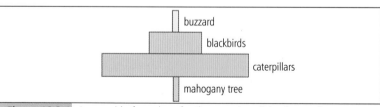

**Figure 18.2.4** A pyramid of numbers for the organisms living in a mahogany tree.

For instance, a mahogany tree and a grass plant each count as one organism. But one mahogany tree can support many more herbivores than one grass plant. As a result some pyramids of numbers can have unusual shapes.

In Figure 18.2.5 the tertiary consumers are parasites. Many of them feed on a single ladybird so this pyramid is inverted and it looks top heavy.

# Pyramids of biomass

One way to overcome the problem of size is to measure **biomass** instead of numbers. Biomass is the mass of living material. So a biomass pyramid shows the actual weight or mass of living things at each trophic level.

To draw a biomass pyramid the data first needs to be collected. A sample of the organisms from each trophic level is taken and weighed. The average mass for the sample is calculated. The average mass is then multiplied by the estimated number of organisms present in the community.

The dry mass is determined for the plant matter by drying it in an oven until it reaches a constant mass (see page 179). It is usually possible to estimate the dry mass of animals as approximately 65% of their body mass is water and this does not change as it does in plants. Dry mass tells us how much useful biological material is present as carbohydrates, proteins and fats as food for the organisms in the community. The data is usually expressed in grams per square metre.

The dry mass recorded is taken at one instant in time. Biomass pyramids do not take into account how fast an organism grows. For instance, grass often grows at a fast rate, but because it is grazed by animals, such as grasshoppers and cattle, its biomass at any instant in time will be low. This means it is better to calculate the biomass produced over a period of time, e.g. over a year or a growing season.

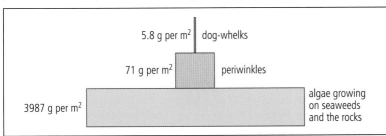

**Figure 18.2.6** A pyramid of biomass for a rocky seashore community.

Phytoplankton consists of tiny photosynthetic organisms that float in water – both freshwater (lakes and ponds) and in the sea. The plankton grow quickly at times of the year when there are nutrients and the sea is warm with plenty of light. They only live for a few days as they are grazed by animal plankton. So their biomass at any one time is small. But over say a year, their biomass is huge. This biomass pyramid records only a few days' growth and so is inverted:

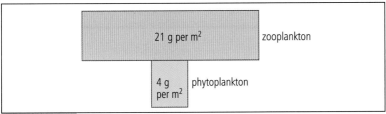

**Figure 18.2.7** Biomass pyramid for the English Channel.

Biomass can vary with the seasons. In temperate latitudes deciduous trees shed their leaves in winter. Their biomass is greater in summer than it is in winter as they will have leaves, flowers, fruits and seeds.

**KEY POINTS**

1 Pyramids of numbers show how many individuals there are at each trophic level but give no indication of their size.

2 Pyramids of biomass indicate the mass of living material at each trophic level, but give no indication of the rate of growth.

**SUMMARY QUESTIONS**

1 Draw two pyramids of numbers with different shapes. Explain their shapes.

2 Draw a pyramid of biomass for an ecosystem and explain its shape. Make sure that you include the unit of measurement for biomass on your pyramid.

3 What criticisms have been made about pyramids of numbers and pyramids of biomass?

# Shortening the food chain

## Pyramids of energy

The best way to show what is happening in the feeding relationships of a community is to use **energy pyramids**. These show the energy transferred from one trophic level to the next. This energy pyramid shows that 87 000 kJ per m² per year is passed to the tadpoles from the plant plankton. The tadpoles pass on 14 000 kJ per m² per year to the small fish, and so on.

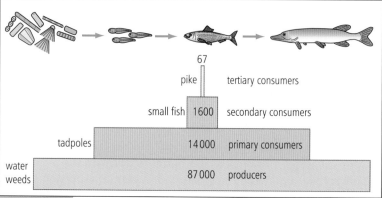

| water weeds | 87 000 | producers |
| tadpoles | 14 000 | primary consumers |
| small fish | 1600 | secondary consumers |
| pike | 67 | tertiary consumers |

**Figure 18.3.1** An energy pyramid for a lake. Figures are in kJ per m² per year.

The tadpoles obtain 87 000 kJ per m² per year from the water plants but only pass on 14 000 kJ of this to the small fish. The remaining 73 000 kJ per m² per year has been lost from the food chain. The tadpoles will have used a lot of energy in swimming and they will have passed out some in waste – urine and faeces. The only energy that they do pass on to the small fish is the energy in their biomass – their muscles and other organs that the fish eats every time it swallows a tadpole.

Energy is always 'lost' in this way as it passes from one trophic level to the next. Of the 87 000 kJ per m² per year of energy in the producers only 67 kJ of it becomes energy in the flesh of the top carnivore, the pike. Since only some of the energy is passed from one trophic level to the next an energy pyramid is never inverted. Its shape is not affected by the size of the organisms or how many of them there are since it simply looks at the energy that is passed on.

**EXAMINER SAYS...**

Pyramids of energy show energy transfer in an ecosystem. Another way is a flow chart as shown opposite. This shows the energy losses to respiration and decomposers. You should be able to interpret flow charts that show energy flow.

**EXAMINER SAYS...**

As you will know from Physics, energy transfer processes are never 100% efficient. Much energy is lost as heat. Respiration is no exception. Birds and mammals retain this heat to maintain a constant body temperature (see page 132).

## Energy losses

Energy flow through ecosystems is relatively inefficient. At best, plants absorb only 2 to 5% of the light energy that strikes their leaves. Much of this energy is not trapped in photosynthesis because it is reflected from the surface of the leaves, passes straight through them, or is green light which they cannot absorb.

Plants use much of the energy they trap in photosynthesis in their own respiration. As an energy transfer process, respiration is about 40%

Extension

efficient so about 60% of the energy is lost as heat to the plant and then to the atmosphere. Much of the plant's biomass is lost to decomposers in the form of dead leaves, twigs, fruits, etc. About 10% of the energy trapped by the plant is available to secondary consumers. Much of what they eat is not very edible or easy to digest. So primary consumers only make available about 10% of what they have eaten to secondary consumers. However, the animal flesh in primary consumers, for example grasshoppers and gazelles, is easier to digest and carnivores may obtain slightly more than 10% of the energy.

At each trophic level, energy is lost as heat to the environment and consumers lose energy in their faeces and urine to decomposers which means that there is less for the next trophic level. Food chains on land rarely have more than four trophic levels. Some in the sea are longer because the producers (plant plankton) are so small.

When farmers grow crops, such as rice, for human consumption all of the energy in the grain is available to us as primary consumers. Livestock farmers grow or buy plant food to feed their animals. They may buy cereals such as barley or maize or they may grow fodder crops, such as grass, alfalfa and clover, for grazing. Animals, such as pigs, cattle and chickens, use up much of the energy in their food. This means that there is not as much energy available to us.

A vegetarian diet can support far more people. If we cut down the number of links in the food chain more individuals at the end of the food chain can be fed. This is because we are cutting down the 90%

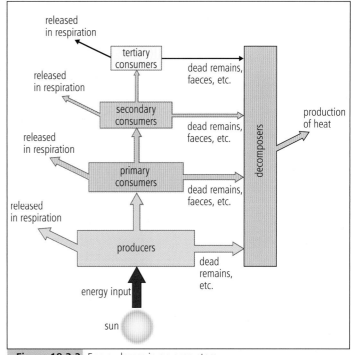

**Figure 18.3.2** Energy losses in an ecosystem.

'wastage' of energy that occurs between each trophic level, i.e. the energy that is uneaten, undigested or used in respiration at each level.

People in many countries tend to have diets that mainly consist of food of plant origin with some meat or fish. In the Western developed countries many people have a varied diet which includes a higher proportion of meat from poultry, fish, lamb, beef and pork.

The human population is increasing. If farmers are to provide enough food for everyone, our diet may have to change to one that includes more plant foods and less food of animal origin.

## SUMMARY QUESTIONS

1 a   What is the ultimate form of energy input in a food chain?
  b   Give two ways in which energy is 'lost' from food chains.

2 Explain why food chains usually have fewer than five trophic levels.

3 a   Explain why it is efficient, in terms of energy transfer, to supply green plants as human food.
  b   Explain why a diet rich in meat products is relatively inefficient in terms of energy loss.

## KEY POINTS

1 Energy losses occur between trophic levels as a result of respiration, and in waste materials produced.

2 More energy is available in foods for human consumption if we feed as primary consumers rather than as secondary consumers.

3 A vegetarian diet can support far more people than one that includes meat products.

# Nutrient cycles

- Describe the role of bacteria and fungi in decomposition
- Describe the different stages of the water cycle

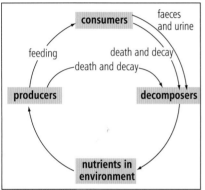

**Figure 18.4.1** The role of decomposers in ecosystems.

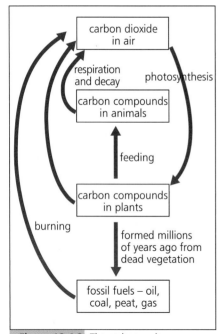

**Figure 18.4.2** The carbon cycle.

## Nutrient cycling

So far we have been concerned with food and energy. There is a constant flow of energy into ecosystems from the Sun, and energy flows through the different trophic levels and is then lost to the atmosphere. This section and the next are about some of the elements that comprise living organisms and how they are cycled in nature.

Most living matter (95%) is made up of six elements: carbon, hydrogen, oxygen, nitrogen, phosphorus and sulfur. Living things must have a constant supply of these elements if they are to make proteins, carbohydrates, fats and other organic materials. Unlike energy, there is no infinite source of these nutrients. Life has existed on Earth for millions of years. For it to continue, these elements must be recycled or they will become locked up in dead bodies and life will become extinct.

**Bacteria** and **fungi** feed on dead and decaying matter. They also feed on the waste matter of animals (urine and faeces). They feed by breaking down carbohydrates, fats and proteins into small molecules that they absorb. Many of these are respired. To do this they require water and a warm temperature as the processes of digestion and respiration are catalysed by enzymes. They also need oxygen for aerobic respiration.

Decomposers release carbon as carbon dioxide when they respire. They also break down amino acids releasing ammonia into their surroundings. In this way they recycle carbon and nitrogen – two of the most important elements for organisms. Simple compounds are absorbed by plants and converted into complex compounds.

These nutrients are then passed on to animals when they eat the plants. We say that **nutrients** are **cycled**.

These elements are found in the substances that living things take in. For instance, carbon is found in carbon dioxide, nitrogen is found in nitrate ions and hydrogen is found in water. If these elements were not recycled then living things would not have the elements that they need.

### The carbon cycle

Carbon is used to make carbohydrates, proteins, fats, DNA and other important biological molecules. The carbon comes from carbon dioxide in the air. Plants absorb carbon dioxide from the atmosphere and use it in photosynthesis to make food. Animals get the carbon compounds by eating plants.

Carbon dioxide gets into the air in the following ways.

- Plants and animals use some of their food for respiration, releasing carbon dioxide (as well as water and energy).
- Decomposers use dead plants and animals for food. They also use some of the decaying material for respiration, releasing carbon dioxide (plus water and energy).

- Fossil fuels like oil, peat, coal, and natural gas contain carbon. When they are burned, carbon dioxide is one of the gases released into the air.

These processes release carbon dioxide into the air and this balances the uptake by photosynthesis so the concentration of carbon dioxide in the atmosphere remains constant.

## The water cycle

The water cycle demonstrates how important water is to life on Earth.

Follow the arrows on the diagram to see how the world's water moves between living organisms and their environment.

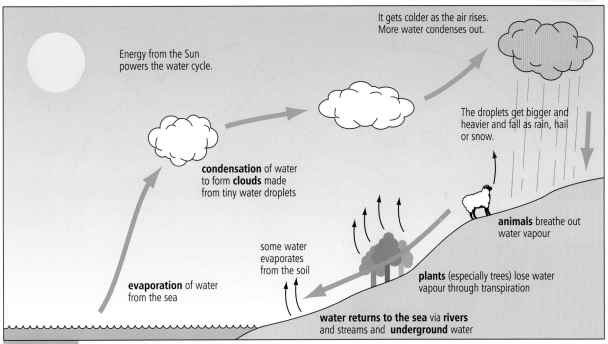

Energy from the Sun powers the water cycle.

It gets colder as the air rises. More water condenses out.

The droplets get bigger and heavier and fall as rain, hail or snow.

**condensation** of water to form **clouds** made from tiny water droplets

**animals** breathe out water vapour

some water evaporates from the soil

**plants** (especially trees) lose water vapour through transpiration

**evaporation** of water from the sea

**water returns to the sea** via **rivers** and streams and **underground** water

**Figure 18.4.3** The water cycle.

### SUMMARY QUESTIONS

1 a Describe what is meant by the term *cycle*, in the context of nutrients and living organisms.

  b State two substances that are absorbed and recycled by living organisms.

  c Name the six elements that make up 95% of living matter.

2 State the roles of the following in nutrient cycles:

  a decomposers, b green plants, c animals.

3 Look at the diagram of the water cycle above.

  a State three ways in which water gets into the atmosphere.

  b Explain why it rains when clouds rise.

  c State the source of the energy that powers the water cycle.

### KEY POINTS

1 Decomposers, like bacteria and fungi, have an important role to play in the recycling of nutrients.

2 Carbon is cycled through ecosystems by processes such as photosynthesis and respiration.

3 Evaporation and condensation are important processes in the water cycle.

## Nitrogen

Nitrogen is an element required for many biologically important molecules. Amino acids, proteins, DNA and chlorophyll contain nitrogen. Approximately 80% of the air is nitrogen gas ($N_2$) but it is inert and very few organisms can make use of it. Plants, animals and most microorganisms cannot use it in this form. It has to be available to them as fixed nitrogen in the form of compounds such as amino acids and proteins, and as ions such as nitrate and ammonium ions.

The diagram below shows the nitrogen cycle which summarises all the changes that happen to nitrogen as it is recycled.

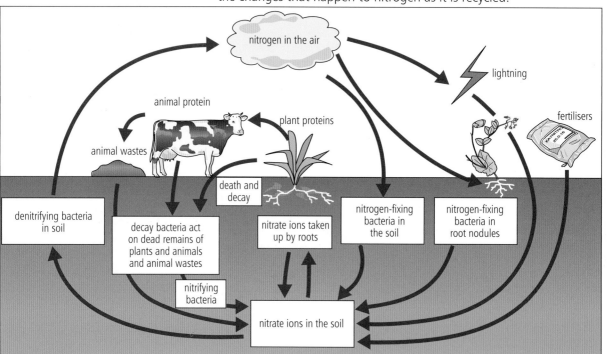

**Figure 18.5.1** The nitrogen cycle.

Most of the nitrogen that plants obtain they absorb in the form of nitrate ions ($NO_3^-$). They use this to make amino acids in their leaves. The amino acids are used to form proteins, such as enzymes. Animals eat plants and so obtain their nitrogen in the form of plant protein. Nitrogen is then recycled from dead plant and animal matter and from animal wastes by decomposers. This part of the cycle is dominated by microorganisms.

### Parts of the nitrogen cycle

**Decomposers** (bacteria and fungi) break down dead remains and animal wastes releasing ammonium ions ($NH_4^+$) into the soil. Bacteria also break down urea in urine to ammonium ions. This process is sometimes called ammonification.

**Nitrifying bacteria** in the soil change ammonium ions into nitrate ions. These bacteria gain their source of energy from this oxidation reaction instead of absorbing light or feeding as a decomposer.

If you are tracing the cycle in the diagram you will realise we are back where we started with absorption of nitrate ions by plants.

Two other groups of microorganisms help to recycle nitrogen.

**Nitrogen-fixing bacteria** are found in the soil. These can convert nitrogen gas from the air into compounds of nitrogen that they use themselves. When they die and are decomposed, this fixed nitrogen is available to plants.

Nitrogen-fixing bacteria are also found in the roots of legume plants like peas, beans, alfalfa and clover and many tropical trees, such as flame trees (see page 176). The bacteria are inside swellings on the roots called **root nodules**. These bacteria change nitrogen gas into ammonia that the legume plants can use to make amino acids. In return the legume plants provide a suitable environment for the bacteria (in the nodules) and also provide all the sugars that they need. Nitrogen fixation requires a lot of energy.

**Denitrifying bacteria** live in water-logged soil. They change nitrate ions to nitrogen gas. It is thought that they balance the uptake of nitrogen gas by nitrogen-fixing bacteria.

**Lightning** causes nitrogen and oxygen to react together at high temperatures. Nitrogen oxides are formed in the reactions. These are washed into the soil by rain where they form nitrate ions.

Nitrate ions are lost from the soil before plants can absorb them as they can be washed out of the soil by rainwater. This is called **leaching**.

Farmers add fertilisers containing nitrogen, e.g. ammonium nitrate. These are manufactured from ammonia made in the Haber process and add extra sources of nitrate ions for crop plants. The fertilisers replace the nitrate absorbed by the plants and removed at harvest. Some farmers do not use inorganic fertilisers, but instead use natural fertilisers such as manure. This provides dead material that enters the nitrogen cycle at the point where the decomposers act.

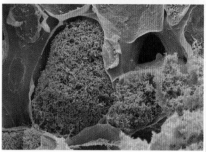

The top photo shows some nitrogen-fixing root nodules. In the bottom photo you can see the cells of a root nodule broken open to reveal the thousands of nitrogen-fixing bacteria that live inside.

## SUMMARY QUESTIONS

1 List four substances present in living organisms that contain the element nitrogen.

2 Describe the roles of microorganisms (bacteria and fungi) in the following processes:
   a  decomposition,       b  nitrification,
   c  nitrogen fixation,   d  denitrification.

3 Explain how nitrogen in the protein of dead animals and plants is made available to plants in the form of nitrate ions.

4 Explain how farmers can increase the quantity of nitrate available to crop plants.

## KEY POINTS

1 Nitrogen is in the atmosphere as a gas ($N_2$) but is not available to most organisms as it is not reactive.

2 Some bacteria fix nitrogen ($N_2$) converting it to ammonia. Some of these live inside root nodules of legumes. They are called nitrogen-fixing bacteria.

3 Bacteria decompose protein and urea to ammonia. Nitrifying bacteria convert ammonia to nitrate ions.

4 Denitrifying bacteria convert nitrate ions to nitrogen gas ($N_2$).

5 Plants absorb nitrate ions and convert them to amino acids which they use to make proteins. Animals obtain the amino acids they need by eating and digesting plant or animal protein.

1 Define the following terms:

   *producer, primary consumer, secondary consumer, decomposer, carnivore, ecosystem.*

2 Explain what is meant by the term *trophic level*.

3 Draw a food chain involving at least four organisms. State the trophic level occupied by each organism in the food chain.

   Annotate your food chain by describing the roles of organisms at each trophic level in your food chain.

4 There are very few large carnivores, such as lions, tigers and great white sharks, in ecosystems. Explain why this is so.

5 Explain the essential difference between nutrient flow and energy flow in an ecosystem.

6 The diagram shows pyramids of numbers for two ecosystems. Explain why they are different.

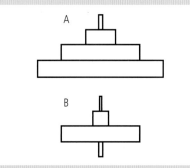

7 Make a flow diagram to show how carbon is recycled. Annotate your diagram to explain the changes that occur at each stage.

8 Explain how energy is lost between trophic levels in a food chain.

9 The element nitrogen exists in many biologically important compounds, such as proteins, DNA, amino acids, urea and nitrate ions. Outline what happens to nitrogen-containing compounds in the following processes:

   (a) protein synthesis,

   (b) deamination (see page 85),

   (c) ammonification,

   (d) nitrification,

   (e) denitrification,

   (f) nitrogen fixation.

1 From which food chain is *most* energy lost?

   A maize → beef cattle → humans

   B soya beans → humans

   C grass → dairy cattle → humans

   D phytoplankton → mollusc larvae → small fish → tuna → humans

   *(Paper 1)*                                    [1]

2 The diagram shows a pyramid of numbers for an ecosystem. Which level indicates the tertiary consumers?

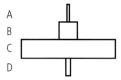

   *(Paper 1)*                                    [1]

3 An ecosystem is all the:

   A organisms in an area

   B organisms in an area and the physical factors that influence them

   C physical factors that influence organisms in an area

   D plants and animals in an area and the interactions between them

   *(Paper 1)*                                    [1]

4 The table shows the total biomass formed in 1 square metre of grassland during one year.

   The figures were obtained by measuring the dry mass and not the fresh mass of the living material.

| organisms | dry mass (g per m² per year) |
|---|---|
| green plants | 480 |
| herbivores | 0.9 |
| carnivores | 0.1 |

   (a) Calculate the percentage decrease in the biomass between green plants and herbivores. Show your working. [2]

   (b) Explain why the biomass formed during the year decreases between trophic levels. [3]

   (c) Explain the advantage of measuring dry mass rather than fresh mass when investigating biomass production in different ecosystems. [3]

   *(Paper 2)*

**5** The diagram shows the passage of energy along a food chain in a grassland ecosystem. The light energy that strikes the leaves of the grass each year is 400 000 kJ per m².

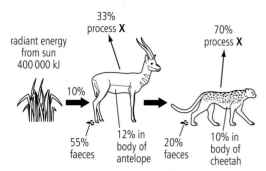

**(a)** The plant only absorbs about 1% of the energy that strikes the plant and uses it in photosynthesis to make simple sugars.

   **(i)** State two compounds that are produced in plants from the simple sugars. [2]

   **(ii)** State three ways in which the leaves of plants are adapted to trap as much light as possible. [3]

**(b)** Only about 10% of the energy trapped by the plant in photosynthesis is passed to herbivores like antelopes.

   **(i)** State two ways in which the plant uses the energy that is not available to the herbivores. [2]

   **(ii)** Calculate how much energy reaches the antelopes each year. Express your answer as kJ per m². Show your working. [3]

**(c)** Name process **X**. [1]

**(d)** Suggest why the antelope loses more of its energy intake as faeces compared with the cheetah. [2]

**(e)** This food chain has three trophic levels in it. Explain why there are no more. [4]

*(Paper 3)*

**6** The following are biologically important substances that contain the element nitrogen:

urea, ammonia ($NH_3$), amino acids, nitrite ions, nitrate ions

**(a)** Choose one of the substances from the list to match the statements **(i)** to **(v)**. You may use each one once, more than once or not at all.

   **(i)** the main nitrogen-containing excretory product of animals

   **(ii)** absorbed by plants

   **(iii)** a product of deamination

   **(iv)** synthesised into proteins

   **(v)** the end product of nitrification [5]

**(b)** Nitrogen gas ($N_2$) in the atmosphere is inert. Unlike carbon dioxide and oxygen very few organisms are able to use it. Describe how nitrogen gas ($N_2$) present in the atmosphere is made available to be used by organisms. [4]

*(Paper 3)*

**7** The table shows the energy flow through a crop of potatoes. Units are kJ per m² per year.

| | |
|---|---|
| solar energy that strikes the leaves of the potato plants | 1 000 000 |
| energy that cannot be absorbed by the chloroplasts in the leaves | 600 000 |
| energy that is reflected from the leaf surfaces | 2400 |
| energy that passes through the leaves | 2400 |
| energy trapped by photosynthesis and used to make simple sugars | 214 500 |
| energy transferred and lost to the environment as heat | 190 000 |
| energy stored in biomass and available to the next trophic level | 24 500 |

**(a)** Calculate the energy stored in biomass as a percentage of the energy that strikes the leaves of the potato plants. Show your working. [2]

**(b)** Use the table to explain why very little solar energy becomes available in the stored biomass. [4]

**(c)** The potatoes are harvested and sold in the market. Explain the ways in which a farmer could maximise his profits by increasing the yield of the potatoes. [4]

**(d)** Explain why feeding crops to livestock is an inefficient way to provide food for humans. [5]

*(Paper 3)*

## 19.1 Populations

Wildebeest and zebras in East Africa.

### Population growth

A **population** is a group of individuals of the same species living in the same habitat at the same time. All the individuals in a population may interbreed. Sometimes it is difficult to tell the geographical limits of a population. This is easiest where the organisms live in a restricted area, such as on an island, like Komodo dragons on islands in Indonesia, or on a mountain, like *Protea kilimanjaro*, or they are highly visible, like wildebeest in the game parks of East Africa.

Some species are very widely distributed and it is difficult to divide them into separate populations. However, there are usually barriers to reproduction, such as rivers and mountains, that divide them into separate populations. Some individuals migrate across these barriers, so there is interbreeding between populations.

The table shows some animal and plant examples.

| population | habitat | place |
|---|---|---|
| creole wrasse | coral reef | reefs around Tobago in the Caribbean |
| wildebeest | grassland | East Africa |
| Komodo dragon | dry grassland and forest | Komodo Island in Indonesia |
| *Nepenthes rajah* – carnivorous plant | mountain forest | Mount Kinabalu in Malaysia |
| *Protea kilimanjaro* | shrubland | Mount Kilimanjaro in Kenya |

### Population size

The diagram shows the factors that determine the size of a population. The number of births adds to the population and the number of deaths decreases it. Individuals may enter or leave a population from neighbouring populations.

Animals migrate so there is mixing between populations. Flowering plants are fixed so you would think that migration is not possible. However, plants use seed dispersal to colonise new areas and in this way individuals leave one population of plants to join another (see page 176).

### Bacterial growth

The growth of a bacterial population is a good way to show how the size of a population changes over time. A small number of bacteria are placed into a flask with a warm nutrient solution which is aerated so the bacteria may respire aerobically. Bacteria grow and divide under these conditions.

**Figure 19.1.1** Factors influencing population size.

immigration

+

birth + → population size − → death

−

emigration

Some species of bacteria divide every 20 minutes if conditions are ideal. One cell divides to give two cells, two cells divide to give four, and so on. You can work out how many cells there will be after 4 hours and you will quickly reach a very large number.

During this phase of rapid growth there are no factors to limit population growth. But after a while factors, such as lack of food and build up of wastes, limit population growth which slows down and stops. If the flask is left then the numbers will decline as bacteria die. The curve shown in the graph is known as the **sigmoid growth curve**.

Some species show this population growth in the wild. When resources become available, species that can reproduce rapidly like algae grow exponentially. When the resources are used up, most of them die (see page 248 for an example). Most species do not do this – their populations remain fairly stable over time.

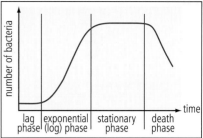

**Figure 19.1.2** Growth of a bacterial colony.

## Phases in bacterial growth

If you look at the graph above you can see four main phases in the growth of a bacterial colony.

- The **lag phase**, when doubling of the numbers has little effect as the numbers are so small. Bacteria take up water and nutrients, make new cytoplasm, DNA and enzymes.
- The **exponential** (or **log**) **phase** when the population is increasing rapidly. The population increases by doubling and there are no limiting factors, such as food or water.
- The **stationary phase**, when bacterial cells are dying at the same rate at which they are being produced. This may be because of shortage of food or because waste products are building up.
- The **death phase**, when more cells are dying than are being produced, so the population declines. Causes of death may be lack of food, shortage of oxygen or a build-up of toxic waste products.

## Checks on population increase

- **Competition**. Plants compete for light, space, water and soil nutrients. Animals compete for food, space (territory) and mates. Competition for food is a common limiting factor for species of herbivores, such as wildebeest in East Africa.
- **Predation**. A **predator** is an animal that feeds by hunting and killing its prey. Often predators take young, sick individuals or less well-adapted individuals. Predators may limit the growth of a population of prey animals, but it is more often the case that the numbers of prey animals limit the population size of the predator.
- **Disease**. Disease is an important control factor when populations increase. Pathogens are transmitted between individuals more easily when organisms live close together. Disease can cause population crashes if the species has no resistance or immunity.

1 A population is a group of individuals of the same species, living in the same habitat at the same time.

2 Populations increase in size due to births and immigration and decrease due to deaths and emigration.

3 The growth and final size of a population is influenced by the availability of food, by predation and by disease.

1 a Define the term *population*.

   b Give three examples of populations in natural ecosystems.

   c State the ways in which populations may increase and decrease.

2 Explain how each of the following can act to limit the growth of a population, giving an example in each case:

   a food supply
   b predation
   c disease.

3 With reference to the sigmoid population growth curve above, describe and explain each of the following phases:

   a lag  b exponential (log)
   c stationary  d death.

# Human populations

- Describe and explain the increase in the human population
- Interpret graphs and diagrams of human population growth

## Human population growth

At present the number of people on the planet is growing at an alarming rate. In early 2009, there were estimated to be about 6.75 billion people in the world. For thousands of years there was only a slow increase in the human population. Lack of food and shelter together with the effects of malnutrition, diseases and wars meant that mortality rates were high and people did not live long.

Six thousand years ago the world's population was about 0.2 billion people. People lived in small scattered communities and much of the world was unaffected by human activities. However, people were beginning to make an impact on their environment by clearing forests, growing crops and keeping livestock. They relied less on hunting and collecting food from the wild, although these were still important and remain so in the case of the fishing industry.

Look at the graph:

the human population has increased exponentially over the past 300 years for the following reasons.

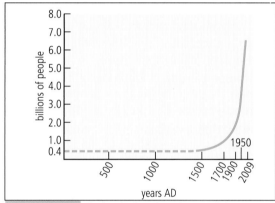

**Figure 19.2.1** Notice the long lag phase and short exponential phase with no sign of a stationary phase.

- Improved agriculture means that most people are better fed. Better nutrition means they are better defended against diseases, especially those caused by malnutrition.
- Public health has improved. There are clean water supplies, drainage of waste and sewage treatment. This has decreased epidemics of waterborne diseases such as cholera.
- Medical care has improved. Since the 1940s doctors have used antibiotics; people are also vaccinated against many infectious diseases, such as diphtheria and polio.

The effects of these improvements have been:

- decrease in the infant and child mortality rates (infancy is the first year of life),
- decrease in death rates from starvation and malnutrition,
- increase in life expectancy – people are now living much longer. In Europe and North America the average life expectancy is 76 years for men and 80 years for women. In India, average life expectancy is 68 years.

In spite of these improvements there are huge inequalities in food, housing, water and health services. Many of the world's human population live in poverty with high infant and child mortality rates and life expectancies that are half those mentioned above.

## Controlling human population growth

There are still controls on population increase. Famines, epidemics, floods, wars, tsunamis, earthquakes, and other disasters, lead to loss of life. But the overall trend is a rapid increase in the world's population. It is estimated that it could double in the next 30 years, but with the population in some regions increasing rapidly and in others remaining stable or even decreasing.

In Europe and North America the population is virtually stable. In other places populations continue to grow. The Earth has limited resources and limited space and the population will have to stabilise and even decrease at some time in the future. The most obvious way to do this is to reduce the birth rate. But many groups of people have strongly held religious or moral views on birth control and family size. This means they may often have large families. China has had a 'one-child' policy since 1979 and it is claimed this has restricted population growth in that country. No other country has such a policy.

The base of the population pyramids below show the percentage of children below the age of 5 years. The oldest people appear at the top. The rate of increase in populations is most influenced by the proportion of child-bearing women in the population.

Increasing human population size brings greater demands on resources and problems for the environment, such as the supply of food, housing, transport and energy needs. There is also the problem of how to dispose of our rubbish.

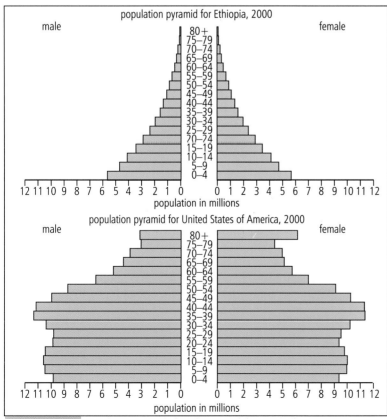

**Figure 19.2.2** Population pyramids for Ethiopia and the USA in the year 2000.

**SUMMARY QUESTIONS**

1 Study the population pyramids on the left.

   a State which country has the greater proportion of i young people, ii old people.

   b Suggest reasons for the differences between the populations of the two countries.

   c Suggest what you think will happen in each country to i the numbers of women of child-bearing age in 10 years' time, and ii the birth rate in 10 years' time.

   d Outline the likely effects that your answers to part c will have on the two countries in the future.

2 Explain why infant and child mortality rates have decreased and why people are living much longer.

# Resources

An open cast coal mine. Coal is an important fossil fuel.

The pressure of an increasing world population has significant effects on the resources of the planet. Some of these resources are:

- fossil fuels – oil, coal and natural gas
- food resources, e.g. staple foods such as wheat, rice and maize
- land for agriculture
- land for housing, transport, industry and human leisure activities
- land and bodies of water for disposal of waste.

As the population of the world increases, so more raw materials are being used up. Raw materials fall into two main categories.

1. **Renewable resources** are those that are replaced as fast as plants and animals grow and reproduce. Examples are timber for building and for making paper, and fish and molluscs harvested from the sea and from lakes.

2. **Non-renewable resources** include energy sources such as fossil fuels and minerals, e.g. copper, zinc and lead ores. When we have used these resources, they cannot be replaced; they are gone forever.

Alternative energy sources, including solar power, hydroelectric power and wind power, are called **renewable resources**. Sugar cane is grown in Brazil to provide sugar for fermentation to make alcohol which is mixed with petrol to make gasohol. Fast-growing willow trees are grown in the UK for burning in power stations.

Nuclear power is used in a number of industrialised countries, such as France, using uranium in power stations. But supplies of uranium will also run out eventually.

We use natural ecosystems for harvesting food and disposal of waste. Here are some examples:

- the oceans have been overfished, reducing fish stocks considerably
- toxic waste has been dumped into the oceans
- rivers are used for disposal of waste
- forests are felled for timber and for growing crops.

## Deforestation

Humans have been clearing forests for over 10 000 years to grow food and provide land for settlements and provide transport links. There are now very few forests left in temperate regions that have not been affected. Tropical forests in South-East Asia and South America have been cut down over the past 100 years. Many of these are rainforests.

There has been large-scale deforestation to provide the following:

- timber as building materials
- paper for newsprint and other forms of paper and cardboard

- land for farms, cattle ranches and plantations of oil palms, sugar cane and soya beans
- land for roads, towns and factories
- firewood and charcoal as fuels.

Deforestation has resulted in a number of environmental problems.

- Soils in tropical rainforests are very thin and when the vegetation is removed the soil is easily washed away. This causes soil erosion, formation of gullies and loss of plant nutrients.
- Local weather patterns change, with more frequent and severe storms.
- Flooding happens more frequently as water runs off the land much quicker and is not absorbed by plants and transpired into the atmosphere. Forests act as 'stores' of water, their leaves slow down the rate of evaporation from the soil and decrease the rate at which water reaches the soil.
- Destruction of the rainforests means the loss of many habitats and the extinction of species.
- Carbon dioxide is added to the atmosphere because vegetation is burnt.

Rainforests are being cut down at an alarming rate.

## Carbon dioxide

*Extension*

Rainforests have no effect on maintaining the correct balance of carbon dioxide and oxygen in our atmosphere. They produce about as much carbon dioxide as they use in photosynthesis, and there is such a huge reserve of oxygen in the atmosphere that the quantity produced by all plants on Earth makes little difference to the overall oxygen concentration of the atmosphere. There is no evidence that the rainforests are the 'lungs' of the Earth. There are, however, plenty of other reasons to stop cutting them down.

There are ecosystems that absorb carbon dioxide from the atmosphere and will help counter the effects of burning fossil fuels. **Carbon sinks** are areas that store carbon in long-lived plant materials, and where there is little decomposition so dead vegetation forms peat that 'locks up' carbon for a long time. Examples are forests in northern latitudes in Asia and North America and peat bogs.

## SUMMARY QUESTIONS

1 Outline some of the effects that an increasing human population has had on the environment.

2 Distinguish between renewable and non-renewable resources.

3 It is estimated that between 1880 and 1980 about 40% of all tropical rainforest was destroyed.

   a  Give three reasons for large-scale deforestation.

   b  Outline some of the effects that deforestation has on the environment.

4 Explain the effects that loss of ecosystems may have on the carbon dioxide concentration of the atmosphere.

*Extension*

### KEY POINTS

1 Deforestation is due to the world demand for timber and paper. The land is also cleared for farms, cattle ranches and new roads.

2 Deforestation leads to soil erosion, severe storms, flooding, the destruction of habitats and extinction of species.

3 Rainforests have no effect on maintaining the concentrations of carbon dioxide and oxygen in the atmosphere, but forests and peat bogs in northern latitudes remove carbon dioxide from the atmosphere.

*Extension*

# Pollution

## LEARNING OUTCOMES

- State the sources and effects of air pollutants such as sulfur dioxide, carbon dioxide and methane
- State the sources and effects of some water pollutants
- Describe the dangers of nuclear fall-out
- Describe the effects of non-biodegradable plastics on the environment

The human population has expanded so much in the past 300 years that it has put pressure on the Earth's resources. This is not only in terms of providing us with materials, such as fossil fuels and minerals. It is also in terms of disposing of our waste and absorbing the materials that we use, such as fertilisers and pesticides.

**Pollution** is the harm done to the environment by the release of substances produced by human activities. The table shows some of these pollutants, their sources and the effects that they have on the environment.

| pollutant | sources | undesirable effects of pollutant on the environment |
|---|---|---|
| sulfur dioxide | burning fossil fuels | cause of acid rain (see page 246) |
| carbon dioxide | burning fossil fuels | enhances greenhouse effect (see page 244) |
| methane | Cattle and paddy fields for growing rice, coal and oil extraction | enhances greenhouse effect (see page 244) |
| nitrogen oxides | motor vehicles, fertilisers | cause of acid rain (see page 246) |
| sewage | human and livestock waste contains urea, ammonia, protein, carbohydrates, fats and pathogens | reduces oxygen concentration in rivers, destruction of freshwater communities (see page 248) |
| industrial chemical waste – includes variety of toxic substances including lead, mercury and cyanide | factories | can be fatal to wildlife and humans; can accumulate in organisms |
| fertilisers (mostly N and P) | arable agriculture | eutrophication in fresh water (rivers, lakes) |
| herbicides for killing weeds | arable agriculture | spray drift kills harmless plants, persist in the environment |
| pesticides for killing pests and diseases | arable and livestock agriculture | accumulates in food chains, kills harmless (non-pest) species |
| solid waste (biodegradable and non-biodegradable rubbish) | domestic and industrial waste | buried in ground (landfill) or left on rubbish tips. Health hazard, leakage of toxic liquids and release of methane |
| non-biodegradable plastics | packaging | buried in ground, does not decay so takes up space |
| nuclear fall out (beta and gamma radiation) | atomic bomb, accidents at nuclear power stations, nuclear tests | death with high exposure, cancers in humans, mutations in non-human species |

# Radiation

Natural radiation from our surroundings, e.g. from rocks and building materials, influences living organisms and is a cause of mutation (see page 216). Human-produced radiation comes from the testing and use of nuclear weapons and leakages from nuclear reactors. Certain atoms are unstable and their nuclei can break down, releasing small particles or rays. These atoms are said to be radioactive. The particles are **alpha** and **beta** particles and the rays are **gamma rays**.

In 1986, there was an accident at the Chernobyl nuclear power station in what is now Ukraine. A huge cloud of radioactive material was released into the atmosphere. The winds blew the cloud across Europe. Radioactive chemicals were deposited in countries such as Sweden and Poland. Two of these radioactive chemicals were iodine and caesium.

Radioactive iodine has a half life of 8 days so does not last long in the environment. However, if absorbed it is concentrated in the thyroid gland in the neck. This caused many thyroid cancers among children living in the areas immediately around the reactor. Radioactive caesium has a half life of 30 years and this has made agricultural land in the countries of Ukraine and Belarus unusable for many years.

The safe disposal of radioactive nuclear waste is a major problem and a potential threat to the environment. Radiation interferes with cell division and cell growth. Exposure to high doses of radiation is fatal, but lower exposure causes sickness, skin burns, loss of hair and cancers, such as leukaemia. Evidence collected from survivors of the atomic bombs dropped on Hiroshima and Nagasaki in 1945 shows that there has not been any increase in the number of inherited mutations, although these may take several generations to appear.

## Waste plastics

Some materials we throw away are broken down in the environment by decomposers – these are called **biodegradable**. Some are not and these are called **non-biodegradable**. Plastics are used for packaging because they last a long time and do not decay easily. But this becomes a problem when it comes to disposing of plastics. Most plastic waste goes into landfill sites or rubbish dumps where they take up a lot of space. Biodegradable plastics are designed to break down more quickly than conventional non-biodegradable plastics once they are dumped. For example, some plastics now have starch incorporated into their structures which is digested by bacteria in the soil.

We can recycle many thermoplastics that we use by melting them and remoulding them into new shapes. Burning plastics in incinerators reduces the volume of waste, but many plastics produce toxic gases as they burn.

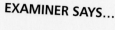

Most plastic bottles have a recycling symbol with a category number. These bottles are in category 1 as they are made of polyethylene terephthalate (PET or PETE) which can be recycled to make products such as packaging materials and carpets.

EXAMINER SAYS...

The table on the previous page summarises what you need to know for Paper 2. If you are taking Paper 3, it is an introduction to the rest of this unit.

## KEY POINTS

1 Pollution is the harm done to the environment by the release of substances produced by human activities.

2 Pollutants affect the air, ecosystems on land and aquatic ecosystems like rivers and the sea.

3 Nuclear fall-out comes from the testing and use of nuclear weapons and leakages from nuclear reactors.

4 Some plastics are biodegradable; others are non-biodegradable but some can be recycled.

## SUMMARY QUESTIONS

1 List three pollutants of each of the following:

  a   the atmosphere

  b   aquatic ecosystems

  c   the land.

2 a   State the main sources of radiation.

  b   Describe the undesirable effects of nuclear fall-out.

3 Explain the problems caused to the environment by non-biodegradable plastics.

243

# The greenhouse effect

## LEARNING OUTCOMES

- Describe the contribution of the greenhouse gases carbon dioxide and methane to global warming

- Explain how air pollution by greenhouse gases causes global warming

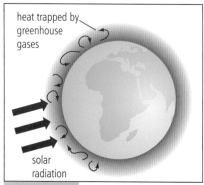

heat trapped by greenhouse gases

solar radiation

**Figure 19.5.1** The greenhouse effect.

Factories, oil refineries and power stations release huge quantities of carbon dioxide into the atmosphere when they burn fossil fuels.

## EXAMINER SAYS...

There are several air pollutants that you need to know. Look back to the table on page 242 to remind yourself of these.

## Greenhouse gases

The atmosphere is like a blanket surrounding the Earth keeping it warm. Some of the gases in the atmosphere act like a greenhouse to keep in heat that otherwise would be radiated into space. These are the so-called **greenhouse gases** which are carbon dioxide, water vapour and methane. Some man-made air pollutants, such as CFCs (chlorofluorocarbons), are greenhouse gases as well as the cause of other problems.

These greenhouse gases allow solar energy to pass through to the Earth's surface. Some energy enters food chains and is eventually lost to the atmosphere as heat, which is radiated away from the Earth's surface.

Some heat energy escapes into space, but much is reflected back towards the Earth. Greenhouse gases keep our atmosphere at the temperatures that allow life to exist.

It is important to understand that the greenhouse effect is a natural process and without it the average temperature on the Earth would be about −17 °C. However, over the last 100 years, there has been a build-up of greenhouse gases.

Power stations, factories, domestic heating and transport use fossil fuels and release huge amounts of carbon dioxide into the atmosphere. As we have seen, deforestation has resulted in large areas of forest being removed. In South America the trees are cleared for farming and they are burnt, which releases carbon dioxide into the atmosphere. Roots and other remaining tree parts are decomposed by microbes in the soil, producing even more carbon dioxide.

There has also been a significant increase in methane (another greenhouse gas) due to the expansion of rice cultivation and cattle rearing. Methane is released by cattle and also by bacteria in the anaerobic conditions found in flooded rice fields and natural wetlands. Rotting material in landfill sites and rubbish tips, as well as the extraction of oil and natural gas, are other sources of methane.

Of all the greenhouse gases the largest increase has been in carbon dioxide, which has risen by 10% in the last 30 years. However, methane and CFCs cannot be ignored as they are much more effective greenhouse gases than carbon dioxide.

## The greenhouse effect

The diagram shows in more detail how the greenhouse effect works.

- Solar radiation passes through the atmosphere and warms the Earth's surface.

- The Earth radiates heat energy back into space. This is mainly infra-red radiation.

- Some of this heat energy is absorbed by the greenhouse gases.

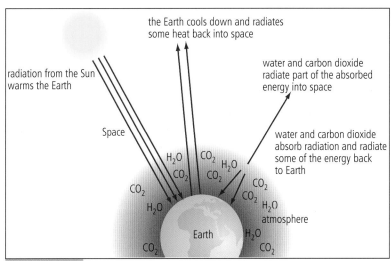

**Figure 19.5.2** How the greenhouse effect works.

This causes the air to warm up. Without carbon dioxide and water vapour the heat energy would pass straight back out into space. Human activity is causing a large increase in the atmosphere of carbon dioxide and other greenhouse gases such as methane, which has a greater impact than carbon dioxide (see question 7 on page 255).

(see question 7 on page 255)

### Global warming

*Extension*

Human activities are causing an increase in the concentration of greenhouse gases so the atmosphere is getting warmer. This is causing the **enhanced greenhouse effect**. The surface of the Earth has warmed by 0.7 °C over the past century. There are fears that this warming is increasing.

If the temperature of the Arctic and Antarctic was to rise above 0 °C then the polar ice would start to melt. This would cause a rise in sea level and flooding of many low-lying areas, for example in Bangladesh. These would include some of the capital cities of the world.

There could also be a change in wind patterns and the distribution of rainfall leading to more extreme weather. Some parts are expected to become very dry. Some of these are important agricultural areas, such as parts of the USA and Asia, so that warming of the climate could mean a massive reduction in the grain crops of Central Asia and North America. The pattern of the world's food distribution could be affected with economic and political consequences.

Measures to reduce the effects of global warming involve reducing carbon emissions. This may be done by encouraging public transport, using energy more efficiently, recycling and changing the diet of cattle to stop them releasing methane.

One method is to use fossil fuels more efficiently as happens in a combined heat and power plant in which the heat is used for domestic heating.

**KEY POINTS**

1 The naturally occurring greenhouse gases act as a blanket around the Earth and prevent some heat energy escaping into space.

2 Air pollution by carbon dioxide and methane has increased the greenhouse effect and this is contributing to global warming.

3 The possible consequences of global warming could be a rise in sea level, flooding of low-lying areas, changes in the world's climate and a reduction in crop production in some areas.

**SUMMARY QUESTIONS**

1 Copy and complete:

**warms  absorbed  air energy  space  radiates infra-red  atmosphere**

Solar _____ passes through the _____ and _____ the Earth's surface. The Earth _____ heat energy back into _____

This is mainly _____ radiation. Some of the heat energy is _____ by the greenhouse gases. This causes the _____ to warm up.

2 List the gases that contribute to the enhanced greenhouse effect and in each case give one human activity that acts as a source of the gas.

3 a Describe the likely consequences of global warming.

b Describe the ways in which people and their governments can reduce the emission of greenhouse gases and attempt to reduce the effects of global warming.

*Extension*

# 19.6 Acid rain

**Sulfur dioxide** ($SO_2$) is released when fossil fuels are burnt. Together with nitrogen oxides ($NO_x$) from exhaust fumes, they cause **acid rain**. Rain is naturally acidic as the water dissolves carbon dioxide. However, when sulfur dioxide and nitrogen oxides dissolve in water in the atmosphere and react with oxygen they produce sulfuric and nitric acids which lower the pH. In some places the pH of the rain may be as low as 3.0.

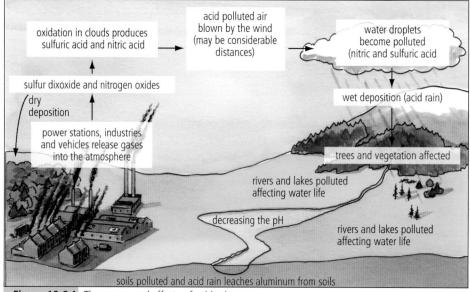

**Figure 19.6.1** The causes and effects of acid rain.

These gases can be carried over large distances by winds before being deposited as dry particles or dissolved in the rain. The term 'acid rain' refers to both of these types of deposition.

When acid rain falls on trees it kills the leaves and reduces their ability to resist disease. Many trees in central European forests have been killed by acid rain.

Vegetation is affected by high concentrations of sulfur dioxide. Most sensitive are lichens, which are composed of algae and fungi living together. They absorb all their water and nutrients from the atmosphere. Some species are very sensitive to sulfur dioxide and only grow where the air is free of the gas and some can tolerate high concentrations. Others can tolerate intermediate concentrations. Lichens are useful indicators of pollution. By looking at the species growing in an area, you can deduce the average concentration of sulfur dioxide.

Increasing concentration of sulfur dioxide in the atmosphere ⟶

When acid rain falls on soils on limestone or chalk there is little effect, because the soils are alkaline and this neutralises the acid. When it falls on soils on hard rocks, such as granite, the soil is already acidic and there is nothing to neutralise the acid rain. Acid rain causes plant nutrients, such as potassium and calcium, to become soluble and wash out of soils leaving them infertile.

Aluminium compounds in soils become soluble below pH 5.5. Acidified water that enters lakes, streams and rivers lowers the pH of these bodies of water. The aluminium concentration can increase considerably. Species of invertebrates and fish that live in these ecosystems cannot tolerate water with a low pH, and aluminium ions are toxic. Lakes in Canada, Scotland and Norway have been badly affected by acid rain and some have very few or no animals in them.

Trees in Central Europe killed by acid rain.

The technology exists to combat acid rain such as:

- **low sulfur fuels** could be used. Crushing coal and washing it with a solvent that dissolves the sulfur compounds reducing its sulfur content
- **flue gas desulfurisation** removes the sulfur from power station chimneys by treating the waste gases with wet powdered limestone, neutralising the acidic gases before they can escape,
- **catalytic converters** can be fitted to reduce the nitrogen oxides in the exhaust fumes of cars.

These solutions are expensive, but are being introduced gradually to stop the damage from acid rain. At a time when Europe and North America are cleaning up some of the damage done by acid rain, China's rapid industrial expansion and use of coal in its many power stations means that the country has problems with acid rain.

## SUMMARY QUESTIONS

1 Copy and complete the following sentences using the words below:

**acid rain   fossil fuels   nitric   nitrogen oxides   dioxide   sulfuric**

When _____ containing sulfur are burned the pollutant gases sulfur _____ and _____ are released into the atmosphere. These gases dissolve in the rain to form _____ acid and _____ acid.

This is known as _____.

2 a Explain why normal rainfall is slightly acidic.
  b Name the gases which dissolve in the water in clouds to form acid rain.
  c State the sources of these gases.
  d Explain the effects of acid rain on:
     i coniferous trees
     ii soils
     iii fish and invertebrates.
  e Explain what can be done to reduce the effects of acid rain.

## KEY POINTS

1 Sulfur dioxide from the burning of fossil fuels and nitrogen oxides from car exhausts are the main causes of acid rain.

2 Acid rain dissolves useful nutrients out of the soil making it infertile and also causes the release of aluminium ions that are toxic to fish.

3 Acid rain damages leaves and kills trees. Fish and invertebrates die if lakes become acidic.

4 Measures taken to reduce acid rain include removing sulfur from fuels and acidic gases from waste gases.

# Water pollution

In many parts of the world raw sewage drains into rivers.

## Pollution of rivers and seas

Domestic and industrial pollutants are often discharged straight into rivers and into the sea.

Rivers empty toxic wastes into the sea.

- Fertilisers and sewage encourage the growth of algae that release toxins.
- Pesticides are concentrated in the tissues of some molluscs (shellfish).
- Radioactive chemicals are found in higher concentrations around coastal nuclear power stations.
- Toxic metals, such as mercury, copper and lead, are found in tissues of marine organisms.

**Sewage** is the biggest single pollutant. It encourages the growth of algae and bacteria which use up lots of oxygen, killing fish and small invertebrates. If raw untreated sewage is dumped in a river it encourages the growth of bacteria that feed on the organic matter. The shortage of oxygen means that many freshwater organisms cannot survive so die or migrate away.

As water travels downstream, the water gradually improves as suspended wastes settle out and are decomposed by bacteria. If no more sewage is dumped in the river, the community recovers as the oxygen concentration of the water increases. In many countries sewage is treated so that raw sewage is not deposited into rivers (see page 252).

**Fertilisers** drain from the land into rivers and lakes. We have seen how using fertilisers can increase the yield of crops. But farmers need to know the best type of fertiliser to use for their particular soil and crop and how much of the fertiliser to add. Problems can occur if a farmer uses too much fertiliser or if the fertiliser is added at the wrong time e.g. before a period of heavy rain.

The result of either of these is that fertilisers can cause water pollution resulting in **eutrophication**, which means that the water is enriched with plant nutrients. This is the sequence of events.

- Fertiliser can be washed through the soil into rivers and streams – this is called **leaching**. The rivers may flow into a lake.
- Once in the water this stimulates population growth of algae. Nutrients in the fertilisers are usually in low concentration in the water and so limit the growth of the algae.
- Animals that eat the algae do not multiply fast enough to control their growth.
- Algae cover the surface layers of water, reducing the light reaching plants at the bottom of the lake.

- These plants eventually die and rot on the river bed.
- Algae also die as there is competition for resources and many are shaded by the algae on the surface.
- Decomposers, such as bacteria, feed on dead plants and algae.
- Bacteria respire aerobically, multiply rapidly and use up a lot of dissolved oxygen.
- The concentration of oxygen decreases and this kills fish and invertebrates that cannot respire properly.

The same chain of events can happen if sewage gets into waterways. Bacteria multiply quickly, use up oxygen in respiration, which can result in the death of fish.

The problems of eutrophication are caused by nitrate and phosphate. These ions are in short supply in most natural aquatic ecosystems, so they act as a limiting factor to the growth of plants. When they are added in the form of fertilisers, plant growth increases.

Farmers are encouraged to reduce the fertilisers they apply and to make sure that they are applied at a time when crops will take them up. Phosphate tends to remain in soils and much of the phosphate in water comes from domestic sources. Removing phosphate from detergents has helped to reduce this type of pollution. Similar events happen in the sea – nitrate in the sea causes growth of algae, many of which produce toxins and kill other marine life.

## Pesticides in food chains

**Insecticides** are chemicals used to kill insect pests. Without insecticides and other pesticides there would be a large decrease in crop yield. DDT is a very effective pesticide. Only small amounts are needed to kill any insect. DDT has saved millions of people from disease and starvation. It has been used to control the mosquitoes that spread malaria. It also helps reduce the numbers of insects that eat food crops.

However, DDT is considered dangerous as it does not break down easily so stays in the environment for a long time and remains in fat stores in animals. It is also accumulated by organisms in food chains.

Clear Lake in California was sprayed with DDD (a chemical similar to DDT) to control biting insects called midges. A few years later fish-eating birds called grebes began to die in large numbers. Their bodies had large amounts of DDD in them.

DDT and DDD are not easily broken down by organisms. This means that they accumulated it in their bodies. DDD was first taken up by plant plankton. Planktonic animals fed on many individual plant plankton so the level of DDD built up in their bodies. Each fish fed on many planktonic animals. Each grebe fed on many fish so that DDD reached a lethal level in the grebes. The pesticide had built up along the food chain. This is called **bioaccumulation**.

Herbicides are sprayed on fields to kill weeds but they may also kill wild plants, many of which may be helpful to farmers by providing food for natural predators of pests.

Fertilisers caused algae to grow and turn this water green.

**SUMMARY QUESTIONS**

1 a Define the terms *pesticide*, *insecticide* and *herbicide*.

   b Explain why they are used.

   c Explain how pesticides can damage the environment.

2 a Explain why farmers use fertilisers containing nitrate and phosphate on their fields.

   b Explain how fertiliser that was spread on a wheat field could have caused the death of fish in a nearby pond.

Carnivorous plants like the pitcher plant, *Nepenthes raja*, catch insects to gain fixed nitrogen. This is the largest species and is only found on Mount Kinabalu in Malaysia.

Habitats are destroyed due to increased land-use for building, quarrying, dumping waste and agriculture. Human populations are creating greater demands upon food resources and energy reserves, and producing more waste.

It is important that we conserve the environment for the benefit of future generations. We have a duty of care to maintain the **biodiversity** and protect endangered species. Biodiversity is a catalogue of all the species in an area, a country or even the whole world. But it also includes the different habitats in an area and the genetic diversity within each species.

We should conserve ecosystems, habitats and species for the following reasons.

- Ecosystems provide us with services such as treating waste, providing food and fuels and giving us areas for recreation. They provide us with useful substances such as medicines.
- Ecosystems help to maintain the balance of life on the planet, e.g. nutrient cycles.
- Habitats support a wide variety of organisms that interact in ways we do not fully understand. This is often to the benefit of life on this planet, for example by keeping pests and diseases in check.
- Other species have as much right to live on this planet as we do. We have a role as guardians of the planet.

No species lives in isolation, so we have a duty to conserve ecosystems and habitats. Here are some ways in which this is done.

- National Parks – large tracts of land that are set aside for wildlife but which may be occupied by people and which are patrolled by wardens, e.g. the game parks of East Africa such as Masai Mara in Kenya and Serengeti in Tanzania.
- Marine parks protect areas of the sea from damage by fishing and pollution, e.g. Goat Island Marine Reserve in New Zealand.
- Rescuing endangered animals and breeding them in captivity and then returning them to the wild. Many species of *Partula* snails became extinct on Pacific islands during the twentieth century. Some are now kept in captivity and prepared for release back into their habitats. The Arabian oryx was bred in zoos and reintroduced to Oman where previously it had become extinct.
- Growing endangered plants in botanical gardens and re-establishing them in the wild.
- Reducing habitat destruction, e.g. issuing licences for logging in forests or preventing it altogether.
- Re-establishment of ecosystems where land has become degraded, e.g. establishing dry forest in Guanacaste National Park in Costa Rica which may take up to 300 years to achieve!

- Preventing trade in endangered species. CITES, the Convention of International Trade in Endangered Species, imposed a worldwide ban on the ivory trade in 1989. This led to an increase in elephant populations in countries like Kenya.
- Encouraging sustainable management of ecosystems. In forests, remove trees but allow natural replacement or replant, but do not destroy habitats by clearing large areas.
- Seed banks are cold stores that conserve seeds of endangered or valuable species. Seed banks around the world hope to collect and store seeds from many species in case they become extinct in the wild. Their genes may be useful for crop improvement in the future or to produce valuable products such as drugs.

The Arabian oryx, *Oryx leucoryx*, has been bred in zoos and then reintroduced into the wild with mixed success.

These wardens in Papua New Guinea are conserving the eggs of leatherback turtles.

Resources need to be conserved as well. We have already discussed how fossil fuels may be conserved, by burning them efficiently and using energy much more efficiently. Recycling materials, such as aluminium, iron, glass and paper, reduces energy consumption and damage to the environment by creating less waste, and saves on raw materials. Water consumption globally has increased considerably and many sources of water are becoming exhausted or polluted. Water must not be wasted and must be used sensibly so that everyone may have some.

## SUMMARY QUESTIONS

1 Explain the meaning of each of the following:
   a conservation, b biodiversity, c endangered species.

2 Explain why it is necessary to conserve habitats and ecosystems.

3 State two species that are endangered in your region or country. Describe the steps being taken to conserve them.

4 Explain the part played by each of the following in conservation:
   a zoos, b botanical gardens, c seed banks.

## KEY POINTS

1 Many of the world's species of animals and plants need to be conserved, along with their natural habitats.

2 We also need to conserve our diminishing supplies of non-renewable fuels, mineral ores and water.

# 19.9

# Sewage treatment and recycling

Activated sludge treatment.

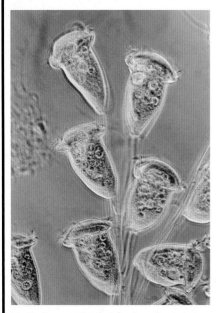

*Vorticella*, a protist that feeds on bacteria in sewage works.

## Sewage treatment

Raw sewage is made up of a number of unpleasant materials, not just faeces and urine, but industrial waste and run-off from roads and paths. Not only is it unpleasant, but it is also a major health hazard.

There are three main stages in the treatment of **sewage**.

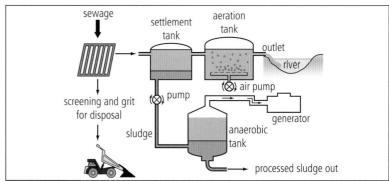

**Figure 19.9.1** A sewage treatment plant.

• **Primary treatment** involves removing large solids, like paper and twigs, by means of filters or screens. Then the grit and organic solids are allowed to settle out in large tanks.

• **Secondary treatment** involves microbes, mainly bacteria, decomposing material suspended in water. This may happen in two ways:

– the **activated sludge process**, in which air is pumped through the sewage with a community of bacteria, fungi and protists. These respire in aerobic conditions and break down carbohydrates, proteins and fats to carbon dioxide. Hydrogen sulfide is changed to sulfate ions and urea is broken down to ammonia and then converted to nitrate ions,

– **trickle filters** are beds of gravel covered with microbes. The liquid from the primary treatment is sprayed over these beds from large rotating arms. As the liquid trickles through the gravel, the microbes break down the organic matter.

• **Tertiary treatment** involves a period of settling. The liquid from the secondary process passes into large tanks. Here microbes and any remaining organic material settle out to form **sludge**. This sludge may be used as a 'starter culture' for the next secondary treatment or may go through an anaerobic stage in which bacteria break down waste matter to methane in anaerobic conditions. The methane is burnt as a fuel in the sewage works to provide energy for operating the machinery. Otherwise, sludge undergoes further treatment before disposal, which may involve dumping at sea or spreading on the land as a soil conditioner. The water leaving the plant will be treated in a variety of ways to make it safe. For example it may be treated with chlorine or ozone to kill all microorganisms. Water leaving the process is now safe to return to the environment or for human use.

# Recycling our waste

Another consequence of an increasing population is the production of more waste. Unless this waste is properly handled and disposed of, it may cause pollution which can harm animals, plants and ourselves. Dumping waste in landfill sites also deprives plants and animals of their habitats.

The solution to the problem of conserving useful materials is to **recycle** them. Glass, metals, paper and plastics can all be recycled. This saves raw materials because the recyclable materials do not have to be made in such large quantities and less energy is used to recycle than to make the material from raw materials. For example, there is a 95% saving in energy if you compare recycled aluminium to the same mass of aluminium extracted from its ore, bauxite.

Paper is a resource in limited supply as it is made from wood. However, paper can be collected and recycled. This means that less paper pulp from trees is required. The waste paper is collected, pulped, the dyes are removed and the pulp is then rolled into sheets. These sheets are dried and converted into newsprint, paper towels, toilet paper and other paper products.

Waste paper is bundled up and shredded. This saves it being thrown into landfill sites, like this one.

## SUMMARY QUESTIONS

1 Recycling means using materials again.
   a Make a list of materials that can be recycled.
   b Describe the effects that recycling of these materials have on the following:
      i the raw materials used to manufacture goods
      ii the energy needed to manufacture these goods
      iii landfill sites and rubbish dumps.

2 a Make a list of the different types of packaging that are used by shops.
   b In what ways does this packaging cause problems for society?
   c Explain how recycling of paper helps the environment.

3 Describe the main processes involved in the treatment of sewage and the recycling of safe water.

## KEY POINTS

1 Sewage treatment involves the use of microbes to break down organic matter and produce water that is safe to use.

2 Aeration ensures that microbes can respire in aerobic condition to break down carbon compounds to carbon dioxide.

3 Recycling materials such as paper saves money and energy and reduces pollution by waste.

1 Define the term *population*.

2 (a) Sketch a graph to show the increase in a population of an organism when there are no limiting factors. Show the three stages of sigmoid growth and label them on your curve.

(b) Show on your graph what happens to the population when nutrients are in short supply.

3 (a) Sketch a graph to show the change in the human population over the last 300 years. Make sure that you indicate the years on the horizontal axis of your graph.

(b) Explain the shape of the graph.

(c) Discuss the consequences for the planet if this growth continues at the same rate.

4 (a) Explain what is meant by the term *limiting factor* as it applies to population growth.

(b) List four limiting factors for population growth.

5 (a) Define the term *pollution*.

(b) List three different ecosystems. Describe three ways in which humans have influenced each ecosystem – for good or bad.

6 (a) State the consequences of deforestation on the environment.

(b) Describe the consequences for the environment of the misuse of fertilisers.

**Extension**

7 Annotate the graph you drew in question 2 to explain why the population size changes in the ways shown.

8 Explain why humans should conserve ecosystems, habitats and species.

9 Describe the impact of the following gases on the planet:

(a) carbon dioxide,

(b) methane,

(c) sulfur dioxide.

1 What is the best explanation for the change in population size shown in the graph?

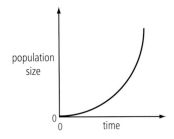

A birth rate and death rate are the same

B emigration

C an outbreak of disease

D no limiting factors

*(Paper 1)* [1]

2 The boll weevil shown below is an important pest of cotton plants. What should be used to control the boll weevil?

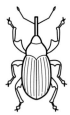

A fungicide

B herbicide

C insecticide

D molluscicide

*(Paper 1)* [1]

3 What is an undesirable effect of the over-use of fertilisers on farmland?

A acid rain

B eutrophication

C global warming

D more photosynthesis

*(Paper 1)* [1]

4 Which pair of gases contributes to the enhanced greenhouse effect?

A carbon dioxide and methane

B oxygen and carbon dioxide

C sulfur dioxide and water vapour

D water vapour and oxygen

*(Paper 1)* [1]

**5** The Asian elephant, *Elephas maximus*, is a large herbivorous animal. It is classified by the International Union for Conservation of Nature as an endangered animal. In January 2009, researchers published the first estimate of the population in the Taman Negara National Park in the centre of Peninsular Malaysia. The researchers counted piles of dung to estimate the population. Their estimate was 631.

(a) Suggest why the researchers could not count the elephants, but had to count piles of dung instead. [3]

(b) Suggest why it is important for conservationists to have reliable estimates of the population sizes of endangered species. [3]

(c) It has been estimated that Asian elephant populations can increase at a rate of 2% per year if there are no limiting factors.

  (i)  List four factors that are likely to limit the population growth of Asian elephants in a National Park such as Taman Negara. [4]

  (ii) Explain why it is important to conserve large herbivorous animals, such as the Asian elephant, but not allow the population in a National Park to increase too much. [5]

*(Paper 2)*

**6** Some students investigated the growth of yeast cells which were kept in a container with a glucose solution. They took samples of the population of yeast at 2 hourly intervals. Their results are shown in the table.

| time (hours) | number of yeast cells |
|---|---|
| 0 | 10 |
| 2 | 25 |
| 4 | 50 |
| 6 | 150 |
| 8 | 350 |
| 10 | 535 |
| 12 | 660 |
| 14 | 685 |
| 16 | 660 |
| 18 | 550 |

(a) Draw a graph of the results shown in the table. [5]

(b) Label on your graph the four phases of population growth. [4]

(c) Explain why the population did not grow in number throughout the 18 hour period. [2]

*(Paper 2)*

**7** The table shows how the concentrations of two gases have increased between 1890 and 1990. It also shows how effective they are as greenhouse gases compared with carbon dioxide.

| gas | concentration in the atmosphere in certain years (parts per million) | | | relative effect as greenhouse gas compared with $CO_2$ |
|---|---|---|---|---|
| | 1890 | 1990 | 2030 | |
| carbon dioxide ($CO_2$) | 290 | 354 | 400–500 | 1 |
| methane ($CH_4$) | 0.9 | 1.7 | 2.2–2.5 | 30 |
| nitrous oxide ($N_2O$) | 0.28 | 0.3 | 0.33–0.35 | 160 |

(a) Calculate the percentage increase in the concentration of carbon dioxide in the atmosphere between 1890 and 1990. Show your working. [2]

(b) The main sources of nitrous oxide are motor vehicles and fertilisers.

Explain why the concentrations of **(i)** carbon dioxide, and **(ii)** methane increased in the twentieth century. [4]

(c) Explain how the gases shown in the table may cause global warming. [5]

(d) Suggest why it is important to know the relative effects of these gases as shown in the table. [3]

*(Paper 3)*

**8 (a)** Discuss **(i)** the impact of non-biodegradable plastics on the environment, and **(ii)** the reasons for recycling paper. [5]

(b) Describe, in outline, how sewage is treated so that it is safe to flow into rivers. [5]

(c) Explain why it is important for sewage to be treated before it enters the environment. [4]

*(Paper 3)*

## Experimental skills and abilities for assessment

**1** Use techniques, apparatus, and materials (including following a sequence of instructions, where appropriate).

**2** Make and record observations and measurements.

**3** Interpret and evaluate experimental observations and data.

**4** Plan and carry out investigations, evaluate methods and suggest possible improvements (including the selection of techniques, apparatus and materials).

These skills are tested together in an alternative to practical paper or practical test such as the one below.

## QUESTION 1

Pancreatin is a mixture of enzymes, including trypsin, that will digest proteins. Pancreatin will make a sample of skimmed milk turn from white to clear. Two students, A and B, are given dried milk powder.

They are given the following instructions:

1 Dissolve the milk powder in water and stir until there is no powder left.

2 Mix the dissolved milk and a pancreatin solution together.

3 Record the time taken for the milk to go clear.

The table on the left shows their results when they carried out their experiment at five different temperatures.

**a** Plot the results obtained for student B in the form of a suitable graph. [4]

| temperature (°C) | time for the solution to clear (minutes) | |
|---|---|---|
| | student A | student B |
| 20 | 14.0 | 10.0 |
| 25 | 11.5 | 8.0 |
| 30 | 10.0 | 6.5 |
| 35 | 7.0 | 4.0 |
| 40 | 6.0 | 2.5 |

**LEARNING OBJECTIVES**

- Following a sequence of instructions

- Interpret experimental data:
  - Select suitable scales and axes from graphs
  - Draw graphs from given data.

Tips for drawing the graph:
- Scale chosen to make the graph as large as possible and to be easy to read.
- Plots are clear but not too large. Line is clear but not too thick.
- Scale labelled.
- Plots joined with ruled straight lines.
- Axis labelled with units. Note that the axis labels are the same as the table headings.

Example 1

**EXAMINER SAYS...**

Examination questions requiring a graph include the grid printed on the examination paper.

This graph gains full marks. Note that the variable that we change in this experiment is the temperature. This is the independent variable and is used as the left-hand column of the table and the x-axis of the graph.

The 'time to go clear' is the dependent variable which goes into the right hand column of the table and the y-axis of the graph.

## Example 2

The plots in this graph are perfect but there are eight errors. What are they?* In biology graphs points are joined with ruled straight lines, not with freehand lines. Lines of best fit can be used if requested in the question, but normally they are not used in biology. Uncertainty is common in biology where there is genetic variation and it can be difficult to control all other variables. This uncertainty is shown by joining points with ruled lines. In physics, chemistry and mathematics there is less uncertainty and then graphs are drawn with lines of best fit. Example 2 has used different plot markers for the two curves. This is good practice when two curves are required on the same grid.

* Answer
1 Curves for both students were plotted, even though only one was asked for.
2 The plot markers for student A shown in red are too large.
3 The red line is too thick.
4 There are no units on the y-axis and the x-axis scale has no numbers on it.
5 The x-axis scale has not been chosen well and the graph is not as large as it could be.
6 Lines of best fit have been used.
7 The lines are extrapolated.

**b** From your graph describe and explain the effect of temperature on this enzyme between 20°C and 35°C. *[3]*

## Example 1

*The greater the temperature the less time is needed for the milk to go clear. The reaction time at 20°C is 10 minutes and 4 minutes at 35°C. This means that the reaction is faster by 6 minutes at the higher temperature. At 35°C the molecules have more energy so are moving faster and the milk molecules are more likely to collide with the enzyme.*

**EXAMINER SAYS...**

Notice that the question asks for a description and an explanation. Both are needed for full marks.
A good description of a graph trend should say how the dependent variable changes as we changed the independent variable. In this case 'The greater the temperature the less time is needed for the milk to go clear'. The answer also includes at least two figures from the graph to illustrate the change as well as a calculation. In a question such as this, it is good practice to carry out a calculation of the rate of change without being directly asked to do so.
The two ideas of molecules moving faster at higher temperatures and of collisions being more likely gives 2 marks (of the maximum 3 marks).

## Example 2

*The reaction time at 20 is 10 minutes and 2.5 minutes at 40. This means that the reaction rate falls at the higher temperature. At very high temperatures enzymes will denature so the rate of reaction falls.*

**EXAMINER SAYS...**

Example 2 makes two mistakes when trying to describe the effect. First, we do not know what 20 and 40 refer to because units are not given. This is a very common mistake. Units should always be given in an answer.
Second the question asks for the effect between 20°C and 35°C but the answer describes the effect between '20' and '40', so the example has not answered the question.
'This means that the reaction rate falls at the higher temperature' seems to be confusing time with rate of reaction.
The discussion of enzymes denaturing is true but it is not relevant to this graph.    No marks.

- Interpret and evaluate experimental observations and data
- Recall simple physiological experiments

Join points on a graph with ruled straight lines.

<table>
</table>

## LEARNING OBJECTIVES

- Interpret and evaluate experimental observations and data
- Evaluate methods used in an investigation

**c** Suggest reasons for differences between the results of the two students. *[3]*

> **Example**
>
> *Student B may have used more milk powder or less water to dissolve the milk in.*
> *Student B may have used a greater volume of the enzyme solution.*
> *They may have had a different pH.*
>
> **EXAMINER SAYS…**
> This answer would gain 2 out of the 3 marks.
> The first two sentences correctly identify that other variables, such as milk concentration and enzyme volume, have not been controlled. Temperature and pH can change the rate of enzyme reactions so the suggestion that the reactions were carried out at a different pH is good. Take care to write pH and not PH or ph.
> In these results student B has the smaller times so the larger rate of reaction. It must be clear from the answer whether concentrations are greater or smaller.

## LEARNING OBJECTIVES

- Interpret and evaluate experimental observations and data

**d** Suggest and explain what would happen if student A carried out the experiment at 80°C. *[2]*

> **Example 1**
>
> *The enzyme will be denatured.*
>
> **Example 2**
> *The milk would not go clear at all because the enzyme will be denatured. This means that the active sites of the enzymes do not work anymore.*
>
> **EXAMINER SAYS…**
> Example 1 only gives an explanation so only scores 1 mark. Example 2 makes a correct suggestion and then goes on to give a correct, more detailed explanation so gains 2 marks.

### QUESTION 2

The banded snail exists as two forms within a single population. These forms can breed with each other and lay eggs. A pair of banded snails was allowed to breed together and their eggs placed in a glass tank with food. Two months after the eggs hatched the number of snails was counted.

Banded snail.

Non-banded snail.

**Figure 2.1**

**a i** Count the number of banded snails and non-banded snails in the tank shown in figure 2.1 and complete the banded and non-banded columns in the table below. *[2]*

|  | Banded | Non-banded | Total number of snails |
|---|---|---|---|
| Number of snails in figure 2.1 |  |  |  |

**ii** Calculate the total number of snails and complete the table above. *[1]*

**Example 1**

|  | Banded | Non-banded | Total number of snails |
|---|---|---|---|
| Number of snails in figure 2.1 | *18* | *6* | *24* |

**EXAMINER SAYS…**

Tip: cross out each snail in pencil as you count so that you do not count one twice or miss one.

**iii** Calculate the fractions of banded snails in the sample. *[2]*

*Fraction of banded snails =*
*Answer =*

**Example 1**

*Fraction of banded snails =* $\dfrac{\text{number of banded snails}}{\text{total number of snails}}$

*Answer =* $\dfrac{2}{3}$

**Example 2**

*Fraction of banded snails =* $\dfrac{\text{number of banded snails}}{\text{total number of snails}}$

*Answer =* $\dfrac{18}{24}$

**EXAMINER SAYS…**

Example 1 gains 2 marks for showing how the fraction was calculated and the correct answer. Fractions do not have units but other calculations in the alternative to practical paper may require units. Example 2 gains only 1 mark because the fraction given is not simplified.
Care is needed that hand written numbers are clear.

**b** Suggest and explain what these results in the table above indicate about the inheritance of the banding pattern in snails. *[3]*

**EXAMINER SAYS…**

This is another example of a question that tests interpretation of experimental data. Marks would be given for:

1. Recognising a 3:1 ratio, banded : non-banded.
2. Banded is dominant.
3. Non-banded is recessive.
4. The original parents were heterozygous, or the non-banded snails were homozygous.
5. Correct use of the term 'allele'; e.g. the banded allele is dominant.

To a maximum of 3 marks.

## LEARNING OBJECTIVES

- Make and record observations
- Make a clear labelled drawing of a specimen from a photograph

**c** Make a labelled drawing of the head of the thrush. Ensure that your drawing has a x2 magnification compared with the photograph. *[3]*

The natural predator of this type of snail is the thrush.

## DRAWING TIP

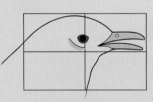

Draw a grid with a ruler over the relevant part of the photograph and draw the same grid lightly onto the answer space. This will help you get the proportions and magnification correct.

### Magnification

You could be asked to calculate the magnification of your drawing:

$$Magnification = \frac{drawing\ size}{actual\ size}$$

If the photograph already has a magnification, do not forget to include that in your final answer.

## TOP TIPS

Use smooth lines without too much shading for drawings.

### Example 1

eye
nostril
beak
eye markings

### EXAMINER SAYS…

- The drawing is of the head only at a x2 magnification.
- The beak is in perfect proportion and the eye and nostril are in the correct place.
- There is minimum shading.

- The lines are smooth giving a clear outline.
- The label lines are clear and go precisely to the part labelled. Tip: avoid arrows.
- The drawing is accurately labelled. 3 marks

### Example 2

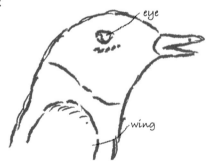

eye
wing

### EXAMINER SAYS…

- The drawing includes some of the body and the head part is not x2 magnification.
- The beak is out of proportion and the eye and nostril are in the wrong places.
- There is too much shading.

- The lines are not smooth; they do not give a clear outline.
- The label lines do not go precisely to the part labelled.
- The line for the eye goes to the feathers above the eye and the wing is labelled but the question asks for a drawing of the head. No marks

Describe an investigation to compare the rate of water loss between plants in the light and plants in the dark, using the apparatus in Figure 3.1. In your answer describe how you will make the results as reliable and valid as possible. [5]

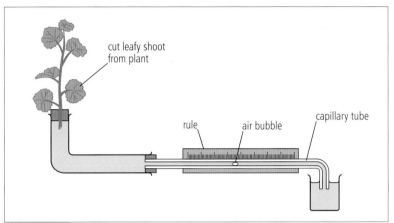

**Figure 3.1** Shows a potometer that is used to measure the rate of water uptake by leafy shoots.

**TOP TIPS**

Keep controlled variables constant in an investigation.

Good investigations always involve taking repeated readings to improve the reliability of the data collected.

## Example 1

*You collect your results by measuring the distance travelled by the bubble in 2 minutes. Divide the distance by 2 and you will get the rate in mm per minute.*
*Make sure your apparatus has no leaks and that the temperature and wind speed are kept the same. Use the same piece of plant.*
*Do the experiment in the light three times, check for anomalies and take an average.*
*Do the same in the dark. Draw a bar chart to compare the averages.*
*If you know the diameter of the capillary tube you can work out the rate as mm³ of water lost per minute.*

**EXAMINER SAYS...**

✓ Measuring the movement of the bubble (dependent variable) is explained.
✓ Gives 2 minutes as the standard time and explains how rate is measured.
✓ Shows the need to prevent leaks. This student has used the apparatus.
✓ Three control variables, temperature, wind speed and the piece of plant are controlled. Humidity could also have been mentioned.
✓ The need to carry out repeat readings, check for anomalies and calculation of the average is stated.
✓ A bar chart is suggested because there are only two values of the independent variable.
✓ Further detail about rates is given. Candidates should be careful when writing superscript numbers by hand.

A maximum of 5 marks is given.

## Example 2

*You have one set of apparatus with the plant in the dark and another with the plant in the light.*
*Measure the distance the bubble moves. When we did this experiment the bubble did not move at all because our apparatus was broken.*
*It is important to keep everything the same.*
*Measure the time with a stop watch.*
*Do the whole experiment three times and take an average.*

**EXAMINER SAYS...**

• The first sentence simply repeats the question.
✓ How to measure the dependent variable by measuring the movement of the bubble is explained.
✓ Time measured with stopwatch.
• Variables kept the same need to be named.
✓ 'Do the experiment 3 times' is acceptable as referring to repeat readings.
• 'Take an average' is too vague, which figures are averaged?

3 marks awarded out of 5.

# Revision checklist

This list is to help you check that you have completed and understood all the sections of the course. When you think you have understood each statement below put a tick in the appropriate box in pencil. When you start to revise for the examination you can rub out the tick and repeat the process.

**(Extension shaded in green here)**

## Unit 1 Characteristics and classification of living organisms

I can:

| | |
|---|---|
| list and describe the characteristics of living organisms | |
| describe how to use the binomial system to name organisms | |
| write out the scientific name of an organism using the binomial system | |
| list the external features of nematodes, annelids and molluscs | |
| list the external features of arthropods | |
| list the external features of four classes of arthropod: insects, crustaceans, arachnids and myriapods | |
| define the term *vertebrate* | |
| list the main features of the following vertebrate groups: bony fish, amphibians, reptiles, birds and mammals | |
| describe the main features of flowering plants | |
| state the differences between dicotyledons and monocotyledons | |
| describe how the animals and plants described in this unit are adapted to their environment. | |
| state the main features of the three groups of microorganisms: bacteria, fungi and viruses | |
| describe how bacteria, fungi and viruses are adapted to their environment | |
| use simple dichotomous keys to identify plants and animals | |
| identify the external features of animals and plants that are useful for making keys | |
| explain that there are other ways of classifying organisms using features such as DNA and RNA | |

## Unit 2 Cells

I can:

| | |
|---|---|
| state that organisms are made of cells | |
| describe the structures of plant and animal cells as seen under a light microscope | |
| describe the differences in structure between plant and animal cells | |
| state the functions of the structures in plant and animal cells that are visible in the light microscope | |
| identify different types of specialised plant and animal cells from diagrams and photographs and state their functions | |
| calculate the magnification and actual size of biological specimens using millimetres as units | |
| define the terms *tissue*, *organ* and *organ system* and describe examples in plants and animals | |

## Unit 3 Movement in and out of cells

I can:

| | |
|---|---|
| define the term *diffusion* and describe the importance of diffusion of gases and solutes in organisms | |
| describe the importance of water as a solvent | |
| define the term *osmosis* and describe the effect of certain factors on osmosis | |
| describe how water can enter and leave plant cells by osmosis | |
| describe how osmosis affects animal cells | |
| explain the movement of water into and out of plant cells using the term *water potential* | |
| define the term *active transport* | |
| explain the importance of active transport as an energy-consuming process | |
| describe the active transport of ions in plant roots | |
| describe the active uptake of glucose by epithelial cells in villi | |

## Unit 4 Enzymes

I can:

| | |
|---|---|
| define the term *catalyst* | |

| | |
|---|---|
| define enzymes as proteins that act as biological catalysts | |
| explain how an enzyme works using the 'lock and key' model | |
| describe how to design experiments to investigate the effects of temperature and pH on enzyme activity | |
| describe the effects of temperature and pH on enzyme activity | |
| explain the effects of temperature and pH on enzyme activity | |
| describe the role of enzymes in the breakdown of stored materials in seeds during germination | |
| describe the role of enzymes in malting | |
| describe the role of enzymes in biological washing powders and the role of pectinase in the production of fruit juices | |
| describe the roles of microorganisms and fermenters in the production of the antibiotic penicillin and enzymes for washing powders | |
| state that the fungus *Penicillium* is used to produce penicillin | |

## Unit 5 Nutrition

**I can:**

| | |
|---|---|
| define the term *nutrition* and list the different nutrients in a human diet | |
| explain the importance of the nutrients in the diet | |
| list the chemical elements present in carbohydrates, fats and proteins | |
| describe the synthesis of large molecules from smaller molecules (e.g. starch from glucose) | |
| state how to carry out chemical tests for starch, reducing sugars, protein and fat | |
| state some foods that are good sources of the nutrients in a balanced diet | |
| describe the symptoms of a deficiency of the following nutrients in the diet: vitamins C and D and the minerals iron and calcium | |
| describe the use of bacteria in yoghurt production | |

| | |
|---|---|
| describe the use of a fungus in the production of mycoprotein (single cell protein) | |
| describe the uses and benefits of food additives | |
| describe the health hazards associated with food additives | |

## Unit 6 Plant nutrition

**I can:**

| | |
|---|---|
| define the term *photosynthesis* | |
| write out the word equation for photosynthesis | |
| explain the role of chlorophyll in photosynthesis | |
| write out a balanced equation for photosynthesis using symbols | |
| describe how to test a green leaf for starch | |
| name the raw materials for photosynthesis as water and carbon dioxide and describe how they are taken into plants | |
| state the products (oxygen and glucose) that are produced in photosynthesis | |
| describe how to show that oxygen is produced in photosynthesis | |
| describe the experiments that show that chlorophyll, carbon dioxide and light are needed for photosynthesis | |
| describe how to investigate the effects of changes in light intensity, carbon dioxide concentration and temperature on the rate of photosynthesis | |
| describe the effects of varying light intensity, carbon dioxide concentration and temperature on the rate of photosynthesis | |
| explain the term *limiting factor* and use the term to explain the effects of varying light intensity, carbon dioxide concentration and temperature on the rate of photosynthesis. | |
| explain the use of carbon dioxide enrichment, optimum light and optimum temperature in glasshouse systems | |
| identify and label the parts of a leaf as seen in a cross-section under the light microscope | |
| describe the functions of epidermis, mesophyll, xylem and phloem in a leaf especially with respect to photosynthesis | |

# Revision checklist

| | |
|---|---|
| state that nitrate ions are needed to make proteins and magnesium ions are needed to make chlorophyll | |
| explain the effects of deficiencies of nitrate ions and magnesium ions on plant growth | |
| describe the uses of nitrogen fertilisers | |

## Unit 7 Animal nutrition

I can:

| | |
|---|---|
| define the term *balanced diet* | |
| describe balanced diets based on age, sex and activity of people | |
| describe the effects of starvation | |
| explain how malnutrition is linked to coronary heart disease | |
| explain how malnutrition may lead to obesity and list the health risks associated with obesity | |
| explain the role of roughage (fibre) in the diet and state that a deficiency may lead to constipation | |
| discuss ways in which modern technology has resulted in increased food production | |
| discuss the problems of world food supplies and the problems that contribute to famine | |
| define the terms *ingestion*, *digestion*, *absorption*, *assimilation* and *egestion* | |
| distinguish between *mechanical digestion* and *chemical digestion* | |
| identify the main regions of the alimentary canal and the liver and pancreas on diagrams | |
| describe the functions of the regions of the alimentary canal, liver and pancreas in ingestion, digestion, absorption, assimilation and egestion of food | |
| state the sites of secretion and the functions of the enzymes amylase, protease and lipase, listing their substrates and end-products | |
| describe chewing and swallowing of food including the action of saliva | |
| identify the types of human teeth from photographs and diagrams | |
| describe the structure and functions of human teeth | |

| | |
|---|---|
| state the causes of dental decay and describe the proper care of teeth | |
| describe how fluoride reduces tooth decay and explain arguments for and against fluoridation of drinking water supplies | |
| describe the roles of circular and longitudinal muscles in peristalsis | |
| describe the digestion of food in the stomach | |
| describe the digestion of food in the small intestine including the role of bile in emulsifying fats | |
| explain that villi increase the surface area of the small intestine for efficient absorption of food | |
| describe the structure of a villus | |
| state that the small intestine and colon absorb water | |
| state the role of the hepatic portal vein in the transport of absorbed food from ileum to liver | |
| describe the role of the liver in storage of glucose as glycogen, the production of proteins from amino acids and the destruction of excess amino acids | |
| define the term *deamination* and state that it happens in the liver | |
| state that the liver breaks down alcohol and other toxins | |
| state the role of fat as an energy storage substance | |

## Unit 8 Plant transport

I can:

| | |
|---|---|
| state the functions of xylem and phloem | |
| identify the positions of xylem and phloem in transverse sections of roots, stems and leaves | |
| identify root hairs as seen under the microscope and state their functions of uptake of water and ions | |
| relate the structure and function of roots hairs to their surface area and to their functions | |
| state the pathway taken by water through root, stem and leaf | |
| define the term *transpiration* | |

| | |
|---|---|
| describe how water evaporates on cell surfaces in leaves and then diffuses through air spaces and stomata into the atmosphere | |
| describe how variations in temperature, humidity and light intensity can affect the rate of transpiration | |
| describe how wilting occurs | |
| describe how to use a stain to show the pathway of water through stems, leaves and flowers of plants | |
| explain the cohesion-tension mechanism for water transport in the xylem ('transpiration pull') | |
| describe the adaptations of the leaves, stems and roots of plants to pond, garden and desert environments | |
| define the term *translocation* | |
| describe the translocation of applied chemicals, such as systemic pesticides, throughout plants | |
| compare transpiration with translocation in transporting substances from sources to sinks in different seasons | |

## Unit 9 Transport in humans

I can:

| | |
|---|---|
| describe the one-way flow of blood around the body through the pulmonary (lungs) and systemic (rest of body) circuits | |
| describe the double circulation as a low pressure flow to the lungs and a high pressure flow to the body tissues ad relate to the functions of the two circuits | |
| describe the structure of the heart to include muscular walls, septum and valves | |
| describe the heart as a pump for the flow of blood and the role of valves to permit only one-way flow | |
| state the sequence of events that take place during one heart beat | |
| name the main blood vessels to and from the heart, lungs, liver and kidney | |
| describe the structure and function of arteries, veins and capillaries | |

| | |
|---|---|
| explain how the structure of arteries, veins and capillaries adapts them to their functions | |
| describe how to investigate the effect of physical activity on pulse rate | |
| state and explain the effect of physical activity on pulse rate | |
| describe coronary heart disease in terms of blockage of coronary arteries | |
| state the possible causes of coronary heart disease and ways to prevent it | |
| list the main components of blood | |
| identify red and white blood cells in diagrams, photographs and under the microscope | |
| describe the role of red blood cells and haemoglobin in oxygen transport | |
| describe the functions of plasma in transport | |
| describe how white blood cells such as lymphocytes and phagocytes protect the body from disease | |
| describe the roles of the immune system in antibody production, tissue rejection and phagocytosis | |
| state that platelets cause blood to clot | |
| describe the process of blood clotting | |
| describe the exchange of materials between capillaries and tissue fluid | |
| describe the functions of the lymphatic system in circulating lymph and producing lymphocytes | |

## Unit 10 Respiration

I can:

| | |
|---|---|
| define the term *respiration* | |
| state the uses of energy released in respiration in humans | |
| define the term *aerobic respiration* | |
| write out the word equation for aerobic respiration | |
| write out a balanced equation for aerobic respiration using symbols | |
| define the term *anaerobic respiration* | |

| | |
|---|---|
| write out the word equation for anaerobic respiration in muscles during hard exercise | |
| write out a balanced equation for anaerobic respiration in muscles using symbols | |
| describe the effect of lactic acid in muscles during exercise | |
| write out the word equation for anaerobic respiration in yeast | |
| write out the balanced equation for anaerobic respiration in yeast using symbols | |
| describe the role of anaerobic respiration in yeast during brewing and bread making | |
| compare the amounts of energy released in aerobic and anaerobic respiration | |
| compare the composition of inspired and expired air | |
| describe how to investigate the difference in carbon dioxide concentration in inspired and expired air using lime water | |
| list the features of gas exchange surfaces in animals | |
| describe gas exchange in an alveolus in the lungs | |
| identify on diagrams the larynx, trachea, bronchi, bronchioles, alveoli and associated capillaries | |
| describe the functions of all the structures named above | |
| describe how the ribs, diaphragm and internal and external intercostal muscles produce volume and pressure changes that lead to ventilation of the lungs | |
| explain the role of mucus and cilia in protecting the respiratory system from pathogens and dust particles | |
| describe how to investigate the effects of physical exercise on the rate and depth of breathing | |
| describe the effects of physical exercise on the rate and depth of breathing | |
| describe how the effects of exercise increase carbon dioxide concentration and lower ph in the tissues and how this affects the rate and depth of breathing | |

## Unit 11 Homeostasis and excretion

I can:

| | |
|---|---|
| define the term *homeostasis* | |
| explain the concept of negative feedback | |
| describe how insulin and glucagon released by the pancreas stimulate the liver to control the blood glucose concentration | |
| identify different structures on a diagram of the skin | |
| describe how the body temperature is kept constant | |
| define the term *excretion* | |
| name the excretory organs and list the excretory products | |
| describe the structure of the urinary system | |
| describe the function of the kidney in reabsorbing glucose and some salts and removing urea and excess water | |
| describe the internal structure of the kidney | |
| describe the structure of a kidney tubule | |
| describe the role of the kidney tubule in filtration, removal of urea and excess water and the reabsorption of glucose and some salts | |
| describe the process of kidney dialysis and explain how it controls the concentrations of glucose, urea and protein in the blood | |
| discuss how dialysis occurs in kidney machines | |
| discuss the advantages and disadvantages of kidney transplants, compared with kidney dialysis | |

## Unit 12 Coordination and response

I can:

| | |
|---|---|
| describe the structure of the nervous system divided into the central and peripheral nervous systems | |
| distinguish between voluntary and involuntary actions | |
| describe a reflex action as a fast, automatic response to a stimulus | |
| identify sensory, relay and motor neurones on a diagram of a reflex arc | |

describe the functioning of these neurones in a reflex action

state that muscles and glands are effectors

describe the action of antagonistic muscles in movement of the lower arm

define sense organs as groups of receptor cells responding to particular stimuli

describe the external and internal structure of the eye

describe the functions of the eye including the pupil reflex and accommodation (focusing)

distinguish between rods and cones, in terms of function and distribution

define the term *hormone*

state the role of adrenaline in control of body metabolism

compare the nervous system with the endocrine systems

discuss the use of hormones in food production

define the terms *geotropism* and *phototropism*

describe how to investigate geotropic and phototropic responses

explain the chemical control of plant growth by auxins

explain the effect of synthetic plant hormones used as weedkillers

## Unit 13 Drugs

I can:

define the term *drug*

describe the use of antibiotics in the treatment of bacterial infection

explain why antibiotics kill bacteria but not viruses

describe the effects of the abuse of heroin

describe the problems of addiction to heroin, severe withdrawal symptoms and problems such as crime and hiv infection

describe the effects of drinking excessive quantities of alcohol

describe the long-term effects of alcohol on the body

describe the effects of the components of tobacco smoke (tar, nicotine, carbon monoxide and smoke particles) on the gas exchange system and the heart

## Unit 14 Reproduction in plants

I can:

define the terms *asexual reproduction* and *sexual reproduction*

describe asexual reproduction in bacteria, spore formation in fungi and tuber formation in potatoes

discuss the advantages and disadvantages to a plant species of asexual and sexual reproduction

draw and describe the structure of an insect-pollinated flower

state the functions of sepals, petals, anthers, stigmas and ovaries

draw and describe the structure of a wind-pollinated flower

identify the different parts in a flower that you may not have seen before

compare different types of pollen grains

define the term *pollination* and name the agents of pollination

compare the different structural adaptations of insect-pollinated and wind-pollinated flowers

Distinguish between self-pollination and cross-pollination and discuss their significance

Describe the events leading up to and including fertilisation

Describe what happens when seeds and fruits are formed

Describe the structure of a seed as an embryo (plumule, radicle and two cotyledons) surrounded by a testa (seed coat)

State that seed and fruit dispersal by wind and by animals provides a means of colonising new areas

Describe examples of dispersal by wind and by animals

# Revision checklist

| Define the terms *growth* and *development* | |
| Describe the germination of seeds | |
| State the environmental conditions that affect the germination of seeds | |

## Unit 15 Sexual reproduction in humans

I can:

| identify on diagrams the parts of the male reproductive system and state their functions | |
| compare male and female gametes | |
| identify on diagrams the parts of the female reproductive system and state their functions | |
| describe the roles of testosterone and oestrogen in developing secondary sexual characteristics at puberty | |
| describe the menstrual cycle in terms of changes in the uterus and ovaries | |
| explain the roles of hormones (FSH, LH, oestrogen and progesterone) in controlling the menstrual cycle | |
| describe sexual intercourse in humans | |
| describe fertilisation in humans | |
| describe the early development of the zygote to form a ball of cells that is implanted into the uterus wall | |
| state the sites of production of oestrogen and progesterone and their roles in pregnancy | |
| describe the development of the fetus | |
| describe the functions of the placenta and umbilical cord | |
| state the functions of the amnion and amniotic fluid | |
| describe the ante-natal care of pregnant women | |
| describe the processes involved in labour and birth | |
| describe the advantages and disadvantages of breast milk and formula milk | |
| describe artificial insemination and the use of hormones in fertility drugs and discuss their social implications | |
| outline the following methods of birth control: natural, chemical, mechanical and surgical | |

| describe the methods of transmission of HIV and the ways in which HIV/AIDS can be prevented from spreading | |
| describe how HIV affects the immune system in a person with HIV/AIDS | |
| describe the symptoms, signs, effects and treatment of gonorrhoea | |

## Unit 16 Inheritance

I can:

| define the term *inheritance* | |
| State the meaning of the terms *chromosome*, *gene* and *DNA* | |
| define mitosis and state its importance in growth, repair, replacement and asexual reproduction | |
| define meiosis and state its importance in the formation of gametes and in producing genetic variation | |
| state the difference between haploid and diploid nuclei in terms of sets of chromosomes | |
| describe the inheritance of sex based upon the X and Y chromosomes in humans | |
| distinguish between genes and alleles | |
| use the following terms to describe the inheritance of a characteristic: *dominant*, *recessive*, *genotype*, *homozygous*, *heterozygous* and *phenotype* | |
| draw genetic diagrams to explain examples of monohybrid inheritance | |
| use genetic diagrams to explain 1:1 and 3:1 ratios | |
| explain the term *co-dominance* | |
| describe the inheritance of the ABO blood group system | |

## Unit 17 Variation and selection

I can:

| state the differences between continuous and discontinuous variation | |
| identify and explain examples of variation | |
| define the term *mutation* | |
| describe down's syndrome as an example of mutation | |

| describe the possible effects of radiation and certain chemicals on the rate of mutation | |
|---|---|
| describe sickle cell anaemia as an example of mutation and explain that people heterozygous for the condition have a resistance to malaria. use this information to explain the similarity between its global distribution and that of malaria | |
| define natural selection as the greater chance that the best adapted individuals survive to pass on their genes to their offspring | |
| state that competition leads to survival of those best adapted to the environment | |
| assess the importance of natural selection as the mechanism for evolution | |
| describe antibiotic resistance in some strains of bacteria as an example of natural selection | |
| describe the role of artificial selection in producing varieties of animals and plants with increased economic importance | |
| define the term *genetic engineering* | |
| outline how bacteria are genetically engineered to produce human insulin and explain why this was done | |

## Unit 18 Energy and nutrient transfer

I can:

| state that the Sun is the ultimate source of energy in most biological systems | |
|---|---|
| define and use the following terms: *food chain, food web, trophic level, producer, consumer, herbivore, carnivore, decomposer* and *ecosystem* | |
| draw, describe and interpret pyramids of numbers and pyramids of biomass | |
| compare pyramids of numbers and biomass | |
| explain energy losses between trophic levels in food chains | |
| explain in terms of energy loss why food chains have fewer than five trophic levels | |
| explain the increased efficiency in supplying green plants as human food compared to feeding crop plants to animals | |
| describe the different stages of the water cycle | |
| describe the different stages of the carbon cycle | |

| describe the role of bacteria and fungi in decomposing nitrogen-containing substances, such as protein and urea, into ammonia | |
|---|---|
| describe the roles of bacteria in nitrogen fixation, nitrification and denitrification | |
| describe the absorption of nitrate ions by plants and their use in making proteins that enter food chains | |

## Unit 19 Human influences on the ecosystem

I can:

| define the term *population* | |
|---|---|
| state the factors affecting the growth of a population and describe their importance | |
| describe the different phases of growth in a population growth curve | |
| describe the increase in the human population and the social implications of this increase | |
| interpret graphs and diagrams of human population growth | |
| explain how limiting factors control the phases of the sigmoid curve of population growth | |
| state the sources and effects of air pollutants such as sulfur dioxide, methane and carbon dioxide | |
| explain how air pollution by greenhouse gases is thought to contribute to global warming | |
| describe the causes and effects of acid rain | |
| state the preventative measures to combat acid rain | |
| describe the dangers of nuclear fall-out | |
| describe the need for conservation of species and their habitats | |
| describe how endangered species can be protected | |
| describe the need for conserving water and non-renewable resources, such as fossil fuels | |
| describe how limited and non-renewable resources like paper can be recycled | |
| describe how sewage treatment can make water safe to return to the environment or fit for human use | |

# Glossary

This glossary provides definitions of some of the important biological terms used in this book. The underlined words are key terms as defined in the syllabus, which you are required to know for the examinations. You may, however, be expected to explain terms other than these.

## A

**Absorption** movement of digested food molecules through the wall of the intestine into the blood or lymph.

**Accommodation** the adjustment of the shape of the lens so as to focus light onto the retina.

**Active site** part of the surface of an enzyme molecule into which the substrate fits.

**Active transport** the movement of molecules or ions in or out of a cell through the cell membrane from a region of their lower concentration to a region of their higher concentration against a concentration gradient, using energy released from respiration.

**Acid rain** rain or snow which is acidic. Polluting gases such as sulfur dioxide and the oxides of nitrogen react with water in the atmosphere to form acid rain.

**Adaptation** a feature that helps an organism to survive in its environment.

**Addiction** when a person has taken a drug so regularly that they cannot do without it.

**Adrenaline** a hormone produced by the adrenal glands that prepares the body for emergencies and stress, for example by increasing the glucose concentration of the blood.

**Aerobic respiration** the process that happens in cells to release a relatively large amount of energy from food substances, such as glucose, in the presence of oxygen.

**AIDS** Acquired immunodeficiency syndrome – a collection of diseases that result from a weakening of the body's immune system following infection by HIV.

**Allele** any of two or more alternative forms of a gene.

**Alveolus** a tiny air sac in the lungs where exchange of gases between the air and blood occurs.

**Amino acid** a molecule made up of carbon, hydrogen, oxygen and nitrogen. Amino acids link together by chemical bonds to form protein molecules. Some amino acids also contain sulfur.

**Amnion** the membrane that surrounds the developing fetus in the uterus.

**Amniotic fluid** the liquid that is contained within the amnion and which protects the fetus from mechanical damage.

**Anaerobic respiration** the process that happens in cells to release a relatively small amount of energy from glucose in the absence of oxygen.

**Anaemia** a disorder of haemoglobin in the red blood cells which means that the blood cannot carry sufficient oxygen.

**Annelids** the phylum of animals that consists of segmented worms.

**Antagonistic muscles** a pair of muscles which brings about movement at a joint. When one contracts, the other relaxes, e.g. the biceps and triceps which move the lower arm.

**Anther** the part of a flower where pollen grains are produced.

**Antibiotic** a drug that is taken to kill or stop the growth of bacteria.

**Antibody** a protein released by lymphocytes to protect against pathogens.

**Antitoxin** a chemical released by lymphocytes that neutralises the poisonous waste products (toxins) produced by bacteria.

**Arthropods** the phylum that consists of animals that have jointed legs and a protective exoskeleton.

**Asexual reproduction** reproduction without the formation of gametes. New individuals are genetically identical (clones) of the parent.

**Assimilation** the movement of digested food molecules into the cells of the body where they are used, becoming part of the cells.

**Artery** a blood vessel through which blood travels away from the heart.

**Arteriole** type of blood vessel between artery and capillaries. Contraction and relaxation of muscle in the wall controls flow of blood into capillaries. See vasoconstriction and vasodilation.

**Atrium** a chamber of the heart that receives blood from veins and pumps it to a ventricle (plural atria).

**Artificial selection** the selection of plants and animals for breeding because of their useful characteristics, e.g. high crop yield. Also called selective breeding.

**Atherosclerosis** a narrowing of the arteries caused by deposits of cholesterol in the internal walls of arteries which slows down the rate of blood flow.

**Auxin** a plant growth hormone which controls cell elongation.

## B

**Bacterium** a type of microorganism consisting of single cells. Each bacterial cell has cytoplasm surrounded by a cell membrane and cell wall, but has no nucleus.

**Balanced diet** a diet that provides sufficient energy for a person's needs and all the food nutrients in the correct proportions.

**Bile** an alkaline fluid made in the liver and stored in the gall bladder. It is released into the small intestine through the bile duct to help with the digestion and absorption of fats.

**Binary fission** a type of asexual reproduction in which one cell divides into two. Bacteria reproduce by binary fission.

**Binomial system** a method for naming organisms in which each is given two names: a genus name and a trivial name, e.g. *Homo sapiens* for humans.

**Biomass** the mass of living material in a particular area.

**Biodegradable** something that can be broken down by biological processes. Some plastics are biodegradable.

**Bladder** a muscular sac that stores urine and passes it out through the urethra.

**Brain** the part of the central nervous system that coordinates most activities of the body.

**Bronchiole** a small branch of a bronchus which ends in alveoli (air sacs).

**Bronchus** one of the two tubes that branch off the trachea and pass into the lungs (plural bronchi).

### C

**Capillary** the smallest blood vessel with walls only one cell thick. Substances are exchanged through capillary walls between blood and tissue fluid.

**Camouflage** something that makes it difficult to detect an organism by sight.

**Cancer** a disease resulting from the uncontrolled division of cells in one or more parts of the body.

**Carbohydrase** an enzyme that digests carbohydrates to simple sugars, e.g. amylase digests starch to sugars.

**Carbohydrate** a class of food substance that provides energy, e.g. starch and glucose. Composed of carbon, hydrogen and oxygen.

**Carbon cycle** the flow of carbon compounds through plants, animals, decomposers and their environment.

**Carbon dioxide** the gas produced as a waste product during respiration and absorbed by plants and used during photosynthesis to make simple sugars.

**Carnivore** an animal that eats other animals – a meat-eater.

**Carrier** (1) an individual who has a recessive allele for a genetic

disease and can transmit it to the next generation; (2) a person who is infected by the pathogen for an infectious disease, does not have the symptoms of the disease, but is able to transmit it to others.

**Catalyst** a substance that speeds up a chemical reaction and is not changed by the reaction.

**Cell** structural and functional unit of living organisms. All organisms are composed of cells. Viruses are not.

**Cell membrane** the boundary of the cell which controls the materials that pass into and out of it.

**Cell sap** the liquid that fills the vacuole of a plant cell.

**Cell wall** the outer layer of a plant cell made of cellulose, which supports the cell and gives it shape.

**Cellulose** a complex carbohydrate that makes up the cell walls of plant cells.

**Central nervous system** brain and spinal cord.

**Chlorophyll** the green pigment found in many plant cells that absorbs light for photosynthesis.

**Chloroplast** small structure containing chlorophyll that is found in plant cells. Carries out photosynthesis.

**Cholesterol** a lipid-based chemical made in the liver and found in the blood. High levels of cholesterol in the blood are linked to an increased risk of atherosclerosis and heart disease.

**Chromosome** a thread-like structure made up of genes. They are found inside the nucleus and are only visible when a cell is dividing.

**Cilium** a tiny process found on cells that line some tubular organs, e.g. airways and oviducts (plural cilia). In the airways, they beat to move dust and microbes out of the lungs and up to the throat.

**Ciliary muscle** a muscle in the eye that controls the shape of the lens during focussing.

**Circulatory system** the organ system made up of blood vessels and the heart that transports blood. Mammals have a double circulation with blood passing through the heart twice in one circuit of the body.

**Cladistics** a method of classifying organisms that often relies on data from the nucleic acids, DNA and RNA.

**Classify** to sort living organisms into groups according to features they have in common.

**Clone** an organism that is genetically identical to its parent.

**Clotting** a series of chemical reactions that cause blood cells to stick together. At a wound this stops the loss of blood and results in the formation of a scab.

**Codominance** the existence of two alleles for a particular characteristic where neither is dominant over the other and both are expressed in heterozygous individuals.

**Colon** the part of the alimentary canal between the small intestine and the rectum where the absorption of water occurs.

**Community** all the animals, plants microorganisms that are found in a particular habitat.

**Competition** contest between organisms for resources such as food, water and mates.

**Compost** decaying plant remains used as a source of nutrients in gardens.

**Cone** a sensory cell in the retina of the eye that responds to light of high intensity and detects colour.

**Concentration gradient** the difference in concentration of a substance between two places, e.g. either side of a cell membrane, between air in the alveolus and blood in the lungs.

**Consumer** an organism that gains its energy by feeding on other organisms.

**Continuous variation** variation in a feature that shows a range of phenotypes between two extremes

# Glossary

with many intermediates, e.g. human height.

**Contraceptive** any device or substance that prevents fertilisation.

**Coronary arteries** arteries that branch from the aorta to supply oxygenated blood to heart muscle.

**Cornea** the transparent layer at the front of the eye which helps to refract light rays onto the retina.

**Coronary heart disease** heart disease caused by blockage of coronary arteries that supply heart muscle with blood.

**Cotyledon** part of the embryo of a flowering plant – a seed leaf. In many plants cotyledons are food stores for the embryo.

**Cuticle** the waxy covering of the epidermis in plant stems and leaves that reduces the loss of water by transpiration.

**Cystic fibrosis** an inherited disease affecting the lungs and the digestive system, caused by a faulty, recessive allele.

**Cytoplasm** jelly-like contents of the cell not including the nucleus.

**D**

**Deamination** the process, which takes place in the liver, where the nitrogen-containing part of amino acids is removed to form ammonia. Ammonia is then converted into urea.

**Decay** the breakdown of dead organisms and waste material by decomposers.

**Decomposers** microorganisms, mainly bacteria and fungi that gain their energy by breaking down dead organisms and waste material.

**Deficiency disease** a condition when an important nutrient, such as a vitamin or mineral, is missing and results in a disease.

**Deforestation** the removal of trees by humans in order to exploit the land.

**Denitrifying bacteria** bacteria which live in anaerobic conditions,

such as water-logged soil, and convert nitrate ions into nitrogen gas.

**Denitrification** conversion of nitrate ions into nitrogen gas by bacteria.

**Development** an increase in complexity as an embryo grows and gains new tissues, organs and organ systems.

**Diabetes** a medical condition in which the blood glucose concentration is not controlled. One cause of diabetes is the failure of the pancreas to secrete insulin.

**Dialysis** the use of a partially permeable membrane to separate substances.

**Diaphragm** sheet of muscular and fibrous tissue that separates the thorax from the abdomen. Its movements cause air to flow in and out of the lungs.

**Dicotyledon** a type of flowering plant with an embryo that has two cotyledons and a net-like arrangement of veins in its leaves. (Also known as eudicotyledon.)

**Diffusion** the net movement of molecules or ions, from a place with a high concentration to a place with a lower concentration down a concentration gradient as a result of random movement.

**Digestion** the breakdown of large, insoluble food molecules into small, water-soluble molecules using mechanical and chemical processes.

**Digestive system** the organ system that breaks down food and absorbs it into the blood.

**Diploid nucleus** a nucleus containing two sets of chromosomes (e.g. in body cells).

**Discontinuous variation** limited number of phenotypes for a feature with no intermediates, e.g. human blood groups.

**Dominant** an allele that is expressed if it is present (e.g. T or G).

**Down's syndrome** a genetic condition resulting from a chromosome mutation. The most

common cause is having an extra chromosome 21.

**Drug** any substance taken into the body that modifies or affects chemical reactions in the body.

**Duodenum** the first part of the small intestine.

 **E**

**Ecosystem** all the living organisms (the community) in a place and the interactions between them and their physical environment.

**Egestion** the removal of undigested food.

**Embryo** the early stage of an animal or plant as it develops from a fertilised egg.

**Emphysema** a medical condition in which the walls of the alveoli are broken down. This reduces the surface area for gas exchange and means that the person cannot get enough oxygen into their blood.

**Emulsification** the breakdown of large fat globules into many tiny globules.

**Energy transfer** the transfer of energy from one trophic (feeding) level to the next.

**Enhanced greenhouse effect** increase in concentration of greenhouse gases in the atmosphere leading to global warming.

**Enzymes** biological catalysts that speed up the rate of chemical reactions in the body.

**Eudicotyledon (see dicotyledon)**

**Eutrophication** the enrichment of waters with plant nutrients that can stimulate growth of algae and plants.

**Evolution** the process in which inherited features change in populations of organisms over time.

**Excretion** the removal from organisms of toxic materials, the waste products of metabolism and substances in excess of requirements.

**Extinct** when a species no longer exists on the Earth.

# Glossary

## F

**Fats** lipid molecules that consist of glycerol and three fatty acids. Fats are energy rich as they contain a high proportion of carbon and hydrogen atoms.

**Fatty acids** molecules that combine with glycerol to form fats.

**Fermentation** (1) anaerobic respiration in which glucose is converted into ethanol and carbon dioxide; (2) an industrial process in which microorganisms are used to make a useful product.

**Fermenter** a large container in which fungi or bacteria are grown under sterile, controlled conditions.

**Fertilisation** the fusion of the male and female sex cells, e.g. sperm and egg, to form a zygote (fertilised egg) that grows into a new individual.

**Fertilisers** chemicals that provide plant nutrients and are put on the land to increase the growth of a crop and produce a higher yield.

**Fertility drug** a drug that is used to increase the chances of a woman becoming pregnant.

**Fetus** a stage during development of a mammal when all the major organs are recognisable.

**Fibre** indigestible plant material, mainly cellulose and lignin that provides bulk to assist the passage of food through the gut by peristalsis.

**Flaccid** a plant cell that has lost water by osmosis so that the cell contents no longer push outwards against the cell wall is described as flaccid.

**Fluoridation** adding fluoride to drinking water to reduce teeth decay in the population.

**Food additives** chemicals that are added to improve the taste, appearance or shelf-life of foods. They include flavourings, colourings, preservatives, antioxidants and chemicals that improve the texture of a food.

**Food chain** this shows the feeding relationships in a community beginning with a producer. Each organism is fed on by the next organism in the chain. Food chains show the flow of energy and nutrients.

**Food web** a network of interconnected food chains showing the energy flow through an ecosystem.

**Fruit** After fertilisation, the ovary of a plant develops into a fruit which contains the seeds.

## G

**Gall bladder** a sac in the liver which stores bile before it is released down the bile duct into the small intestine.

**Gametes** sex cells with the haploid number of chromosomes.

**Gas exchange system** organ system comprising trachea, bronchi and lungs that involves moving air into the alveoli where oxygen and carbon dioxide are exchanged with the blood.

**Gene** a length of DNA, found on a chromosome, that codes for a particular characteristic.

**Genetic engineering** taking a gene from one species and placing it into the DNA of another species.

**Genotype** the genetic make up of an organism in terms of the alleles it possesses (e.g. Tt or GG).

**Genus** a group of species with similar characteristics, e.g. the lion, *Panthera leo* and the tiger, *Panthera tigris* are in the same genus.

**Geotropism** a growth response by a plant to the stimulus of gravity.

**Glucagon** a hormone produced by the pancreas that stimulates the liver to convert glycogen to glucose and so increase the concentration of glucose in the blood.

**Glycogen** a complex carbohydrate found as an energy store in the liver and muscles.

**Gonorrhoea** a sexually transmitted bacterial disease.

**Greenhouse effect** the Earth is kept warm because carbon dioxide and other greenhouse gases in the atmosphere reduce the escape of heat energy into space. Greenhouse gases radiate heat towards the Earth and maintain the temperature higher than it would be otherwise.

**Growth** a permanent increase in size and dry mass by an increase in cell number or cell size or both.

## H

**Haemoglobin** the red pigment in red blood cells that combines with oxygen to form oxyhaemoglobin.

**Haploid nucleus** a nucleus containing a single set of unpaired chromosomes (e.g. sperm and egg).

**Hepatic portal vein** the vein through which absorbed food travels from the small intestine to the liver.

**Herbicide** a chemical that kills weeds.

**Herbivore** an animal that feeds on plants.

**Heroin** a highly addictive, depressant drug derived from opium extracted from poppies.

**Heterozygous** a genotype where the two alleles of a gene are different.

**HIV (Human immunodeficiency virus)** the virus that causes AIDS. HIV attacks and destroys lymphocytes reducing the body's ability to defend itself against disease.

**Homeostasis** maintenance of a constant internal environment. This involves controlling factors, such as temperature and the concentration of glucose in the blood.

**Homologous chromosomes** a pair of matching chromosomes that carry genes for the same characteristics in the same positions.

**Homozygous** a genotype where both alleles of a gene are identical.

**Hormone** a chemical messenger produced by an endocrine gland that is transported in the blood and alters the activity of one or more specific target organs. Hormones are destroyed by the liver.

**Hypha** thin thread-like structure that is part of the body (mycelium) of a mould fungus (plural hyphae).

# Glossary

**Ileum** the part of the small intestine between the duodenum and the colon, the major function of which is the absorption of digested food.

**Immune system** tissues, cells and chemicals that act together to give a defence against pathogens.

**Immunity** protection against disease provided by the immune system, including lymphocytes and antibodies.

**Implantation** the embedding of an embryo into the lining of the uterus.

**Ingestion** the process of taking in food.

**Inheritance** the transmission of genetic information from one generation to the next.

**Inherited disorders** disorders caused by dominant or recessive alleles that are passed from one generation to the next.

**Insulin** a hormone produced by the pancreas that stimulates the liver and muscles to store glucose as glycogen so causing a reduction in the concentration of glucose in the blood.

**Involuntary action** an action that we do not have to think about.

**Iris** the coloured part of the eye around the pupil. It alters the size of the pupil and so controls the amount of light entering the eye.

**Joint** the place where two bones meet. Movable joints allow movement to occur, e.g. the hinge joint at the elbow.

**K**

**Kidney** the organ that filters waste chemicals out of the blood and controls the water and salt levels in the body.

**L**

**Lactation** the secretion of milk from the mammary glands of a female mammal.

**Lacteal** a lymph capillary found inside a villus, which contains absorbed fats.

**Lactic acid** the chemical produced in muscles when glucose is respired anaerobically. Some bacteria also produce lactic acid during anaerobic respiration.

**Large intestine** the final parts of the alimentary canal that absorb water and store faeces.

**Leaching** the loss of plant nutrients from soils in water that drains from the land.

**Leaf** the plant organ that absorbs light energy to convert into chemical energy during photosynthesis.

**Lens** part of the eye that focuses light rays onto the retina.

**Ligament** a strong structure that binds bones together at a joint.

**Limiting factor** the factor that is in the shortest supply and restricts processes, such as the rate of photosynthesis or the rate of growth.

**Lipase** the enzyme that digests fats to fatty acids and glycerol.

**Liver** the organ in the abdomen that produces bile, breaks down amino acids into ammonia, converts ammonia into urea, stores glucose in the form of glycogen and carries out detoxification of toxic chemicals, e.g. alcohol.

**Lymph** the fluid formed when tissue fluid drains into lymph vessels.

**Magnesium** the element needed for the synthesis of chlorophyll. It is absorbed by the roots in the form of magnesium ions.

**Malnutrition** the condition caused by eating an unbalanced diet. Undernutrition occurs when a diet is deficient in one or more food types. Overnutrition can lead to obesity and coronary heart disease.

**Meiosis** a type of division of the nucleus to reduce the chromosome number by half. Diploid nuclei give rise to haploid nuclei. Also called a reduction division.

**Menstrual cycle** the sequence of events, that occurs in a woman, where the lining of the uterus thickens in order to receive a fertilised egg after ovulation. The cycle is controlled by hormones from the pituitary gland and the ovaries.

**Menstruation** the breakdown of the soft lining of the uterus, discharging blood and cells through the vagina.

**Metabolism** all the chemical reactions that take place inside a living organism.

**Mineral salts** inorganic nutrients such as iron and calcium that are needed for a balanced diet. Also required by plants to make compounds, such as amino acids.

**Mitosis** a type of division of the nucleus that gives rise to genetically identical cells in which the chromosome number is maintained by the exact duplication of chromosomes.

**Molluscs** the phylum that includes animals with soft, unsegmented bodies. Many molluscs have a shell and move by means of a muscular foot.

**Microorganism (microbe)** microscopic organisms, such as bacteria, fungi and viruses.

**Monocotyledon** a type of flowering plant with an embryo with one cotyledon and parallel veins in its leaves.

**Monohybrid inheritance** the inheritance of one gene with two or more alleles.

**Motor (effector) neurone** a neurone that transmits impulses away from the brain or spinal cord to effector organs, e.g. muscles and glands.

**Movement** an action by an organism or part of an organism causing a change of position or place.

**Mucus** a slimy, sticky substance that traps dusts and some microbes in the air pathways.

It also acts as a lubricant to help the passage of food along the gut.

**Muscle** tissue that is capable of contracting and relaxing to bring about movement of bones at joints. Muscle tissue also moves food along our gut and keeps our heart beating.

**Mutation** a change in a gene or in a chromosome.

**Mycelium** a network of thin threads (hyphae) that make up the body of a fungus.

**N**

**Natural selection** factors such as competition and predation affect the survival of a species. As a result, only those individuals adapted to survive have the greater chance to pass on their genes to the next generation.

**Nematodes** the phylum that consists of roundworms with long, thread-like bodies.

**Nerve** a bundle of nerve cells (neurones) which pass from the central nervous system to a certain part of the body.

**Neurone** a nerve cell.

**Nitrifying bacteria** bacteria found in the soil that convert ammonium ions into nitrite ions and nitrite ions into nitrate ions.

**Nitrification** conversion of ammonium ions to nitrate ions by bacteria.

**Nitrogen-fixing bacteria** bacteria found both in the soil and in the roots of legume plants that convert atmospheric nitrogen into nitrogen-containing compounds such as amino acids.

**Nitrogen** an element needed for healthy plant growth, taken up by plant roots in the form of nitrate ions. Chemical fertilisers often supply nitrate ions.

**Non-biodegradable** materials that will not break down in the environment, e.g. many plastics.

**Nucleus** the part of the cell which contains genetic information in the form of chromosomes. The nucleus controls the activities of the cell. Nuclei may be haploid or diploid.

**Nutrition** taking in of nutrients which are organic substances and mineral ions, containing raw materials or energy for growth and tissue repair, absorbing and assimilating them.

**O**

**Obesity** when a person is extremely overweight (see page 74 for two ways in which this is determined).

**Oesophagus** the muscular tube connecting the mouth with the stomach. Food passes down the oesophagus by a wave of muscular contraction called peristalsis.

**Oestrogen** a hormone secreted by the ovaries that stimulates the development of secondary sexual characteristics in females and helps to control the menstrual cycle.

**Organ** a number of tissues working together to carry out a function in the body.

**Organ system** a number of different organs that work together to carry out functions for the body.

**Osmoregulation** the control of the water content of the body.

**Osmosis** the diffusion of water molecules through a partially permeable membrane, from a region of high concentration of water molecules to a region of lower concentration of water molecules [or from a region of high water potential to a region of lower water potential.]

**Ovary** female sex organ where ova or eggs are produced.

**Ovulation** the release of an ovum (egg) from the ovary.

**Ovule** the structure inside the ovary of a plant that contains the female gamete. After fertilisation an ovule develops into a seed.

**Ovum** the female sex cell (gamete) produced in the ovary. Also called the egg.

**Oxygen debt** the extra oxygen that is needed by the body to respire lactic acid produced during anaerobic respiration.

**P**

**Palisade mesophyll** tissue in leaves that contain many chloroplasts and are the main site of photosynthesis.

**Pancreas** the organ in the abdomen that produces digestive enzymes and makes insulin and glucagon that regulate the concentration of glucose in the blood.

**Partially permeable membrane** a membrane that allows small molecules to pass through, but does not allow large molecules to pass through.

**Pathogen** an organism that causes a disease.

**Pericarp** the outer layers of a fruit that develop from an ovary after fertilisation.

**Peripheral nervous system** nerves that arise from the brain and spinal cord and go to all the organs of the body.

**Peristalsis** a wave of muscular contraction that squeezes food down the oesophagus to the stomach.

**Pesticide** a chemical that kills pests.

**Phagocyte** a type of white blood cell that ingests and destroys pathogens.

**Phagocytosis** the ingestion of food particles into a cell.

**Phenotype** the physical or other features of an organism due to both its genotype and its environment.

**Photosynthesis** a complex set of reactions in which plants convert light energy and use it to convert carbon dioxide into simple sugars.

**Phototropism** a growth response of a plant to the direction of light.

**Phloem** the plant tissue that transports sugars and amino acids.

**Pituitary gland** a gland at the base of the brain that secretes hormones to control the activity of other organs, e.g. kidneys, testes and ovaries.

# Glossary

**Placenta** the organ that connects a mammalian embryo to its mother and through which it receives food and oxygen and removes carbon dioxide and chemical waste.

**Plaque** (1) a mixture of food remains, saliva and bacteria which can build up on the surface of teeth; (2) fatty deposit in the lining of an artery.

**Plasma** the liquid part of the blood which transports dissolved foods, urea, carbon dioxide and hormones.

**Platelets** small pieces of cells that release substances to cause blood to clot.

**Plumule** the part of a plant embryo that will grow into the shoot.

**Pollination** the transfer of pollen from the anther of a flower to the stigma.

**Pollution** the release by humans of materials or energy that will harm the environment.

**Population** a group of individuals of the same species living in the same habitat at the same time.

**Population growth** growth in numbers of a population. In absence of limiting factors growth is usually exponential.

**Predators** animals that hunt and kill other animals for their food.

**Prey** animals that are hunted and killed for food by predators.

**Producers** an organism that makes its own organic nutrients, usually using energy from sunlight through photosynthesis.

**Progesterone** a hormone secreted by the ovaries and by the placenta that maintains the lining of the uterus during the second half of the menstrual cycle and during pregnancy.

**Protease** an enzyme that breaks down proteins to amino acids.

**Proteins** compounds made up of amino acids, which are needed for growth and repair of tissues in the body. They contain the elements carbon, hydrogen, oxygen, nitrogen and sulfur.

**Puberty** the age at which secondary sexual characteristics appear in boys and girls.

**Pulse** when the left ventricle of the heart contracts, it forces blood out of the heart along the arteries. The arteries swell and this can be felt as a pulse in various parts of the body such as the wrist.

**Pupil** the hole through which light enters the eye. The size of the pupil is controlled by the iris.

**Pyramid of biomass** a way to show biomass at each trophic level in an ecosystem. The area of each horizontal bar is proportional to the mass of living material at each trophic level.

**Pyramid of numbers** a way to show numbers of organisms at each trophic level in an ecosystem. The area of each horizontal bar is proportional to the number of individuals at each trophic level.

## R

**Radicle** the part of a plant embryo that will grow into the root.

**Receptor** cells or organs that are sensitive to a stimulus.

**Recessive** an allele that is only expressed when there is no dominant allele of the gene present (e.g. t or g).

**Rectum** the last part of the large intestine where faeces are stored before passing out through the anus.

**Recycle** to convert material back into a form that can be useful to humans.

**Reflex action** an automatic, rapid response to a stimulus which is often protective.

**Relay (connector) neurone** a neurone in the central nervous system that transmits impulses from sensory to motor neurones.

**Renal dialysis** the use of a machine to remove the body's waste chemicals when the kidneys fail.

**Reproduction** processes that make more of the same kind of organism.

**Respiration** a complex series of reactions, taking place in all living cells, that break down nutrients molecules to release energy from food.

**Response** the reaction of an organism to a particular stimulus.

**Retina** the part of the eye that contains light sensitive cells.

**Rod** a sensory cell in the retina of the eye that responds to light of low intensity.

**Root** the organ that anchors plants into the ground and absorbs water and mineral salts.

**Root hairs** specialised cells in a root that provide a large surface area for the absorption of water and mineral salts.

## S

**Sclerotic** the tough, white outer layer of the eye which keeps it in shape.

**Secretion** the release of useful substances by cells.

**Sense organ** a receptor organ that is sensitive to a particular stimulus or stimuli, e.g. touch, light, sound, temperature and chemicals..

**Sensitivity** the ability to detect changes in the environment (stimuli) and make responses.

**Sensory neurone** a neurone that transmits impulses from receptors to the brain or spinal cord.

**Sex chromosomes** the pair of chromosomes that determine a person's sex. In humans, XX is female and XY is male.

**Sexual reproduction** the process involving fusion of haploid nuclei to form a diploid zygote and the production of genetically dissimilar offspring.

**Sickle cell anaemia** an inherited disease affecting haemoglobin, which alters the shape of the red blood cells and results in severe anaemia.

**Single cell protein** food high in protein that is produced by microbes, e.g. mycoprotein is produced by fungi.

**Small intestine** the region of alimentary canal that completes digestion and absorbs digested food.

**Solute** a substance that dissolves in a solvent.

**Solvent** a liquid that dissolves substances.

**Species** a group of organisms with similar characteristics which are capable of interbreeding and producing fertile offspring.

**Sperm** the male sex cell or gamete.

**Starch** an insoluble carbohydrate made from glucose molecules. An energy store in plant cells and an important component of the human diet.

**Stem** the organ that supports the leaves, flowers and fruits of a plant. It contains xylem tissue to transport water and mineral salts and phloem tissue to transport sugars and amino acids.

**Stimulus** (plural stimuli) a change in the environment that is detected by a sense organ.

**Stoma** (plural stomata) a small hole in the epidermis of leaves that allows gases to diffuse in and out. The size of the hole is controlled by guard cells.

**Stomach** a muscular sac at the end of the oesophagus that mixes food with gastric juice. The chemical digestion of protein begins in the stomach.

**Suspensory ligaments** fibres that hold the lens in the eye in place and alter its shape when the ciliary muscles contract and relax.

**Sustainable development** development that is able to conserve natural resources so that they are available in the future.

**Sweat glands** coiled glands found in the dermis of the skin which secrete sweat to lose heat by evaporation.

**Synapse** a gap between two neurones across which a chemical transmitter is released to stimulate an impulse in the second neurone.

**Synovial fluid** fluid present at a synovial joint which lubricates the joint and reduces friction.

**Synovial joint** a joint between two bones which allows free movement.

**T**

**Tendon** an inelastic band of fibres that attaches a muscle to a bone.

**Testa** the hard outer coat that protects a seed.

**Testis** (plural testes) the male sex organs where sperm cells and testosterone are produced.

**Testosterone** the hormone, produced by the testes, that stimulates the development of secondary sexual characteristics in males and the development of sperm cells.

**Tissue** a group of similar cells that act together to perform the same function.

**Tissue culture** a cloning technique that involves growing new plants without the need for gametes. The new plants are genetically identical to the parent plant.

**Tissue fluid** the fluid that bathes the cells when plasma and some white blood cells pass out of the capillaries.

**Toxin** a poisonous substance. Bacteria release toxins as waste products which bring about the symptoms of a disease, e.g. high fever.

**Translocation** the movement of sucrose and amino acids in the phloem.

**Transpiration** the evaporation of water from the surfaces of mesophyll cells in leaves followed by diffusion of water vapour through stomata into the atmosphere.

**Trophic level** the position of an organism in a food chain, food web, pyramids of numbers, biomass or energy. For example, herbivores are primary consumers and form the second trophic level.

**Tropism** a growth response by part of a plant to a stimulus, e.g. light or gravity.

**Thrombosis** a blood clot that occurs in a vein or an artery.

**Tuber** a swollen stem of a potato for food storage and asexual reproduction.

**Turgor** the pressure exerted by a plant cell onto its cell wall. Turgid cells are firm because they are full of water; this can support plant organs such as stems.

**U**

**Umbilical cord** the cord connecting the placenta to the fetus. It contains two umbilical arteries and a vein.

**Urea** a waste product formed from excess amino acids in the liver. It is filtered out of the blood in the kidneys and passed out in the urine.

**Ureter** a tube through which urine passes from the kidney to the bladder.

**Urethra** a tube that passes urine from the bladder to the outside at intervals.

**Urinary system** organ system that filters blood, produces and stores urine.

**Urine** an excretory fluid produced in the kidneys and stored in the bladder. It contains excess water, urea, and excess salts.

**Uterus** the womb, a muscular chamber with a soft lining in which the fetus develops.

**V**

**Vaccine** a preparation containing mild or dead pathogenic microorganisms to stimulate the production of antibodies and give immunity.

**Vaccination** giving a vaccine to provide immunity.

**Vacuole** fluid-filled sac containing cell sap present in most plant cells.

**Vagina** a tube leading from the uterus to the outside. It receives the erect penis during sexual intercourse and is the birth canal.

**Variation** differences between individuals in features that may show continuous variation or discontinuous variation.

# Glossary

**Vasoconstriction** contraction of muscles in arterioles to reduce blood flow through capillaries.

**Vasodilation** relaxation of muscles in arterioles that increases blood flow through capillaries.

**Vein** a blood vessel through which blood travels towards the heart.

**Ventricle** the lower, more muscular chamber of the heart. In mammals, the right ventricle pumps blood to the lungs and the left ventricle pumps blood to the rest of the body.

**Vertebrate** an animal with a backbone.

**Villus** (plural villi) tiny, finger-like projection from the wall of the small intestine. Villi increase the surface area of the small intestine for absorption of digested food.

**Virus** a microorganism that cannot be seen under the light microscope. Smaller than bacteria, they consist of nucleic acid (e.g. DNA) surrounded by a protein coat. They can only reproduce inside living cells.

**Vitamin** a micronutrient, needed in small amounts in the diet. If not enough is provided in the diet a deficiency disease can result.

**Voluntary action** an action that we decide to make.

**Water potential** the tendency for water molecules to move by diffusion. Water diffuses from an area of high water potential to an area of lower water potential.

**White blood cells** they form part of the body's defence system. Lymphocytes release antibodies and antitoxins to combat pathogens. Phagocytes ingest and kill pathogens.

**Wilting** loss of turgor causes plant leaves to droop if water is lacking.

**Withdrawal symptoms** side effects that a person feels when they give up an addictive drug.

**Yeast** a single-celled fungus that ferments sugar to produce ethanol and carbon dioxide.

**Yield** the quantity of product from a crop or from a fermentation process.

**Xylem** the plant tissue that transports water and mineral salts from roots to leaves, flowers and fruits.

**Zygote** a fertilised egg.

# Index

# Index

# Index

# Acknowledgements

The authors and publishers wish to thank Julietta Fosbery for her assistance on the research and commenting on the manuscript and Paul Connell for his work on the Alternative to practical paper section.

The authors and publisher are grateful to the following for permission to reproduce photographs in this book.

**Alamy** /**Arcoimages GmbH** 260, /**Peter Arnold Inc.** 174 (bottom), /**Juniors Bildarchiv** 251 (top), /**blickwinkel** 171, /**Juanvi Carrasco** 9 (top), /**Nigel Cattlin** 65 (bottom), /**CuboImages srl** 211, /**Custom Medical Stock Photo** 215 (top right), /**Chad Ehlers** 241, /**Michael Freeman** 148, /**Blaine Harrington III** 236, /**imagebroker** 74 (middle), /**Ern Mainka** 88 (top), /**Elliot Nichol** 224, /**Photofusion Picture Library** 152, /**John Potter** 242, /**Ian Shaw** 214, /**Lourens Smak** 253 (middle), /**Sean Sprague** 198, /**Stockbyte** 216 (bottom), /**Frank Walker** 170 (bottom), /**Rob Walls** 216 (top); **Martyn Chillmaid** 116; **Corbis** /**Underwood & Underwood** 164; **Gene Cox** 89 (middle), 89 (bottom), 90 (right); **Fotolia** 58 (left); **Getty Images** 127 (top), 240, /**John Giustina** 220 (middle), /**Michele Westmorland** 220 (bottom); **iStockphoto** 2, 3, 4, 6 (middle), 7 (bottom), 8 (middle), 49, 60 (bottom), 66, 74 (top), 94 (bottom), 108 (bottom), 124, 132, 163, 194, 195, 202 (top), 208, 217 (top), 243, 253 (left), 258 (bottom); **Natural Visions/Heather Angel** 8 (top); **Nature Picture Library** /**Adrian Davies** 176; **Noel Sturt** 89(top); **Oxford Scientific** /**Mike Birkhead** 9 (bottom), /**Phil Fisk** 146 (bottom), /**Peter O'Toole** 50 (bottom); **Photofusion/ Chapman Wiedelphoto** 161(bottom); **Photolibrary/Michael Fogden** i; **Mike Samworth** 31 (top), 31 (bottom); **Science Photo Library** 218 (top), /**Steve Allen** 94 (middle), /**Anatomical Travelogue** 189 (top), 189 (middle), /**AJ Photo/Hop Americain** 138, /**David Aubrey** 6 (bottom right), 21 (bottom), /**Biology Media** 111, /**Biophoto Associates** 56, 92 (bottom left), 92 (bottom right), 96, 106 (top), 144 (top), 144 (bottom), 207, /**Ian Boddy** 80, /**Martin Bond** 77, 246 (left), /**Dr Jeremy Burgess** 92 (top), 173, 249, /**Mark Burnett** 215 (top left), /**Tony Camacho** 218 (bottom), /**Nigel Cattlin** 155, /**Clay Coleman** 5 (middle), /**CNRI** 5(top), 27, 106 (bottom), 118, 202 (bottom), /**Darwin Dale** 172, /**Mike Danson** 95, /**Michel Delarue, ISM** 204, /**Alain Dex, Publiphoto Diffusion** 160, /**Gregory Dimijian** 11, /**Martin Dohrn** 60 (top), /**Georgette Douwma** 5 (bottom), 258 (top), /**John Durham** 159, /**Eye of Science** 252 (bottom), /**Mauro Fermariello** 94 (top), 146 (top), 158, 191 (top), /**Fletcher & Baylis** 218 (middle), /**Simon Fraser/Northumbrian Environmental Management Ltd.** 253 (right), /**Adam Gault** 146 (middle), /**Gilbert S. Grant** 177 (bottom), /**Steve Gschmeissner** 51 (top), 110, 183 (top), /**Gustoimages** 74 (bottom), 126, /**John Heseltine** 246 (right), /**Innerspace Imaging** 84, /**Manfred Kage** 18, /**Geoff Kidd** 68, /**Ted Kinsman** 6 (top), /**Mehau Kulyk** 143, /**Francis Leroy, Biocosmos** 217 (bottom), /**Living Art Enterprises** 165 (bottom), /**Helen McArdle** 191 (bottom), /**Andrew McClenaghan** 53, /**Will & Deni McIntyre** 247, /**Doug Martin** 69, /**Astrid & Hanns-Frieder Michler** 131, /**Cordelia Molloy** 51 (bottom), 58 (right), /**Moredun Animal Health Ltd** 165 (top), /**Dr G. Moscoso** 190, /**John Moss** 220 (top), /**Dr Gopal Murti** 10, 21 (top), /**Susumu Nishinaga** 174 (top), /**David Nunuk** 248, /**D.Phillips** 183 (bottom), /**Louisa Preston** 88 (bottom), /**Philippe Psaila** 177 (top), / **Ed Reschke, Peter Arnold Inc.** 108 (top), /**J.C. Revy** 36, /**Revy, ISM** 210, /**Rosenfeld Images Ltd** 65 (top), 127 (bottom), 252 (top), /**David Scharf** 117, 170 (top), /**SCIMAT** 50 (top), /**Scubazoo** 251 (bottom), /**M.H. Sharp** 7 (top), 8 (bottom), /**Joe Sohm/Visions of America** 244, /**Hugh Spencer** 233 (top), /**Sinclair Stammers** 12 (left), 250, /**Volker Steger** 40, 97, /**James Stevenson** 189 (bottom), /**Bjorn Svensson** 12 (right), /**Andrew Syred** 19, 90 (left), 233 (bottom), /**Merlin Tuttle** 177 (middle), /**Jerome Wexler** 154, 215 (bottom), /**Dirk Wiersma** 246 (middle), /**Stuart Wilson** 6 (bottom left); **Wellcome Images** 161.